Albert Harkness

A Complete Latin Course for the First Year

Albert Harkness

A Complete Latin Course for the First Year

ISBN/EAN: 9783337400804

Printed in Europe, USA, Canada, Australia, Japan

Cover: Foto ©Paul-Georg Meister /pixelio.de

More available books at **www.hansebooks.com**

A

COMPLETE LATIN COURSE

FOR THE

FIRST YEAR,

COMPRISING

AN OUTLINE OF LATIN GRAMMAR, AND A SERIES OF
PROGRESSIVE EXERCISES IN READING AND
WRITING LATIN, WITH FREQUENT
PRACTICE IN READING
AT SIGHT.

BY

ALBERT HARKNESS, Ph.D., LL.D,

PROFESSOR IN BROWN UNIVERSITY.

REVISED EDITION.

NEW YORK:
D. APPLETON AND COMPANY,
1, 3, AND 5 BOND STREET.
1888.

Entered, according to Act of Congress, in the year 1883, by
ALBERT HARKNESS,
In the Office of the Librarian of Congress at Washington.

Entered, according to Act of Congress, in the year 1888, by
ALBERT HARKNESS,
In the office of the Librarian of Congress at Washington.

PREFACE

TO THE REVISED EDITION.

In this edition, the Latin Course for the First Year has been thoroughly revised and in part rewritten. In its present form it aims to introduce the beginner to the Latin language as a means of expressing thought, and not as a mere system of grammatical forms and rules, to make his first lessons as simple and attractive as possible, and then to conduct him by easy stages to such a practical and working knowledge of the language as will enable him to read Caesar or Vergil with some little facility and with some degree of pleasure.

The following are a few of the leading features of the revised edition.

1. The beginner is introduced, at the outset, to complete Latin sentences, and is informed how he may best ascertain their meaning.

2. He learns no arbitrary rules. He is allowed to see the various Latin usages exemplified in the language itself, and is thus prepared to recognize in each rule of syntax, to which his attention is called, only a simple statement of the facts in the case.

3. He is instructed that his chief object must be to read and appreciate the language itself, and that the grammar will be useful mainly as it aids him in this work. An attempt is made to enable him to understand and enjoy the thought in the original, to see that Latin words are not mere equivalents for corresponding English words, but that they have a meaning of their own, that Latin nouns, for instance, are the actual names of real persons and things.

4. The grammatical information, which will be of immediate and constant use to the learner in reading and understanding Latin, is given in the lessons themselves, while other grammatical facts which ought to be within his reach, but which should not be allowed to burden his memory, are placed in the introduction for reference.

In conclusion, the learner is advised to make faithful use of the Suggestions, which he will find in the latter part of the book, beginning on page 261. It is hoped that they will greatly aid him in his work.

BROWN UNIVERSITY, *July*, 1888.

PREFACE.

The volume now offered to the public is intended to furnish the pupil a complete course for his first year in the study of Latin. It conducts the beginner through the common forms and inflections of the language, introduces him to the leading principles of its syntax, and aims to prepare him to enter with success upon the consecutive study of Caesar or of any of the less difficult Latin authors. It comprises an Outline of Latin Grammar, Progressive Exercises in Reading and Writing Latin, eighteen pages of Connected Discourse from Caesar, Directions for Reading at Sight, Suggestions to the Learner, Notes, a Latin-English and an English-Latin Vocabulary.

The Paradigms and Rules are introduced in the exact form and language of the author's Grammar. Thus the great objection to many First Latin Books, that they fill the memory of the pupil with forms of statement that must be laid aside as soon as he passes to his Grammar, is entirely obviated in this volume.

The *Latin Exercises* are taken chiefly from Caesar's Commentaries on the Gallic War. They are made so strictly progressive, that the learner will find it perfectly easy, in the latter part of the volume, to make the transition from classified sentences to connected discourse. The

English Exercises are modelled after the Latin, and involve the same constructions and the same vocabulary.

The *Exercises in Reading at Sight* consist of easy passages of connected discourse from Caesar's Commentaries. They are so arranged that all the words and constructions involved in any given exercise are introduced and used in previous lessons. The pupil, therefore, who has learned all the vocabularies, and has been faithful in his other work, will find little difficulty in reading at sight in accordance with the directions given him. The important point is not that he should translate any given passage absolutely at sight, but that he should master it without help from any source whatever. The exercises are intended to encourage independent work, to promote self-reliance in study, and to give facility in reading and appreciating Latin.

The *Suggestions to the Learner* are intended not only to point out to the beginner the process by which he may most readily and surely reach the meaning of a Latin sentence, but also to aid him in expressing that meaning in idiomatic English. Experience has abundantly shown the need of such directions. The beginner's first efforts to solve the problem presented by a Latin sentence are too often little better than a series of unsuccessful conjectures, while his first translations are purely mechanical renderings, with little regard either to the thought of his author or to the proprieties of his mother-tongue.

I am happy in this connection to acknowledge my obligations to my esteemed friend, Mr. Edward H. Cutler, the accomplished Head-Master of the Newton High School. His accurate scholarship and large professional experience have contributed greatly to the value of every part of the work. The vocabularies are all from his hand.

The work which appears entire in this volume is also published without the *Grammatical Outline*, under the title: *Progressive Exercises in Reading and Writing Latin, with*

PREFACE. vii

Frequent Practice in Reading at Sight, intended as a Companion Book to the Author's Latin Grammar.

Teachers who use the author's Latin Series in connection with the Standard Edition[1] of his Latin Grammar, may now choose for their classes during the first year of their Latin studies any one of the following courses: —

1. *The Complete Latin Course for the First Year.*
2. *The Grammar, and the Progressive Exercises in Reading and Writing Latin.*
3. *The Grammar, and the New Latin Reader.*

Each of these courses will be found to furnish an adequate preparation for the reading of any of the less difficult Latin authors. In making the selection, teachers will have an opportunity to gratify their individual preferences, and to consult the special needs of their schools.

---

[1] Those who retain the earlier edition of the Grammar will find the *Introductory Latin Book* and the *Latin Reader* adapted to it. The editions of Latin Authors may be had with references to either edition of the Grammar, at the option of the instructor.

BROWN UNIVERSITY, PROVIDENCE, R.I.,
July, 1883.

CONTENTS.

		PAGE
INTRODUCTION.	Pronunciation. — Quantity. — Accentuation	1
	Sentences. — Verbs	11
LESSON I.	Parts of Speech. — Nouns	15
II.	Cases	17
III., IV.	Sentences. — Verbs. — First Conjugation	19
V.	First Declension	22
VI.	Subject Nominative. — Agreement of Verbs	23
VII.	Direct Object	26
VIII., IX.	Questions	28
X., XI.	Certain Forms of the Second Conjugation. — Appositives. — Genitive with Nouns	30
XII., XIII.	Second Declension	33
XIV.	Adjectives. — First and Second Declension. — Agreement of Adjectives	37
XV.	Adjectives. — Certain Forms of *Sum*	39
XVI., XVII.	Adjectives. — *Liber.* — *Aeger*	40
XVIII., — XXIV.	Third Declension	43
	Dative with Verbs	47
	Predicate Nouns	51
XXV.	Gender in Third Declension. — Cases with Prepositions	56
XXVI.	Certain Forms of the Third Conjugation. — Use of Adverbs	60
XXVII., XXVIII.	Certain Forms of the Fourth Conjugation. — Perfect Tense. — Ablative of Means	62
XXIX., XXX.	Adjectives of the Third Declension	66
	Comparison of Adjectives	70
XXXI.	Ablative with Comparatives	71
XXXII	Fourth Declension. — Fifth Declension. — Time	74

CONTENTS.

Lesson XXXIII.	Numerals. — Accusative of Time and Space.	77
XXXIV.—XXXVI.	Pronouns	81
	Questions—Answers	87
XXXVII.	Agreement of Pronouns	88
XXXVIII.	Present and Imperfect Subjunctive Active, and Present Imperative Active, in Conjugations I. and II., and in *Sum*. — Use of Indicative	91
XXXIX.	Subjunctive of Desire, Command. — Imperative	94
XL., XLI.	Present and Imperfect Subjunctive Active, and Present Imperative Active, in Conjugations III. and IV. — Sequence of Tenses. — Purpose	97
XLII.	Result	102
XLIII.	Moods in Indirect Clauses	106
XLIV.	Present Infinitive Active. — Use of Infinitive. — Certain Forms of *Possum*.	109
XLV.	Directions for Reading at Sight. — Exercise in Reading at Sight.	112
XLVI., XLVII.	*Sum*	115
	Dative with Adjectives	118
XLVIII. — L.	First Conjugation. — Indicative Active	120
LI., LII.	First Conjugation. — Active Voice	123
	Two Accusatives — Same Person	126
LIII. — LV.	First Conjugation. — Indicative Passive. — Separation, Source, Cause	128
LVI., LVII.	First Conjugation. — Subjunctive Passive. — Supine in *um*.	133
LVIII.	First Conjugation.—Passive Voice.—Accusative and Infinitive. — Subject of Infinitive	135
LIX.	Exercise in Reading at Sight	140
LX.	Second Conjugation. — Indicative Active	141
LXI. — LXIII.	Second Conjugation. — Active Voice	143
	Place in Which	147
LXIV., LXV.	Second Conjugation. — Indicative Passive. — Use of Vocative	151
LXVI. — LXVIII.	Second Conjugation. — Passive Voice	153

Lesson LXIX.	Exercise in Reading at Sight	160
LXX.	Third Conjugation. — Indicative Active	161
LXXI., LXXII.	Third Conjugation. — Active Voice	163
LXXIII. — LXXV.	Third Conjugation. — Passive Voice	169
LXXVI.	Exercise in Reading at Sight	176
LXXVII.	Fourth Conjugation. — Indicative Active	177
LXXVIII., LXXIX.	Fourth Conjugation. — Active Voice	179
	Ablative of Specification	183
LXXX. — LXXXII.	Fourth Conjugation. — Passive Voice	185
	Ablative of Difference	188
	Ablative Absolute	190
LXXXIII.	Exercise in Reading at Sight	193
LXXXIV.	Third Conjugation. — Verbs in *iō.* — Active Voice. — Supine in *ū*	194
LXXXV.	Third Conjugation. — Verbs in *iō.* — Passive Voice. — Conditional Sentences	198
LXXXVI.	Concessive Clauses	202
LXXXVII.	Deponent Verbs. — Ablative in Special Constructions	205
LXXXVIII.	Indirect Discourse	209
LXXXIX.	Periphrastic Conjugations. — Exercise in Reading at Sight	211
XC. — XCV.	Irregular Verbs. — *Possum*	215
	Ferō	216
	Volō. — *Nōlō.* — *Mālō.* — Two Accusatives	220
	Fīō. — *Eō.* — Accusative of Limit. — Place from Which	224
XCVI., XCVII.	Impersonal Verbs. — Two Datives	229
	Accusative and Genitive	232
XCVIII.	Exercise in Reading at Sight	235
XCIX., C.	Gerunds, Gerundives, and Participles	236
Narratives from Caesar. — The Helvetii		242
Invasion of Britain		253
Suggestions on Exercises in Latin Composition		260
Suggestions to the Learner		261
Latin-English Vocabulary		271
English-Latin Vocabulary		305
Appendix. — General Rules of Syntax		321

FIRST YEAR'S LATIN COURSE.

INTRODUCTION.

NOTE. — The teacher will doubtless deem it advisable to begin with Lesson I., page 15, and to use the introduction for reference.

LATIN ALPHABET.

1. LATIN GRAMMAR treats of the principles of the Latin language.
2. The Latin alphabet is the same as the English, with the omission of *w*.
3. Letters are divided according to the position of the vocal organs at the time of utterance into two general classes, vowels and consonants,[1] and these classes are again divided into various subdivisions, as seen in the following

CLASSIFICATION OF LETTERS.

I. VOWELS.

1. OPEN VOWEL[2] . . . . . . a
2. MEDIAL VOWELS . . . . . e   o
3. CLOSE VOWELS[3] i   y   u

---

[1] If the vocal organs are sufficiently open to allow an uninterrupted flow of vocal sound, a vowel is produced, otherwise a consonant; but the least open vowels are scarcely distinguishable from the most open consonants.

[2] In pronouncing the open vowel *a* as in *father*, the vocal organs are fully open. By gradually contracting them at one point and another we produce in succession the medial vowels, the close vowels, the semivowels, the nasals, the aspirate, the fricatives, and finally the mutes, in pronouncing which the closure of the vocal organs becomes complete.

[3] *E* is a *medial* vowel between the open *a* and the close *i*; *o* a *medial*

II. CONSONANTS.[1]

	GUTTURALS.	DENTALS.	LABIALS.
1. SEMIVOWELS, *sonant*[2]	i or j = y		v = w
2. NASALS, *sonant*	n[3]	n	m
3. ASPIRATE, *surd*[2]	h		
4. FRICATIVES, comprising:			
1. *Liquids, sonant*		l, r	
2. *Spirants, surd*		s	f
5. MUTES, comprising:			
1. *Sonant mutes*	g	d	b
2. *Surd mutes*	c, k, q	t	p

NOTE. — $X = cs$, and $z = ds$, are double consonants, formed by the union of a mute with the spirant *s*.

4. Diphthongs are formed by the union of two vowels in one syllable.

NOTE. — The most common diphthongs are *ae*, *oe*, *au*, and *eu*. *Ei*, *oi*, and *ui* are rare.

PHONETIC CHANGES.

22. Vowels are often weakened, *i.e.*, are often changed to weaker vowels.

The order of the vowels, from the strongest to the weakest, is as follows:

---

vowel between the open *a* and the close *u*; *y* was introduced from the Greek.

[1] Observe that the consonants are divided:
  I. According to the ORGANS chiefly employed in their production, into
    1. Gutturals — *throat letters*, also called Palatals.
    2. Dentals — *teeth letters*, also called Linguals.
    3. Labials — *lip letters*.
  II. According to the MANNER in which they are uttered, into
    1. Sonants, or *voiced letters*.
    2. Surds, or *voiceless letters*.

[2] The distinction between a *sonant* and a *surd* will be appreciated by observing the difference between the sonant *b* and its corresponding surd *p* in such words as *bad, pad*. *B* is vocalized, *p* is not.

[3] With the sound of *n* in *concord, linger*. It occurs before gutturals. *congruenter*, suitably.

$$\text{a,} \quad \text{o,} \quad \text{u,} \quad \text{e,} \quad \text{i.}^1$$
Thus a is changed to o ... u ... e ... i.
o to u ... e ... i.
u to e ... i.
e to i.[2]

Carmen,[3] *carmenis*, *carminis*, a song, of a song; *faciō*, *cŏn-faciō*, *cŏn-ficiō*, I make, I accomplish; *factus*, *in-factus*, *in-fectus*, made, not made; *teneō*, *con-teneō*, *con-tineō*, I hold, I contain; *tuba*, *tuba-cen*, *tubi-cen*, a flute, a flute-player.

30. A Guttural — **c, g, q, (qu)** or **h,** — before **s** generally unites with it and forms **x**:

Ducs, dux, leader; *pācs, pāx*, peace; *rēgs, rēcs, rēx*, king; *lēgs, lēcs, lēx*, law: *coquŭsi, cocsi, coxi*, I have cooked; *trahsi, tracsi, traxi*, I have drawn.

31. **S** is generally changed to **r** when it stands between two vowels:

Flōsēs, flōrēs, flowers; *jūsa, jūra*, rights; *mēnsāsum, mēnsārum*, of tables; *agrōsum, agrōrum*, of fields; *esam, eram*, I was; *esāmus, erāmus*, we were.

33. PARTIAL ASSIMILATION. — A consonant is often partially[4] assimilated by a following consonant. Thus before the surd **s** or **t,** a sonant **b** or **g** is generally changed to its corresponding surd, **p** or **c**:

Scribsi, scripsi, I have written; *scribtus, scriptus*, written; *rēgsi, rēcsi, rēxi* (30), I have ruled; *regtus, rectus*, ruled.

---

[1] The change from *a* through *o* to *u* is usually arrested at *o*, while *a* is often changed directly through *e* to *i* without passing through *o* or *u*. Thus the open *a* is changed either to the close *u* through the medial *o*, as seen on the right side of the following vowel-triangle, or to the close *i* through the medial *e*, as seen on the left side:

Open vowel . . . . *a*
Medial vowels . . . . . . *e* *o*
Close vowels . . . . . . *i* *u*

[2] But *u, e*, and *i* differ so slightly in strength that they appear at times to be simply interchanged.

[3] Here *e* in *carmen* becomes *i* in *carminis*, *a* in *faciō* becomes *i* in *cŏn-ficiō*, etc.

[4] That is, it is adapted or accommodated to it, but does not become the same letter.

PRONUNCIATION OF LATIN.[1]

I. *Roman Method of Pronunciation.*[2]

5. VOWELS. — The vowel sounds are the following: —

	LONG.				SHORT.		
ā like	a	in father:	*ā'-ris.*[3]	a like	a	in Cuba:[5]	*a'-met.*
ē "	e	" prey;[4]	*ē'-di.*	e "	e	" net:	*re'-get.*
ī "	i	" machine:[4]	*i'-ri.*	i "	i	" cigar:	*vi'-det.*
ō "	o	" old:	*ō'-ras.*	o "	o	" obey:	*mo'-net.*
ū "	u	" rule:[4]	*ū'-no.*	u "	u	" full:	*su'-mus.*

1. A short vowel in a long syllable is pronounced short: *sunt,*[6] *u* as in *sum, su'-mus.* But see 16, note 2.

3. I preceded by an accented *a, e, o,* or *y,* and followed by another vowel, is a semivowel with the sound of *y* in *yet* (7): *A-chā'-ia* (A-kā'-yä).

4. U in *qu,* and generally in *gu* and *su* before a vowel, has the sound of *w: qui* (kwē), *lin'-gua* (lin'-gwä), *suā'-sit* (swä'-sit).

---

[1] In this country three distinct methods are recognized in the pronunciation of Latin. They are generally known as the *Roman,* the *English,* and the *Continental Methods.* Recent researches have revealed laws of phonetic change of great value in tracing the history of Latin words. Accordingly, whatever method of pronunciation may be adopted for actual use in the class-room, the pupil should sooner or later be made familiar with the leading features of the Roman Method, which is at least an approximation to the ancient pronunciation of the language. The pupil will, of course, at present study only the method adopted in the school.

[2] Those who adopt the English Method will now turn to page 6; those who adopt the Continental Method to page 8. Strictly speaking, there is no Continental Method, as every nation on the Continent of Europe has its own method.

[3] The Latin vowels marked with the *macron* ¯ are *long in quantity,* i.e. in the duration of the sound (16); those not marked are *short in quantity;* see 16, note 3. Observe that the *accent* is also marked. For the laws of *accentuation,* see 17 and 18 in this introduction.

[4] Or *ē* like *ā* in made, *ī* like *ē* in me, and *ū* like *oo* in moon.

[5] The short vowels can be only imperfectly represented by English equivalents. In theory they have the same sounds as the corresponding long vowels, but occupy only half as much time in utterance.

[6] Observe the difference between the *length* or *quantity* of the vowel and the *length* or *quantity* of the syllable. Here the vowel *u* is short, but the syllable *sunt* is long; see 16, I. In syllables long irrespective of the length

PRONUNCIATION.

6. Diphthongs. — In diphthongs each vowel retains its own sound:

    ae (for *ai*) like the English ay (yes): *měn'-sae*.[1]
    au   like *ow* in how: *cau'-sa*.
    oe (for *oi*) like *oi* in coin: *foe'-dus*.[2]

7. Consonants. — Most of the consonants are pronounced nearly as in English, but the following require special notice:

    c like *k* in king: *cē'-lēs* (kay-lace), *ci'-vi* (kē-wē).
    g " *g* " get: *re'-gunt, re'-gis, ge'-nus*.
    j " *y* " yet: *jŭ'-stum* (yoo-stum), *ja'-cet*.
    s " *s* " son: *sa'-cer, so'-ror, A'-si-a*.
    t " *t* " time: *ti'-mor, tŏ'-tus, ăc'-ti-ŏ*.
    v " *w* " we: *va'-dum, vi'-ci, vi'-ti-um*.[3]

8. Syllables. — In dividing words into syllables,

1. Make as many syllables as there are vowels and diphthongs: *mō'-re, per-suā'-dē, měn'-sue*.

2. Join to each vowel as many of the consonants which precede it — one or more — as can be conveniently pronounced at the beginning of a word or syllable:[4] *pa'-ter, pa'-tres, ge'-ne-ri, do'-mi-nus, men'-sa, bel'-lum*. But —

3. Compound words must be separated into their component parts, if the first of these parts ends in a consonant: *ab'-es, ob-ī'-re*.[5]

---

of the vowels contained in them, it is often difficult and sometimes absolutely impossible to determine the *natural quantity* of the vowels; but it is thought advisable to treat vowels as short in all situations where there are not good reasons for believing them to be long.

[1] Combining the sounds of *a* and *i*.
[2] *Ei* as in *veil, eu* with the sounds of *e* and *u* combined, and *oi = oe*, occur in a few words: *dein, neu'-ter, proin*.
[3] There is some uncertainty in regard to the sound of *v*. Corssen gives it at the beginning of a word the sound of the English r.
[4] By some grammarians any combination of consonants which can begin either a Latin or a Greek word is always joined to the following vowel, as *o'-mnis, i'-pse*. Others, on the contrary, think that the Romans pronounced with each vowel as many of the following consonants as could be readily combined with it.
[5] Those who adopt the *Roman Pronunciation*, omitting the *English* and the *Continental Method*, will now turn to Lesson I., page 15.

II. *English Method of Pronunciation.*

9. Vowels. — Vowels generally have their long or short English sounds.

10. Long Sounds. — Vowels have their long English sounds — a as in *fate*, e in *mete*, i in *pine*, o in *note*, u in *tube*, y in *type* — in the following situations: —

1. In final syllables ending in a vowel: —

Se, si, ser'-vi, ser'-ro, cor'-nu, mi'-sy.

2. In all syllables, before a vowel or diphthong: —

De'-us, de-o'-rum, de'-ae, di-e'-i, ni'-hi-lum.[1]

3. In penultimate[2] syllables before a single consonant, or before a mute followed by a liquid: —

Pa'-ter, pa'-tres, ho-no'-ris, A'-thos, O'-thrys.

4. In unaccented syllables, not final, before a single consonant, or before a mute followed by a liquid: —

Do-lo'-ris, cor'-po-ri, con'-su-lis, a-gric'-o-la.

1. **A** *unaccented*, except before consonants in final syllables (11, 1), has the sound of *a final* in *America: men'-sa, a-cu'-tus, a-ma'-mus.*[3]

2. **I** and **y** *unaccented*, in any syllable except the first and last, generally have the short sound: *nob'-i-lis* (nob'-e-lis), *Am'-y-cus* (Am'-e-cus).

3. **I** preceded by an accented *a, e, o,* or *y,* and followed by another vowel, is a semivowel with the sound of *y* in *yet: A-cha'-ia* (A-ka'-ya), *Pom-pe'-ius* (Pom-pe'-yus), *La-to'-ia* (La-to'-ya), *Har-py'-ia* (Har-py'-ya).

4. **U** in *qu*, and generally in *gu* and *su* before a vowel, has the sound of *w: qui* (kwi), *qua; lin'-gua* (lin'-gwa); *sua'-de-o* (swa'-de-o).

11. Short Sounds. — Vowels have their short English sounds — a as in *fat*, e in *met*, i in *pin*, o in *not*, u in *tub*, y in *myth* — in the following situations: —

---

[1] In these rules no account is taken of the aspirate *h:* hence the first *i* in *nihilum* is treated as a vowel before another vowel; for the same reason, *ch, ph,* and *th* are treated as single mutes; thus *th* in *Athos* and *Othrys.*

[2] Penultimate, the last syllable but one.

[3] Some give the same sound to *a final* in monosyllables: *da, qua;* while others give it the *long* sound, according to 10, 1.

PRONUNCIATION.

1. In final syllables ending in a consonant: —
A'-mat, a'-met, rex'-it, sol, con'-sul, Te'-thys; except *post, es final*, and *os final* in plural cases: *res, di'-es, hos, a'-gros.*

2. In all syllables before *x*, or any two consonants except a mute followed by a liquid (10, 3 and 4): —
Rex'-it, bel'-lum, rex-e'-runt, bel-lo'-rum.

3. In all accented syllables, not penultimate, before one or more consonants: —
Dom'-i-nus, pat'-ri-bus. But —

1) A, e, or o before a single consonant (or a mute and a liquid), followed by *e, i,* or *y* before another vowel, has the long sound: *a'-ci-es, a'-cri-a, me'-re-o, do'-ce-o.*

2) U, in any syllable not final, before a single consonant or a mute and a liquid, except *bl*, has the long sound: *Pu'-ni-cus, sa-lu'-bri-tas.*

12. DIPHTHONGS. — Diphthongs are pronounced as follows:

Ae like *e*: *Cae'-sar, Daed'-a-lus.*[1] | Au as in author: *au'-rum.*
Oe like *e*: *Oe'-ta, Oed'-i-pus.*[1] | Eu[2] as in neuter: *neu'-ter.*

13. CONSONANTS. — The consonants are pronounced in general as in English. Thus: —

I. C and G are *soft* (like *s* and *j*) before *e, i, y, ae,* and *oe,* and *hard* in other situations[3]: *ce'-do* (se'-do), *ci-vis, Cy'-rus, cae'-do, coe'-pi, a'-ge* (a'-je), *a'-gi; ca'-do* (ka-do), *co'-go, cum, Ga'-des.*

II. S, T, and X are generally pronounced as in the English words *son, time, expect: sa'-cer, ti'-mor, rex'-i* (rek'-si). But —

1. *S, T,* and *X* are aspirated before *i* preceded by an accented syllable and followed by a vowel, — *s* and *t* taking the sound of *sh,* and *x* that of *ksh: Al'-si-um* (Al'-she-um), *ar'-ti-um* (ar'-she-um), *anx'-i-us* (ank'-she-us).

---

[1] The diphthong has the *long sound* in *Cae'-sar* and *Oe'-ta,* according to 10, 3, but the *short sound* in *Daed'-a-lus* (Ded'-a-lus) and *Oed'-i-pus* (Ed'-i-pus). according to 11, 3, as *e* would be thus pronounced in the same situations.

[2] *Ei* and *oi* are seldom diphthongs, but when so used they are pronounced as in *height, coin: hei, proin. Ui,* as a diphthong, with the long sound of *i,* occurs in *cui, hui, huic.*

[3] *C* has the sound of *sh* —
1. Before *i* preceded by an accented syllable and followed by a vowel: *so'-ci-us* (so'-she-us);
2. Before *eu* and *yo* preceded by an accented syllable: *ca-du'-ce-us* (ca-du'-she-us), *Sic'-y-on* (Sish'-y-on)

2. *S* is pronounced like *z* —

1) At the end of a word, after *c*, *ae*, *au*, *b*, *m*, *n*, *r* : *spes, pracs, laus, urbs, hi'-ems, mons, pars ;*

2) In a few words after the analogy of the corresponding English words: *Cae'-sar*, Caesar; *cau'-sa*, cause; *mu'-sa*, muse; *mi'-ser*, miser, miserable, etc.

3. *X* at the beginning of a word has the sound of *z* : *Xan'-thus.*

14. Syllables. — In dividing words into syllables —

1. Make as many syllables as there are vowels and diphthongs: *mo'-re, per-sua'-de, men'-sae.*

2. Distribute the consonants so as to give the proper sound to each vowel and diphthong, as determined by previous rules (10–12): *pa'-ter, pa'-tres, a-gro'-rum, au-di'-ri, gen'-e-ri, dom'-i-nus.*

III. *Continental Method of Pronunciation.*

5. Vowels. — The vowel sounds are the following : — .

Long.				Short.			
ā like *ä* in father:	ū'-ris.[1]		a like *a* in Cuba:[3]	a'-met.
ē " *e* " prey:[2]	ē'-di.		e " *e* " net:	re'-get.
ī " *ī* " machine:[2]	ī'-ri.		i " *i* " cigar:	vi'-det.
ō " *ō* " old:	ō'-ras.		o " *o* " obey:	mo'-net.
ū " *u* " rule:[2]	ū'-no.		u " *u* " full:	su'-mus.

1. A short vowel in a long syllable is pronounced short: *sunt*,[4] *u* as in *sum, su'-mus*. But see 16, note 2.

6. Diphthongs. — In diphthongs each vowel retains its own sound: —

    ae (for *ai*) like the English **ay** (yes): *men'-sae*.[5]
    au   like *ow* in how: *cau'-sa*.
    oe (for *oi*) like *oi* in coin: *foe'-dus*.[6]

---

[1] The Latin vowels marked with the *macron* ¯ are *long in quantity*, i.e. in the duration of the sound (16); those not marked are *short in quantity*; see 16, note 3.

[2] Or *ē* like *ā* in made, *ī* like *ē* in me, and *ū* like *oo* in moon.

[3] The sounds of the vowels and diphthongs are the same as in the Roman method; see pages 4 and 5.

[4] See foot-note 6, page 4.   [5] See foot-note 1, page 5.

[6] See foot-note 2, page 5.

QUANTITY.

13. CONSONANTS. — The consonants are pronounced in general as in English; see 13, I., II. 1, 2, page 7.

14. SYLLABLES. — In dividing words into syllables make as many syllables as there are vowels and diphthongs: *mō'-re, per-suā'-dē, měn'-sae.*[1]

QUANTITY.

16. Syllables are in quantity or length either long, short, or common.[2]

I. LONG. — A syllable is long in quantity —

1. If it contains a diphthong or a long vowel: *haec, rēs.*[3]
2. If its vowel is followed by *x* or *z* or any two consonants, except a mute and a liquid:[4] *dux, rēx, sunt.*[5]

II. SHORT. — A syllable is short, if its vowel is followed by another vowel, by a diphthong, or by the aspirate *h: di-ēs, vi-ae, ni''-hil.*[6]

---

[1] Join to each vowel as many of the consonants which precede it — one or more — as can be conveniently pronounced at the beginning of a word or syllable: *pa'-ter, pa'-trēs, ge'-ne-rī, do'-mi-nus, měn'-sa, bel'-lum.* But compound words must be separated into their component parts, if the first of these parts ends in a consonant: *ab'-es, ob-ī'-re.*

[2] Common, *i.e.* sometimes long and sometimes short.

[3] See note 3, below.

[4] That is, in the order here given, with the mute before the liquid; if the liquid precedes, the syllable is long.

[5] Observe that the vowel in such syllables may be either long or short. Thus it is long in *rēx*, but short in *dux* and *sunt.*

[6] By referring to pages 4 and 8, it will be seen, that, in the Roman Method and in the Continental, *quantity* and *sound* coincide with each other: a vowel long in quantity is long in sound, and a vowel short in quantity is short in sound. But, by referring to 10 and 11, it will be seen, that, in the English Method, the quantity of a vowel does not at all affect its sound, except in determining the accent (18). Hence, in this method, a vowel long in quantity is often short in sound, and a vowel short in quantity is often long in sound. Thus in *rēx* and *sōl*, the vowels are long in quantity; but by 11, 1, they have the short English sounds: while in *are, mare*, the vowels are all short in quantity; but by 10, 1 and 3, they all have the long English sounds. Hence, in pronouncing according to the English Method, determine the place of the accent by the quantity, according to

III. Common. — A syllable is common, if its vowel, naturally[1] short, is followed by a mute and a liquid: *a-gri*.

Note 1. — Vowels are also in quantity either long, short, or common; but the quantity of the vowel does not always coincide with the quantity of the syllable.[2]

Note 2. — Vowels are long before *ns*, *nf*, *gn*, and *gm*; *cŏn'-sul*, *in-fē'-lix*, *rĕg'-num*, *āgmen*.

Note 3. — The signs ¯, ˘ are used to mark the quantity of vowels, the first denoting that the vowel over which it is placed is *long*, the second that it is *common*, i.e. sometimes long and sometimes short: *a-mā-bŏ*. All vowels not marked are to be treated as short.[3]

ACCENTUATION.

17. Words of two syllables are always accented on the first: *mēn'-sa*.

18. Words of more than two syllables are accented on the *Penult*,[4] if that is long in quantity;[5] otherwise on the *Antepenult*:[4] *ho-nō'-ris*, *cŏn'-su-lis*.[6]

3. A secondary or subordinate accent is placed on the second or third syllable before the primary accent — on the second, if that is the first syllable of the word, or is long in quantity, otherwise on the third: *mo'-nu-ē'-runt*, *mo'-nu-e-rā'-mus*,[7] *in-stau'-ra-vē'runt*.

18, and then determine the sounds of the letters irrespective of quantity, according to 10-13.

[1] A vowel is said to be *naturally* short, when it is short in its own *nature*; i.e. in itself, without reference to its position.

[2] Thus in long syllables the vowels may be either long or short, as in *rēx*, *dux*, *sunt* (see foot-note 6, p. 4). But in short syllables the vowels are also short.

[3] See p. 4, foot-note 6. In many works short vowels are marked with the sign ˘: *rĕgis*.

[4] The penult is the last syllable but one; the antepenult, the last but two.

[5] Thus the quantity of the *syllable*, not of the *vowel*, determines the place of the accent: *regen'-tis*, accented on the penult, because that syllable is *long*, though its *vowel* is *short*: see 16, I., 2.

[6] In the subsequent pages, the pupil will be expected to accent words in pronunciation according to these rules.

[7] In the English Method divide thus: *mon'-u-ĕ'-runt*, *mon-u-e-ra'-mus*.

SENTENCES. — VERBS.

346. A sentence is a combination of words expressing either a single thought or two or more thoughts.

347. A SIMPLE SENTENCE expresses a single thought:
Deus mundum aedificāvit, *God made (built) the world.* Cic.

348. A COMPLEX SENTENCE expresses one leading thought with one or more dependent thoughts:
Dōnec eris fēlix, multōs numerābis amīcōs, *so long as you shall be prosperous, you will number many friends.*[1] Ovid.

349. A COMPOUND SENTENCE expresses two or more independent thoughts:
Sōl ruit et montēs umbrantur, *the sun hastens to its setting and the mountains are shaded.* Verg.

356. The SIMPLE SENTENCE in its MOST SIMPLE FORM consists of two distinct parts, expressed or implied: —

1. The SUBJECT, or that of which it speaks;
2. The PREDICATE, or that which is said of the subject:
Cluilius moritur, *Cluilius dies.*[2] Liv.

NOTE. — In Latin, both subject and predicate may be contained or implied in a single word, if that word is a verb:
Amās,[3] *thou lovest.* Amat,[3] *he loves.*

357. The SIMPLE SENTENCE in its MOST EXPANDED FORM consists of these same parts with their various modifiers:

---

[1] In this example two simple sentences — (1) '*you will be prosperous,*' and (2) '*you will number many friends*' — are so united that the first only specifies the *time* of the second: *You will number many friends so long as you shall be prosperous.* The part of the complex sentence which makes complete sense of itself — *multōs numerābis amīcōs* — is called the *Principal* or *Independent Clause ;* and the part which is dependent upon it — *dōnec eris fēlix* — is called the *Subordinate* or *Dependent Clause.*

[2] Here *Cluilius* is the subject, and *moritur* the predicate.

[3] The ending *s* shows that the subject is of the *second person singular*, THOU, while *t* shows that it is of the *third person singular*, HE.

In his castris Cluilius, Albānus rēx, moritur, *Cluilius, the Alba king, dies in this camp.*¹ Liv.

192. Verbs in Latin, as in English, express existence condition, or action: *est*, he is; *dormit*, he is sleeping *legit*, he reads.

193. Verbs comprise two principal classes:—

I. TRANSITIVE VERBS admit a direct object of the action *servum verberat*, he beats the slave.²

II. INTRANSITIVE VERBS do not admit such an object *puer currit*, the boy runs.²

194. Verbs have *Voice, Mood, Tense, Number and Person*

195. There are two voices:

I. The ACTIVE VOICE³ represents the subject as ACTING or EXISTING: *pater filium amat*, the father loves his son *est*, he is.

II. The PASSIVE VOICE represents the subject as ACTED UPON by some other person or thing: *filius ā patre amātus* the son is loved by his father.

196. There are three moods:⁴—

I. The INDICATIVE MOOD either asserts something as *fact* or inquires after the *fact:*

Legit, HE IS READING. *Legitne*, IS HE READING? *Servius rēg nāvit, Servius* REIGNED. *Quis ego sum, who* AM I?

---

¹ Here *Cluilius, Albānus rēx*, is the subject in its enlarged or modifie form: *in his castris moritur*, the predicate in its enlarged or modified form

² Here *servum*, 'the slave,' is the object of the action; *beats* (what? *the slave*. The object thus *completes* the meaning of the verb. *He beat* is incomplete in sense, but *the boy runs* is complete, and accordingly doe not admit an object.

³ *Voice* shows whether the subject *acts* (Active Voice), or is *acted upo* (Passive Voice). Thus, with the Active Voice, '*the father loves his son* the subject, *father*, is the one who *performs the action, loves*, while wit the Passive Voice, '*the son is loved by the father*,' the subject, *son*, merel *receives the action, is acted upon, is loved.*

⁴ *Mood*, or *Mode*, means *manner*, and relates to the manner in whic the meaning of the verb is expressed, as will be seen by observing th force of the several moods.

VERBS.

II. The Subjunctive Mood expresses not an actual fact, but a *possibility* or *conception*.

Amēmus patriam, LET US LOVE *our country.* *Sint* beāti, MAY THEY BE *happy.* *Quaerat* quispiam, *some one* MAY INQUIRE.

III. The Imperative Mood expresses a *command* or an *entreaty:*

Jūstĭtĭam *cole,* PRACTISE *justice.* Tū nē cēde malis, DO *not* YIELD *to misfortunes.*

197. There are six tenses:[1]

I. Three Tenses for Incomplete Action: —
1. Present: *amō,* I love, I am loving.
2. Imperfect: *amābam,* I was loving, I loved.
3. Future: *amābō,* I shall love, I will love.

II. Three Tenses for Completed Action:
1. Perfect: *amāvī,* I have loved, I loved.
2. Pluperfect: *amāveram,* I had loved.
3. Future Perfect: *amāverō,* I shall have loved.

198. Tenses are also distinguished as —

I. Principal or Primary Tenses:
1. Present: *amō,* I love.
2. Present Perfect: *amāvī,* I have loved.
3. Future: *amābō,* I shall love.
4. Future Perfect: *amāverō,* I shall have loved.

II. Historical or Secondary Tenses:
1. Imperfect: *amābam,* I was loving.
2. Historical Perfect: *amāvī,* I loved.
3. Pluperfect: *amāveram,* I had loved.

199. In *Verbs,* as in Nouns (44), there are two numbers, Singular and Plural, and three persons, First, Second, and Third.

Note. — The various verbal forms which have voice, mood, tense, number, and person, make up the *finite verb.*

---

[1] *Tense* means *time.* The tense of a verb shows the *time* of the action.

200. Among verbal forms are included the following verbal nouns and adjectives:

I. The INFINITIVE is a verbal noun. It is sometimes best translated by the English *Infinitive*, sometimes by the *verbal noun in* ING, and sometimes by the *Indicative:*

Exīre ex urbe volŏ, *I wish* TO GO *out of the city.* Gestiō scīre omnia, *I long* TO KNOW *all things.* Haec scīre juvat, TO KNOW *these things affords pleasure.*

II. The GERUND gives the meaning of the verb in the form of a verbal noun of the second declension,[1] used only in the *genitive, dative, accusative,* and *ablative singular.* It corresponds to the English verbal noun in ING:

Amandī, OF LOVING. *Amandī* causā, *for the sake* OF LOVING. Ars vivendi, *the art* OF LIVING. *Ad discendum* propēnsus, *inclined* TO LEARN, or TO LEARNING.

III. The SUPINE gives the meaning of the verb in the form of a verbal noun of the fourth declension.[2] It has a form in **um** and a form in **ū**:

Amātum, TO LOVE, FOR LOVING. *Amātū,* TO BE LOVED, FOR LOVING, IN LOVING. Auxilium *postulātum* vēnit, *he came* TO ASK *aid.* Difficile *dictū* est, *it is difficult* TO TELL.

IV. The PARTICIPLE in Latin, as in English, gives the meaning of the verb in the form of an adjective. It is sometimes best translated by the English *Participle* or *Infinitive,* and sometimes by a *Clause:*

Amāns, LOVING. *Amātūrus,* ABOUT TO LOVE. *Amātus,* LOVED. *Amandus,* DESERVING TO BE LOVED. Platō *scrībēns* mortuus est, *Plato died* WHILE WRITING, or WHILE HE WAS WRITING.

NOTE. — A Latin verb may have four participles: two in the Active, the Present and the Future, *amāns, amātūrus;* and two in the Passive, the Perfect and the Gerundive, *amātus, amandus.*

201. Regular verbs are inflected, or conjugated, in four different ways, and are accordingly divided into Four Conjugations.

---

[1] See 32. [1]   [2] See 92. 116.

LESSONS AND EXERCISES.

LESSON I.

PARTS OF SPEECH.—NOUNS.

1. *Lesson from the Grammar.*[1]

38. In Latin, as in English, words are divided, according to their use, into eight classes, called *Parts of Speech,* viz.: *Nouns, Adjectives, Pronouns, Verbs, Adverbs, Prepositions, Conjunctions,* and *Interjections.*[2]

NOUNS.

39. A Noun or Substantive is a name, as of a person, place, or thing: *Cicerŏ,* Cicero; *Rōma,* Rome; *domus,* house.

1. A PROPER NOUN is a proper name, as of a person or place: *Cicerŏ; Rōma.*

2. A COMMON NOUN is a name common to all the members of a class of objects: *vir,* man; *equus,* horse.

40. Nouns have *Gender, Number, Person, and Case.*

---

[1] The lessons are from the author's Latin Grammar, and the numerals at the side of the page, 38, 39, etc., designate articles in that work. It is advised that the Introduction be used mainly for reference, but that such parts of it be learned from time to time as the interests of the class may require. For pronunciation the pupil must at first depend upon his teacher, but he will soon be able to profit by the rules contained in the Introduction.

[2] In general, the use of the Parts of Speech is the same in Latin as in English.

I. Gender.

41. There are three genders:[1] *Masculine*, *Feminine*, and *Neuter*.

NOTE.—In some nouns, gender is determined by signification; in others, by endings.

42. GENERAL RULES FOR GENDER.

I. Masculines:—

1. Names of *Males;* *Cicerŏ;* vir, man; *rēx*, king.
2. Names of *Rivers, Winds*, and *Months:* *Rhēnus*, Rhine; *Notus*, south wind; *Mārtius*, March.

II. Feminines:—

1. Names of *Females:* *mulier*, woman; *leaena*, lioness.
2. Names of *Countries, Towns, Islands*, and *Trees: Graecia*, Greece; *Rōma*, Rome; *Dēlos*, Delos; *pirus*, pear-tree.

II. Person and Number.

44. The Latin, like the English, has three persons and two numbers. The first person denotes the speaker; the second, the person spoken to; the third, the person spoken of. The singular number denotes one; the plural, more than one.

2. *In this exercise give the* GENDER *and* NUMBER *of each noun, and tell whether it is* COMMON *or* PROPER.

1. Caesar (*Caesar*), Alexander (*Alexander*), Graecia (*Greece*). 2. Mātrēs (*mothers*), māter (*a mother*), Hispānia (*Spain*). 3. Pater (*a father*), patrēs (*fathers*), Rhēnus (*the river Rhine*). 4. Puer (*a boy*), puerī (*boys*), puella (*a girl*), puellae (*girls*). 5. Sicilia (*Sicily*), Sparta (*the city Sparta*), mīles (*a soldier*), mīlitēs (*soldiers*).

---

[1] In English, *gender* denotes *sex*. Accordingly, masculine nouns denote *males;* feminine nouns, *females;* and neuter nouns, objects which are *neither male nor female*. In Latin, however, this natural distinction of gender is applied only to the names of *males* and *females;* while, in all other nouns, gender depends upon an artificial distinction, according to grammatical rules.

LESSON II.

NOUNS.—CASES.

3. *Lessons from the Grammar.*

45. The Latin has six cases:[1] —

NAMES.	ENGLISH EQUIVALENTS.
Nominative,	Nominative.
Genitive,	Possessive, or Objective with *of*.
Dative,	Objective with *to* or *for*.
Accusative,	Objective.
Vocative,	Nominative Independent.
Ablative,	Objective with *from*, *with*, *by*, *in*.

Thus in general the English cases are represented in Latin as follows:

1. The *Nominative*, by the *Nominative* in Latin:

THE QUEEN is praised. *Regina laudatur.*[2]

2. The *Possessive* and the *Objective* with *of*, by the *Genitive* in Latin:

THE QUEEN's daughter is praised.   Filia *reginae* laudatur.[3]
The daughter OF THE QUEEN is praised.   Filia *reginae* laudatur.

3. The *Objective* with *to* or *for*, by the *Dative* in Latin; the *Objective without a preposition*, by the *Accusative:*

They give a BOOK TO THE QUEEN. *Reginae librum donant.*[4]

---

[1] The *case* of a noun shows the relation which that noun sustains to other words: as, *John's book.* Here the *possessive case* shows that John sustains to the book the relation of *possessor.*

[2] Observe that the English words to be illustrated are printed in SMALL CAPITALS and the corresponding Latin in *Italics.* QUEEN is in the *Nominative,* and is the subject of the verb *is praised,* and *regina,* the corresponding word in the Latin, is also in the *Nominative* and is the subject of the Latin verb *laudatur.* The Latin has no article; accordingly *regina* may mean *a queen, the queen,* or simply *queen.*

[3] Here *daughter,* the subject of the English sentence, and *filia,* the subject of the Latin sentence, are both in the *Nominative,* but the possessive *queen's,* or its equivalent, *of the queen,* becomes in the Latin *reginae,* the *Genitive* of *regina.*

[4] *Book,* the object of *give,* is in the *Objective* case, and the correspond-

4. The *Nominative Independent* in an address, by the *Vocative* in Latin:

They praise you, O QUEEN. Tē, rēgīna, laudant.[1]

5. The *Objective* with *from, with, by, in,* by the *Ablative* in Latin:

They are fortifying the city WITH A WALL. Urbem vallō mūniunt.[2]
They are walking IN THE GARDEN. In hortō ambulant.

NOTE 1. The Genitive, Dative, Accusative, and Ablative are called the *Oblique Cases*.

NOTE 2. The Latin has also a few remnants of another case, called the *Locative*, denoting the *place in which*.

4. *In this exercise give the* GENDER, NUMBER, *and* CASE *of each Noun, and tell whether it is* COMMON *or* PROPER.

1. Rēx (*the king*) laudātur (*is praised*). 2. Fīlius (*the son*) rēgis (*of the king*) laudātur (*is praised*). 3. Fīliī (*the sons*) rēgis (*of the king*) laudantur (*are praised*). 4. Fīliī (*the sons*) rēgum (*of kings*) laudantur (*are praised*). 5. Rēx (*the king*) fīliam (*his*[3] *daughter*) amat (*loves*). 6. Rēx (*the king*) fīliās (*his daughters*) amat (*loves*). 7. Caesar (*Caesar*) mīlitēs (*the soldiers*) laudat (*praises*). 8. Mīlitēs (*the soldiers*) laudantur (*are praised*).

---

ing Latin, *librum*, the object of the Latin verb *dōnant*, is in the Accusative, but the words *to the queen* are rendered by *rēgīnae*, the *Dative* of *rēgīna*. Observe the order of the words:

ENGLISH ORDER: They give a book to the queen.
LATIN ORDER: To the queen a book they give.

[1] *O queen* is rendered by the Vocative *rēgīna;* and *you*, the object of praise, by the Accusative *tē*, the object of *laudant*. Here again observe the order of the words.

[2] *With a wall* is rendered by the Ablative *vallō*, but *in the garden* by the Ablative with *in: in hortō*. Observe the order of the words:

ENGLISH ORDER: They are fortifying the city with a wall.
LATIN ORDER: The city with a wall they are fortifying.
ENGLISH ORDER: They are walking in the garden.
LATIN ORDER: In the garden they are walking.

Observe that in all these examples the verb in Latin stands at the end of the sentence.

[3] In Latin the possessive pronouns, meaning *his, her, their*, when not emphatic, are seldom expressed if they can be supplied from the context.

LESSON III.

SENTENCES.—VERBS.—CERTAIN FORMS OF THE FIRST CONJUGATION.

5. *Lesson from the Grammar.*

356. Every SENTENCE consists of two distinct parts, expressed or implied:—

1. The SUBJECT, or that of which it speaks;
2. The PREDICATE, or that which is said of the subject:

Cluilius moritur, Cluilius dies.¹ Liv.

NOTE.—In Latin, both subject and predicate may be contained or implied in a single word, if that word is a verb :

Amās,² *thou lovest.* Amat,² *he loves.*

201. Regular verbs ³ are conjugated in four different ways, and are accordingly divided into Four Conjugations.

6. In Verbs of the FIRST CONJUGATION, the THIRD PERSON in the *singular* and *plural* of the *present, imperfect,* and *future* tenses of the *indicative mood* has the following —

ENDINGS.

PRESENT.	IMPERFECT.	FUTURE.
Singular, at,	ābat,	ābit.
Plural, ant,	ābant,	ābunt.

PARADIGM.

SINGULAR.	PLURAL.
Pres. am**a**t, *he loves ;* ⁴	am**a**nt, *they love.*
Imp. am**ābat**, *he was loving ;* ⁵	am**ābant**, *they were loving.* ⁵
Fut. am**ābit**, *he will love ;*	am**ābunt**, *they will love.* ⁶

---

¹ *Cluilius* is the subject, and *moritur* the predicate.

² The ending *s* shows that the subject is of the *second person singular,* THOU, while *t* shows that it is of the *third person singular,* HE.

³ For *verbs, mood, tense, number,* and *person,* see pages 12 and 13.

⁴ The subject of each of these verbs may be, in English, either *he, she,* or *it : amat, he loves, she loves,* or *it loves.* The suffix, *t,* shows the number and person of the subject, but not its gender.

⁵ Or, *he loved ;* plural, *they loved.* See page 13, 197.

⁶ Each of these Latin forms, *amat, amant,* etc., consists of two distinct elements—(1) the *stem,* which gives the *general meaning* of the verb;

7. In English, the *tenses, numbers,* and *persons* of verbs are indicated by certain *words* or *signs;* as,

PRESENT.	IMPERFECT.	FUTURE.
He loves,	he *was* loving,	he *will* love.
They love,	they *were* loving,	they *will* love.

In Latin, however, no such *signs* are used; but their place is supplied by the *endings* of the verb. Hence, in translating English into Latin, omit these signs, and express the *tense, number,* and *person* of the verb by the *proper endings:*

	PRESENT.	IMPERFECT.	FUTURE.
Eng.	*He* loves,	he *was* loving,	he *will* love,
Lat.	Am*at*,	am*ābat*,	am*ābit*.

LESSON IV.

CERTAIN FORMS OF THE FIRST CONJUGATION.—EXERCISES.

8. *Vocabulary.*[1]

Ambulat,	*he walks, he is walking.*[2]
Arat,	*he ploughs, he is ploughing.*
Dēlĭberat,	*he deliberates, he is deliberating.*
Equitat,	*he rides, he is riding.*
Lacrĭmat,	*he weeps, he is weeping.*
Nāvigat,	*he sails, he is sailing.*
Rēgnat,	*he reigns, he is reigning.*

---

and (2) the *suffix,* added to the *stem,* to designate *tense, number,* and *person.* Thus in

ama-t	ama-nt
amā-bat	amā-bant
amā-bit	amā-bunt

the stem is *amā,* and the suffixes are *t, nt, bat, bant, bit, bunt;* but as in some verbal forms the final vowel of the stem has become inseparably united with the suffix, it is impossible to keep the two elements of the word distinct. We accordingly give the *endings* produced by the union of this final vowel with the suffix, as above, *at, ant,* etc.

The *final vowel of the stem* is called the *stem characteristic.*

[1] It is recommended that the Vocabularies be so carefully and accurately learned that the pupil shall be able to give with promptness either the English for the Latin or the Latin for the English.

[2] Or, *she walks,* etc.

FIRST CONJUGATION. 21

9. *In this exercise, first pronounce the several sentences with care, then give the* TENSE, NUMBER, *and* PERSON *of each Verb, and finally translate the whole into English.*

1. Regnat,[1] regnant. 2. Deliberabat, deliberabant. 3. Lacrimabit, lacrimabunt. 4. Ambulant, arant, equitant. 5. Equitat, equitabat, equitabit. 6. Navigat, navigabat, navigabunt. 7. Ambulat, ambulabunt, ambulabat. 8. Regnant, regnabit, regnabant. 9. Navigant, ambulabit, equitabant.

10. *Translate into Latin.*

1. He was reigning, they will reign, she will reign.[2] 2. They are walking, he will walk, they were walking. 3. She is weeping, they will weep, he was weeping. 4. They will ride, he will sail. 5. He is deliberating, they will deliberate. 6. He was ploughing, they will plough. 7. They were ploughing, he will plough. 8. They were sailing, they are deliberating.

---

[1] In preparing this exercise, notice carefully the endings of the words; even a Roman could not understand this Latin without attending to these endings. What, then, is the meaning of the endings *at, ant,* in *regnat, regnant?* They show that in the first the *subject,* or *agent,* of the action is in the third person singular, *he, she,* or *it;* and, in the second, in the third person plural, *they.* But these endings also show that the verbs are in the present tense. How does that fact help you to understand the meaning? It tells you that the action is now taking place : *He is reigning.*

Again, what is the meaning of *ābat, ābant,* in *dēlīberābat, dēlīberābant,* and of *ābit, ābunt,* in *lacrimābit, lacrimābunt?* What do these endings tell you about the *subjects* of these verbs? What about their *tense?* What about the *time of each action?* The endings *ābat* and *ābant* assure you that the action of the verb was taking place at some past time; *ābit* and *ābunt* that it will be taking place or will take place at some future time.

In these exercises you may use at pleasure either *he* or *she* as subject, if the sense permits: *he reigns, he is reigning,* or *she reigns, she is reigning.* You should, however, accustom yourself to think of all the possible meanings of a Latin word, or of a Latin sentence, before you attempt to translate it. This habit, if early formed, will be of great value to you in your subsequent work.

[2] Observe that the English pronouns, *he, she, it, they,* are not to be rendered by separate Latin words, as the Latin verb contains a pronominal subject in itself. Hence, 'he reigns,' *regnat;* 'they reign,' *regnant.*

3

LESSON V.

NOUNS. — CASES. — FIRST DECLENSION.

11. *Lesson from the Grammar.*

46. DECLENSIONS. — The process by which the several cases of a word are formed is called Declension. It consists in the addition of certain suffixes to one common base called the stem.[1] In Latin there are five declensions.

FIRST DECLENSION. — A NOUNS.

48. Nouns of the first declension end in a and ē—*feminine*; ās and ēs—*masculine*.[2]

Nouns in *a* are declined as follows:

SINGULAR.

EXAMPLE.	MEANING.	CASE-ENDING.[4]
Nom. mēnsa,	*a table*,[3]	a
Gen. mēnsae,	*of a table*,	ae
Dat. mēnsae,	*to, for a table*,	ae
Acc. mēnsam,	*a table*,	am
Voc. mēnsa,	*O table*,	a
Abl. mēnsā,	*from, with, by a table*,	ā

PLURAL.

Nom. mēnsae,	*tables*,	ae
Gen. mēnsārum,	*of tables*,	ārum
Dat. mēnsīs,	*to, for tables*,	īs
Acc. mēnsās,	*tables*,	ās
Voc. mēnsae,	*O tables*,	ae
Abl. mēnsīs,	*from, with, by tables*.	īs

---

[1] Thus each case-form contains the *stem*, which gives the general meaning of the word, and the *case-suffix*, which shows its relation to some other word. In *rēg-is*, 'of a king,' the general idea, *king*, is denoted by the stem, *rēg*; the relation *of*, by the suffix *is*. When the stem ends in a vowel, the *case-suffix* is seen only in combination with that vowel. The ending thus produced is called a *case-ending*, and the final vowel of the stem is called the *stem characteristic* or simply the *characteristic*.

[2] That is, nouns of this declension in *a* and *ē* are feminine, and those in *ās* and *ēs* are masculine, unless their gender is determined by their *signification* according to the General Rules: see page 16, 42.

[3] *Mēnsa* may be translated *a table*, *table*, or *the table*.

[4] These *case-endings* should be carefully studied and compared, as

FIRST DECLENSION. 23

1. **Stem.** — In nouns of the first declension, the stem ends in ā.[1]
2. In the PARADIGM, observe that the stem is *mēnsā*,[1] and that the several cases are distinguished by their case-endings.[2]
3. **Examples for Practice.** — Like *mēnsa* decline : —
Āla, wing; aqua, water; causa, cause; fortūna, fortune.
4. **Locative.** — Names of towns and a very few other words have a Locative Singular in ae, denoting the *place in which* (p. 18, note 2): *Rōmae*, at Rome; *mīlitiae*, in war.

LESSON VI.

NOUNS. — FIRST DECLENSION. — NOMINATIVE CASE. — RULES III. AND XXXVI.

12. *Examine carefully the following examples.*

1. Rēgnat,   He, she, or it reigns.[3]
2. Numa rēgnat,   Numa reigns.[4]
3. Rēgnat,   He reigns.
4. Victōria rēgnat, Victoria reigns.
5. Rēgnat,   She reigns.
6. Rēginae rēgnant, Queens reign.
7. Rēgnant,   They reign.[4]

---

they will serve as a practical guide to the learner in distinguishing the different cases and in ascertaining the meaning of words.

[1] Remember that the final vowel of the *stem* forms a part of the *case-ending*. See page 22, foot-note, 1.

[2] Observe also (1) that the *Nominative* and *Vocative* are alike, (2) that the *Dative* and *Ablative* plural are alike, and (3) that the *Genitive* and *Dative* singular and the *Nominative* and *Vocative* plural are all alike.

[3] This is the full meaning of *rēgnat* when there is nothing in the context to restrict it, but take notice that in the third example it is rendered *he reigns*, because we make it refer to *Numa*, the king, while in the fifth example it is rendered *she reigns*, because we make it refer to *Victōria*.

[4] Observe (1) that *rēgnant*, 'they reign,' differs from *rēgnat*, 'he, she, or it reigns,' only in having *nt*, meaning *they*, as its ending, while *rēgnat* has simply *t*, meaning *he, she, it*; and (2) that, though the forms of the verb thus contain a pronoun, yet a substantive may at any time be introduced as subject, and that then the pronoun is not translated. Thus *rēgnat*, 'he, she, or it reigns,' but *Numa rēgnat*, 'Numa reigns' (*not* 'Numa he reigns'), *Victōria rēgnat*, 'Victoria reigns,' *rēgnant*, 'they reign,' but *rēginae rēgnant*, 'queens reign.'

Note 1. — Observe (1) that in the first, third, fifth, and seventh examples the subjects are pronouns implied in the endings *at*, *ant*, or, more strictly, *t*, *nt*, *he*, *she*, *it*, *they*, and (2) that in the second example the subject is *Numa*, in the fourth *Victoria*, and in the sixth *reginae*, and that these three subjects are all in the Nominative case. This is in accordance with general Latin usage,[1] expressed in the following

RULE III. — Subject Nominative.

368. The subject of a finite verb[2] is put in the Nominative.

Note 2. — Observe that in the examples at the head of this lesson the verb is in the singular if the subject is singular, and in the plural if the subject is plural. Thus, in the second example, the singular verb, *regnat*, is used, because the subject, *Numa*, is singular, while in the sixth example the plural verb, *regnant*, is used, because the subject, *reginae*, is plural. Observe also that these verbs are in the third person, because their subjects, *Numa* and *reginae*, are in the third person.[3] This is in accordance with general Latin usage, expressed in the following

RULE XXXVI. — Agreement of Verb with Subject.

460. A finite verb agrees with its subject in NUMBER and PERSON.

13. *Vocabulary.*

Agricola, ae,[4] *m.*[5]	*husbandman.*[6]
Incola, ae, *m.* or *f.*	*inhabitant.*

---

[1] English usage is the same.

[2] That is, Latin writers always put a noun or pronoun in the Nominative case when they wish to use it as the subject of a finite verb, i.e. of any part of the verb except the Infinitive. This Rule is a simple statement of that fact.

[3] See page 13, 199. If the subject was a pronoun of the *first* or of the *second* person, the verb would be in the *first* or the *second* person; as we shall see when we take up those parts of the verb.

[4] The ending *ae* is the case-ending of the Genitive: *agricola;* Genitive, *agricolae.*

[5] Gender is indicated in the vocabularies by *m.* for *masculine*, *f.* for *feminine*, and *n.* for *neuter*.

[6] In learning Latin it is not enough to find English equivalents for Latin words, the pupil must early learn to see the meaning in the Latin itself, without even thinking of the English. The Latin nouns in this

Nauta, ae, m.	sailor, seaman.
Poëta, ae, m.	poet.
Puella, ae, f.	girl, maiden.
Pugnat,	he is fighting.
Regina, ae, f.	queen.
Victoria, ae, f.	Victoria, queen of England.

14. *Give the* GENDER, NUMBER, PERSON, *and* CASE *of each Noun, and the* TENSE, NUMBER, *and* PERSON *of each Verb, and translate the whole into English.*

1. Puella[1] lacrimat. 2. Puellae[1] lacrimant. 3. Agricola arabat. 4. Agricolae arabant. 5. Poëta equitabit. 6. Puellae ambulabunt. 7. Victoria regnat. 8. Regnabit.[2] 9. Regnabat. 10. Victoria deliberat. 11. Incolae deliberant. 12. Nauta navigabat. 13. Nautae navigabunt. 14. Incolae deliberabunt. 15. Nautae pugnabant. 16. Nautae navigant. 17. Poëtae navigabunt.

15. *Translate into Latin.*

1. Victoria was reigning. 2. She is reigning. 3. The[3] inhabitants were deliberating. 4. They will deliberate. 5. The[3] girls are riding. 6. They will ride. 7. The sailors were walking. 8. They are walking. 9. The poet was sailing. 10. He will walk. 11. The husbandman is ploughing. 12. Husbandmen plough. 13. The poets are deliberating. 14. The queen will reign. 15. Queens reign.

---

vocabulary, for instance, must represent to him not *words*, but *living persons*. *Agricola* should suggest to him, not the English WORD *husbandman*, but the *husbandman himself*, not the *name*, but the *man*.

[1] As the Latin has no article, a noun may, according to the connection in which it is used, be translated (1) without the article: as, *puella*, girl; *puellae*, girls; (2) with the indefinite article *a* or *an*: as, *puella*, a girl; (3) with the definite article *the*: as, *puella*, the girl.

[2] See page 23, foot-note, 3.

[3] The pupil will remember that the English articles, *a*, *an*, and *the*, are not to be rendered into Latin at all.

LESSON VII.

VERBS. — SUBJECT. — DIRECT OBJECT. — RULE V.

16. *Examine carefully the following examples.*

1. Regina laudat.   The queen praises.
2. Regina puellam laudat. The queen praises THE GIRL.
3. Puella reginam laudat. The girl praises THE QUEEN.

NOTE 1. — In the example *regina laudat*, "the queen praises," the thought is not entirely complete, as we are not told *what* the queen praises, but in the example *regina puellam laudat*, "the queen praises (what?) the girl," the sense is complete. The noun which thus completes the meaning of a verb is called the *Direct Object*.

NOTE 2. — Observe that in English the object follows the verb: thus in the examples above, the objects, *the girl* and *the queen*, follow the verb, *praises;* but in Latin the object usually precedes the verb; thus *puellam* and *reginam* precede the verb *laudat*.

NOTE 3. — Again compare the second and third examples. Observe that *laudat* is common to both, that *regina* in the second becomes *reginam* in the third, and that *puellam* in the second becomes *puella* in the third. Notice now the *effect* of these simple changes upon the *meaning* of the sentences. You thus learn that when the Romans spoke of a *queen* as the *subject* of an action, they used the form *regina*, but when they spoke of a *queen* as the *object* of an action they used *reginam*. These forms, *regina*, *reginam*, are types or examples of a large class of Latin nouns which in the singular end in *a* when used as subject and in *am* when used as object.

NOTE 4. — Observe that *puellam*, the Direct Object in the second example, and *reginam*, the Direct Object in the third example, are both in the *Accusative*. This is in accordance with general Latin usage, expressed in the following

RULE V. — Direct Object.

371. The Direct Object of an action is put in the Accusative.

17. *Vocabulary.*

Amat,   he loves.
Amicitia,   friendship.
Delectat,   he delights.

Epistula, ae, *f.*   *letter, epistle.*
Filia, ae, *f.*   *daughter.*
Jūstitia, ae, *f.*   *justice.*
Laudat,   *he praises.*

18. *Translate into English.*

1. Rēgīna puellās laudābat.[1] 2. Puellae rēgīnam laudābant. 3. Rēgīna incolās laudat. 4. Incolae rēgīnam laudant. 5. Poētae amīcitiam laudant. 6. Poētae rēgīnam laudābunt. 7. Rēgīna poētās laudābit. 8. Nauta poētam laudābat. 9. Poēta nautam laudābit. 10. Poētae nautās laudant. 11. Poēta dēlīberābit. 12. Poētae dēlīberābant. 13. Puellae ambulābant. 14. Rēgīna fīliam[2] amat. 15. Fīliam amābit.[2] 16. Epistula rēgīnam dēlectat.

19. *Translate into Latin.*

1. The poet praises the queen. 2. He was praising the queen. 3. The poet will praise friendship. 4. The letter delights the girl. 5. The girl praises the letter. 6. The girls were praising the poet. 7. The girls love the queen. 8. The queen loves the girls. 9. The husbandman will

---

[1] In taking up a Latin sentence, remember that the meaning must be learned in part from the vocabulary, and in part from the endings of the words. In this sentence, for example, we first learn the general meaning of the words from the vocabulary. We then ascertain the number and case of *rēgīna* from its ending. We find that it is in the singular number, and that in *form* it may be either a *Nominative* or a *Vocative*. As a *Nominative* it would mean that *the queen* is the *subject* of the action, as that is the only use of the Nominative which we have thus far learned; as a *Vocative*, that *the queen is addressed*. We next notice *puellās*. This must be an *Accusative Plural*, and it accordingly represents *the girls* as the *object* of an action; *puellās*, then, must be the object of the action of which *rēgīna* is the subject. The ending *ābat* in *laudābat* shows that the verb is in the imperfect tense, third person singular, and that it accordingly represents the action as taking place in past time, and as having one person for its subject. We are now prepared to translate the sentence: *The queen was praising the girls.* See *Suggestions*, I. to X., page 261.

[2] Render *her daughter*. In Latin the possessive pronouns, meaning *his, her, their*, when not emphatic, are seldom expressed.

[3] Render *she will love*, thus making the pronoun refer to *rēgīna*.

plough. 10. The husbandmen were ploughing. 11. The poets are deliberating. 12. The husbandman loves his daughter.

LESSON VIII.

SUBJECT. — DIRECT OBJECT. — QUESTIONS.

20. In questions the interrogative particles, *-ne, nōnne,* and *num,* are often used in Latin.

1. Questions with *-ne* ask for information: *Rēgatne,*[1] 'is he reigning?'
2. Questions with *nōnne* expect the answer 'yes': *Nōnne rēgnat,* 'is he not reigning?'[2]
3. Questions with *num* expect the answer 'no': *Num rēgnat,* 'is he reigning?'[2]

21. *Vocabulary.*

Artemīsia,	*Artemisia,* queen of Caria.
Corōna, ae, *f.*	*crown.*
Exspectat,	*he expects, awaits.*
Fābula, ae, *f.*	*story, fable.*
Jūlia, ae, *f.*	*Julia,* a Roman name.
Nōn,	*not.*
Sapientia, ae, *f.*	*wisdom.*

22. *Translate into English.*

1. Nōnne Artemīsia rēgnābat?[2] 2. Rēgnābat. 3. Nōnne poēta rēgīnam laudābit? 4. Rēgīnam laudābit. 5. Num poēta nāvigābat? 6. Nōn nāvigābat. 7. Nōnne poētae sapientiam laudant? 8. Sapientiam laudant. 9. Ambulantne?[3] 10. Nōn ambulant. 11. Equitantne? 12. Equitant. 13. Nōnne rēgīna corōnam amābat? 14. Corōnam amābat. 15. Nōnne fābulae puellās dēlectābant? 16. Puellās dēlectābant. 17. Fābula nautās dēlectat. 18. Fābulae nautam dēlectant. 19. Nautae nāvigābunt.

---

[1] The particle *-ne* is always thus appended to some other word.

[2] Observe in 2 and 3 that the auxiliary *is* stands at the beginning of the question in English, and that the subject follows: is he not *reigning?* is he *reigning? Does* and *do* often introduce questions in the same way, and in the past tense *was* and *did:* was he not *reigning, nōnne rēgnābat?*

[3] *Ambulantne = ambulant* and the interrogative particle *-ne.*

23. *Translate into Latin.*

1. Does not Julia praise the queen? 2. She praises the queen. 3. Will the girls love Julia? 4. They will love Julia. 5. Is not Victoria reigning? 6. She is reigning. 7. Is the sailor expecting letters? 8. He is not expecting letters. 9. Does the poet love his daughters? 10. He loves his daughters. 11. Will not the letters delight the queen? 12. They will delight the queen. 13. Were not the inhabitants deliberating? 14. They were deliberating. 15. The story will delight the poet.

LESSON IX.

SUBJECT. — DIRECT OBJECT. — QUESTIONS.

24. *Vocabulary.*

Accūsat,	*he accuses.*
Armat,	*he arms.*
Familia, ae, *f.*	*family, servants.*
Gallia, ae, *f.*	*Gaul, now France.*
Honōrat,	*he honors.*
Patria, ae, *f.*	*country, one's country.*
Probat,	*he approves.*
Sententia, ae, *f.*	*opinion, sentiment.*
Tullia, ae, *f.*	*Tullia, a Roman name.*

25. *Translate into English.*

1. Nōnne agricolae patriam amābant? 2. Patriam amābant. 3. Num incolae rēgīnam accūsābunt? 4. Nōn rēgīnam accūsābunt. 5. Rēgīnam amant. 6. Rēgīna nautās armābit. 7. Nōnne familiam armābat? 8. Familiam armābat. 9. Num Artemīsia incolās armābat? 10. Nōn incolās armābat. 11. Rēgnābatne? 12. Rēgnābat. 13. Incolae nautās accūsābunt. 14. Nōnne agricolae nautās accūsābant? 15. Nautās accūsābant. 16. Nōnne rēgīna sententiam probābat? 17. Sententiam probābat. 18. Nōnne incolae sententiam probābunt?

26. *Translate into Latin.*

1. Was Artemisia reigning? 2. She was not reigning. 3. Victoria was reigning. 4. Do the husbandmen love Gaul? 5. They do[1] not love Gaul. 6. Will not the queen honor the poet? 7. She will honor the poet. 8. The inhabitants honor the queen. 9. Do they not love their country? 10. They love their country. 11. Will the queen approve the opinion? 12. She will approve the opinion. 13. She approves the opinion. 14. Was not Gaul arming its inhabitants? 15. Gaul was arming its inhabitants. 16. Did not Artemisia accuse[2] her servants? 17. She accused[2] her servants.

LESSON X.

CERTAIN FORMS OF THE SECOND CONJUGATION. — RULES II. AND XVI.

27. In verbs of the SECOND CONJUGATION, the THIRD PERSON in the *singular* and *plural* of the *present, imperfect,* and *future* tenses of the *indicative* mood has the following

ENDINGS.

	PRESENT.	IMPERFECT.	FUTURE.
Singular,	et,	ēbat,	ĕbit.
Plural,	ent,	ēbant,	ēbunt.[3]

PARADIGM.

SINGULAR.	PLURAL.
Pres mon**et**, *he advises;*[4]	mon**ent**, *they advise.*
Imp monē**bat**, *he was advising;*[5]	monē**bant**, *they were advising.*[5]
Fut. monē**bit**, *he will advise;*	monē**bunt**, *they will advise.*

---

[1] Omit *do* in rendering into Latin, as that language has no separate words for the English auxiliaries, *does, do, did.*

[2] Use the imperfect; see page 19, foot-note 5.

[3] Observe that these endings all begin with the stem-characteristic *e*.

[4] Or, *she advises, it advises;* see page 23, foot-note 3.

[5] Or, *he advised;* plural, *they advised;* see page 19, foot-note 5.

APPOSITIVES.

28. *Examine the following examples.*

1. Artemisia rēgnat.   Artemisia reigns.
2. Artemisia *rēgīna* rēgnat.   Artemisia the queen reigns.
3. Poëta Artemisiam laudat.   The poet praises Artemisia.
4. Artemisiam *rēgīnam* laudat.   He praises Artemisia THE QUEEN.
5. Corōnam laudat.   He praises the crown.
6. Corōnam *rēgīnae* laudat.   He praises the crown OF THE QUEEN.

NOTE 1. — A noun or pronoun used to qualify or identify another noun or pronoun, denoting the *same* person or thing, as *rēgīna* in the second example and *rēgīnam* in the fourth, is called an appositive. *Rēgīna*, "the queen," is an appositive, showing the rank or office of Artemisia, — *Artemisia* THE QUEEN.

NOTE 2. — Observe that in the second example, where *Artemisia* is in the Nominative, the appositive, *rēgīna* is also in the Nominative, while in the fourth example, where *Artemisiam* is in the Accusative, the appositive is also in the Accusative. This usage is expressed in the following

RULE II. — Appositives.

363. An Appositive agrees in CASE with the noun or pronoun which it qualifies.[1]

NOTE 3. — Observe that in the sixth of the above examples the genitive *rēgīnae* limits or qualifies *corōnam* by showing whose crown is meant, *the crown* OF THE QUEEN. This usage is expressed in the following

RULE XVI. — Genitive with Nouns.

395. Any noun, not an appositive, qualifying the meaning of another noun, is put in the Genitive.[1]

397. The PARTITIVE GENITIVE designates the whole of which a part is taken.

Gallōrum fortissimī, *the bravest of the Gauls.*

---

[1] The pupil must not fail to notice that the Appositive always denotes the *same* person or thing as the noun or pronoun which it qualifies, while the Genitive always denotes a *different* person or thing. The Appositive follows its noun as in examples 2 and 4 above. The Genitive generally follows its noun as in example 6, but when *emphatic* it is placed before that noun.

LESSON XI.

CERTAIN FORMS OF THE SECOND CONJUGATION.

29. *Vocabulary.*

Dēlet,	he [1] destroys.
Docet,	he teaches.
Habet,	he has.
Luxuria, ae, *f.*	luxury.
Monet,	he advises.
Pecūnia, ae, *f.*	money.
Rōma, ae, *f.*	Rome, the city Rome.
Tacet,	he is silent.
Timet,	he fears.
Videt,	he sees.

30. *Translate into English.*[2]

1. Poēta filiam docēbat. 2. Filiam docēbit. 3. Nōnne

---

[1] See page 23, foot-notes 3 and 4.

[2] The pupil has already learned that in the first declension a noun in *a* is always in the Nominative or Vocative singular, and he has observed that in the previous exercises the Nominative is always the subject of a verb. He has now learned a new use for the Nominative, viz. that it may be an Appositive qualifying another Nominative.

Again, he has learned that a noun in *am* is in the Accusative singular and a noun in *ās* in the Accusative plural, and he has observed that in previous exercises the Accusative is the direct object, i.e. the object of some action, but he has now learned a new use for the Accusative, viz. that it may be an Appositive qualifying another Accusative. Hence, in future, in preparing his exercises, he must remember that a *Nominative* may be either the *subject* of a verb or an *Appositive*, and that an *Accusative* may be either the *object* of an action or an *Appositive*, but he will have little difficulty in distinguishing the *Appositive* from the *subject* or *object*, if he remembers that it follows another noun or pronoun in the same case, as in examples 2 and 4 under 28.

The pupil has also learned that a noun may be qualified by another noun denoting a different person or thing, and that the qualifying noun is in the Genitive, as in the sixth and seventh examples under 28, but the Genitive may also be used as an Appositive to another Genitive; hence the pupil must remember when he sees a Genitive that it may either qualify another noun, denoting a different person or thing, or may be an Appositive to another Genitive. See Suggestion VI., page 262.

SECOND CONJUGATION.   33

agricolae[1] fīliās docēbunt? 4. Fīliās docēbunt. 5. Artemīsia rēgīna[2] tacēbat. 6. Victōria rēgīna jūstitiam laudat. 7. Incolae Victōriam rēgīnam[3] honōrant. 8. Nōnne poēta fīliam Jūliam[3] docēbit? 9. Fīliam Jūliam docēbit. 10. Nōnne poēta Victōriam rēgīnam vidēbit? 11. Rēgīnam vidēbit. 12. Poēta pecūniam habet. 13. Nōnne Jūlia, fīlia poētae,[4] pecūniam habēbit? 14. Pecūniam habēbit. 15. Num agricolae tacēbant? 16. Nōn tacēbant. 17. Nōnne luxuria Rōmam dēlēbat? 18. Luxuria Rōmam dēlēbat. 19. Tullia, fīlia rēgīnae, fīliam poētae amat. 20. Nōnne Jūlia Tulliam, fīliam rēgīnae, amābit?

31. *Translate into Latin.*

1. The queen was advising her daughter. 2. Was not Victoria advising her daughters? 3. Victoria the queen was advising her daughters. 4. Will not the poet praise Victoria the queen? 5. He will praise Victoria the queen. 6. He is praising the daughter of the queen. 7. He praises the daughters of Victoria the queen.

8. Did Artemisia the queen fear the sailors? 9. She did not fear the sailors. 10. Did not the husbandmen fear the queen? 11. They were fearing Artemisia the queen. 12. Will not the girls see the queen? 13. They will see the queen. 14. Will they not see the crown?

LESSON XII.

NOUNS. — SECOND DECLENSION.

32. *Lesson from the Grammar.*

51. Nouns of the second declension end in

er, ir, us, and **os** —*masculine;* **um,** and **on**—*neuter.*

---

[1] In *form* where may *agricolae* be found? In what case is it in this sentence? See Suggestion VII., page 263.

[2] Which nominative is subject and which appositive?

[3] Which accusative is object and which appositive?

[4] In *form* where may *poëtae* be found? In what case is it here?

SECOND DECLENSION.

Nouns in *er, ir, us,* and *um* are declined as follows:

Servus, *slave.*   Puer, *boy.*   Ager, *field.*   Templum, *temple.*

SINGULAR.

Nom. servus	puer	ager	templum
Gen. servī	puerī	agrī	templī
Dat. servō	puerō	agrō	templō
Acc. servum	puerum	agrum	templum
Voc. serve	puer	ager	templum
Abl. servō	puerō	agrō	templō

PLURAL.

Nom. servī	puerī	agrī	templa
Gen. servōrum	puerōrum	agrōrum	templōrum
Dat. servīs	puerīs	agrīs	templīs
Acc. servōs	puerōs	agrōs	templa
Voc. servī	puerī	agrī	templa
Abl. servīs	puerīs	agrīs	templīs

1. STEM. — In nouns of the second declension, the stem ends in o.
2. In the PARADIGMS, observe —
1) That the stems are *servo, puero, agro,* and *templo.*
2) That the characteristic o becomes u in the endings *us* and *um,* and e in *serve;* that it disappears by contraction in the endings *a, i,* and *is* (for *o-a, o-i,* and *o-is*), and is dropped in the forms *puer* and *ager.*
3) That the case-endings, including the characteristic o,[1] are as follows: —

	SINGULAR.		PLURAL.	
	MASC.	NEUT.	MASC.	NEUT.
Nom.	us[2]	um	*Nom.* i	a
Gen.	i	i	*Gen.* ōrum	ōrum
Dat.	ō	ō	*Dat.* is	is
Acc.	um	um	*Acc.* ōs	a
Voc.	e	um	*Voc.* ī	a
Abl.	ō	ō	*Abl.* is	is

3. EXAMPLES FOR PRACTICE. — Like SERVUS: *dominus,* master. Like PUER: *gener,* son-in-law. Like AGER: *magister,* master. Like TEMPLUM: *bellum,* war.

---

[1] For the *characteristic,* and for the distinction between *case-endings* and *case-suffixes,* see 11 with foot-note.

[2] The endings of the Nominative and Vocative Singular are wanting in nouns in *er.* Thus *puer* is for *puerus.*

SECOND DECLENSION.

5. Nouns in **ius** generally contract **ii** in the Genitive Singular and **ie** in the Vocative Singular into **ī** without change of accent; *Claudī* for *Claudii*, of Claudius, *filī* for *filiī*, of a son; *Mercúrī* for *Mercúrie*, Mercury, *filī* for *filie*, son.

6. LOCATIVE.— Names of towns, and a few other words, have a Locative Singular in **ī**, denoting the *place in which* (page 23, 4). *Corinthī*, at Corinth; *humī*, on the ground.

33. Vocabulary.

Ager, agrī, m.	field.
Crassus, ī, m.	Crassus, a Roman name.
Discipulus, ī, m.	pupil, learner.
Dominus, ī, m.	master, owner.
Filius, ī, m.[1]	son.
Liber, librī, m.	book.
Liberat.	he liberates, liberates.
Puer, puerī, m.	boy.
Servus, ī, m.	slave.
Templum, ī, n.	temple.
Tyrannus, ī, m.	tyrant.

34. Translate into English.[2]

1. Filia tyrannī tacēbat. 2. Filiae tyrannī tacent. 3. Servus agrum arat. 4. Servī agrum arābunt. 5. Servī rēgīnae agrōs arābant. 6. Rēgīna servōs laudābit. 7. Nōnne puer librum habet? 8. Librum habet. 9. Nōnne puerī librōs habēbunt? 10. Librōs habēbunt. 11. Discipulus librōs habēbat.[3] 12. Nōnne discipulī librōs habēbant? 13. Librōs habēbant. 14. Tullia, filia rēgīnae, discipulōs laudābat. 15. Discipulī Tulliam, filiam rēgīnae, laudant. 16. Crassus agrōs habēbat. 17. Nōnne servōs habēbat? 18. Servōs habēbat. 19. Nōnne servōs liberābat? 20. Servōs liberābat. 21. Poēta servum habet. 22. Nōnne servum līberībit? 23. Servum līberābit.

---

[1] *Filī* for *filiī*; see 32, 5.

[2] It is important that the pupil should early learn to recognize Latin words by their *sounds* as well as by their *forms*. Many teachers, therefore, frequently read the Latin to their classes, and require them to translate with closed books. [3] *Had = was having*; see page 19, foot-note 5.

35. *Translate into Latin.*

1. The story delights the boy. 2. Stories delight boys. 3. The stories will delight the boys. 4. The boy was expecting a letter. 5. The boys were expecting letters. 6. The queen praises her daughter. 7. The queen will praise the daughter of the tyrant.
8. Is not the husbandman ploughing the field? 9. He is ploughing the field. 10. The husbandman will plough the fields. 11. Did not the slave love his master? 12. He loved his master Crassus. 13. Will not the boys see the temple? 14. They will see the temple.

LESSON XIII.

SECOND DECLENSION.

36. *Vocabulary.*

Amīcus, ī, *m.*	*friend.*
Dōnum, ī, *n.*	*gift, present.*
Fortūna, ae, *f.*	*fortune.*
Gener, generī, *m.*	*son-in-law.*
Nātūra, ae, *f.*	*nature.*
Pīsistratus, ī, *m.*	*Pisistratus,* tyrant of Athens.
Socer, socerī, *m.*	*father-in-law.*
Terret,	*he terrifies, frightens.*
Verbum, ī, *n.*	*word.*

37. *Translate into English.*

1. Verba tyrannī rēgīnam terrēbant. 2. Verba Pīsistratī tyrannī rēgīnam terrēbant. 3. Servus puerum terret. 4. Servī puerōs terrēbunt. 5. Verba servī puerum terrent. 6. Socer tyrannī tacēbat. 7. Puerī servōs rēgīnae timent. 8. Puer librum habet. 9. Puer librōs habēbit. 10. Puerī librōs habēbunt. 11. Rēgīna tyrannum timēbat. 12. Tyrannum timēbit. 13. Pīsistratum timēbant.
14. Pīsistratum tyrannum timēbant. 15. Puer amīcum habēbat. 16. Nōnne amīcum amābat? 17. Amīcum amā-

bat. 18. Amīcōs habēbit. 19. Puerī amīcōs habent. 20. Tullia amīcōs exspectābat. 21. Servīne[1] dominum exspectābunt? 22. Dominum exspectābunt. 23. Nōnne epistula Crassī rēgīnam dēlectābat? 24. Rēgīnam dēlectābat. 25. Rēgīna sapientiam, dōnum nātūrae, habet.

38. *Translate into Latin.*

1. Will the boy see the crown of the tyrant? 2. He will see the crown. 3. Did not the gift delight Tullia? 4. It delighted Tullia, the daughter of the queen?[2] 5. Did not Tullia praise the gifts? 6. She praised the gifts. 7. Did not the letter of Tullia delight her father-in-law? 8. It delighted her father-in-law. 9. Did not the tyrant terrify the son-in-law of the queen? 10. He terrified the son-in-law of the queen. 11. The slave was ploughing the field. 12. The slaves are ploughing the field. 13. The slaves will plough the fields. 14. The son-in-law has the letter. 15. He will have the letters. 16. The tyrant will see the letter. 17. He will see the letter of the queen.

LESSON XIV.

ADJECTIVES. — FIRST AND SECOND DECLENSIONS. — RULE XXXIV.

39. *Lesson from the Grammar.*

146. The Adjective is the part of speech which is used to qualify nouns: *bonus*, good; *magnus*, great.

NOTE. — The form of the adjective in Latin depends in part upon the gender of the noun which it qualifies: *bonus puer*, a good boy; *bona puella*, a good girl; *bonum templum*, a good temple.

147. Some adjectives are partly of the first declension, and partly of the second, while all the rest are entirely of the third declension.

---

[1] *Servīne* = *servī* with the interrogative particle *ne*.
[2] In what case should the Latin word for *daughter* be put? The word for *of the queen?* See 28, Rule II. and Rule XVI.

ADJECTIVES.

FIRST AND SECOND DECLENSIONS: **A** AND **O** STEMS.

148. Bonus, *good.*[1]

SINGULAR.

	MASC.	FEM.	NEUT.
Nom.	bonus	bona	bonum
Gen.	bonī	bonae	bonī
Dat.	bonō	bonae	bonō
Acc.	bonum	bonam	bonum
Voc.	bone	bona	bonum
Abl.	bonō	bonā	bonō

PLURAL.

	MASC.	FEM.	NEUT.
Nom.	bonī	bonae	bona
Gen.	bonōrum	bonārum	bonōrum
Dat.	bonīs	bonīs	bonīs
Acc.	bonōs	bonās	bona
Voc.	bonī	bonae	bona
Abl.	bonīs	bonīs	bonīs

Servus Bonus, *a good slave.*[2]

SINGULAR.

Nom. servus bonus,	*a good slave.*
Gen. servī bonī,	*of a good slave.*
Dat. servō bonō,	*for a good slave.*
Acc. servum bonum,	*a good slave.*
Voc. serve bone,	*O good slave.*
Abl. servō bonō,	*from a good slave.*

PLURAL.

Nom. servī bonī,	*good slaves.*
Gen. servōrum bonōrum,	*of good slaves.*
Dat. servīs bonīs,	*for good slaves.*
Acc. servōs bonōs,	*good slaves.*
Voc. servī bonī,	*O good slaves.*
Abl. servīs bonīs,	*from good slaves.*

---

[1] BONUS is declined in the Masc. like *servus* of Decl. II., (32, 51,) in the Fem. like *mēnsa* of Decl. I., (11, 48), and in the Neut. like *templum* of Decl. II., (32, 51). The stems are *bono* in the Masc. and Neut., and *bonā* in the Fem.

[2] In English the adjective usually precedes its noun, but in Latin it sometimes precedes and sometimes follows, though when not *emphatic* it more frequently follows.

AGREEMENT OF ADJECTIVES.

40. *Examine the following examples.*

1. Servus bonus.   A good slave.
2. Servi boni.   Of a good slave.
3. Servis bonis.   For good slaves.
4. Vērae amicitiae.[1]   TRUE *friendships.*
5. Templum pulchrum. A beautiful temple.

NOTE. — In these examples, observe that the adjectives are all in the same *Gender*, *Number*, and *Case* as their nouns. This usage is expressed in the following

RULE XXXIV. — Agreement of Adjectives.

438. An adjective agrees with its noun in GENDER, NUMBER, and CASE.

LESSON XV.

ADJECTIVES. — FIRST AND SECOND DECLENSIONS. — RULE XXXIV. — EXERCISES.

41. *Certain Forms of the Verb Sum, I am.*

SINGULAR.	PLURAL.
Pres. est, *he, she,* or *it is;*	sunt, *they are.*
Imp. erat, *he, she,* or *it was;*	erant, *they were.*
Fut. erit, *he, she,* or *it will be;*	erunt, *they will be.*

42. *Vocabulary.*

Aureus, a, um,	golden, of gold.
Bonus, a, um,	good.
Fidus, a, um,	faithful.
Glōria, ae, *f.*	glory.
Magnus, a, um,	great, large.
Multus, a, um,	much; plural, many.
Novus, a, um,	new.
Sanctus, a, um,	sacred.
Superbus, a, um,	proud, haughty..

43. *Translate into English.*

1. Nōnne corōna aurea[2] rēgīnam dēlectat? 2. Rēgīnam bonam dēlectat. 3. Corōna aurea est. 4. Corōnae sunt

---

[1] *Vērae* is emphatic: See page 38, foot-note 2.
[2] On the position of the adjective in Latin, see page 38, foot-note 2.

aureae.¹ 5. Nōnne rēgīna bona corōnam laudābat. 6. Corōnam auream laudābat. 7. Puellae rēgīnam bonam amant. 8. Puellae bonae rēgīnam amant. 9. Puellae bonae rēgīnam bonam amābunt. 10. Discipulus novum² librum habet. 11. Discipulī librōs novōs habēbunt. 12. Nōnne discipulī multōs librōs habent? 13. Nōn habent. 14. Librōs multōs habēbunt. 15. Poēta glōriam habet. 16. Poētae glōriam māgnam habēbunt. 17. Poēta māgnus glōriam māgnam habēbat. 18. Glōria est māgna. 19. Templum erat sanctum.

44. *Translate into Latin.*

1. Tullia has many³ books. 2. Are the books new?³ 3. They are not new. 4. Has not the poet a faithful friend?⁴ 5. He has many friends. 6. Are the friends faithful? 7. They are faithful. 8. The good queen has many friends. 9. The slave loves his good master. 10. Do not good masters have good slaves?

11. They have good slaves. 12. Tullia was praising the great poet. 13. The great poet will praise the good queen. 14. Great poets have great glory. 15. The haughty tyrant terrified the poet. 16. Tullia feared the haughty tyrant. 17. Tullia loves faithful friends. 18. The sailor will see the sacred temple.

LESSON XVI.

ADJECTIVES. — FIRST AND SECOND DECLENSIONS.

45. *Lesson from the Grammar.*

---

¹ While in general the verb in Latin occupies the last place in the sentence, *est* and *sunt* often stand between the subject and the predicate adjective, as in this sentence. Some freedom of arrangement is, however, allowed. Thus *Corōnae sunt aureae* might be *corōnae aureae sunt*, and *corōna aurea est*, above, might be *corōna est aurea*.

² *Novum* is *emphatic*.

³ Put the adjective in the right form to agree with its noun.

⁴ In translating English into Latin, the pupil is expected, in the arrangement of words, to imitate the order followed in the Latin Exercises.

ADJECTIVES.

149. Liber, *free*.[1]

SINGULAR.

	MASC.	FEM.	NEUT.
Nom.	līber	lībera	līberum
Gen.	līberī	līberae	līberī
Dat.	līberō	līberae	līberō
Acc.	līberum	līberam	līberum
Voc.	līber	lībera	līberum
Abl.	līberō	līberā	līberō

PLURAL.

Nom.	līberī	līberae	lībera
Gen.	līberōrum	līberārum	līberōrum
Dat.	līberīs	līberīs	līberīs
Acc.	līberōs	līberās	lībera
Voc.	līberī	līberae	lībera
Abl.	līberīs	līberīs	līberīs

150. Aeger, *sick*.

SINGULAR.

	MASC.	FEM.	NEUT.
Nom.	aeger	aegra	aegrum
Gen.	aegrī	aegrae	aegrī
Dat.	aegrō	aegrae	aegrō
Acc.	aegrum	aegram	aegrum
Voc.	aeger	aegra	aegrum
Abl.	aegrō	aegrā	aegrō

PLURAL.

Nom.	aegrī	aegrae	aegra
Gen.	aegrōrum	aegrārum	aegrōrum
Dat.	aegrīs	aegrīs	aegrīs
Acc.	aegrōs	aegrās	aegra
Voc.	aegrī	aegrae	aegra
Abl.	aegrīs	aegrīs	aegrīs

151. IRREGULARITIES. — Nine adjectives have in the singular **īus** in the Genitive and **ī** in the Dative:

Alius, a, ud, another; *nūllus, a, um*, no one; *sōlus*, alone; *tōtus*, whole; *ūllus*, any; *ūnus*,[2] one; *alter, -tera, -terum*, the other; *uter, -tra, -trum*, which (of two); *neuter, -tra, -trum*, neither.

---

[1] In the Masculine *liber* is declined like *puer* (32, 51), *aeger*, like *ager* (32, 51).   [2] For declension see page 78.

LESSON XVII.

ADJECTIVES. — FIRST AND SECOND DECLENSIONS. EXERCISES.

46. *Vocabulary.*

Aeger, aegra, aegrum,   *ill, sick.*
Beātus, a, um,   *happy, blessed.*
Ēgregius, a, um,   *excellent, distinguished.*
Grātus, a, um,   *acceptable, pleasing.*
Hōra, ae, f.   *hour.*
Longus, a, um,   *long, lasting.*
Pulcher, pulchra, pulchrum, *beautiful.*
Vērus, a, um,   *true.*
Victōria, ae, f.   *victory.*
Vīta, ae, f.   *life.*

47. *Translate into English.*

1. Agricola agrum pulchrum habet. 2. Estne beātus? 3. Beātus est. 4. Agricola beātus agrum arābat. 5. Nōnne agricolae beātī sunt? 6. Beātī sunt. 7. Puella pulchra pulchram rēgīnam amat. 8. Puellae pulchrae rēgīnam bonam amābant. 9. Nōnne rēgīna bona puellās pulchrās amābit? 10. Puellās pulchrās amābit.

11. Poēta servum ēgregium habēbat. 12. Servus Tulliae ēgregius erat. 13. Dominus superbus ēgregiōs servōs habet. 14. Suntne hōrae longae? 15. Nōn longae sunt. 16. Estne vīta longa? 17. Nōn est longa. 18. Puer erat aeger. 19. Puerī erant aegrī. 20. Suntne puellae aegrae? 21. Nōn sunt aegrae. 22. Vīta agricolae est beāta.

48. *Translate into Latin.*

1. The present is beautiful. 2. Is it acceptable? 3. It is acceptable. 4. Presents are acceptable. 5. Beautiful presents are acceptable. 6. Victory will be acceptable. 7. The glory of the victory will be great. 8. Is the story true? 9. It is not true. 10. Many stories are true. 11. Is the slave of the poet ill? 12. He is not ill.

THIRD DECLENSION.

13. Julia, the beautiful daughter of the poet, is ill. 14. Tullia was praising the beautiful daughter of the poet. 15. The temple is beautiful. 16. Many temples are beautiful. 17. Tullia will see the beautiful temples. 18. Will not the pupils have beautiful books? 19. They will have beautiful books. 20. Friends will be faithful.

LESSON XVIII.

THIRD DECLENSION — CONSONANT AND I NOUNS.

49. *Lesson from the Grammar.*

55. Nouns of the third declension end in

a, e, ĭ, ŏ, y, c, l, n, r, s, t, and x.

56. Nouns of this declension may be divided into two classes:

I. Nouns whose stem ends in a *Consonant*.
II. Nouns whose stem ends in I.

Class I. — Consonant Stems.

57. Stems ending in a Labial: B or P.

Princeps, m., *a leader, chief.*

			Case-Suffixes.
	SINGULAR.		
Nom.	princeps,	a leader,	s
Gen.	principis,	of a leader,	is
Dat.	principi,	to, for a leader,	i
Acc.	principem,	a leader,	em
Voc.	princeps,	O leader,	s
Abl.	principe,	from, with, by a leader,	e
	PLURAL.		
Nom.	principēs,	leaders,	ēs
Gen.	principum,	of leaders,	um
Dat.	principibus,	to, for leaders,	ibus
Acc.	principēs,	leaders,	ēs
Voc.	principēs,	O leaders,	ēs
Abl.	principibus,	from, with, by leaders.	ibus

1. STEM AND CASE-SUFFIXES. — In this Paradigm observe —

1) That the stem is *princep*, modified before an additional syllable to *princip*; see p. 2, 22, and 49, 57, 2.

2) That the case-suffixes appear distinct and separate from the stem;[1] see 11, 46, with foot-note.

2. VARIABLE VOWEL. — In the final syllable of disyllabic consonant stems, short *e* or *i* generally takes the form of *e* in the Nominative and Vocative Singular, and that of *i* in all the other cases. Thus *princeps*, *principis*, and *jūdex*, *jūdicis* (53, 59), alike have *e* in the Nominative and Vocative Singular, and *i* in all the other cases.

58. STEMS ENDING IN A DENTAL: D OR T.

Lapis, M., *stone*.   Aetās, F., *age*.   Mīles, M., *soldier*.

SINGULAR.

Nom.	lapis	aetās	mīles
Gen.	lapidis	aetātis	mīlitis
Dat.	lapidī	aetātī	mīlitī
Acc.	lapidem	aetātem	mīlitem
Voc.	lapis	aetās	mīles
Abl.	lapide	aetāte	mīlite

PLURAL.

Nom.	lapidēs	aetātēs	mīlitēs
Gen.	lapidum	aetātum	mīlitum
Dat.	lapidibus	aetātibus	mīlitibus
Acc.	lapidēs	aetātēs	mīlitēs
Voc.	lapidēs	aetātēs	mīlitēs
Abl.	lapidibus	aetātibus	mīlitibus

Nepōs, M., *grandson*.   Virtūs, F., *virtue*.   Caput, N., *head*.

SINGULAR.

Nom.	nepōs	virtūs	caput
Gen.	nepōtis	virtūtis	capitis
Dat.	nepōtī	virtūtī	capitī
Acc.	nepōtem	virtūtem	caput
Voc.	nepōs	virtūs	caput
Abl.	nepōte	virtūte	capite

---

[1] Thus, *princep-s*, *princip-is*, etc. In the first and second declensions, on the contrary, the suffix can not be separated from the final vowel of the stem in such forms as *mēnsis*, *puerī*, *agrīs*, etc.

THIRD DECLENSION.

PLURAL.

Nom. nepōtēs	virtūtēs	capita
Gen. nepōtum	virtūtum	capitum
Dat. nepōtĭbus	virtūtĭbus	capitĭbus
Acc. nepōtēs	virtūtēs	capita
Voc. nepōtēs	virtūtēs	capita
Abl. nepōtĭbus	virtūtĭbus	capitĭbus

1. **STEMS AND CASE-SUFFIXES.** — In these Paradigms observe —

1) That the stems are *lapid, aetāt, milit, nepōt, virtūt,* and *caput.*
2) That *miles* has the variable vowel, e, i, and *caput,* u, i.
3) That the dental d or t is dropped before s: *lapis* for *lapids, aetŭs* for *aetŭts, miles* for *milets, virtūs* for *virtūts.*
4) That the case-suffixes, except in the *neuter, caput,* 'head,' are the same as those given above; see **49, 57.**
5) That the *neuter, caput,* has no case-suffix in the Nominative, Accusative, and Vocative Singular, a in the Nominative, Accusative, and Vocative Plural, and the suffixes of masculine and feminine nouns in the other cases.

LESSON XIX.

THIRD DECLENSION. — CLASS I.

50. *Vocabulary.*

Caput, capitis, *n.*	*head.*
Comes, comitis, *m.* and *f.*	*companion.*
Hospes, hospitis, *m.*	*guest, host.*
Lapis, lapidis, *m.*	*stone.*
Miles, militis, *m.*	*soldier.*
Nepōs, nepōtis, *m.*	*grandson.*
Princeps, principis, *m.*	*leader, chief, chieftain.*
Virtūs, virtūtis, *f.*	*virtue, valor, bravery.*

51. *Translate into English.*

1. Nōnne mīlitēs pūgnābunt? 2. Pūgnābunt. 3. Nōnne sunt fīdī? 4. Sunt fīdī. 5. Princeps nepōtem laudat. 6. Nōnne mīlitem laudat? 7. Mīlitem laudat. 8. Estne superbus? 9. Superbus est. 10. Mīlitēs principem laudant. 11. Virtūtem principis laudant.

12. Virtūs mīlitum. 13. Virtūte mīlitum. 14. Virtūtem mīlitum timet. 15. Tyrannus virtūtem mīlitum timēbat. 16. Rēgīna virtūtem mīlitum laudat. 17. Fīlia rēgīnae mīlitēs laudābit. 18. Mīlitēs fīliam rēgīnae laudant. 19. Pīsistratum tyrannum accūsat. 20. Pīsistratum tyrannum accūsābant. 21. Mīles dōnum pulchrum videt. 22. Mīlitēs dōna pulchra vident. 23. Tyrannus prīncipēs timēbat.

52. *Translate into Latin.*

1. The chief praises his companion. 2. Has he many companions? 3. He has many companions. 4. Did the chiefs approve the opinion? 5. They approved the opinion. 6. The chief praised his grandson. 7. The queen praises her guest. 8. She has many guests. 9. The boy has a large head. 10. The chief praises the valor of his soldiers.

11. The companions of Tullia, the queen. 12. For the companions of Tullia, the queen. 13. They accuse Tullia, the queen. 14. They were accusing the companions of Tullia, the queen. 15. They fear the tyrant. 16. They will fear the grandson of the tyrant. 17. The friends of the queen praise the chief. 18. The friend of the queen was praising the good chiefs.

LESSON XX.

THIRD DECLENSION.—CLASS I.—RULE XII.

53. *Lesson from the Grammar.*

59. Stems ending in a Guttural: C or G.

	Rēx, m., king.	Jūdex, m. & f., judge.	Rādīx, f., root.	Dux, m. & f., leader.
		SINGULAR.		
Nom.	rēx	jūdex	rādīx	dux
Gen.	rēgis	jūdicis	rādīcis	ducis
Dat.	rēgī	jūdicī	rādīcī	ducī
Acc.	rēgem	jūdicem	rādīcem	ducem
Voc.	rēx	jūdex	rādīx	dux
Abl.	rēge	jūdice	rādīce	duce

THIRD DECLENSION.

PLURAL.

Nom.	rēgēs	jūdicēs	rādīcēs	ducēs
Gen.	rēgum	jūdicum	rādīcum	ducum
Dat.	rēgĭbus	jūdicĭbus	rādīcĭbus	ducĭbus
Acc.	rēgēs	jūdicēs	rādīcēs	ducēs
Voc.	rēgēs	jūdicēs	rādīcēs	ducēs
Abl.	rēgĭbus	jūdicĭbus	rādīcĭbus	ducĭbus

1. STEMS AND CASE-SUFFIXES. — In the Paradigms observe —

1) That the stems are *rēg, jūdic, rādic,* and *duc; jūdic* with the variable vowel, *i, e*; see **49, 57, 2.**
2) That the case-suffixes are those given in **49, 57.**
3) That *s* in the Nominative and Vocative Singular unites with *c* or *g* of the stem, and forms *x*; see p. 3, 30.

54. *Examine the following examples.*

1. *Imperiō pāret.*   *He is obedient* TO (obeys) AUTHORITY.
2. *Hōc mihī placet.*   *This is pleasing* TO (pleases) ME.
3. *Nōbīs vīta data est.*   *Life has been given* TO US.
4. *Lēgēs cīvitātī scripsit.*   *He wrote laws* FOR THE STATE.

NOTE.—In these examples *imperiō,* 'to authority,' *mihī,* 'to me,' *nōbis,* 'to us,' and *cīvitātī,* 'for the state,' are examples of what is called the *Indirect Object.* The first is the Indirect Object of *pāret,* the second of *placet,* the third of *data est,* and the fourth of *scripsit.* If the verb is transitive (p. 12, 193), as in the last example, an *Accusative* of the *Direct Object* (16, 371) may be used in addition to the *Indirect Object.* Observe that in these examples the *Indirect Objects* are all in the *Dative Case.* This is in accordance with the following

RULE XII. — Dative with Verbs.

384. The INDIRECT OBJECT of an action is put in the Dative. It is used —

I. With INTRANSITIVE and PASSIVE Verbs:

Serviunt populō, they are devoted TO THE PEOPLE.[1] Cic. *Imperiō pārēbant, they were obedient* TO (obeyed) AUTHORITY. Caes. *Tempori*

---

[1] *Populō,* 'to the people,' is in the Dative, and is the Indirect Object of *serviunt,* 'they serve' or 'are devoted;' *plēbi,* 'to the common people,' is the Indirect Object of the transitive verb *dedit,* 'he gave,' which also takes the Direct Object *agrōs,* 'fields,' 'lands.'

cēdit, *he yields to the time.* Cic. Labōrī student, *they devote themselves to labor.* Caes. Mundus deo pāret, *the world obeys God.* Cic. Nōbis vita data est, *life has been granted to us.* Cic.

II. With TRANSITIVE Verbs, in connection with the DIRECT OBJECT:

Agrōs plēbī[1] dedit, *he gave lands* TO THE COMMON PEOPLE. Cic. Tibī grātiās agō, *I give thanks* TO YOU. Cic. Pōns iter hostībus dedit, *the bridge gave a passage to the enemy.* Liv. Lēgēs civitātibus suis scripsērunt, *they prepared laws for their states.* Cic.

LESSON XXI.

THIRD DECLENSION. — CLASS I. — EXERCISES.

55. *Vocabulary.*

Divīnus, a, um,	*divine.*
Dōnat,	*he presents.*
Hūmānus, a, um,	*human.*
Iniquus, a, um,	*unjust.*
Jūdex, jūdicis, *m.* and *f.*	*judge.* [Central Italy.
Latīnus, ī, *m.*	*Latinus,* King of the Laurentians in
Lāvinia, ae, *f.*	*Lavinia,* daughter of King Latinus.
Lēx, lēgis, *f.*	*law.*
Nūntiat,	*he announces.*
Pāret,	*he obeys.*
Placet,	*he pleases.*
Rēx, rēgis, *m.*	*king.*
Superbus, a, um,	*proud.*

56. *Translate into English.*

1. Mīlitēs prīncipī pārēbant. 2. Lēgī pārent. 3. Lēgibus pārent. 4. Rēgem bonum laudant. 5. Rēx jūdicēs bonōs laudat. 6. Mīles victōriam nūntiat. 7. Rēgī victōriam nūntiat. 8. Jūdex erat inīquus. 9. Rēgīna rēgī librum pulchrum dōnābit. 10. Prīnceps sapientiam rēgis laudābat. 11. Rēx bonus lēgibus pārēbat. 12. Rēgēs bonī lēgibus pārēbunt.

---

[1] See foot-note, page 47. [2] In what case? See 54, Rule XII.

13. Lex divīna rēgī bonō placet. 14. Lēgēs bonae jūdicī placent. 15. Jūdex bonus rēgem superbum timet. 16. Rēgem superbum timēbit. 17. Rēgēs superbōs timēbunt. 18. Rēgīna jūdicem bonum laudābat. 19. Jūdex rēgem bonum laudābit. 20. Rēgīna bona jūdicem inīquum timēbat. 21. Jūdex puerō librum dōnat. 22. Fīlia rēgīnae puellīs librōs dōnābit.

57. *Translate into Latin.*

1. The judge praises the law. 2. Does he obey the law? 3. The king will present a beautiful gift to the judge. 4. The soldiers praise the judge. 5. The poet praises the king.[1] 6. The good poet was praising the daughter of the king. 7. The poets praise Lavinia, the daughter of Latinus, the king.

8. They were praising the virtues of the good king. 9. The queen was praising the bravery of the soldier. 10. The poets will praise the bravery of the soldiers. 11. The soldiers will obey the laws.[1] 12. The king will present a golden crown[1] to the queen.[1]

LESSON XXII.

THIRD DECLENSION.—CLASS I.

58. *Lesson from the Grammar.*

60. Stems ending in L, M, N, or R.

	Sōl, M., sun.	Cōnsul, M., consul.	Passer, M., sparrow.	Pater, M., father.
		SINGULAR.		
Nom.	sōl	cōnsul	passer	pater
Gen.	sōlis	cōnsulis	passeris	patris
Dat.	sōlī	cōnsulī	passerī	patrī
Acc.	sōlem	cōnsulem	passerem	patrem
Voc.	sōl	cōnsul	passer	pater
Abl.	sōle	cōnsule	passere	patre

[1] In what case will you put the Latin word for *king?* 16, Rule V.; the Latin words for *laws, crown, to the queen?* 54, 384, I. and II.

PLURAL.

Nom.	sŏlēs[1]	cōnsulēs	passerēs	patrēs
Gen.	sŏlum	cōnsulum	passerum	patrum
Dat.	sŏlĭbus	cōnsulĭbus	passerĭbus	patrĭbus
Acc.	sŏlēs	cōnsulēs	passerēs	patrēs
Voc.	sŏlēs	cōnsulēs	passerēs	patrēs
Abl.	sŏlĭbus	cōnsulĭbus	passerĭbus	patrĭbus

	Pástor, M., shepherd.	Leō, M., lion.	Virgŏ, F., maiden.	Carmen, N., song.

SINGULAR.

Nom.	pástor	leō	virgŏ	carmen
Gen.	pástōrĭs	leōnĭs	virginĭs	carminĭs
Dat.	pástōrī	leōnī	virginī	carminī
Acc.	pástōrem	leōnem	virginem	carmen
Voc.	pástor	leō	virgŏ	carmen
Abl.	pástōre	leōne	virgine	carmine

PLURAL.

Nom.	pástōrēs	leōnēs	virginēs	carmina
Gen.	pástōrum	leōnum	virginum	carminum
Dat.	pástōrĭbus	leōnĭbus	virginĭbus	carminĭbus
Acc.	pástōrēs	leōnēs	virginēs	carmina
Voc.	pástōrēs	leōnēs	virginēs	carmina
Abl.	pástōrĭbus	leōnĭbus	virginĭbus	carminĭbus

1. STEMS AND CASE-SUFFIXES. — In the Paradigms observe —

1) The stems are *sŏl, cōnsul, passer, patr, pástŏr, leŏn, virgon, carmen.*
2) *Virgŏ* (virgon) has the variable vowel, o, i, and *carmen,* e, i.
3) In the Nominative and Vocative Singular s, the case-suffix, is omitted, the stem *pástŏr* shortens o, while *leŏn* and *virgon* drop n.

61. STEMS ENDING IN S.

	Flōs, M., flower.	Jūs, N., right.	Opus, N., work.	Corpus, N., body.

SINGULAR.

Nom.	flōs	jūs	opus	corpus
Gen.	flōrĭs	jūrĭs	operĭs	corporĭs
Dat.	flōrī	jūrī	operī	corporī
Acc.	flōrem	jūs	opus	corpus
Voc.	flōs	jūs	opus	corpus
Abl.	flōre	jūre	opere	corpore

---

[1] Many monosyllables want the Genitive Plural.

THIRD DECLENSION.   51

PLURAL.

Nom.	flōrēs	jūra	opera	corpora
Gen.	flōrum	jūrum	operum	corporum
Dat.	flōribus	jūribus	operibus	corporibus
Acc.	flōrēs	jūra	opera	corpora
Voc.	flōrēs	jūra	opera	corpora
Abl.	flōribus	jūribus	operibus	corporibus

1. STEMS AND CASE-SUFFIXES. — In the Paradigms observe —

1) That the stems are *flōs, jūs, opos,* and *corpos.*
2) That *opus* has the variable vowel, e, u, and *corpus,* o, u.
3) That s of the stem becomes r between two vowels: *flōs, flōris* (for *flōsis*).
4) That the Nominative and Vocative Singular omit the case-suffix; see 58, 60, 1, 3).

LESSON XXIII.

THIRD DECLENSION. — RULE I. — EXERCISES.

59. *Examine the following examples.*

1. Servius rēx.   *Servius* THE KING.
2. Servius rēx erat.   *Servius was* KING.
3. Artemisia, Mausōli uxor. *Artemisia,* THE WIFE *of Mausolus.*
4. Artemisia Mausōli uxor erat. *Artemisia was* THE WIFE *of Mausolus.*

NOTE 1. — In the first example *rēx* is an Appositive; see 28, Rule II. In the second example, however, *rēx* is predicated or affirmed of *Servius,* — Servius was king, — and is called a Predicate Noun. *Rēx erat* is the Predicate of the sentence of which *Servius* is the subject. In the third example *uxor* is an *Appositive,* while in the fourth it is a *Predicate Noun,* predicated of *Artemisia.*

NOTE 2. — In the second and fourth examples observe that *rēx* and *uxor* are in the same case as the nouns of which they are predicated, *i.e.* in the Nominative. This usage is expressed in the following

RULE I. — Predicate Nouns.[1]

362. A noun predicated of another noun denoting the same person or thing agrees with it in CASE:

---

[1] Compare this Rule with Rule II.; see 28.

THIRD DECLENSION.

Brūtus cūstōs[1] libertātis fuit, *Brutus was the* GUARDIAN *of liberty.* Liv. Servius rēx est dēclārātus, *Servius was declared* KING. Liv. Orestem sē esse dixit, *he said that he was* ORESTES. Cic.

60. Vocabulary.

Bellum, i, n.	war.
Brūtus, i, m.	Brutus, a Roman name.
Cāria, ae, f.	Caria, a country in Asia Minor.
Catō, ōnis, m.	Cato, a Roman name.
Causa, ae, f.	cause.
Cicerō, ōnis, m.	Cicero, a Roman orator and states-
Exsul, ulis, m. and f.	exile. [man.
Frāter, frātris, m.	brother.
Herodotus, i, m.	Herodotus, a Greek historian.
Historia, ae, f.	history.
Imperātor, ōris, m.	general, commander.
Libertās, ātis, f.	liberty, freedom.
Mausōlus, i, m.	Mausolus, King of Caria.
Numa, ae, m.	Numa, second of the legendary kings
Ōrātor, ōris, m.	orator. [of Rome.
Uxor, ōris, f.	wife.
Victor, ōris, m.	conqueror.
Vindex, vindicis, m. and f.	defender.

61. Translate into English.

1. Cicerō exsul erat. 2. Nōnne cōnsul bellum timēbat? 3. Bellum timēbat. 4. Numa erat bonus rēx. 5. Cicerō cōnsul victōrem laudat. 6. Numa rēx patriam amābat. 7. Orātor Numam laudat. 8. Cicerō cōnsul erat. 9. Vindex lībertātis.[2] 10. Brūtus, vindex lībertātis. 11. Brūtus est vindex[3] lībertātis. 12. Poēta imperātōrem laudat. 13.

---

[1] In these examples *cūstōs, rēx,* and *Orestem* are all predicate nouns, and agree in case respectively with *Brūtus, Servius,* and *sē*.

[2] *Libertātis* is in the Genitive, depending upon *vindex,* according to 28, Rule XVI. The Genitive generally follows its noun, as in this instance, but sometimes, especially when emphatic, it precedes, as in *belli causa* below.

[3] *Vindex* in 10 is an *Appositive,* according to 28, Rule II., but in 11 it is a *Predicate Noun,* according to 59, Rule I.

Tullia bellī causa erat. 14. Tullia, rēgis fīlia.¹ 15. Herodotus, pater historiae. 16. Catŏ, magnus imperātor. 17. Catŏ magnus imperātor erat.

18. Jūstitia, rēgīna virtūtum. 19. Jūstitia est rēgīna virtūtum. 20. Artemīsia rēgis² uxor erat. 21. Artemīsia Mausōlī, Cariae rēgis,³ uxor erat. 22. Virtūs est comes sapientiae. 23. Virtūtēs sunt comĭtēs sapientiae. 24. Jūdex virtūtem rēgis laudat. 25. Virtūtēs rēgis bonī laudābat. 26. Poētae virtūtēs Numae, rēgis bonī, laudābunt. 27. Rēx bonus⁴ est. 28. Pater jūdicis rēgem bonum laudābit. 29. Tulliam, rēgis fīliam,⁵ accūsābant.

62. *Translate into Latin.*

1. Cicero was an orator. 2. He was a great orator. 3. Mausolus was king. 4. Was he not king of Caria? 5. He was king of Caria. 6. Poets will praise the great commander. 7. They praise the father of history. 8. Does not the consul praise his brother? 9. He praises his brother.

10. The soldiers fear the king. 11. Latinus was the king.⁶ 12. Lavinia was the daughter of Latinus. 13. Lavinia was the daughter of Latinus, the king.⁷ 14. The daughter of the king was praising the faithful slave. 15. The orator will praise the wisdom of the judge. 16. Cicero, the orator, praises the bravery of the conqueror. 17. Cicero, the consul, praises the bravery of the soldiers. 18. The judge praises the wisdom of Cicero, the consul.

---

[1] *Filia* governs *rēgis*, according to Rule XVI., but is itself in apposition with *Tullia*, according to Rule II. The *appositive* generally follows its noun.

[2] Remember that the Genitive sometimes precedes the governing word, especially when it is emphatic.

[3] What is the construction of *rēgis?* See 28, Rule II.

[4] See 40, Rule XXXIV.

[5] Explain the case of *filiam*. See 28 and 16, Rules II. and V.

[6] A Predicate Noun. See 59, Rule I.

[7] In what case will you put the Latin word? See 28, Rule II.

LESSON XXIV.

THIRD DECLENSION. — CLASS II. — I STEMS.

63. *Lesson from the Grammar.*

CLASS II. — I STEMS.

62. STEMS ENDING IN I. — *Nouns in* is *and* ēs, *not increasing in the Genitive.*[1]

	Tussis, F., cough.	Turris, F., tower.	Ignis, M., fire.	Hostis, M. & F., enemy.	Nūbēs, F., cloud.
			SINGULAR.		
Nom.	tussis	turris	ignis	hostis	nūbēs
Gen.	tussis	turris	ignis	hostis	nūbis
Dat.	tussī	turrī	ignī	hostī	nūbī
Acc.	tussim	turrim, em	ignem	hostem	nūbem
Voc.	tussis	turris	ignis	hostis	nūbēs
Abl.	tussī	turrī, e	ignī, e	hoste	nūbe
			PLURAL.		
Nom.	tussēs	turrēs	ignēs	hostēs	nūbēs
Gen.	tussium	turrium	ignium	hostium	nūbium
Dat.	tussibus	turribus	ignibus	hostibus	nūbibus
Acc.	tussēs, īs	turrēs, īs	ignēs, īs	hostēs, īs	nūbēs, īs
Voc.	tussēs	turrēs	ignēs	hostēs	nūbēs
Abl.	tussibus	turribus	ignibus	hostibus	nūbibus

I. PARADIGMS. — Observe —

1. That the stems are *tussi, turri, igni, hosti,* and *nūbi.*

2. That the case-endings, including the characteristic i, which disappears in certain cases, are as follows: —

	SINGULAR.	PLURAL.
Nom.	is, ēs	ēs
Gen.	is	ium
Dat.	i	ibus
Acc.	im, em	ēs, is
Voc.	is	ēs
Abl.	i, e	ibus

---

[1] That is, having as many syllables in the Nominative Singular as in the Genitive Singular.

THIRD DECLENSION. 55

63. Stems ending in I.—*Neuters in* e, al, *and* ar.

Mare, *sea*.   Animal, *animal*.   Calcar, *spur*.

		SINGULAR.		CASE-ENDINGS.
Nom.	mare	animal	calcar	e— [1]
Gen.	maris	animālis	calcāris	is
Dat.	marī	animālī	calcārī	ī
Acc.	mare	animal	calcar	e—
Voc.	mare	animal	calcar	e—
Abl.	marī	animālī	calcārī	ī
		PLURAL.		
Nom.	maria	animālia	calcāria	ia
Gen.	marium	animālium	calcārium	ium
Dat.	maribus	animālibus	calcāribus	ibus
Acc.	maria	animālia	calcāria	ia
Voc.	maria	animālia	calcāria	ia
Abl.	maribus	animālibus	calcāribus	ibus

1. Paradigms. — Observe—

1) That the stem-ending i is changed to e in the Nominative, Accusative, and Vocative Singular of *mare*, and dropped in the same cases of *animal* (for *animāle*) and *calcar* (for *calcāre*).

2) That the case-endings include the characteristic i.

64. Stems ending in I.—*Nouns in* s *and* x *generally preceded by a consonant.*

Cliēns, M. & F.,   Urbs, F.,   Arx, F.,   Mūs,[2] M.,
client.   *city.*   *citadel.*   *mouse.*

		SINGULAR.		
Nom.	cliēns	urbs	arx	mūs
Gen.	clientis[3]	urbis	arcis	mūris
Dat.	clientī	urbī	arcī	mūrī
Acc.	clientem	urbem	arcem	mūrem
Voc.	cliēns	urbs	arx	mūs
Abl.	cliente	urbe	arce	mūre

[1] The dash here implies that the case-ending is sometimes wanting.

[2] *Cliēns* is for *clientis*, *urbs* for *urbis*, *arx* for *arcis*, and *mūs* for *mūsis*. *Mūs*, originally an *s*-stem, Greek μῦς, became an *i*-stem in Latin by assuming *i*.

[3] The vowel e is here short before *nt*, but long before *ns*; see p. 9, 10, note 2. Indeed, it seems probable that *nt* and *nd* shorten a preceding vowel, as *ns* lengthens it.

THIRD DECLENSION.

PLURAL.

Nom.	clientēs	urbēs	arcēs	mūrēs
Gen.	clientium	urbium	arcium	mūrium
Dat.	clientibus	urbibus	arcibus	mūribus
Acc.	clientēs, ĭs	urbēs, ĭs	arcēs, ĭs	mūrēs, ĭs
Voc.	clientēs	urbēs	arcēs	mūrēs
Abl.	clientibus	urbibus	arcibus	mūribus

I. PARADIGMS. — Observe —

1) That the stems are *clienti, urbi, arci,* and *mūri.*

2) That these nouns are declined in the singular precisely like consonant-stems, and in the plural precisely like all other masculine and feminine *i*-stems.

65. SUMMARY OF I-STEMS. — To I-stems belong —

1. All nouns in **is** and **ēs** which do not increase[1] in the Genitive; see **63, 62.**

2. Neuters in **e, al** (for **ālis**), and **ar** (for **āris**); see **63, 63.**

3. Many nouns in **s** and **x** — especially (1) nouns in **ns** and **rs**, and (2) monosyllables in **s** and **x** preceded by a consonant; see **63, 64.**

66, 4. LOCATIVE. — Many names of towns have a Locative Singular in **ī** or **e** denoting the *place in which* (11, 40, 4). *Karthāgini* or *Karthāgine,* at Carthage, *Tiburi* or *Tibure,* at Tibur.

LESSON XXV.

GENDER IN THIRD DECLENSION. — RULE XXXIII. — EXERCISES.

64. *Lesson from the Grammar.*

GENDER IN THIRD DECLENSION.

99. Nouns in the third declension ending in

ŏ, or, ōs, er, and in **ĕs** and **es**

increasing in the Genitive,[1] are masculine: *sermŏ,* discourse; *dolor,* pain; *mōs,* custom; *agger,* mound; *pēs,* Genitive *pedis,* foot.

---

[1] That is, have no more syllables in the Genitive than in the Nominative.

THIRD DECLENSION.

105. Nouns of the third declension ending in

ās, as, is, ys, x, in **ēs**

not increasing in the Genitive, and in **s** *preceded by a consonant,* are feminine: *aetās,* age; *nāvis,* ship; *chlamys,* cloak; *pāx,* peace; *nūbēs,* cloud; *urbs,* city.

111. Nouns of the third declension ending in

a, e, i, y, c, l, n, t, ār, ar, ur, ūs, and **us**

are neuter:[1] *poēma,* poem; *mare,* sea; *lāc,* milk; *animal,* animal; *carmen,* song; *caput,* head; *corpus,* body.

65. *Examine the following examples.*

1. Apud *concilium.*   *In the presence of* THE COUNCIL.
2. Post *castra.*   *Behind* THE CAMP.
3. Ab *urbe.*   *From* THE CITY.
4. Prō *castris.*   *Before* THE CAMP.

NOTE. — Observe that in the first and second of these examples, the nouns after the prepositions *apud* and *post* are in the *Accusative*, and that in the third and fourth the nouns after *ab* and *prō* are in the *Ablative*. This general usage is expressed in the following

RULE XXXIII. — Cases with Prepositions.

432. The Accusative and Ablative may be used with prepositions:[2]

---

[1] Nouns whose gender is determined by *Signification* (1, 42) may be exceptions to these rules for gender as determined by *Endings*.

[2] The Preposition is the part of speech which shows the relation of objects to each other: *apud jūdicem dīxit,* 'he spoke in the presence of the judge'; *prō castris,* 'before the camp.' Here *apud* and *prō* are prepositions. In the Vocabulary, each preposition, as it occurs, will be marked as such; and the case which may be used with it will be specified. The following examples illustrate the use of prepositions: in Asiam profūgit, *he fled into Asia;* in Italiā fuit, *he was in Italy;* sub montem, *toward the mountain;* sub monte, *at the foot of the mountain;* ad urbem, *to the city;* apud concilium, *in the presence of the council;* contrā nātūram, *contrary to nature;* ab urbe, *from the city;* ex Asiā, *out of Asia.*

Ad amīcum scripsī, *I have written to a friend.* Cic. In cūriam, *into the senate-house.* Liv. In Ĭtaliā,[1] *in Italy.* Nep. Prō castris, *before the camp.* Caes.

66. *Vocabulary.*

Aedĭfĭcat,	*he builds.*
Ante, *prep. w. acc.*	*before.*
Apŭd, *prep. w. acc.*	*in the presence of, among, in; of an author, in the works of.*
Caesar, ăris, *m.*	*Caesar, the celebrated Roman statesman and general.*
Cīvis, cīvis, *m.*[2]	*citizen.*
Cīvĭtās, ātis, *f.*	*state.*
Contrā, *prep. w. acc.*	*against, contrary to.*
Habĭtat,	*he resides, lives, dwells.*
Hostis, is, *m. and f.*	*enemy.*
In, *prep. w. acc. and abl.*	*into, in.*
Lūx, lūcis, *f.*	*light.*
Multus, a, um,	*much, many.*
Nāvis, is, *f.*[3]	*ship.*
Oppūgnat,	*he assaults, attacks, storms.*
Patria, ae, *f.*	*native country.*
Prō, *prep. w. abl.*	*for, before.*
Pūgnat,	*he fights.*
Rōmŭlus, ī, *m.*	*Romulus, the legendary founder of Rome.*
Superat,	*he conquers.*

67. *Translate into English.*

1. Cīvĕs rēgem laudant. 2. Rēx cīvēs laudat. 3. Puer leōnem timēbit. 4. Leō puerum terret. 5. Urbs est māgna. 6. Estne pulchra? 7. Est pulchra. 8. Rēx hostēs superābit. 9. Caesar multās navēs habēbat. 10. Apud Herodotum sunt fābulae. 11. Apud Herodotum, patrem historiae, sunt multae fābulae. 12. Mīlitēs prō patriā pūgnābant. 13.

---

[1] Here the Ablative *Ĭtaliā* is used with *in*, though, in the second example, the Accusative *cūriam* is used with the same preposition. The rule is, that the Latin preposition *in* is used with the Accusative when it means *into*, and that it is used with the Ablative when it means *in*.

[2] Decline *cīvis* like *ignis*; *nāvis* like *turris*.

[3] See Rule XXXIII., 432.

Mīlitēs prō lībertāte pūgnant. 14. Cīvis bonus lēgibus patriae pāret.
15. Cōnsul in urbe habitābat. 16. Hostēs urbem oppūgnābant. 17. Rēx urbēs multās oppūgnābit. 18. Caesar hostēs superābat. 19. Cōnsul virtūtem hostium timēbat. 20. Mīlitēs cōnsulibus pārēbunt. 21. Caesar turrim oppūgnābat. 22. Rēx turrēs oppūgnābit. 23. Hostēs arcem oppūgnābunt. 24. Hostēs nāvēs multās habent. 25. Caesarī pūgnam nūntiant. 26. Cīvēs bonī lēgibus pārent. 27. Cōnsulēs virtūtem hostium timent.

68. *Translate into Latin.*

1. The consul was attacking the tower. 2. He had (*was having*) many soldiers. 3. The king had a beautiful ship. 4. The consul had many ships. 5. The ships of the consul were large. 6. The commander destroyed the city. 7. He destroyed the city contrary to the law.[1] 8. Caesar conquers the king. 9. The citizens praise the law. 10. They praise the laws. 11. They praise the laws of the state. 12. The judge will obey the laws. 13. The citizens will obey the laws of the state. 14. The consul was building a large ship.
15. The citizens will build many ships. 16. The king has a good ship. 17. The soldiers were fighting for liberty. 18. The consul will attack the city. 19. He will conquer the enemy. 20. The conqueror is in the city. 21. The father of the king resides in the city. 22. The father of the good queen will reside in the city. 23. Good citizens will fight for their country. 24. The soldiers of the good king were assaulting many cities of the enemy.

---

[1] See 65, Rule XXXIII. The words *contrary to* are to be rendered by a single Latin preposition. We have already learned that the English prepositions *of*, *to*, *by*, *with*, etc., may generally be rendered into Latin without prepositions by simply using the proper case; but many prepositions, as *before*, *between*, *behind*, *around*, *contrary to*, must be rendered by corresponding prepositions.

LESSON XXVI.

CERTAIN FORMS OF THE THIRD CONJUGATION.

69. In verbs of the THIRD CONJUGATION, the THIRD PERSON in the *singular* and *plural* of the *present*, *imperfect*, and *future* tenses of the *indicative* mood has the following

ENDINGS.

	PRESENT.	IMPERFECT.	FUTURE.
Singular,	it	ēbat	et
Plural,	unt	ēbant	ent

PARADIGM.

SINGULAR.
Pres. regit, *he rules;*
Imp. regēbat, *he was ruling;*
Fut. reget, *he will rule;*

PLURAL.
regunt, *they rule.*
regēbant, *they were ruling.*
regent, *they will rule.*

70. *Examples.* — *Adverbs.*

1. Miles pūgnat.   *The soldier fights.*
2. Miles *fortiter* pūgnat.   *The soldier fights* BRAVELY.
3. Miles *nōn* pūgnat.   *The soldier does* NOT *fight.*

NOTE.—In these examples *fortiter* (bravely), and *nōn* (not) are adverbs modifying *pūgnat*. The use of adverbs is expressed in the following

RULE LXI.— Use of Adverbs.

551. Adverbs qualify VERBS, ADJECTIVES, and other ADVERBS:

Sapientēs fēlīciter[1] vīvunt, *the wise live happily.* Cic. Facile doctissimus, *unquestionably the most learned.* Cic. Haud aliter, *not otherwise.* Verg.

---

[1] The Adverb is, therefore, the part of speech which is used to qualify verbs, adjectives, and other adverbs. *Fēliciter*, 'happily,' is an adverb qualifying the verb *vīvunt*, 'live' (live *happily*). *Facile*, 'easily,' 'unquestionably,' is an adverb qualifying the adjective *doctissimus*, 'the most learned' (*easily*, i.e. *unquestionably* the most learned). *Haud*, 'not,' is an adverb qualifying the adverb *aliter*, 'otherwise' (*not* otherwise). The adverb in Latin usually stands directly before the word which it qualifies, as in these examples.

THIRD CONJUGATION. 61

71. Adverbs, unlike Nouns and Adjectives, from which they are largely derived, are *indeclinable.* They have a variety of endings, of which we now notice *e, o,* and *ter: modestē,* 'modestly'; *saepe,* 'often'; *tūtō,* 'safely'; *fortiter,* 'bravely.'

72. Vocabulary.

Ad, *prep. with acc.*	*to.*
Breviter, *adv.*	*briefly.*
Dē, *prep. with abl.*	*about, concerning, in regard to.*
Dicit,	*he says, speaks.*
Diligenter, *adv.*	*attentively, diligently.*
Dūcit,	*he leads.*
Fēliciter, *adv.*	*happily.*
Fortiter, *adv.*	*bravely.*
Lēgātus, ī, *m.*	*ambassador; lieutenant.*
Legit,	*he reads.*
Mittit,	*he sends.*
Modestē, *adv.*	*modestly.*
Nōn, *adv.*	*not.*
Numerus, ī, *m.*	*number.*
Ōrātiō, ōnis, *f.*	*oration, speech.*
Regit,	*he rules.*
Saepe, *adv.*	*often.*
Scrībit,	*he writes.*
Simpliciter, *adv.*	*simply.*
Vērum, ī, *n.*	*truth.*
Vīvit,	*he lives.*

73. *Translate into English.*

1. Dīcit, dīcēbant, dīcet. 2. Legunt, legēbat, legent. 3. Dīcunt, scrībunt. 4. Dīcēbat, scrībēbat. 5. Dīcent, scrībent. 6. Dūcit, dūcēbat, dūcet. 7. Regunt, regēbat, regent. 8. Cōnsul modestē dīcēbat. 9. Puerī modestē dīcunt. 10. Rēx breviter dīcet. 11. Cōnsulēs breviter dīcunt. 12. Jūdex fēliciter vīvit. 13. Cīvēs fēliciter vīvēbant. 14. Pāstōrēs simpliciter vīvunt.
15. Jūdex librum legēbat. 16. Jūdicēs ōrātiōnēs Cicerōnis legēbant. 17. Jūdicēs bonī ōrātiōnēs Cicerōnis cōnsulis

dīligenter legēbant. 18. Epistulās cōnsulis dīligenter legent. 19. Hostēs lēgātōs ad Caesarem mittunt. 20. Hostēs lēgātōs ad rēgem mittent. 21. Mīlitēs fortiter pūgnābant. 22. Cōnsul amīcōs multōs habēbat. 23. Cōnsul māgnum amīcōrum numerum habēbat.

74. *Translate into Latin.*

1. He leads, he was leading, he will lead. 2. He rules, he was ruling, he will rule. 3. They lead, they rule. 4. They were leading, they were ruling. 5. They will lead, they will rule. 6. The judge will speak the truth. 7. They speak the truth. 8. They will speak modestly. 9. Cicero was writing to a friend. 10. The boys will write often. 11. Cicero was writing about friendship.
12. The king is writing a book. 13. He will write many books. 14. The boy is writing about virtue. 15. The boys will write about the victory. 16. The king lives happily. 17. The father of the good queen was living happily. 18. He was reading a good book. 19. The boys will read good books. 20. Caesar sends an ambassador to the enemy. 21. The king will send ambassadors to the enemy.

LESSON XXVII.

CERTAIN FORMS OF THE FOURTH CONJUGATION. — PERFECT TENSE.

75. In verbs of the FOURTH CONJUGATION, the THIRD PERSON in the *singular* and *plural* of the *present, imperfect,* and *future* tenses of the *indicative* mood has the following

ENDINGS.

	PRESENT.	IMPERFECT.	FUTURE.
Singular,	it	iēbat	iet
Plural,	iunt	iēbant	ient

FOURTH CONJUGATION.

PARADIGM.

SINGULAR.	PLURAL.
Pres. audit, *he hears;*	audiunt, *they hear.*
Imp. audiēbat, *he was hearing;*	audiēbant, *they were hearing.*
Fut. audiet, *he will hear;*	audient, *they will hear.*

76. In verbs of the FOUR CONJUGATIONS, the THIRD PERSON in the *singular* and *plural* of the *perfect* tense of the *indicative* mood has the following

ENDINGS.

	SINGULAR.	PLURAL.
Conj. I.	āvit	āvērunt
Conj. II.	uit	uērunt
Conj. III.	sit	sērunt
Conj. IV.	īvit	īvērunt

PARADIGM.

SINGULAR.	PLURAL.
I. amāvit, *he has loved;*[1]	amāvērunt, *they have loved.*[1]
II. monuit, *he has advised;*	monuērunt, *they have advised.*
III. rēxit,[2] *he has ruled;*	rēxērunt,[2] *they have ruled.*
IV. audīvit, *he has heard;*	audīvērunt, *they have heard.*

77. In the verb *Sum*, the THIRD PERSON in the *singular* and *plural* of the *perfect* tense of the *indicative* mood has the following forms:

SINGULAR.	PLURAL.
fuit, *he has been, he was;*	fuērunt, *they have been, they were.*

78. *Examples. — Ablative.*

1. Virtūte regnum tenuit.   *He obtained the kingdom* BY MERIT.
2. Oppidum vallō munīvit.   *He fortified the town* BY MEANS OF A RAMPART.

NOTE. — Observe in these examples that *virtūte*, 'by merit,' and *vallō*, 'by means of a rampart,' are both in the *Ablative*. This Latin Idiom is expressed in the following

---

[1] Or *he loved, they loved.*   [2] *Rēxit=rēg-sit, rēxerunt=rēg-sērunt*; p. 3, 30.

FOURTH CONJUGATION.

RULE XXV.—Ablative of Means.

420. INSTRUMENT and MEANS are denoted by the Ablative:

Cornibus tauri se tutantur, bulls defend themselves WITH THEIR HORNS. Cic. *Gloriâ ducitur, he is led* BY GLORY. Cic. *Sol omnia luce collustrat, the sun illumines all things with its light.* Cic. *Lacte vivunt, they live upon milk.* Caes. *Tellus saucia vomeribus, the earth turned* (wounded) *with the ploughshare.* Ovid.

LESSON XXVIII.

FOURTH CONJUGATION AND PERFECT TENSE.— EXERCISES.

79. *Vocabulary.*

Altus, a, um,	*high.*
Artē, *adv.*	*closely, soundly.*
Castra, ōrum, *n. pl.*	*camp.*
Custōdit, 4,[1]	*he guards.*
Discipulus, i, *m.*	*learner, pupil.*
Dormit, 4,	*he sleeps.*
Erudit, 4,	*he instructs.*
Fossa, ae, *f.*	*ditch, moat.*
Fugitivus, i, *m.*	*runaway, deserter.*
Gallia, ae, *f.*	*Gaul,* a country nearly corresponding to France.
Helvetii, ōrum, *m. pl.*	the *Helvetii* or *Helvetians,* a people of Switzerland.
Legio, ōnis, *f.*	*legion.*
Munit, 4,	*he fortifies.*
Murus, i, *m.*	*wall.*
Posteā, *adv.*	*afterward.*
Pugna, ae, *f.*	*fight, battle.*
Rōmānus, i, *m.*	*Roman.*
Sermo, ōnis, *m.*	*discourse, conversation.*
Vallum, i, *n.*	*rampart.*
Vox, vōcis, *f.*	*voice.*

---

[1] As the ending of the third person singular of the present indicative is the same in the fourth conjugation as in the third, verbs of the fourth conjugation for the present will be distinguished in the vocabularies by the numeral 4.

FOURTH CONJUGATION.

80. *Translate into English.*

1. Audiunt, audiēbat, audient, audīvit. 2. Erudit, ērudiēbant, ērudiet, ērudīvērunt. 3. Mūnit, cūstōdit, cūstōdient, mūnient. 4. Puerī dormiēbant. 5. Puer artē dormiēbat. 6. Pāstōrēs artē dormiunt. 7. Mīlitēs artē dormīvērunt. 8. Mīlitēs arcem mūniēbant. 9. Caesar castra mūnīvit. 10. Legiōnēs castra mūniēbant. 11. Hostēs fortiter pūgnāvērunt. 12. Hostēs urbem oppūgnāvērunt. 13. Jūdex bonus tyrannum timuit. 14. Cīvēs Pīsistratum tyrannum timuērunt. 15. Hostēs urbem mūrō mūniēbant. 16. Cōnsul urbem mūrō altō mūnīvit. 17. Rōmānī Helvētiōs superāvērunt. 18. Mīlitēs castra fossā mūniēbant. 19. Caesar castra vallō mūnīvit. 20. Fugitīvī hostibus pūgnam nūntiāvērunt. 21. Rōmānī posteā hostēs superāvērunt. 22. Caesar in Galliā fuit. 23. Hostēs nāvēs multās habuērunt. 24. Cicerō cōnsul epistulās multās scrībit. 25. Cōnsul vōcēs mīlitum audīvit. 26. Puerī sermōnem dē amīcitiā audient.

81. *Translate into Latin.*

1. He hears, he guards. 2. They hear, they guard. 3. He was hearing, they were sleeping. 4. He was sleeping, they were hearing. 5. He will hear, they will hear. 6. They have slept, they have heard. 7. The boys heard the oration. 8. The pupils heard the conversation. 9. They did not hear the oration. 10. The citizens are fortifying the city. 11. They will guard the beautiful city. 12. The soldiers will guard the city. 13. They will guard the temple. 14. The shepherd was sleeping soundly. 15. The shepherds will sleep soundly. 16. Caesar heard the voice of the soldier. 17. Caesar hears the voices of the soldiers. 18. The soldier heard the voice of Caesar. 19. They heard the conversation in regard to the consul. 20. Caesar was fortifying the camp with a rampart. 21. The soldiers will fortify the camp with a moat.

LESSON XXIX.

ADJECTIVES OF THE THIRD DECLENSION.

82. *Lesson from the Grammar.*

152. Adjectives of the third declension may be divided into three classes:

I. Those which have in the Nominative Singular three different forms—one for each gender.

II. Those which have two forms—the masculine and feminine being the same.

III. Those which have but one form—the same for all genders.

153. ADJECTIVES OF THREE ENDINGS in this declension have the stem in **i**, and are declined as follows:

Ācer, *sharp*.[1]

SINGULAR.

	MASC.	FEM.	NEUT.
Nom.	ácer[2]	ácris	ácre
Gen.	ácris	ácris	ácris
Dat.	ácrī	ácrī	ácrī
Acc.	ácrem	ácrem	ácre
Voc.	ácer	ácris	ácre
Abl.	ácrī	ácrī	ácrī

PLURAL.

	MASC.	FEM.	NEUT.
Nom.	ácrēs	ácrēs	ácria
Gen.	ácrium	ácrium	ácrium
Dat.	ácribus	ácribus	ácribus
Acc.	ácrēs, īs	ácrēs, īs	ácria
Voc.	ácrēs	ácrēs	ácria
Abl.	ácribus	ácribus	ácribus

---

[1] Ācer is declined like *ignis* in the Masc. and Fem., and like *mare* (63, 63) in the Neut., except in the Nom and Voc. Sing. Masc., and in the Abl. Sing.

[2] These forms in *er* are like those in *er* of Decl. II. in dropping the ending in the Nom. and Voc. Sing., and in developing final *r* into *er*: *acer* for *acris*, stem *acri*.

ADJECTIVES.

154. ADJECTIVES OF TWO ENDINGS are declined as follows:

Tristis, *sad.*[1]   Tristior, *sadder.*[1]

SINGULAR.

	M. AND F.	NEUT.	M. AND F.	NEUT.
Nom.	tristis	triste	tristior	tristius
Gen.	tristis	tristis	tristioris	tristioris
Dat.	tristī	tristī	tristiōrī	tristiōrī
Acc.	tristem	triste	tristiōrem	tristius
Voc.	tristis	triste	tristior	tristius
Abl.	tristī	tristī	tristiōre (ī)[2]	tristiōre (ī)

PLURAL.

	M. AND F.	NEUT.	M. AND F.	NEUT.
Nom.	tristēs	tristia	tristiōrēs	tristiōra
Gen.	tristium	tristium	tristiōrum	tristiōrum
Dat.	tristibus	tristibus	tristiōribus	tristiōribus
Acc.	tristēs, īs	tristia	tristiōrēs (īs)	tristiōra
Voc.	tristēs	tristia	tristiōrēs	tristiōra
Abl.	tristibus	tristibus	tristiōribus	tristiōribus

83. *Vocabulary.*

Ācer, ācris, ācre,   *sharp, severe.*
Aetās, ātis, *f.*   *age.*
Cōpia, ae, *f.*   *abundance, supply.*
Crūdēlis, e,   *cruel.*
Fertĭlis, e,   *fertile.*
Fortis, e,   *brave.*
Gallus, ī, *m.*   *Gaul.*
Germānus, ī, *m.*   *German.*
Incolit,   *he inhabits.*
Inūtĭlis, e,   *useless.*
Nāvālis, e,   *naval.*
Occupat,   *he seizes, takes possession of.*
Omnis, e,   *all.*
Pābulum, ī, *n.*   *fodder.*
Per, *prep. w. acc.*   *through, on account of, by means*
Post, *prep. with acc.*   *after.*   [*of, by, during, for.*
Singulāris, e,   *remarkable, singular.*
Timor, ōris, *m.*   *fear.*
Utĭlis, e,   *useful.*

---

[1] *Tristis* and *triste* are declined like *ācris* and *ācre*. *Tristior* is the comparative of *tristis*.   [2] Enclosed endings are rare.

ADJECTIVES.

84. *Translate into English.*

1. Cīvis est fortis. 2. Cīvēs fortēs erunt. 3. Rēx est beātus. 4. Estne fortis? 5. Fortis est. 6. Librī sunt ūtilēs. 7. Gallia fertilis erat. 8. Cīvēs fortiter pūgnant. 9. Fertilēs agrōs habent. 10. Verba sunt ūtilia. 11. Lēx ācris est. 12. Lēgēs ācrēs sunt. 13. Mīles est fortis. 14. Mīlitēs sunt fortēs. 15. Cōnsul virtūtem mīlitis fortis laudat. 16. Cōnsul est ōrātor.

17. Catō māgnus imperātor est. 18. Timor omnēs mīlitēs occupāvit. 19. Timor omnēs hostēs occupābit. 20. Gallī fortēs sunt. 21. Caesar Gallōs fortēs superāvit. 22. Germānī agrōs fertilēs incolunt. 23. Pābulī cōpia in agrīs fertilibus erat. 24. Lēgēs sunt ūtilēs. 25. Cīvēs bonī lēgibus ūtilibus pārent. 26. Jūdicēs per aetātem ad pūgnam inūtilēs erant. 27. Timor omnēs cīvēs occupābit. 28. Agrī Gallōrum fertilēs erant. 29. Mīles verba ducis fortis audit.

85. *Translate into Latin.*

1. Will the brave leader obey the words of the consul? 2. He will obey the words of the consul. 3. Is he a good commander? 4. He is a good commander. 5. He is brave. 6. Will not the books be useful? 7. They will be useful. 8. The leaders of the soldiers are brave. 9. The brother of the consul is a brave soldier. 10. The brother of the king was a severe judge. 11. The brother of the orator will be a severe judge.

12. The brave soldiers were guarding the camp. 13. The soldiers will be brave. 14. They will all be brave. 15. Caesar praised the brave soldiers. 16. The soldiers will hear the words of the brave leader. 17. The field is fertile. 18. The fields are fertile. 19. Fear is taking possession of all the citizens. 20. There will be an abundance of fodder in the fields of the Germans.

---

[1] Genitive according to Rule XVI.

LESSON XXX.

ADJECTIVES OF THIRD DECLENSION.—COMPARISON OF ADJECTIVES.

86. *Lesson from the Grammar.*

155. ADJECTIVES OF ONE ENDING generally end in *s* or *x*, but sometimes in *l* or *r*.

156. Audāx, *audacious*.[1]   Fēlix, *happy*.[1]

SINGULAR.

	M. AND F.	NEUT.	M. AND F.	NEUT.
Nom.	audāx	audāx	fēlix	fēlix
Gen.	audācis	audācis	fēlicis	fēlicis
Dat.	audācī	audācī	fēlicī	fēlicī
Acc.	audācem	audāx	fēlicem	fēlix
Voc.	audāx	audāx	fēlix	fēlix
Abl.	audācī (e)	audācī (e)	fēlicī (e)	fēlicī (e)

PLURAL.

	M. AND F.	NEUT.	M. AND F.	NEUT.
Nom.	audācēs	audācia	fēlicēs	fēlicia
Gen.	audācium	audācium	fēlicium	fēlicium
Dat.	audācibus	audācibus	fēlicibus	fēlicibus
Acc.	audācēs (īs)	audācia	fēlicēs (īs)	fēlicia
Voc.	audācēs	audācia	fēlicēs	fēlicia
Abl.	audācibus	audācibus	fēlicibus	fēlicibus

157. Amāns, *loving*.   Prūdēns, *prudent*.

SINGULAR.

	M. AND F.	NEUT.	M. AND F.	NEUT.
Nom.	amāns	amāns	prūdēns	prūdēns
Gen.	amantis	amantis[2]	prūdentis	prūdentis[2]
Dat.	amantī	amantī	prūdentī	prūdentī
Acc.	amantem	amāns	prūdentem	prūdēns
Voc.	amāns	amāns	prūdēns	prūdēns
Abl.	amante (ī)	amante (ī)	prūdentī (e)	prūdentī (e)

---

[1] Observe that *i* in the Ablative Singular, and *ia*, *ium*, and *is* in the Plural, are the regular case-endings for *i*-stems. See 63.

[2] According to Ritschl, Schmitz, and others, the *e* which is long in *prūdēns* before *ns* is short in all other forms of the word, i.e. before *nt*. In the same manner the *a* which is long in *amāns*, is according to Ritschl short in *amantis*, *amanti*, etc.

ADJECTIVES.

PLURAL.

Nom. amantēs	amantia	prūdentēs	prūdentia
Gen. amantium	amantium	prūdentium	prūdentium
Dat. amantibus	amantibus	prūdentibus	prūdentibus
Acc. amantēs (īs)	amantia	prūdentēs (īs)	prūdentia
Voc. amantēs	amantia	prūdentēs	prūdentia
Abl. amantibus	amantibus	prūdentibus	prūdentibus

Note.—The participle *amāns* differs in declension from the adjective *prūdēns* only in the Ablative Singular, where the participle usually has the ending e, and the adjective, ī.

Comparison of Adjectives.

160. Adjectives have three forms, called the Positive degree, the Comparative, and the Superlative: *altus, altior, altissimus*,[1] high, higher, highest. These forms denote different degrees of the quality expressed by the adjective.

161. The Latin, like the English, has two modes of comparison:

I. Terminational Comparison, by endings.

II. Adverbial Comparison, by adverbs.

I. Terminational Comparison.

162. Adjectives are regularly compared by adding to the stem of the positive the endings:

COMPARATIVE.			SUPERLATIVE.		
Masc.	Fem.	Neut.	Masc.	Fem.	Neut.
ior	ior	ius	issimus	issima	issimum

Altus, altior, altissimus: *high, higher, highest.*

Levis, levior, levissimus: *light, lighter, lightest.*

1. Vowel Stems lose their final vowel: *alto, altior, altissimus.*

---

[1] Each of these forms of the adjective is declined. Thus *altus* and *altissimus* are declined like *bonus*, 39, 148: *altus, a, um; alti, ae, i,* etc.; *altissimus, a, um; altissimi, ae, i,* etc. *Altior* is declined like *tristior*, 82, 154; *altior, altius; altiōris,* etc.

ADJECTIVES. 71

165. The following are compared irregularly:

bonus,	melior,	optimus,	*good, better, best.*
magnus,	major,	maximus,	*great, greater, greatest.*
parvus,	minor,	minimus,	*small, smaller, smallest.*

166. POSITIVE WANTING.

citerior,	citimus,	*nearer,*	prior,	primus,	*former,*
deterior,	deterrimus,	*worse,*	propior,	proximus,	*nearer,*
interior,	intimus,	*inner,*	ulterior,	ultimus,	*farther.*
ocior,	ocissimus,	*swifter,*			

II. ADVERBIAL COMPARISON.

170. Adjectives which want the terminational comparison form the comparative and superlative, when their signification requires it, by prefixing the adverbs, *magis*, more, and *maxime*, most, to the positive:

Arduus, magis arduus, maxime arduus.
Arduous, more arduous, most arduous.

LESSON XXXI.

THIRD DECLENSION OF ADJECTIVES. — COMPARISON. —
EXERCISES.

87. *Examples.* — *Comparison.*

1. Aurum gravius est *quam argentum.*   *Gold is heavier* THAN SILVER.
2. Aurum *argento* gravius est.   *Gold is heavier* THAN SILVER.

NOTE. — Observe (1) that in the first example, the Latin construction is the same as the English, and that the two nouns compared, *aurum* and *argentum,* are in the same case, i.e. in the Nominative, and (2) that in the second example *quam* is omitted, and that the second noun is put in the *Ablative*. This Latin idiom is expressed in the following

RULE XXIII. — Ablative with Comparatives.

417. Comparatives without QUAM are followed by the Ablative:

Nihil est amabilius *virtūte*,[1] *nothing is more lovely* THAN VIRTUE. Cic. Quid est melius *bonitāte*,[1] *what is better* THAN GOODNESS? Cic. Scimus sōlem mājōrem esse terrā,[1] *we know that the sun is larger than the earth.* Cic.

1. COMPARATIVES WITH QUAM are followed by the Nominative, or by the case of the corresponding noun before them:

Hibernia minor quam *Britannia* existimātur, *Ireland is considered smaller than* BRITAIN. Caes. Agris quam *urbi* terribilior, *more terrible to the country than* TO THE CITY. Liv.

NOTE.— Conjunctions are mere connectives, and are without inflection. *Quam* is a conjunction.

88. *Comparison of Adverbs.*

Most adverbs are derived from adjectives, and are dependent upon them for their comparison. The comparative is the accusative neuter singular of the adjective, and the superlative changes the ending **us** of the adjective into long **ē**:

altus,	altior,	altissimus,	*lofty.*
altē,	altius,	altissimē,	*loftily.*
prūdēns,	prūdentior,	prūdentissimus,	*prudent.*
prūdenter,	prūdentius,	prūdentissimē,	*prudently.*

89. *Vocabulary.*

Aquilēia, ae, *f.* — *Aquileia,* a town in north-eastern Italy.
Ariovistus, ī, *m.* — *Ariovistus,* a German king.
Aurum, ī, *n.* — *gold.*
Belgae, ārum, *m. pl.* — the *Belgae,* or *Belgians,* a people of [Gaul.
Circum, *prep. w. acc.* — *around, in the vicinity of.*
Clārus, a, um, — *clear, illustrious.*
Cōnsilium, iī, *n.* — *counsel, plan.*
Divitiacus, ī, *m.* — *Divitiacus,* a chieftain of the Aedui in
Duplex, duplicis, — *double.* [Gaul.
Fēlix, fēlicis, — *happy, fortunate.*
Hannibal, alis, *m.* — *Hannibal,* a Carthaginian general.
Hiemat, — *he winters, passes the winter.*
Homō, hominis, *m.* and *f.* — *man, human being, person.*

---

[1] *Virtūte = quam virtūs; bonitāte = quam bonitās; terrā = quam terram* (sc. *esse*).

COMPARISON. 73

Infēlix, infēlicis, — unhappy, unfortunate.
Labiēnus, i, *m.* — Labienus, an officer in Caesar's army in Gaul.
Potēns, potentis, — powerful.
Pretiōsus, a, um, — precious, valuable.
Quam, *conj.* — than.
Sapiēns, sapientis, — wise.

90. *Translate into English.*

1. Ōrātor est clārus. 2. Estne clārissimus? 3. Est clārissimus. 4. Ōrātōrēs fuērunt clārī. 5. Ōrātōrēs clāriōrēs[1] sunt. 6. Ōrātōrēs clārissimī erunt. 7. Cōnsul fēlīx erat. 8. Cōnsulēs fēlīcēs sunt. 9. Caesar rēgem infēlīcem superāvit. 10. Caesar Ariovistum rēgem superāvit. 11. Caesar Ariovistum, infēlīcem Germānōrum rēgem, superāvit. 12. Legiō circum Aquilēiam hiemābit. 13. Hannibal infēlīx erat. 14. Jūdex sapiēns est. 15. Omnēs cīvēs jūdicem sapientem laudant. 16. Sapientēs hominēs cīvitātem regunt.
17. Caesar Labiēnum laudāvit. 18. Jūdex sapientior erat quam rēx. 19. Turris altior est quam mūrus. 20. Cōnsilium clārius est quam lūx. 21. Cōnsilium lūce clārius est. 22. Cōnsilia omnia lūce sunt clāriōra. 23. Belgae fortissimī sunt. 24. Gallōrum omnium fortissimī sunt Belgae. 25. Mīlitēs nōn pūgnābunt. 26. Hostēs castra altissimō mūrō mūnīvērunt.

91. *Translate into Latin.*

1. Gold is valuable. 2. Wisdom is more valuable. 3. The king is unfortunate. 4. Is not the consul ill? 5. The consul is ill. 6. Life is precious. 7. Is not gold useful? 8. It is useful. 9. Cato was wise. 10. The Gauls were brave. 11. The Romans were braver than the Gauls. 12. The Gauls were unfortunate. 13. The Romans conquered the unfortunate Gauls. 14. King Divitiacus was very powerful. He

---

[1] Declined like *tristior*, 82, 154. Comparatives and superlatives, as well as positives, must agree with their nouns, according to 40 Rule XXXIV.

was the most powerful of all the chiefs. He was the most powerful of all the Gauls.

15. Virtue is more valuable than gold. 16. Wisdom is more useful than gold. 17. Virtue is better than wisdom. 18. The soldiers are braver than the general. 19. The wall will be double. 20. The enemy will fortify the city with a double wall. 21. The wall was very high. 22. The Gauls were fortifying the city with a very high wall.

LESSON XXXII.

NOUNS. — FOURTH DECLENSION. — FIFTH DECLENSION.

92. *Lesson from the Grammar.*

FOURTH DECLENSION: **U** NOUNS.

116. Nouns of the fourth declension end in

us—*masculine;* **ū**—*neuter.*

They are declined as follows:

Frūctus, *fruit.*   Cornū, *horn.*

			SINGULAR.	CASE-ENDINGS.	
Nom.	frūct**us**	corn**ū**	us	ū
Gen.	frūct**ūs**	corn**ūs**	ūs	ūs
Dat.	frūct**uī, ū**[1]	corn**ū**	uī, ū[1]	ū
Acc.	frūct**um**	corn**ū**	um	ū
Voc.	frūct**us**	corn**ū**	us	ū
Abl.	frūct**ū**	corn**ū**	ū	ū
			PLURAL.		
Nom.	frūct**ūs**	corn**ua**	ūs	ua
Gen.	frūct**uum**	corn**uum**	uum	uum
Dat.	frūct**ibus**	corn**ibus**	ibus (ubus)[2]	ibus (ubus)
Acc.	frūct**ūs**	corn**ua**	ūs	ua
Voc.	frūct**ūs**	corn**ua**	ūs	ua
Abl.	frūct**ibus**	corn**ibus**	ibus (ubus)	ibus (ubus)

---

[1] Thus *ui* is contracted into *ū: frūctuī, frūctū.*
[2] The enclosed endings occur in a few words.

FIFTH DECLENSION.

1. The STEM in nouns of the fourth declension ends in u: *frūctu, cornu*.

2. The CASE-ENDINGS here given contain the characteristic u, weakened to *i* in *ibus*, but retained in *ubus*; see p. 2, 22.

FIFTH DECLENSION: E NOUNS.

120. Nouns of the fifth declension end in **ēs**—*feminine*, and are declined as follows:

Diēs, *day*.[1]   Rēs, *thing*.

	SINGULAR.		CASE-ENDINGS.
Nom.	diēs	rēs	ēs
Gen.	diēī or diē	rēī or rē	ēī, ē
Dat.	diēī or diē	rēī or rē	ēī, ē
Acc.	diem	rem	em
Voc.	diēs	rēs	ēs
Abl.	diē	rē	ē
	PLURAL.		CASE-ENDINGS.
Nom.	diēs	rēs	ēs
Gen.	diērum	rērum	ērum
Dat.	diēbus	rēbus	ēbus
Acc.	diēs	rēs	ēs
Voc.	diēs	rēs	ēs
Abl.	diēbus	rēbus	ēbus

1. The STEM of nouns of the fifth declension ends in **ē**: *diē, rē*.

2. The CASE-ENDINGS here given contain the characteristic **ē**, which appears in all the cases. It is shortened (1) generally in the ending *ēī* when preceded by a consonant, and (2) regularly in the ending *em*.

93. *Examples.* — *Time.*

1. Urbem *hōc tempore* mūniunt.   They are AT THIS TIME *fortifying the city*.

2. *Sextō annō.*   IN THE SIXTH YEAR.

NOTE.—Observe that *hōc tempore*, 'at this time,' and *sextō annō* 'in the sixth year' are both in the *Ablative*. This Latin idiom is expressed in the following

---

[1] By exception, *diēs* is usually masculine in the singular, and always in the plural.

RULE XXXI.—Time.

429. The TIME of an Action is denoted by the Ablative:

Octōgēsimō annō est mortuus, he died IN HIS EIGHTIETH YEAR. Cic. *Vēre convēnēre,* they assembled IN THE SPRING. Liv.

94. Vocabulary.

Aciēs, aciēī, *f.*	edge, line of battle.
Adventus, ūs, *m.*	approach, arrival.
Avis, is, *f.*	bird.
Cantus, ūs, *m.*	singing.
Comparat,	he prepares, raises.
Cōnspectus, ūs, *m.*	sight, view.
Exercĭtus, ūs, *m.*	army.
Impetus, ūs, *m.*	attack, charge. [*forms the line of battle.*
Instruit,	he constructs, draws up; aciem instruit, he
Magistrātus, ūs, *m.*	magistrate, magistracy. [ibus, in hand.
Manus, ūs, *f.*[1]	hand, a band of soldiers, a force; in manu-
Militāris, e,	military; res militāris, military affairs.
Occāsus, ūs, *m.*	setting; sōlis occāsus, sunset.
Portus, ūs, *m.*	port, harbor.
Posterus, a, um,	following, next.
Redūcit,	he leads back.
Spēs, spĕī, *f.*	hope.
Tenet,	he holds.
Ūsus, ūs, *m.*	use, usage, experience.

95. *Translate into English.*

1. Rēx exercitum comparābat. 2. Aciem instruēbat. 3. Tenetne portum?[2] 4. Portum tenēbit. 5. Impetum timēbat. 6. Opus est māgnum. 7. Timor exercitum occupābat. 8. Portus est bonus. 9. Labiēnus in exercitū[3] Caesaris fuit. 10. Hannibal exercitum māgnum in Italiam dūxit. 11. Caesar exercitūs māgnōs comparāvit. 12. In cōnspĕctū hostium erat.

---

[1] Feminine by exception.
[2] *Tenetne* = *tenet* and interrogative particle *-ne.*
[3] See page 58, foot-note 1.

13. Puer cantum avis audiēbat. 14. Puerī cantūs avium audient. 15. Cōnsul hostium exercitum nōn timēbat. 16. Cicerō cōnsul opus māgnum in manibus habēbat. 17. Hostēs portum tenēbant. 18. Caesar aciem īnstruet. 19. Posterō diē aciem īnstruēbat. 20. Posterō diē in cōnspectū hostium aciem īnstruēbat. 21. Posteā exercitum in castra redūxit. 22. Ariovistus sōlis occāsū exercitum in castra redūxit. 23. Hostēs adventum Caesaris exspectābant. 24. Timor omnem exercitum occupāvit.

96. *Translate into Latin.*

1. At sunset fear seized the army. 2. The next day Caesar conquered the king. 3. The consul will hold the harbor. 4. He has a large army. 5. Will he fortify the harbor? 6. He is fortifying the harbor. 7. Does he expect an attack? 8. He expects an attack. 9. The commander fears the attack of the enemy. 10. The soldiers will fight in sight of the commander. 11. The pupil is writing about the army. 12. The girl hears the singing of the bird.

13. Fear will take possession of the army. 14. Caesar led a large army into Gaul. 15. Ariovistus, the king of the Germans, had a large army in Gaul. 16. The consul will hold the harbor. 17. He was awaiting the approach of Ariovistus, the king of the Germans. 18. The consul has large experience in military affairs. 19. The soldiers of Ariovistus did not have large experience in military affairs.

LESSON XXXIII.

NUMERALS.

97. *Lesson from the Grammar.*

171. Numerals comprise numeral adjectives and numeral adverbs.

172. Numeral adjectives comprise three principal classes:

1. **Cardinal Numbers:**[1] *ūnus*, one; *duo*, two.
2. **Ordinal Numbers:**[1] *prīmus*, first; *secundus*, second.
3. **Distributives:**[1] *singulī*, one by one; *bīnī*, two by two.

174. Partial Table of Numeral Adjectives:

CARDINALS.	ORDINALS.	DISTRIBUTIVES.
1. ūnus, ūna, ūnum, *one*	prīmus, *first*	singulī, *one by one*
2. duo, duae, duo, *two*	secundus, *second*	bīnī, *two by two* [2]
3. trēs, tria, *three*	tertius, *third*	ternī (trīnī), *three by three*
4. quattuor, *four*	quārtus, *fourth*	quaternī, *four by four*
5. quīnque, *five*	quīntus, *fifth*	quīnī, *five by five*
6. sex, *six*	sextus, *sixth*	sēnī, *six by six*
7. septem, *seven*	septimus, *seventh*	septēnī, *seven by seven*
8. octo, *eight*	octāvus, *eighth*	octōnī, *eight by eight*
9. novem, *nine*	nōnus, *ninth*	novēnī, *nine by nine*
10. decem, *ten*	decimus, *tenth*	dēnī, *ten by ten*

Declension of Numeral Adjectives.

175. *Ūnus*, *Duo*, and *Trēs* are declined as follows:

Ūnus, *one*.

	SINGULAR.			PLURAL.	
Nom.	ūnus	ūna	ūnum	ūnī	ūnae	ūna
Gen.	ūnīus	ūnīus	ūnīus	ūnōrum	ūnārum	ūnōrum
Dat.	ūnī	ūnī	ūnī	ūnīs	ūnīs	ūnīs
Acc.	ūnum	ūnam	ūnum	ūnōs	ūnās	ūna
Voc.	ūne	ūna	ūnum	ūnī	ūnae	ūna
Abl.	ūnō	ūnā	ūnō	ūnīs	ūnīs	ūnīs

Duo, *two*.   **Trēs, *three*.**

Nom.	duo	duae	duo	trēs, *m. and f.*	tria, *n.*
Gen.	duōrum	duārum	duōrum [3]	trium	trium
Dat.	duōbus	duābus	duōbus	tribus	tribus
Acc.	duōs, duo	duās	duo	trēs, trīs	tria
Voc.	duo	duae	duo	trēs	tria
Abl.	duōbus	duābus	duōbus	tribus	tribus

---

[1] *Cardinals* denote simply the *number* of objects. *Ordinals* denote the *place* of an object in a *series*. *Distributives* denote the *number* of objects taken at a time.   [2] Or *two each*, *two apiece*.

[3] Instead of *duōrum* and *duārum*, *duūm* is sometimes used.

NUMERALS.

NOTE 1. — The plural of *ūnus* in the sense of *alone* may be used with any noun: *ūni Ubii*, the Ubii alone; but in the sense of *one*, it is used only with nouns plural in form, but singular in sense: *ūna castra*, one camp; *ūnae litterae*, one letter.

176. The Cardinals from *quattuor*, 'four,' to *centum*, 'one hundred,' are indeclinable.

177. Hundreds are declined like the plural of *bonus*; *ducentī, ae, a*, 'two hundred.'

179. Ordinals are declined like *bonus*, and distributives like the *plural* of *bonus*.

98. *Examples. — Duration of Time.*

1. Caecus *annōs* multōs fuit.   *He was blind many* YEARS.
2. Trīgintā *annōs* vīxit.   *He lived thirty* YEARS.
3. Fossa quīndecim *pedēs* lāta.   *A moat fifteen* FEET *broad.*

NOTE. — In these examples observe that *annōs*, 'years,' and *pedēs*, 'feet,' are in the *Accusative*. This Latin idiom[1] is expressed in the following

RULE IX. — Accusative of Time and Space.

379. DURATION OF TIME and EXTENT OF SPACE are expressed by the Accusative:

Rōmulus septem et trīgintā rēgnāvit *annōs*, *Romulus reigned thirty-seven* YEARS. Liv. Quīnque *mīlia* passuum ambulāre, *to walk five* MILES. Cic. *Pedēs* octōgintā distāre, *to be eighty* FEET *distant.* Caes. Nix quattuor *pedēs* alta, *snow four* FEET *deep.* Liv.

99. *Vocabulary.*

Ā, ab, *prep. w. abl.*   *from, by.*
Annus, ī, *m.*   *year.*
Celtae, ārum, *m. pl.*   *Celts, a people of Gaul.*
Circiter, *adv., and prep. w. acc.*   *about.*
Cōnscrībit,   *he enrols.*
Cȳrus, ī, *m.*   *Cyrus, King of Persia.*
Dionȳsius, iī, *m.*   *Dionysius, tyrant of Syracuse.*
Duodecim, *indeclinable,*   *twelve.*

---
[1] The English uses the *Objective* case in the same way.

NUMERALS.

Duodēquadrāgintā, *indeclinable,*	*thirty-eight.*
Merīdiēs, ēī, m.[1]	*midday, noon.*
Oppidum, ī, n.	*town.*
Pars, partis, f.	*part.*
Suessiōnēs, um, m. pl.	*Suessiones,* a Gallic tribe.
Sustinet,	*he sustains, withstands, resists.*
Trigintā, *indeclinable,*	*thirty.*
Ūndecimus, a, um,	*eleventh.*
Usque, *adv.*	*until, even;* usque ad, *even to,*
Vēr, vēris, n.	*spring.* [*until.*
Vīcus, ī, m.	*village.*

100. *Translate into English.*

1. Gallī trēs hōrās pūgnābant. 2. Nōnne fortiter pūgnant? 3. Fortiter pūgnant. 4. Circiter merīdiem exercitum in castra redūcet. 5. Belgae ūnam Galliae partem incolunt. 6. Celtae tertiam Galliae partem incolunt. 7. Caesar duās legiōnēs in Ītaliā cōnscrībit. 8. Trēs legiōnēs circum Aquilēiam hiemābant. 9. Duās legiōnēs in Galliā cōnscrīpsit.[2] 10. Legiōnis nōnae mīlitēs fortiter pūgnāvērunt. 11. Duae legiōnēs, ūndecima et octāva, fortiter pūgnābant. 12. Legiōnis decimae mīlitēs impetum hostium fortiter sustinēbant. 13. Legiōnis octāvae mīlitēs in cōnspectū imperātōris impetum hostium fortiter sustinuērunt. 14. Legiōnēs sex castra mūniēbant. 15. Mīlitēs ab hōrā quārtā usque ad sōlis occāsum fortiter pūgnāvērunt. 16. Suessiōnēs oppida duodecim habent. 17. Cyrus trīgintā annōs rēgnāvit. 18. Dionȳsius duodēquadrāgintā annōs tyrannus fuit.

101. *Translate into Latin.*

1. Numa reigned many years. 2. Did not the Gauls fight bravely? 3. They fought bravely. 4. The boy has thirty books. 5. He will present three to his brother. 6. The legions will attack the tower at sunset. 7. At that time the tenth legion was in Gaul. 8. The soldiers of the

---

[1] Masculine by exception.   [2] *Cōnscrīpsit* = *cōnscrīb-sit;* see 76.

PRONOUNS.

tenth legion were brave. 9. They were the bravest of all. 10. Two legions will guard the camp. 11. Five legions will fortify the camp with a rampart.

12. The soldiers were fortifying one part of the village with a very high wall. 13. The commander was awaiting the arrival of two legions. 14. The two consuls enrolled six legions. 15. The soldiers of two legions did not have large experience in military affairs. 16. The enemy fought bravely for ten hours. 17. They held the harbor for five days.

LESSON XXXIV.

PRONOUNS.

102. *Lesson from the Grammar.*

182. In construction, Pronouns[1] are used either as Substantives: *ego*, I, *tū*, thou; or as Adjectives: *meus*, my, *tuus*, your.

183. Pronouns are divided into six classes:

1. Personal Pronouns: *tū*, thou.
2. Possessive Pronouns: *meus*, my.
3. Demonstrative Pronouns: *hīc*, this.
4. Relative Pronouns: *quī*, who.
5. Interrogative Pronouns: *quis*, who?
6. Indefinite Pronouns: *aliquis*, some one.

I. PERSONAL PRONOUNS.

184. Personal Pronouns,[2] so called because they designate the person of the noun which they represent, are:

---

[1] But in their signification and use, Pronouns differ widely from ordinary substantives and adjectives, as they never *name* any object, action, or quality, but simply *point out* its relation to the speaker, or to some other person or thing.

[2] Also called *Substantive Pronouns*, because they are always used *substantively*.

PRONOUNS.

Ego, *I.* Tū, *thou.* Suī, *of himself,* etc.[1]

SINGULAR.

Nom.	ego	tū	
Gen.	meī	tuī	suī [1]
Dat.	mihī or mī	tibī	sibī
Acc.	mē	tē	sē
Voc.		tū	
Abl.	mē	tē	sē

PLURAL.

Nom.	nōs	vōs	
Gen.	{ nostrum { nostrī	vestrum } vestrī }	suī
Dat.	nōbis	vōbis	sibī
Acc.	nōs	vōs	sē
Voc.		vōs	
Abl.	nōbīs	vōbīs	sē

2. Suī, *of himself,* etc., is often called the *Reflexive* pronoun.
4. REDUPLICATED FORMS. — *Sēsē, tētē, mēmē,* for *sē, tē, mē.*
6. CUM, when used with the *ablative* of a Personal Pronoun, is appended to it: *mēcum, tēcum.*

II. POSSESSIVE PRONOUNS.

185. From *Personal* pronouns are formed the *Possessives:*[2]

meus, a, um, *my;* noster, tra, trum, *our;*
tuus, a, um, *thy, your;* vester, tra, trum, *your;*
suus, a, um, *his, hers, its;* suus, a, um, *their.*

III. DEMONSTRATIVE PRONOUNS.

186. Demonstrative Pronouns, so called because they specify the objects to which they refer, are declined as follows:

---

[1] *Of himself, herself, itself.* The Nominative is not used.

[2] Possessives are declined as adjectives of the first and second declensions; but *meus* has in the Vocative Singular Masculine generally *mī*, sometimes *meus*, and in the Genitive Plural sometimes *meum* instead of *meōrum.*

I. Hic, *this, this one, he.*

	SINGULAR			PLURAL		
	Masc.	Fem.	Neut.	Masc.	Fem.	Neut.
Nom.	hic	haec	hŏc	hī	hae	haec
Gen.	hūjus	hūjus	hūjus	hōrum	hārum	hōrum
Dat.	huic	huic	huic	hīs	hīs	hīs
Acc.	hunc	hanc	hŏc [1]	hōs	hās	haec
Abl.	hōc	hāc	hōc	hīs	hīs	hīs

II. Iste, *that, that of yours, that one, he.*

	SINGULAR			PLURAL		
	Masc.	Fem.	Neut.	Masc.	Fem.	Neut.
Nom.	iste	ista	istud	istī	istae	ista
Gen.	istīus	istīus	istīus	istōrum	istārum	istōrum
Dat.	istī	istī	istī	istis	istis	istis
Acc.	istum	istam	istud	istōs	istās	ista
Abl.	istō	istā	istō	istīs	istīs	istīs

III. Ille, *that, that one, he,* is declined like *iste.*

IV. Is, *he, this, that.*

	SINGULAR			PLURAL		
	Masc.	Fem.	Neut.	Masc.	Fem.	Neut.
Nom.	is	ea	id	eī, iī	eae	ea
Gen.	ējus	ējus	ējus	eōrum	eārum	eōrum
Dat.	eī	eī	eī	eis, iis	eis, iis	eis, iis
Acc.	eum	eam	id	eōs	eās	ea
Abl.	eō	eā	eō	eis, iis	eis, iis	eis, iis

V. Ipse, *self, he.*

	SINGULAR			PLURAL		
	Masc.	Fem.	Neut.	Masc.	Fem.	Neut.
Nom.	ipse	ipsa	ipsum	ipsi	ipsae	ipsa
Gen.	ipsīus	ipsīus	ipsīus	ipsōrum	ipsārum	ipsōrum
Dat.	ipsi	ipsi	ipsi	ipsis	ipsis	ipsis
Acc.	ipsum	ipsam	ipsum	ipsōs	ipsās	ipsa
Abl.	ipsō	ipsā	ipsō	ipsis	ipsis	ipsis

---

[1] The Vocative is wanting in Demonstrative, Relative, Interrogative, and Indefinite Pronouns.

VI. Idem, *the same.*[1]

	SINGULAR			PLURAL		
	Masc.	Fem.	Neut.	Masc.	Fem.	Neut.
Nom.	idem	eadem	idem	eidem / iidem	eaedem	eadem
Gen.	ejusdem	ejusdem	ejusdem	eorundem	earundem	eorundem
Dat.	eidem	eidem	eidem	eisdem / iisdem	eisdem	eisdem
Acc.	eundem	eandem	idem	eosdem	easdem	eadem
Abl.	eodem	eadem	eodem	eisdem / iisdem	eisdem	eisdem

LESSON XXXV.

PRONOUNS. — EXERCISES.

103. *Vocabulary.*

Aequitās, ātis, *f.*   *kindness, calmness, fairness.*
Commemorat,   *he mentions, speaks.*
Commemorătiō, ōnis, *f.*   *remembrance, mentioning, mention.*
Cum, *prep. w. abl.*   *with.*
Diligentia, ae, *f.*   *diligence, carefulness.*
Doctus, a, um,   *learned.*
Hic, haec, hoc,   *this, this one, the latter, he, she, it.*
Hūmānītās, ātis, *f.*   *culture, refinement.*
Ille, illa, illud,   *that, that one, the former, he, she, it.*
Impedimenta, ōrum, *n. pl.*   *baggage.*
Integritās, ātis, *f.*   *integrity, uprightness.*
Iste, ista, istud,   *that of yours, that, that one, he, she, it.*
Longus, a, um,   *long.*
Portat,   *he carries, brings.*
Que, *conj. enclitic,*[2]   *and.*
Semper, *adv.*   *always.*   [*of her, of it.*
Sui,   *of himself, of herself, of itself, of him,*

---

[1] Idem, compounded of *is* and *dem*, is declined like *is*, but shortens *isdem* to *idem*, and *iddem* to *idem*, and changes *m* to *n* before the ending *dem*.

[2] That is, it is always appended to some other word: *virtūs-que*, 'and virtue.' *Que* connects words that are closely related in thought or use. For *conjunctions*, see 88, 417, note.

PRONOUNS.

Suus, a, um, — his, her, hers, its, their, theirs, his own, her own, its own, one's own.
Temperantia, ae, f. — temperance, self-control.
Tum, adv. — then.
Vocat, — he calls, summons, invites.

104. Translate into English.

1. Caesar Divitiacum ad sē vocāvit. 2. Exercitus noster in Galliā hiemābat. 3. Hostēs suam urbem vallō mūniēbant. 4. Gallī hanc urbem vallō fossāque mūniēbant. 5. Mīlitēs omnia impedīmenta sēcum portant. 6. Pater tuus epistulam longam ad tē scrībet. 7. Amīcus tuus trēs epistulās ad mē scrīpsit. 8. Omnēs bonī vōs semper amābunt. 9. Omnēs tē laudant; omnēs dē tuā hūmānitāte commemorant; omnēs aequitātem tuam, temperantiam, integritātemque laudant. 10. Mē commemorātiō tuae virtūtis dēlectāvit. 11. Omnēs bonī omnem ā nōbīs dīligentiam virtūtemque exspectant. 12. Sapientēs hominēs illam cīvitātem regēbant. 13. Doctī hominēs istam cīvitātem regunt. 14. Doctī et sapientēs hominēs hanc cīvitātem regent. 15. Cicerō suā manū epistulam scrīpsit (for *scrīb -sit*).

105. Translate into Latin.

1. The boy praises himself. 2. Many boys praise themselves. 3. Wise men do not praise themselves. 4. Your father loves you. 5. Does he praise me? 6. He praises you. 7. This book is beautiful. 8. These books are new. 9. The queen wrote this letter. 10. That legion was wintering in Italy. 11. Those legions will winter in Gaul. 12. The citizens praise you. 13. All the citizens will praise you. 14. Wise men will always praise your wisdom. 15. Good men will praise your virtue. 16. Good men will always praise your virtue and wisdom. 17. Your father wrote this letter with his own hand. 18. He has written to me. 19. The consul had five legions with him. 20. He was then in Italy. 21. The enemy are fortifying their city with a very high wall.

LESSON XXXVI.

PRONOUNS. — RELATIVE, INTERROGATIVE, INDEFINITE.

106. *Lesson from the Grammar.*

IV. Relative Pronouns.

187. The Relative *quī,* 'who,' so called because it relates to some noun or pronoun, expressed or understood, called its antecedent, is declined as follows:

	SINGULAR.			PLURAL.		
	MASC.	FEM.	NEUT.	MASC.	FEM.	NEUT.
Nom.	qui	quae	quod	qui	quae	quae
Gen.	cūjus	cūjus	cūjus	quōrum	quārum	quōrum
Dat.	cui	cui	cui	quibus	quibus	quibus
Acc.	quem	quam	quod	quōs	quās	quae
Abl.	quō	quā	quō	quibus	quibus	quibus

1. *Quī = quō, quā,* 'with which,' 'wherewith,' is a *Locative* or *Ablative* of the relative *quī.*
2. *Cum,* when used with the Ablative of the relative, is generally appended to it: *quibuscum.*

V. Interrogative Pronouns.

188. The Interrogative Pronouns *quis* and *quī,* with their compounds, are used in asking questions. They are declined as follows:

I. Quis, *who, which, what?*

	SINGULAR.			PLURAL.		
	MASC.	FEM.	NEUT.	MASC.	FEM.	NEUT.
Nom.	quis	quae	quid	qui	quae	quae
Gen.	cūjus	cūjus	cūjus	quōrum	quārum	quōrum
Dat.	cui	cui	cui	quibus	quibus	quibus
Acc.	quem	quam	quid	quōs	quās	quae
Abl.	quō	quā	quō	quibus	quibus	quibus

II. Quī, *which, what?* is declined like the *relative quī.*

1. Quis is generally used substantively, and Quī, adjectively. The forms *quis* and *quem* are sometimes feminine.
2. *Quī,* how? in what way? is a Locative or Ablative of the interrogative *quis.*

VI. Indefinite Pronouns.

189. Indefinite Pronouns do not refer to any definite persons or things. The most important are *quis* and *qui*, with their compounds.

190. *Quis,* 'any one,' and *qui,* 'any one,' 'any,' are the same in form and declension as the interrogatives *quis* and *qui.* But—

1. After *si, nisi, nē,* and *num,* the Feminine Singular and Neuter Plural have *quae* or *qua: si quae, si qua.*

2. From *quis* and *qui* are formed —

aliquis,   aliqua,   aliquid *or* aliquod,   *some, some one.*
quidam,   quaedam,   quiddam *or* quoddam,[1]   *certain, certain one.*

351. An Interrogative Sentence has the form of a question:

Quis loquitur, *who speaks?* Ter. Quis nōn paupertātem extimēscit, *who does not fear poverty?* Cic. Quālis est ōrātiō, *what kind of an oration is it?* Cic. Quot sunt, *how many are there?* Plaut. Ubi sunt, *where are they?* Cic. Vīsne fortūnam experīrī meam, *do you wish to try my fortune?* Cic. Nōnne nōbilitārī volunt, *do they not wish to be renowned?* Cic. Num igitur peccāmus, *are we then at fault?* Cic.

1. Interrogative Words. — Interrogative sentences generally contain some interrogative word — either an interrogative pronoun, adjective, or adverb, or one of the interrogative particles: *-ne, nōnne, num;* see examples above.

Note 1. — Questions with *-ne* ask for information; *Scribitne,* 'is he writing?'

Note 2. — Questions with *nōnne* expect the answer *yes: Nōnne scribit,* 'is he not writing?'

Note 3. — Questions with *num* expect the answer *no: Num scribit,* 'is he writing?'

2. The particle *-ne* is always appended to some other word, generally to the emphatic word of the sentence, i.e. to the word upon which the question especially turns; appended to *nōn,* 'not,' it forms *nōnne:*

Vīsne experīrī, *do you* wish *to try?* Cic. Tūne id veritus es, *did* you *fear this?* Cic. Omnisne pecūnia solūta est, *has* all *the money*

---

[1] *Quidam* changes *m* to *n* before *d: quendam* for *quemdam.*

been paid? Cic. *Unquamne* vidisti, *have you* EVER *seen?* Cic. *Nonne* volunt, *do they* NOT *wish?* Cic.

352. ANSWERS.—Instead of replying to a question of fact with a simple particle meaning *yes* or *no*, the Latin usually repeats the verb or some emphatic word, often with *prōrsus*, *vĕrō*, 'certainly,' 'truly,' and the like, or if negative, with *nōn*, 'not.'

Dixitne causam, *did he state the cause?* Dixit, *he stated it.* Cic. Possumusne tūti esse, *can we be safe?* Nōn possumus, *we can not.* Cic.

353. DOUBLE or DISJUNCTIVE QUESTIONS offer a *choice* or *alternative*, and generally take one of the following forms:

1. The first clause has *utrum* or *-ne*, and the second *an:*

Utrum ea vestra an nostra culpa est, *is that your fault or ours* Cic. Rōmamne veniō an hic maneō, *do I go to Rome, or do I remain here?* Cic.

2. The first clause omits the particle, and the second has *an* or *anne:*

Ēloquar an sileam, *shall I utter it, or keep silence?* Verg.

LESSON XXXVII.

PRONOUNS. — RULE XXXV. — EXERCISES.

107. *Examples.* — *Agreement.*

Rex *quem* omnēs laudant.	*The king* WHOM *all praise.*
Regina *quam* omnēs laudant.	*The queen* WHOM *all praise.*
Iī *quōs* omnēs laudant.	*Those* WHOM *all praise.*
Ego *qui* dicō.	*I* WHO *speak.*

NOTE. — In these examples the pronoun *quem* refers to *rex*, called its antecedent, *quam* to its antecedent *regina*, *quōs* to its antecedent *iī*, and *qui* to its antecedent *ego*. Observe that the pronoun in each instance is in the same gender and number [1] as its antecedent. Thus

---

[1] The *case* of the pronoun is determined by the construction of the clause in which it stands, and not by the case of its antecedent. Thus in these examples, though the antecedents are all in the Nominative, the pronouns *quem, quam,* and *quōs* are all in the Accusative as Direct Objects.

quem is in the *masculine singular*, because *rex* is in that gender and number; *quam* in the feminine singular like *regina*; and *quos* in the masculine plural like *ii*. The pronoun has also the same person as its antecedent. Thus *quem, quam,* and *quos* are all in the third person, like their antecedents *rex, regina,* and *ii,* while *qui* is in the first person, like its antecedent *ego.* This agreement of pronouns with their antecedents applies not only to relatives, but to all pronouns when used as substantives,¹ and is expressed in the following

RULE XXXV.—Agreement of Pronouns.

445. A pronoun agrees with its antecedent in GEN-
DER, NUMBER, and PERSON:
Animal *quod* sanguinem habet, *an animal* WHICH *has blood.* Cic.
Ego, *qui* tĕ cōnfīrmō, *I* WHO *encourage you.* Cic.   Vis est in vir-
tūtibus, *eās* excitā, *there is strength in virtues, arouse* THEM. Cic.

108. *Vocabulary.*

Agit,	*he leads, drives, does, acts, performs, treats, pleads;* grātiās [agit, *he returns thanks.*
Arma, ōrum, *n. pl.*	*arms.*
Britannia, ae, *f.*	*Britain.*
Cis, *prep. w. acc.*	*on this side of.*
Cōnstanter, *adv.*	*consistently, uniformly.*
Cotīdiē, *adv.*	*daily.*
Dēbet,	*he owes; he ought.*
Doctrīna, ae, *f.*	*learning.*
Ex, ē, *prep. w. abl.*	*out of, from, of.*
Ferē, *adv.*	*almost.*
Grātia, ae, *f.*	*gratitude, favor;* grātiae, *pl., [thanks.*
Locus, i, *m., pl.* loca, ōrum, *n.*	*place.*
Nāvigat,	*he navigates, sails.*
Platō, ōnis, *m.*	*Plato,* a celebrated Greek philoso- [pher.
Quīdam, quaedam, quiddam or quoddam,	*a certain, certain one.*
Reliquus, a, um,	*remaining, the other, the rest of.*
Rhēnus, i, *m.*	*the Rhine.*
Suprā, *adv.*	*above.*
Tempus, oris, *n.*	*time.*
Venetī, ōrum, *m. pl.*	*the Veneti,* a tribe of western Gaul.

¹ Pronouns when used as adjectives agree like other adjectives, with the nouns to which they belong, according to 40, Rule XXXIV.

109. *Translate into English.*[1]

1. Gallī ea loca incolunt. 2. Gallī fortēs sunt. 3. Gallī, quī[2] ea loca incolunt, fortēs sunt. 4. Germānī, quī eis Rhēnum incolunt, in armīs sunt. 5. Hostēs urbem,[3] dē quā[3] suprā scrīpsit Caesar, vallō fossāque mūniēbant. 6. Reliquī omnēs Belgae in armīs erant. 7. Iī cōnstanter omnēs idem[4] nūntiant. 8. Venetī nāvēs habent multās, quibus[5] in Britanniam nāvigant. 9. Iī quī vōbīs omnia dēbent, vōs semper amābunt. 10. Cīvēs nōbīs grātiūs cotīdiē agunt.

11. Ille[6] prīnceps doctrīnae, Platō, virtūtem et sapientiam laudat. 12. Iī quī hanc cīvitātem regunt, sapientēs sunt. 13. Quid dīxit? Hōc dīxit. 14. Num haec dīxērunt? Nōn dīxērunt.[7] 15. Omnēs ferē Belgae in armīs fuērunt. 16. Cicerō in illō ipsō[8] librō dē amīcitiā scrīpsit.

110. *Translate into Latin.*

1. Who was the king? 2. Was not[9] Romulus king? He was.[10] 3. Who was the leader of the Romans? Was not

---

[1] In preparing the longer and more difficult sentences in this and in the subsequent exercises, it is recommended that the pupil should follow the Suggestions which are inserted in this volume, page 200, and which are intended to aid him in discerning the *process* by which he may most readily and surely reach the meaning of a Latin sentence.

[2] For *Gender* and *Number*, see 107, Rule XXXV.

[3] In reading this sentence in the Latin slowly and attentively, in accordance with Suggestion IV., which words do you recognize? What *parts of speech* do you find? What *cases, moods, tenses, numbers*, and *persons*? What does each *case, mood, tense, number*, and *person* show you?

[4] Direct Object of *nūntiant*.

[5] *Ablative of Means*. See 78, Rule XXV.

[6] *Ille* is often thus used of what is WELL KNOWN, FAMOUS.

[7] Observe that the auxiliaries *does, do, did*, are often used in interrogative and negative sentences in English, but that no corresponding auxiliaries are used in Latin. Thus, *nōnne dīcit*, does he say? *nōn dīcit*, he does not say. Remember this difference in rendering into Latin, as in 110, 4 and 5, *Did not Cicero*, etc.?

[8] *Illō ipsō*, that very; *ipse* is sometimes best rendered VERY.

[9] What *Interrogative* will you use? See 106, 351, 1, notes.

[10] See 106, 352.

Caesar the leader of the Romans? Caesar was the leader of the Romans. 4. Did not Cicero write this book? He wrote it. 5. Did he write the book that[1] the pupils are reading? He did not write it. Caesar, who conquered the Gauls, wrote that book. 6. Cicero, who wrote these books, was at that time a very renowned orator.

7. The enemy, about whom Caesar wrote above, were Gauls. 8. The Belgae, who were at that time in arms, were the bravest of the Gauls. 9. What did Plato praise? Did he not praise learning and wisdom? He always praised virtue. 10. Who has written in regard to friendship? Cicero, the consul, wrote a book in regard to friendship.

LESSON XXXVIII.

PRESENT AND IMPERFECT SUBJUNCTIVE ACTIVE, AND PRESENT IMPERATIVE ACTIVE, IN CONJUGATIONS I. AND II., AND IN THE VERB *Sum*. — RULE XXXVII.

111. *Lesson from the Grammar.*

196. The SUBJUNCTIVE MOOD[2] expresses not an actual fact, but a *possibility* or *conception*. It is best translated —

1. Sometimes by the English auxiliaries, *let, may, might, should, would:*

Amēmus patriam, LET US LOVE our country. Sint beāti, MAY THEY BE happy. Quaerat quispiam, *some one* MAY INQUIRE. Hōc nēmō dixerit, *no one* WOULD SAY *this.* Ego cēnseam, *I* SHOULD THINK, or *I* AM INCLINED TO THINK.

2. Sometimes by the English *Indicative*, especially by the Future forms with *shall* and *will:*

Huic cēdāmus, SHALL WE YIELD *to this one?* Quid diēs ferat incertum est, *what a day* WILL BRING FORTH *is uncertain.* Quaesivit si licēret, *he inquired whether* IT WAS LAWFUL.

---

[1] For the *Gender, Number* and *Case* of the Latin Pronoun, see 107, Rule XXXV., and 16, Rule V.

[2] For the *Imperative Mood*, see p. 13, 196, III.

92   INDICATIVE, SUBJUNCTIVE, IMPERATIVE.

3. Sometimes by the *Imperative*, especially in prohibitions:

Nē trānsiĕris Hibĕrum, DO not CROSS *the Ebro.*

4. Sometimes by the English *Infinitive:*[1]

Contendit ut vincat, *he strives* TO CONQUER. Missi sunt qui cōnsulerent Apollinem, *they were sent* TO CONSULT *Apollo.*

112. *Examples.* — *Indicative Mood.*

1. Galli ea loca *incolunt.*   *The Gauls* INHABIT *those places.*
2. Hostēs urbem *mūniēbant.*   *The enemy* WERE FORTIFYING *the city.*

NOTE. — Observe in these examples that the verbs *incolunt,* 'inhabit,' and *mūniēbant,* 'were fortifying,' relate to *facts.* They are in the *Indicative Mood,* in accordance with the Latin usage,[2] expressed in the following

RULE XXXVII. — Indicative.

474. The Indicative is used in treating of facts:

Deus mundum aedificāvit, *God made* (built) *the world.* Cic. Nōnne expulsus est patriā, *was he not banished from his country?* Cic. Hōc fēci dum licuit, *I did this as long as it was permitted.* Cic.

113. *Certain Forms of the Subjunctive and Imperative.*

I. In the Verb Sum, *I am.*

SUBJUNCTIVE.

PRESENT.

SINGULAR.		PLURAL.	
sim,	*may I be,*	sīmus,	*let us be,*
sīs,	*mayst thou be,*	sītis,	*be ye, may you be,*
sit,	*let him be, may he be;*	sint,	*let them be.*

---

[1] Observe, however, that the Infinitive here is not the translation of the Subjunctive alone, but of the Subjunctive with its subject and connective: ut vincat, *to conquer* (lit., *that he may conquer*); qui cōnsulerent, *to consult* (lit., *who should* or *would consult*).

[2] All the verbs in the preceding Lessons are in the *Indicative Mood,* and are illustrations of this usage.

SUBJUNCTIVE AND IMPERATIVE.

IMPERFECT.

essem,	I should be,	essēmus,	we should be,
essēs,	thou wouldst be,	essētis,	you would be,
esset,	he would be;	essent,	they would be.

IMPERATIVE.

Pres. es,   be thou, | este,   be ye.

II. In the First Conjugation.

SUBJUNCTIVE.
PRESENT.

SINGULAR.		PLURAL.	
amem,	may I love,	amēmus,	let us love,
amēs,	may you love,	amētis,	may you love,
amet,	let him love;	ament,	let them love.

IMPERFECT.

amārem,	I should love,	amārēmus,	we should love,
amārēs,	you would love,	amārētis,	you would love,
amāret,	he would love;	amārent,	they would love.

IMPERATIVE.

Pres. amā,   love thou; | amāte,   love ye.

III. In the Second Conjugation.

SUBJUNCTIVE.

PRESENT.
May I advise, let him advise.

SINGULAR.	PLURAL.
moneam	moneāmus
moneās	moneātis
moneat	moneant

IMPERFECT.
I should advise, he would advise.

monērem	monērēmus
monērēs	monērētis
monēret	monērent

IMPERATIVE.

Pres. monē,   advise thou; | monēte,   advise ye.

LESSON XXXIX.

SUBJUNCTIVE AND IMPERATIVE ACTIVE IN CONJUGATIONS I. AND II., AND IN THE VERB *Sum*. — RULES XXXVIII. AND XL. — EXERCISES.

114. *Examples.* — *Subjunctive and Imperative.*

1. Amēmus patriam.   LET US LOVE *our country.*
2. Nē audeant.   LET THEM *not* DARE.
3. Sint beāti.   MAY THEY BE *happy.*
4. Jastitiam cole.   PRACTISE *justice.*
5. Perge, Catilina.   Go, *Catiline.*

NOTE 1. — In the first three of these examples, observe that the verbs *amēmus, audeant,* and *sint* all express or imply a *desire* or *wish* on the part of the speaker. These verbs are all in the Subjunctive, in accordance with the Latin usage expressed in the following

RULE XXXVIII. — Subjunctive of Desire, Command.

483. The Subjunctive is used to represent the action NOT AS REAL, but AS DESIRED:

Valeant civēs, MAY *the citizens* BE WELL. Cic. *Amēmus* patriam, LET US LOVE *our country.* Cic. Ā nōbis *diligātur,* LET HIM BE LOVED *by us.* Cic. Scribere nē *pigrēre,* DO *not* NEGLECT *to write.* Cic.

1. The *Subjunctive of Desire* is often accompanied by *utinam,* and sometimes, especially in the poets, by *ut, si, ō si :*

Utinam cōnāta efficere possim, *may I be able to accomplish my endeavors.* Cic. Ut illum dī perdant, *would that the gods would destroy him.* Ter.

2. FORCE OF TENSES. — The Present and Perfect imply that the wish may be fulfilled; the Imperfect and Pluperfect, that it cannot be fulfilled:

Sint beāti, *may they be happy.* Cic. Nē trānsierīs Hibērum, *do not cross the Ebro.* Liv. Utinam possem, utinam potuissem, *would that I were able, would that I had been able.* Cic.

3. NEGATIVES. — With the *Subjunctive of Desire,* the negative is *nē,* rarely *nōn;* with a connective, *nēve, neu,* rarely *neque :*

IMPERATIVE. 95

Nē audeant, *let them not dare.* Cic. Nōn recēdāmus, *let us not recede.* Cic. Nēve minor neu sit prōductior, *let it be neither shorter nor longer.* Hor.

NOTE 2. — In the fourth and fifth of the examples at the head of this lesson, observe that the verbs *cole* and *perge* both denote a command. They are in the *Imperative,* in accordance with the Latin usage expressed in the following

RULE XL. — Imperative.

487. The Imperative is used in COMMANDS, EXHORTATIONS, and ENTREATIES:

Jūstitiam cole, *practise justice.* Cic. Tū nē cēde malis, *do not yield to misfortunes.* Verg. Si quid in tē peccāvi, īgnōsce, *if I have sinned against you, pardon me.* Cic.

1. The PRESENT IMPERATIVE corresponds to the Imperative in English:

Jūstitiam cole, *practise justice.* Cic. Perge, Catilīna, *go, Catiline.* Cic.

115. *Vocabulary.*

Animus, ī, *m.*	*mind, heart, soul.*
Castellum, ī, *n.*	*redoubt.*
Castīcus, ī, *m.*	*Casticus,* a chief of the Sequani.
Cōnfirmat,	*he strengthens, assures, establishes.*
Conjūrat,	*he conspires.*
Ferāx, ācis,	*productive, fertile.*
Frūmentārius, a, um,	*pertaining to grain;* rēs frūmentāria,
Juvat,	*he aids, helps, assists.* [*grain, supplies.*
Lātus, a, um,	*broad, wide, extensive.*
Liber, libera, liberum,	*free.*
Mēns, mentis, *f.*	*mind, intellect.*
Parātus, a, um,	*prepared, ready.*
Pāx, pācis, *f.*	*peace.*
Perturbat,	*he disturbs.*
Propior, propius,	*nearer; sup.* prōximus, a, um, *nearest,*
Quis, quae, quid *or* quod,	[*next, adjacent.* **86, 100.**
indef. pron.	*one, any one, anything.*
Rēgnum, ī, *n.*	*kingdom, regal power.*
Suspiciō, ōnis, *f.*	*suspicion.*
Utinam, *interj.*	*O that!*
Vitat,	*he avoids, shuns.*

SUBJUNCTIVE AND IMPERATIVE.

116. *Translate into English.*

1. Patriam amēmus. 2. Prō patriā pūgnēmus. 3. In cōnspectū imperātōris fortiter pūgnēmus. 4. Mīlitēs in cōnspectū imperātōris fortiter pūgnent. 5. Mīlitēs fortēs sint; fortēs sīmus. 6. Lēgibus[1] pārcāmus. 7. Cīvēs omnēs lēgibus pāreant. 8. Patriam amāte; lēgibus pārēte. 9. Illam urbem oppūgnāte. 10. Hanc urbem oppūgnēmus. 11. Nē[2] Helvētiōs juvēmus. 12. Nē quis Helvētiōs juvet. 13. Suspīciōnem vītēmus. 14. Timōris suspīciōnem vītēs. 15. Omnēs suspīciōnēs vītā. 16. In[3] reliquum tempus omnēs suspīciōnēs vītēmus. 17. Mīlitēs castellum oppūgnent.
18. Cum hīs cīvitātibus[4] amīcitiam cōnfirmēmus. 19. Cum proximīs cīvitātibus pācem et amīcitiam cōnfirmāte. 20. In hōc locō adventum hostium exspectēmus. 21. Hostēs in hōc locō adventum Caesaris exspectent. 22. Utinam parātus ad[5] omnia perīcula sīs.[5] 23. Utinam mīlitēs omnēs fortēs essent.[6] 24. Casticus rēgnum in cīvitāte suā occupet. 25. Hostium impetum sustineāmus. 26. Utinam timor hostium mentēs animōsque perturbet. 27. Lātōs ferācēsque agrōs occupēmus. 28. Rem frūmentāriam comparēmus. 29. Lībera sit Gallia. 30. Nē contrā patriam conjūrēmus.

117. *Translate into Latin.*

1. Let us praise the brave soldiers. 2. May they all fight bravely for themselves and for their country. 3. Let not fear take possession of our army. 4. Let not fear disturb our minds. 5. Let us await the arrival of our army. 6. Let the soldiers obey the commander. 7. Let them not fear the enemy. 8. Let us not fear the enemy. 9. Let us await them in this place.

---

[1] For *Case*, see 54, Rule XII.
[2] For the use of *nē* rather than *nōn*, see 114, 483, 3.
[3] Literally *into;* render FOR.
[4] In accordance with Suggestion XI., for what form will you look in the Vocabulary to find the meaning of *cīvitātibus?*
[5] Literally *to;* render FOR.   [6] For the force of *Tenses*, see 114, 483, 2.

10. Let us aid our friends. 11. Do not aid the enemy. 12. May all the citizens love their country. 13. May they obey all the laws. 14. Let us establish friendship with the Romans. 15. Let the Romans establish peace with the Gauls. 16. Let not the soldiers conspire against the king.

LESSON XL.

PRESENT AND IMPERFECT SUBJUNCTIVE ACTIVE, AND PRESENT IMPERATIVE ACTIVE, IN CONJUGATIONS III. AND IV.—RULES XLI. AND XLII.

118. *Certain Forms of the Subjunctive and Imperative.*

I. In the Third Conjugation.

SUBJUNCTIVE.

PRESENT.

May I rule, let him rule.

SINGULAR.	PLURAL.
regam	regāmus
regās	regātis
regat	regant

IMPERFECT.

I should rule, he would rule.

regerem	regerēmus
regerēs	regerētis
regeret	regerent

IMPERATIVE.

| Pres. rege, *rule thou;* | regite, *rule ye.* |

II. In the Fourth Conjugation.

SUBJUNCTIVE.

PRESENT.

May I hear, let him hear.

SINGULAR.	PLURAL.
audiam	audiāmus
audiās	audiātis
audiat	audiant

SUBJUNCTIVE AND IMPERATIVE.

IMPERFECT.
I should hear, he would hear.

audīrem | audīrēmus
audīrēs | audīrētis
audīret | audīrent

IMPERATIVE.

Pres. audī, *hear thou;* | audīte, *hear ye.*

119. Examples. — Sequence of Tenses. — Subjunctive of Purpose.

1. Nītitur *ut vincat.*   He *strives* TO CONQUER.
2. Nītēbātur *ut vinceret.*   He *was striving* TO CONQUER.
3. Mittuntur quī (= *ut iī*) cōnsulant Apollinem.   They *are sent* TO CONSULT (who may consult) *Apollo.*
4. Missī sunt quī cōnsulerent Apollinem.   They *were sent* TO CONSULT *Apollo.*

NOTE 1. — In these examples observe that after a present tense, as *nītitur, mittuntur,* the verb of the subordinate clause [1] is also *Present,* as *vincat, cōnsulant,*[2] while after a past tense, as *nītēbātur, missī sunt,* the verb in the subordinate clause is in the *Imperfect,* as *vinceret, cōnsulerent.*[2] This adjustment of the tense in the subordinate clause to the tense in the Principal clause [1] is in accordance with the Latin usage expressed in the following

RULE XLI. — Sequence of Tenses.

491. Principal tenses depend upon principal tenses; historical upon historical: [3]

Nītitur ut vincat, *he strives to conquer.*[4] Cic. Nēmō erit quī cēnseat, *there will be no one who will think.*[4] Cic. Quaesierās nōnne

---

[1] For *Principal* and *Subordinate* Clauses, see p. 11, 348, foot note.

[2] If the verb in the Subordinate Clause denotes *completed* action, it must be in the *Perfect* after a Present tense, and in the *Pluperfect* after a Past tense. See 492, 2, and 493, 2.

[3] For *Principal* and *Historical* Tenses, see p. 13, 198.

[4] The Present Subjunctive generally denotes *present time* in relation to the principal verb. Accordingly, *vincat* depending upon the *present, nītitur,* denotes *present* time, while *cēnseat* depending upon the *future, erit,* denotes *future* time.

putārem, *you had asked whether I did not think.* Cic. Ut honōre dignus essem labōrāvi, *I strove to be worthy of honor.* Cic.

492. In accordance with this rule, the Subjunctive dependent upon a principal tense, *present, future, future perfect,* is put —

1. In the PRESENT, to denote *incomplete action:*
Quaeritur cūr dissentiant, *the question is asked, why they disagree.* Cic. Nēmŏ erit qui cēnseat, *there will be no one who will think.* Cic.

2. In the PERFECT, to denote *completed action:*
Quaerāmus quae vitia fuerint, *let us inquire what faults there were.* Cic. Rogitābit me ubi fuerim, *he will ask me where I have been.* Ter.

493. The Subjunctive dependent upon an historical tense, *imperfect, historical perfect, pluperfect,* is put —

1. In the IMPERFECT, to denote *incomplete action:*
Timēbam nē ēvenirent ea, *I was fearing that those things would take place* (i.e. at some future time). Cic. Quaesierās nōnne putārem, *you had inquired whether I did not think* (i.e. at that time). Cic.

2. In the PLUPERFECT, to denote *completed action:*
Themistoclēs, cum Graeciam liberāsset, expulsus est, *Themistocles was banished, though he had liberated Greece.* Cic.

NOTE 2. — In the examples given above, observe that the verbs in the Subordinate clauses, *vincat, vinceret, cōnsulant, cōnsulerent,* all express the *purpose* of the leading action. *He strives* (for what purpose?) *that he may conquer* or *to conquer. They are sent* (for what purpose?) *that they may consult Apollo* or *to consult Apollo.* These verbs are all in the *Subjunctive,* in accordance with the Latin usage expressed in the following

RULE XLII. — Purpose.

497. The Subjunctive is used to denote PURPOSE:

I. With the relative **qui**, and with relative adverbs, as **ubi, unde,** etc.:

Missi sunt qui (=ut ii) cōnsulerent Apollinem, *they were sent* TO CONSULT *Apollo* (who should, *or* that they should). Nep. Missi sunt dēlecti qui Thermopylās occupārent, *picked men were sent* TO TAKE POSSESSION OF *Thermopylae.* Nep. Domum, ubi habitāret, lēgit, *he selected a house where he might dwell* (that he might dwell in it). Cic.

PURPOSE.

II. With **ut, nē, quō, quōminus**:

Ēnītitur ut *vincat*, *he strives that* HE MAY CONQUER. Cic. Pūnit nē *peccētur*, *he punishes that crime* MAY NOT BE COMMITTED. Sen. Lēgum idcircō servī sumus, ut līberī esse possīmus, *we are servants of the law for this reason, that we may be free*. Cic. Medicō dare quō sit studiōsior, *to give to the physician, that* (by this means) *he may be more attentive*. Cic. Nōn recūsāvit quōminus poenam subīret, *he did not refuse to submit to punishment*. Nep.

498. CLAUSES OF PURPOSE readily pass into *Object Clauses*,[1] but they still retain the Subjunctive.

Optō ut id audiātis, *I desire* (pray) *that you may hear this*. Cic. Servīs imperat ut fīliam dēfendant, *he commands his servants to defend his daughter*. Cic. Contendit ut vincat, *he strives to conquer*. Cic.

LESSON XLI.

SUBJUNCTIVE AND IMPERATIVE ACTIVE IN CONJUGATIONS III. AND IV. — EXERCISES.

120. *Vocabulary.*

Addūcit,	*he leads to.*
Cōgnōscit,	*he ascertains.*
Colloquium, iī, *n.*	*conversation, conference, interview.*
Dēdūcit,	*he leads forth, conducts.*
Equitātus, ūs, *m.*	*cavalry.*
Imperat, *w. dative.*	*he orders, gives orders to.*
Implōrat,	*he implores.*
Intellegit,	*he understands.*
Mulier, eris, *f.*	*woman.*
Nūntius, iī, *m.*	*messenger; tidings.*
Obses, idis, *m.* and *f.*	*hostage.*
Pedes, itis, *m.*	*foot-soldier; pl. foot-soldiers, infantry.*
Pedius, iī, *m.*	*Pedius,* a lieutenant in Caesar's army.
Populus, ī, *m.*	*people.*

---

[1] An Object Clause is one which has become virtually the *object* of a verb. Thus, in '*optō ut id audiātis*,' the clause *ut id audiātis* has become the object of *optō*, 'I desire.'

SUBJUNCTIVE AND IMPERATIVE.

Postulat,	*he demands.*
Reddit,	*he gives back, returns.*
Remanet,	*he remains.*
Rogat,	*he asks.*
Rōmānus, a, um,	*Roman.*
Trādit,	*he gives up, surrenders.*

121. *Translate into English.*

1. Mīlitēs timōris suspīciōnem vītent. 2. Mīlitēs ut timōris suspīciōnem vītent[1] in aciē remanent. 3. Ut timōris suspīciōnem vītārent remanēbant. 4. Suam urbem vallō fossāque mūniant. 5. Hunc locum altissimō[2] mūrō mūnīte. 6. Helvētiī prōximās cīvitātēs rogant ut sē juvent.[3] 7. Rogābant ut sē juvārent.[3] 8. Noster equitātus hostium impetum sustineat. 9. Caesar equitātum, quī sustinēret[4] hostium impetum, mīsit.[4] 10. Haec intellegātis. 11. Haec ut intellegātis, audīte Rōmānōs mīlitēs. 12. Cum populō Rōmānō pācem cōnfirment. 13. Castra vallō mūnīte. 14. Mīlitibus imperāvit ut castra vallō mūnīrent.[5] 15. Lēgātī haec dīcant. 16. Gallī lēgātōs mittent quī haec dīcant. 17. Haec cōgnōscite. 18. Gallīs imperābat ut haec cōgnōscerent. 19. Mulierēs patrēs suōs implōrābant nē sē Rōmānīs trāderent. 20. Caesar nē quem peditem ad colloquium addūcat. 21. Ariovistus postulāvit nē quem peditem ad colloquium Caesar addūceret.[6] 22. Caesar postulāvit ut Ariovistus obsidēs redderet. 23. Caesar duās legiōnēs cōnscrīpsit, et Pedium mīsit quī eās in Galliam dēdūceret.[7]

---

[1] *Subjunctive of Purpose.* See 119, Rule XLII.
[2] In accordance with Suggestion XI., for what form will you look in the Vocabulary to find the meaning of *altissimō?* See 86, 162.
[3] Why *juvent* in one case, and *juvārent* in the other? See 119, 492 and 493.
[4] See Suggestion XVII., 3; *mīsit*, sent, the perfect of *mittit*.
[5] *Ut . . . mūnīrent*, an Object Clause. See 119, 498.
[6] *Nē . . . addūceret*. See 119, 498.
[7] For *Mood*, see 119, 497, I.; for *Translation*, see Suggestion XVII., 3.

122. *Translate into Latin.*

1. Let us fortify this city with a high wall.[1] 2. Fortify your cities with moats and walls. 3. He implores you to fortify[2] the city with a very high wall. 4. Let us hear the words of the lieutenant. 5. The soldiers will remain to hear[2] the words of the lieutenant. 6. Let the soldiers remain to hear the words of the king. 7. The soldiers remained[3] to hear the words of Caesar. 8. Let us lead the army back into camp. 9. Let us enrol three legions in Gaul. 10. The commander will send five legions to withstand[4] the attacks of the enemy.

11. He sent three legions to withstand the attack of the enemy. 12. Let him not announce our plans to the enemy. 13. Will he not send a messenger to announce these things to Caesar? 14. Listen to me (*hear me*) that you may understand these things. 15. Caesar demanded that the Germans should not remain in Gaul.[5] 16. The soldiers remained in the city that they might fortify it. 17. He asked us to help you. 18. They demand that you listen to our words. 19. Ariovistus demanded that Caesar should not help the Gauls. 20. They asked Caesar not to give them up to the Germans.

LESSON XLII.

PRESENT AND IMPERFECT SUBJUNCTIVE ACTIVE. — RULE XLIII.

123. *Examples. — Subjunctive in Clauses of Result.*

1. Nōn is sum qui (= ut ego) his *ūtar*.
 I am not such a one AS TO USE *these things.*
2. Ita vīxit ut *esset* cārissimus.
 He so lived that HE WAS *most dear.*

---

[1] In Latin, use the *Ablative of Means.* See 78, Rule XXV.
[2] Use *ut with the Subjunctive.*
[3] Or *were remaining;* use the *imperfect.*
[4] Use the *Relative with the Subjunctive.*
[5] *That . . . in Gaul,* an *Object Clause;* see 119, 498.

NOTE. — In these examples observe that the Subordinate verbs, *ūtar, esset,* express the *Result* of what is stated in the principal clause. They are in the *Subjunctive* in accordance with the Latin usage expressed in the following

RULE XLIII. — Result.

500. The Subjunctive is used to denote RESULT:

I. With the relative quī, and with relative adverbs, as ubī, unde, cūr, etc.:

Nōn is sum quī (= ut ego) his ūtar,[1] *I am not such a one as* TO USE *these things.* Cic. Innocentia est adfectiō tālis animī, quae (= ut ea) noceat nēminī,[1] *innocence is such a state of mind as* INJURES *no one.* Cic.

II. With ut, ut nōn, quīn:

Ita vīxit ut Athēniēnsibus esset cārissimus, *he so lived that* HE WAS *very dear to the Athenians.* Nep. Ita laudō, ut nōn pertīmēscam, *I so praise as not* TO FEAR.[2] Cic.

501. CLAUSES OF RESULT readily pass into *Substantive Clauses,* but they still retain the Subjunctive. Thus the Subjunctive is used —

I. In SUBJECT CLAUSES:

Fit ut quisque dēlectētur, *it happens that every one is delighted.* Cic. Sequitur ut falsum sit, *it follows that it is false.* Cic.

II. In OBJECT CLAUSES:

Sōl efficit ut omnia flōreant, *the sun causes all things to bloom* (i. e., produces that result). Cic.

503. The Subjunctive is used in RELATIVE CLAUSES to *characterize* an *Indefinite* or *General Antecedent:*

Quid est quod tē dēlectāre possit, *what is there which can delight you?* Cic. Sunt quī putent, *there are some who think.* Cic. Nēmō est quī nōn cupiat, *there is no one who does not desire.* Cic.

---

[1] *Is quī,* literally, *he who* = 'such that I.' *Tālis quae,* literally, *such which* = 'such that it.'

[2] Or *that I do not fear.*

RESULT.

124. Vocabulary.

Barbarus, a, um,	barbarous, rude.
Commovet,	he moves, disturbs.
Compellit,	he drives.
Complūrēs, plūra or plūria,	very many, many, several.
Condōnat,	he condones, pardons, forgives.
Cōnflīgit,	he contends, fights.
Contendit, 134, foot-note 2.	he hastens, goes in haste.
Continet,	he restrains, retains, confines, keeps
Eques, ĭtis, m.	horseman; pl. horsemen, cavalry.
Finis, is, m. and f.[1]	end, limit; fīnēs, pl. m. boundaries;
Injūria, ae, f.	injury, wrong. [territory.
Ita, adv.	so, in such a way.
Littera, ae, f.	letter, letter of the alphabet; litterae. pl., letters; a letter, epistle.
Periculum, i, n.	peril, danger.
Prohibet,	he prohibits, checks, prevents, keeps.
Scit, 4,	he knows.
Silva, ae, f.	wood, forest.
Tam, adv.	so, to such an extent.
Tantus, a, um,	so great.
Tempestās, ātis, f.	weather; tempest, storm.

125. Translate into English.

1. Mīlitēs omnēs fortissimē pūgnābant. 2. Tanta mīlitum virtūs fuit ut omnēs fortissimē pūgnārent. 3. Timor māgnus omnem exercitum occupāvit. 4. Timor māgnus mentēs mīlitum omnium perturbābat. 5. Omnium mentēs animōsque perturbāvit. 6. Tantus timor omnem exercitum occupāvit ut omnium mentēs animōsque perturbāret. 7. Caesar nōn is fuit quī hostēs timēret.[2] 8. Erant tempestātēs quae nostrōs[3] in castrīs continērent. 9. Tempestātēs hostem ā pūgnā prohibuērunt. 10. Erant complūrēs diēs[4] tempestātēs quae hostem ā pūgnā prohibērent.

11. Ariovistus nōn tam barbarus fuit ut haec nōn scīret. 12. Hī nūntiī Caesarem ita commovent ut castra vallō fos-

---
[1] Decline like *ignis*, page 54.   [2] See 123, 500.
[3] Lit., *our, ours*; render *our men*; a *Possessive* used *substantively*.
[4] *Accusative of Duration of Time.* See 98, Rule IX.

sāque mūniat. 13. Iī nūntiī littcraeque Caesarem ita commovent ut in fīnēs Belgārum contendat. 14. Equitēs hostium cum equitātū nostrō ita cōnflīgunt ut nostrī[1] eōs in silvās compellant. 15. Tanta Divitiacī apud Caesarem grātia fuit ut injūriam condōnāret. 16. Utinam in reliquum tempus timōris suspīciōnem vītētis. 17. Imperātor sex legiōnēs mīsit quae hanc urbem oppūgnārent. 18. Utinam hae cīvitātēs in armīs essent. 19. Utinam omnēs mīlitēs nostrī fortiter pūgnārent.

126. *Translate into Latin.*

1. Our soldiers fought so bravely that they conquered[2] the enemy. 2. The courage of our soldiers is so great that they always fight bravely, and withstand all the attacks of the enemy. 3. They are not so barbarous as not to help (*that they do not help*) their friends. 4. He is not one who (*that one who*) would announce our counsels to the enemy. 5. So great fear took possession of the commander that he led the army back into camp. 6. So great fear took possession of the Gauls that they fortified their camp with a moat and a rampart.

7. The fear of the enemy was so great that they gave up the hostages. 8. The soldiers of the tenth legion were so brave that they did not fear the enemy. 9. Our soldiers are so brave that they are prepared for[3] all dangers. 10. Fear so disturbs your minds that you do not listen to (*hear*) me. 11. For[4] the future let us avoid all suspicions. 12. For the future our soldiers will fight so bravely that they will avoid suspicion of fear. 13. Would that all our citizens were in arms. 14. The enemy sent a large army to assault our city.

---

[1] See foot-note 2, page 104.
[2] What *Mood* will you use in Latin? See 123, Rule XLIII.
[3] Use *ad*. See 116, foot-note on *ad*.
[4] Use *in*. See 116, foot-note on *in*.

LESSON XLIII.

PRESENT AND IMPERFECT SUBJUNCTIVE ACTIVE. — RULE LV.

127. *Examples.* — *Indirect Questions.*

1. Quaeris *cūr dissentiant.* *You ask* WHY THEY DISAGREE.
2. Quaesīvit *salvusne esset clipeus.* *He asked* WHETHER HIS SHIELD WAS SAFE.

NOTE. — In these examples observe that the Subordinate clauses *cūr dissentiant*, 'why they disagree,'[1] and *salvusne esset clipeus*, 'whether the (his) shield was safe,'[1] involve questions without directly asking them. Such clauses are called *Indirect Questions*. The verbs in these Indirect Questions are in the Subjunctive, in accordance with the Latin usage expressed in the following

RULE LV. — Moods in Indirect Clauses.

529. The Subjunctive is used —

I. In indirect questions:

Quaeritur, cūr doctissimi homines dissentiant, *it is a question, why the most learned men disagree.* Cic. Quaesieras, nonne putārem, *you had asked whether I did not think.* Cic. Quālis sit animus, animus nescit, *the soul knows not what the soul is.* Cic. Quid dies ferat incertum est, *what a day will bring forth is uncertain.* Cic.

II. Often in clauses dependent upon an Infinitive or upon another Subjunctive:

Nihil indignius est quam eum qui culpā *careat* suppliciō nōn carēre, *nothing is more shameful than that he who* IS FREE *from fault should not be exempt from punishment*. Cic. Vereor ne, dum minuere *velim* labōrem, augeam, *I fear that while I* WISH *to diminish the labor, I shall increase it.* Cic.

3. Indirect double questions are generally introduced by the same interrogative particles as are direct double questions (106, 353).

---

[1] The Indirect question. *cūr dissentiant,* involves the Direct question, *Cūr dissentiunt?* 'why do they disagree?' *Salvusne esset clipeus* involves the Direct question: *Salvusne est clipeus?* 'is the shield safe?'

SUBJUNCTIVE.

Thus they generally take *utrum* or *-ne* in the first member, and *an* in the second:

Quaeritur virtūs suamne propter dignitātem an propter frūctūs aliquōs expetātur, *it is asked whether virtue is sought for its own worth, or for certain advantages.* Cic.

128. Vocabulary.

Arar, aris,[1] m.	the *Arar*, a river in southeastern Gaul,
Atque, *conj.*	and. [the modern *Saône*.
Captīvus, i, *m.*	captive.
Condūcit,	he leads together, brings together.
Dēcertat,	he contends, struggles, fights.
Fluit,	it flows.
Gerit,	he carries on, does, wages.
Igitur, *conj.*	therefore.
Interior,[2] us,	interior, inner.
Jūdicat,	he judges.
Ob, *prep. w. acc.*	on account of, for.
Officium, ii, *n.*	duty.
Proelium, ii, *n.*	battle, engagement.
Pudor, ōris, *m.*	shame, respect.
Quaerit,	he inquires, asks, seeks.
Quantus, a, um,	how great.
Quot, *indeclinable*,	how many.
Rēmi, ōrum, *m. pl.*	The *Remi*, a tribe of northern Gaul.
Uter, tra, trum, 45, 151.	which (of two). [ence.
Valet,	he avails, prevails, has force or influ-

129. Translate into English.

1. Quae cīvitātēs in armīs sunt? Ab hīs lēgātīs quaerit quae cīvitātēs in armīs sint.[3] 2. Quae cīvitātēs quantaeque[4] in armīs sunt? Ab hīs quaerēbat quae cīvitātēs quantaeque in armīs essent. 3. Quid dīcit Ariovistus? Quid dīcat Ariovistus cōgnōscite. Hīs lēgātīs imperāvit ut, quid dīceret

---

[1] Accusative *Ararem* or *Ararim*, Ablative *Arare* or *Arari*.
[2] See 86, 166.
[3] *Quae . . . sint*, an *Indirect Question*. What would be the *Direct Question?* For Translation, see Suggestion XVII., 2.
[4] *Quantaeque*, composed of *quantae* and the conjunction *que*, 'and.'

SUBJUNCTIVE.

Ariovistus, cōgnōscerent. 4. In utram partem¹ fluit Arar? In utram partem fluat Arar jūdicēmus.

5. Quam ob rem¹ Ariovistus proeliō nōn dēcertat? Caesar ex captīvīs quaerēbat quam ob rem Ariovistus proeliō nōn dēcertāret. 6. Omnem exercitum in ūnum locum condūcāmus. 7. Nōnne pudor apud vōs valet? Num apud vōs timor valet? Utrum apud vōs pudor atque officium an timor valet? Intellēgāmus utrum apud vōs pudor atque officium an timor valeat. 8. Quid gerunt Belgae? 9. Quid gerēbant Belgae? Imperātor sciēbat quid gererent Belgae. 10. Trēs legiōnēs igitur in interiōrem Galliam mittat.

130. *Translate into Latin.*

1. For what reason are the Gauls fortifying their cities? Let us ascertain for what reason the Gauls are fortifying² their camp. 2. Let us inquire of³ the ambassadors how many Germans there are in Gaul. 3. Caesar knew how many Germans there were in Gaul. 4. Let us inquire of the captives how many states of Gaul are in arms. 5. Did Caesar know⁴ how many states of Gaul were in arms? He knew⁴ which states were in arms. 6. Inquire in which direction the Rhine flows.

7. Caesar knew how large the states of Gaul were. Did he then know how brave the Belgians were? He knew who were the bravest of all the Gauls. 8. The Gauls did⁵ not understand who their enemies were. So great fear took possession of the Gauls that they did not understand who their enemies were.⁶ 9. He inquired of the captives into what place Ariovistus was leading his army.⁵

---

¹ *Partem,* lit. *part;* render *direction; rem,* lit. *thing;* render *reason.*
² What *Mood* will you use in Latin? See 127, 529, I.
³ Or *from;* render by *ab.* This preposition has the form *ab* before vowels and *h;* the form *ā* or *ab* before the other letters.
⁴ What Tense will you use? See 129, 9.
⁵ *Did not understand,* continued action like *sciēbat* in 129, 9; *inquired,* i. e., repeatedly = *was inquiring,* as in 129, 2.
⁶ For Moods, see 123, Rule XLIII., and 127, Rule LV.

LESSON XLIV.

PRESENT INFINITIVE ACTIVE. — RULE LVI.

131. The *Present Infinitive*[1] of the verb *Sum* is *esse*, 'to be.' In the four conjugations, the *Present Infinitive Active* has the following

ENDINGS.

CONJ. I.	CONJ. II.	CONJ. III.	CONJ. IV.
āre,	ēre,	ere,	īre,

PRESENT INFINITIVE ACTIVE.

First conjugation,	amāre, *to love.*
Second conjugation,	monēre, *to advise.*
Third conjugation,	regere, *to rule.*
Fourth conjugation,	audīre, *to hear.*
Verb sum,	esse, *to be.*

132. *Examples. — Infinitive.*

1. Haec vitāre cupit.   *He desires* TO AVOID *these things.*
2. Vincere scit.   *He knows how* TO CONQUER.
3. Gestiunt scire omnia.   *They long* TO KNOW *all things.*

NOTE. — In these examples observe that *vitāre* depends upon the verb *cupit*, 'he desires to avoid,' *vincere* upon *scit*, and *scire* upon *gestiunt.* They are all in the infinitive, in accordance with the Latin usage expressed in the following

RULE LVI. — Infinitive.

533. Many verbs admit an Infinitive to complete or qualify their meaning:

Audeō dicere, *I dare say* (I venture to say). Cic. Haec vitāre cupimus, *we desire to avoid these things.* Cic. Cōnstituit nōn prōgredī, *he decided not to advance.* Caes. Crēdulī esse coepērunt, *they began to be credulous.* Cic. Vincere scis, *you know how to conquer* (you know to conquer). Liv. Victōriā ūtī nescis, *you do not know how to use victory.* Liv.

---

[1] For the *Infinitive,* see p. 14, 200, I.

INFINITIVE.

133. In the Irregular verb *Possum,* 'I am able,' a compound of *Sum,*[1] the THIRD PERSON in the *singular* and *plural* of the *present, imperfect, future,* and *perfect* of the *indicative* has the following forms:

PARADIGM.

SINGULAR.	PLURAL.
Pres. potest, *he is able;*	possunt, *they are able.*
Imp. poterat, *he was able;*	poterant, *they were able.*
Fut. poterit, *he will be able;*	poterunt, *they will be able.*
Perf. potuit, *he has been able;*	potuērunt, *they have been able.*

134. *Vocabulary.*

Altitūdŏ, ĭnis, *f.*	*height, depth.*
Autem, *conj.*, foot-note p. 316.	*but.*
Citerior, ius, 86, 106,	*nearer;* citerior Gallia, Cisalpine Gaul, Gaul south of the Alps.
Cŏgit,	*he drives together, brings together, collects; he forces, compels.*
Comportat,	*he brings together, gathers.*
Cōnstituit, *pres.* and *per'ect,*[2]	*he determines, has determined, determined.*
Diū, diūtius, diūtissimē, *adv.*	*for a long time.*
Dubitat,	*he hesitates, doubts.*
Expūgnat,	*he takes by storm.*
Frūmentum, ī, *n.*	*grain.*
Ibi, *adv.*	*there.*
Ītalia, ae, *f.*	*Italy.*
Lătitūdŏ, ĭnis, *f.*	*width, thickness.*
Mātūrat, *with infinitive,*	*he hastens.*[3]
Pēs, pedis, *m.*	*foot.*
Potest,	*he is able, can.*
Propter, *prep. w. acc.*	*on account of.*
Renovat,	*he renews.*
Vastat,	*he lays waste.*
Venetia, ae, *f.*	*Venetia, the country of the Veneti.*
Vērŏ, *adv.*	*in truth, indeed;* as conj., *but.*

---

[1] Compounded of *potis,* 'able,' and *sum,* 'I am.'

[2] In a few verbs the third person singular has the same form in the *perfect* as in the *present.* Thus cōnstituit in the present tense means *he determines;* in the perfect, *he has determined,* or *he determined.* Contendit, 124, is also either *present* or *perfect.*

[3] Thus dicere mātūrat, he hastens to write.

INFINITIVE.

135. *Translate into English.*

1. Caesar hōc oppidum propter lātitūdinem fossae mūrīque altitūdinem expūgnāre nōn poterat. 2. Hostēs impetum nostrōrum mīlitum diūtius sustinēre nōn poterant. 3. Gallī adventum Rōmānōrum ibī exspectāre cōnstituērunt. 4. Mīlitēs omnia impedīmenta sēcum[1] portāre dēbent. 5. Mīlitēs sēsē[2] diūtius sustinēre nōn poterant. 6. Caesar autem castra in altitūdinem pedum[3] duodecim vallō mūnīre cōnstituit. 7. Imperātor hanc urbem māgnam oppūgnāre nōn dubitāvit. 8. Imperātor hunc locum altissimō mūrō mūnīre dēbet. 9. Venetī cōnstituērunt oppida mūnīre, frūmenta ex agrīs in oppida comportāre, nāvēs in Venetiam cōgere. 10. Tum vērō Caesar manūs[4] māgnās cōgere cōnstituit. 11. Gallī multīs dē causīs bellum renovāre cōnstituērunt. 12. Rōmānī agrōs nostrōs vastāre nōn dēbent. 13. Imperātor duās legiōnēs in citeriōre Galliā cōnscrībere mātūrāvit. 14. Hostēs omnem exercitum in ūnum locum condūcere mātūrāvērunt.

136. *Translate into Latin.*

1. Are the enemy able to take our city by storm? They can (*are able to*) attack the city, but on account of the valor of the citizens, and the height of the wall, they cannot take it by storm. 2. Caesar hastened to fortify his camp. 3. The soldiers determined to remain and avoid suspicion of fear. 4. The Romans determined to fortify their camp with a rampart. 5. They determined to enrol five legions in Italy. 6. Were the Helvetii able to take their grain with them.[4] They were not able to take all their grain with them.

---

[1] Observe that the preposition *cum* is appended to the pronoun *sē*. See 102, 184, 6.
[2] *Reduplicated* form of the pronoun. See 102, 184, 4.
[3] Construe with *vallō*.
[4] See 94, and 102, 184, 6.

7. The enemy are so brave that they do not hesitate[1] to renew the war. 8. Ought not the commander to ascertain what states are in arms?[2] He has not been able to ascertain what states are in arms. 9. The enemy will not be able to sustain the attacks of our soldiers. 10. The citizens did not hesitate to remain in Italy. 11. Let not the commander hesitate to fortify the city with a high wall. 12. The soldiers ought not to hesitate to remain in line, that they may avoid suspicion of fear.

LESSON XLV.

READING AT SIGHT. — DIRECTIONS. — EXERCISE.

137. *Directions for Reading at Sight.*

I. Read at Sight in the Latin, slowly and attentively, the entire passage that is assigned for the exercise. In this reading

1. Remember that the full and exact meaning of an inflected word contains TWO distinct elements.

1) The *general meaning* of the word, without reference to *case, number, mood, tense,* etc., that is, the meaning of the STEM. See 11, 46.

2) The meaning of the endings which mark *case, number, mood, tense,* etc., that is, the meaning of the SUFFIXES.

2. Recall as vividly as possible the exact meaning of all the words which you recognize.

3. Notice carefully the *ending* of each word, and thus determine which words are nouns, which verbs, etc.

4. Determine from these endings *case, number, voice, mood, tense,* etc., and endeavor to recall the exact force of each.

---

[1] What *Mood* will you use in rendering into Latin? See 123, 500, II.
[2] By what *Mood* will you render *are?* See 127, 529, I.

b. In Complex and Compound Sentences, observe carefully the relation of the clauses to one another, and determine which are *principal*,[1] and which are *subordinate*.[1] Remember that a clause introduced by a conjunction meaning *and, or, but, therefore*, adds a new thought, while a clause introduced by a conjunction meaning *when, since*, etc., only explains or modifies some other clause.

II. Having by this first reading acquired a good general idea of the entire passage, read a second time with the same care. If in this reading, any word should appear unfamiliar, endeavor to recall some passage in which you have previously met it. Be not hasty in turning to the passage, but use the knowledge which you already possess. As a last resort, if you fail to recall the word, turn to the vocabulary for it, and make yourself so familiar with it, that you will always recognize it in future.

III. Having by these two readings thoroughly mastered the entire passage, read the Latin aloud two or three times, for the important purpose of appreciating and enjoying the thought in its original form. By this practice the Latin will become, in time, a second vernacular, and you will enjoy reading a fine passage in Latin as you would enjoy reading one in English.

IV. After having thus read and examined the Latin, write a translation[2] of the passage in good idiomatic English.

138. *Read at Sight, examine carefully, and translate into English.*[3]

Omnēs ferē Belgae contrā populum Rōmānum conjūrāvērunt. Caesar igitur duās legiōnēs in citeriōre Galliā con-

---

[1] On *Principal* and *Subordinate Clauses*, see p. 11, 348, notes.
[2] On Translation, see Suggestions XII, to XIX.
[3] It is hoped that the pupil will enter upon this exercise with the determination to master it without help from any source. He has already had in previous lessons *every word* and *every construction* contained in it. The

scripsit et in interiōrem Galliam qui dēdūceret Pedium lēgātum mīsit. Ipse posteā ad exercitum contendit et Gallis imperāvit ut quid Belgae gererent cōgnōscerent. Hī cōnstanter omnēs nūntiāvērunt: "Belgae manūs māgnās cōgunt, et omnem exercitum in ūnum locum condūcunt." Tum vērō Caesar rem frūmentāriam comparāvit et ad finēs Belgārum contendit. Rēmī autem qui nōn in armīs erant, ad eum lēgātōs mīsērunt qui cum populō Rōmānō pācem et amīcitiam cōnfirmārent, et dīcerent: "Reliquī omnēs Belgae in armīs sunt."

139. *Translate into Latin.*

1. The Remi did not conspire against the Roman people. All the rest of the Belgae did not hesitate to conspire against the Romans. 2. Caesar enrolled many legions in Italy and Gaul. He determined to send a lieutenant to conduct[1] two legions into the interior of Gaul. 3. The Remi hastened to establish peace and friendship with the Roman people. They will announce to the Romans what the rest of the Belgae are doing.

4. Caesar determined to hasten to the army and to ascertain what the Gauls were doing. 5. The tidings so disturbed the commander that he hastened[2] to enrol soldiers and to fortify his camp. 6. Let us prepare supplies of grain and hasten[2] toward the territory of the enemy. 7. Caesar ordered Pedius, the lieutenant, to conduct the legions into Gaul. 8. The Belgae determined to collect large bands of men. 9. The commander determined to send five legions to withstand[1] the attack of the enemy.

---

important point is, not that he should translate it absolutely at sight, but that he should master it entirely by means of his own resources. These exercises in Reading at Sight are intended to encourage independent work, to promote self-reliance in study, and to give facility in reading and appreciating Latin.

[1] What *Mood* should be used in rendering into Latin? See 119, 497, I.
[2] For the choice of words, see 124 and 134.

LESSON XLVI.

VERB *Sum* IN FULL.

140. *Lesson from the Grammar.*

CONJUGATION.

201. Regular verbs are inflected, or conjugated, in four different ways, and are accordingly divided into Four Conjugations. These Four Conjugations are distinguished from one another by the stem characteristics or by the endings of the Infinitive, as follows:

	CHARACTERISTICS.	INFINITIVE ENDINGS.
CONJ. I.	ā	ā-re
II.	ē	ē-re
III.	e	e-re
IV.	ī	ī-re

202. PRINCIPAL PARTS.— The Present Indicative, Present Infinitive, Perfect Indicative, and Supine are called from their importance, the *Principal Parts* of the verb.

203. The ENTIRE CONJUGATION of any regular verb may be readily formed from the Principal Parts by means of the proper endings.[1]

1. SUM, *I am*, is used as an auxiliary in the passive voice of regular verbs. Accordingly, its conjugation, though quite irregular, must be given at the outset. The Principal Parts are —

PRES. INDIC.	PRES. INFIN.	PERF. INDIC.
Sum, *I am*,	esse, *to be*,	fuī, *I have been*.

---

[1] In the Paradigms of regular verbs, the endings which distinguish the various forms are separately indicated, and should be carefully noticed. In the principal tenses each ending contains the characteristic vowel.

VERBS.

204. Sum, *I am.*—STEMS, *es, fu.*

PRINCIPAL PARTS.

Pres. Ind.	Pres. Inf.	Perf. Ind.	Supine.[1]
sum,	esse,	fui,	—

INDICATIVE MOOD.

PRESENT TENSE.

SINGULAR.		PLURAL.	
sum,[2]	*I am,*	sumus,	*we are,*
es,	*thou art,*[3]	estis,	*you are,*
est,	*he is ;*	sunt,	*they are.*

IMPERFECT.

eram,	*I was,*	erāmus,	*we were,*
erās,	*thou wast,*[3]	erātis,	*you were,*
erat,	*he was ;*	erant,	*they were.*

FUTURE.

erō,[4]	*I shall be,*[5]	erimus,	*we shall be,*
eris,	*thou will be,*	eritis,	*you will be,*
erit,	*he will be ;*	erunt,	*they will be.*

PERFECT.

fui,	*I have been,*[5]	fuimus,	*we have been,*
fuisti,	*thou hast been,*	fuistis,	*you have been,*
fuit,	*he has been ;*	fuerunt, fuēre,	} *they have been.*

PLUPERFECT.

fueram,	*I had been,*	fuerāmus,	*we had been,*
fuerās,	*thou hadst been,*	fuerātis,	*you had been,*
fuerat,	*he had been ;*	fuerant,	*they had been.*

FUTURE PERFECT.

fuerō,	*I shall have been,*	fuerimus,	*we shall have been,*
fueris,	*thou will have been,*	fueritis,	*you will have been,*
fuerit,	*he will have been ;*	fuerint,	*they will have been.*

---

[1] The Supine is wanting.

[2] *Sum* is for *esum*, *eram* for *esam*. Whenever *s* of the stem *es* comes between two vowels, *s* is dropped, as in *sum*, *sunt*, or *s* is changed to *r*, as in *eram*, *erō*; see p. 3. 31. The pupil will observe that the endings which are added to the roots *es* and *fu* are distinguished by the type.

[3] Or *you are*, and in the Imperfect, *you were ; thou* is confined mostly to solemn discourse.

[4] In verbs, final *o*, marked *ō*, is generally long.

[5] Or, Future, *I will be ;* Perfect, *I was.*

VERBS.

SUBJUNCTIVE.

PRESENT.

SINGULAR.		PLURAL.	
sim,	may I be,[1]	simus,	let us be,
sis,	mayst thou be,[2]	sitis,	be ye, may you be,
sit,	let him be, may he be;	sint,	let them be.

IMPERFECT.

essem,	I should be,[1]	essēmus,	we should be,
essēs,	thou wouldst be,	essētis,	you would be,
esset,	he would be;	essent,	they would be.

PERFECT.

fuerim,	I may have been,[1]	fuerimus,	we may have been,
fueris,	thou mayst have been,	fueritis,	you may have been,
fuerit,	he may have been;	fuerint,	they may have been.

PLUPERFECT.

fuissem,	I should have been,	fuissēmus,	we should have been,
fuissēs,	thou wouldst have been,	fuissētis,	you would have been,
fuisset,	he would have been;	fuissent,	they would have been.

IMPERATIVE.

Pres.	es,	be thou,	este,	be ye.
Fut.	estō,	thou shalt be,[3]	estōte,	ye shall be,
	estō,	he shall be;[3]	sunto,	they shall be.

INFINITIVE.   PARTICIPLE.

Pres. esse, to be.
Perf. fuisse, to have been.
Fut. futūrus esse,[4] to be about
to be.   Fut. futūrus,[4] about to be.

1. In the Paradigm all the forms beginning with *e* or *s* are from the stem *es*; all others from the stem *fu*.[5]
2. RARE FORMS:—*forem, forēs, foret, forent, fore,* for *essem, essēs, esset, essent*; *futūrus esse*; *siem, siēs, siet, sient,* or *fuam, fuās, fuat, fuant,* for *sim, sis, sit, sint.*

---

[1] On the translation of the Subjunctive, see III, 196, and remember that it is often best rendered by the Indicative. Thus, *sim* may often be rendered *I am*, and *fuerim, I have been.*

[2] Or *be thou,* or *may you be.*

[3] The Fut. may also be rendered like the Pres., or with *let: be thou; let him be.*

[4] *Futūrus* is declined like *bonus.* So in the Infinitive: *futūrus, a, um esse.*

[5] *Es* and *fu* are *roots* as well as *stems.* As the basis of this paradigm they are properly *stems,* but as they are not derived from more primitive forms, they are in themselves *roots.*

LESSON XLVII.

VERB SUM. — RULE XIV. — EXERCISES.

141. *Examples.* — *Dative with Adjectives.*

Patria omnibus cāra est.   *Native country is dear* TO ALL.
Pāx nōbis grāta fuit.   *Peace was acceptable* TO US.

NOTE. — Observe in these examples that *omnibus*, limiting the meaning of *cāra*, 'dear,' and *nōbis* that of *grāta*, 'acceptable,' are both in the *Dative*. This Latin usage is expressed in the following

RULE XIV. — Dative with Adjectives.

391. With adjectives the OBJECT TO WHICH the quality is directed is put in the Dative:

Patriae sŏlum omnibus cārum est, *the soil of their country is dear* TO ALL. Cic. Id aptum est tempori, *this is adapted* TO THE TIME. Cic. Canis similis lupō est, *a dog is similar to a wolf.* Cic.

142. *Vocabulary.*

Continenter, *adv.*	*continually, incessantly.*
Divicŏ, ōnis, *m.*	*Divico, an Helvetian chieftain.*
Flūmen, ĭnis, *n.*	*stream, river.*
Lēgātĭŏ, ōnis, *f.*	*embassy.*
Longē, *adv.*	*by far, far, long.*
Nōbilis, e,	*noble, of high birth.*
Omnīnō, *adv.*	*in all, only.*
Orgetorix, ĭgis, *m.*	*Orgetorix, an Helvetian chieftain.*
Pār, paris,[1]	*equal, a match for.*
Pōns, pontis, *m.*	*bridge.*
Rhodanus, ī, *m.*	*the Rhone.*
Sĕquanus, a, um,	*Sequanian, of the Sequani;* see 211.
Testis, is, *m.* and *f.*[1]	*witness.*
Tōtus,[2] a, um,	*all, the whole of.* [Gaul.[3]
Ulterior, us,[2] *adj. comp.*	*farther;* Gallia ulterior, *Transalpine*

---

[1] Decline *testis* like *hostis;* *par* like *audāx,* i. e., with the same case-endings.   [2] See 45, 151, and 86, 166.

[3] That is, *Gaul beyond the Alps* from Rome, *Gaul west of the Alps.*

DATIVE.

143. *Translate into English.*

1. Belgae, quī Gallōrum[1] omnium fortissimī erant, cum Germānīs continenter bellum gerēbant. 2. Helvētiī lēgātōs ad Caesarem mīsērunt, cūjus[2] lēgātiōnis Divicō prīnceps fuit. 3. Apud Helvētiōs longē nōbilissimus fuit Orgetorix. 4. Fuerat omnīnō in Galliā ūlteriōre legiō ūna. 5. Ad bellum parātī sīmus. 6. Legiōnēs multās cōnscrīpsit ut ad bellum parātus esset.[3]
7. Hūjus reī populus Rōmānus sit testis. 8. Ager Sēquanus erat optimus tōtīus Galliae. 9. Ariovistus, rēx Germānōrum, tertiam partem agrī Sēquanī occupāvit. 10. In[4] eō flūmine pōns erat. 11. Mīlitēs omnēs fortēs esse dēbent. 12. Hostēs parēs esse nostrō exercituī[5] nōn poterant.

144. *Translate into Latin.*

1. You shall be chief of the embassy which the citizens are sending to the enemy. 2. You are the bravest of all the soldiers. 3. Who will be braver than this soldier? 4. Let us all be brave. 5. Did he not say: "All the Gauls were in arms"? He says: "All the Gauls will be in arms." 6. Caesar was in Italy, but his legions were in Gaul. 7. The Helvetii said: "We are the bravest of the Gauls."

8. The Gauls had always been prepared for war. 9. Shall you be prepared to withstand the attack of the enemy? 10. Let us be brave, that we may be prepared to withstand the attacks of the enemy. 11. Were the Gauls a match for the Romans? They were not a match for the Roman soldiers.

---

[1] *Gallōrum* is a Partitive Genitive, governed by *fortissimi* used substantively, according to Rule XVI.; see 28, 397.

[2] *Cūjus* is here an adjective, agreeing with *lēgātiōnis*, according to Rule XXXIV.; see 40.

[3] Why in the *Subjunctive*, and why in the *Imperfect?* See 119, Rules XLI. and XLII.

[4] Render *over*, and observe the difference of idiom between the Latin and the English.   [5] Why in the *Dative?* See 141, Rule XIV.

FIRST CONJUGATION.

LESSON XLVIII.

FIRST CONJUGATION. — INDICATIVE ACTIVE.

145. *Lesson from the Grammar.*

In the verb *Amō* learn the Indicative Mood of the Active voice. See page 124.

LESSON XLIX.

FIRST CONJUGATION. — INDICATIVE ACTIVE. — EXERCISES.

146. *Vocabulary.*

Acceptus, a, um,	*acceptable.*
Aeduī, ōrum, *m. pl.*	*the Aedui, Aeduans,* a tribe of [central Gaul.
Amīcus, a, um,	*friendly.*
Auxilium, ii, *n.*	*aid.*
Collocŏ, āre, āvī, ātum,	*to place, station.*
Divitiacus, ī, *m.*	*Divitiacus,* an Aeduan chieftain.
Dumnorix, igis, *m.*	*Dumnorix,* an Aeduan chieftain.
Ēdūcit,	*he leads out.*
Finitimus, a, um,	*neighboring.*
Graecia, ae, *f.*	*Greece.*
Graviter, *adv.*	*severely.*
Hiberna, ōrum, *n. pl.*	*winter quarters.*
Jam, *adv.*	*already.*
Maximē, *sup. adv.*	*most, very greatly.*
Mōns, montis, *m.*	*mountain.*
Plēbs, plēbis, *f.*	*the common people, populace.*
Profectiŏ, ōnis, *f.*	*departure, starting.*
Senātus, ūs, *m.*	*senate.*
Trāns, *prep. w. acc.*	*across, beyond.* [Gaul.
Trēverī, ōrum, *m. pl.*	*the Treveri,* a tribe of northeastern

147. *Translate into English.*

1. Caesar exercitum in hībernīs collocāvit. 2. Helvētiī in tertium annum[1] profectiōnem lēge[2] cōnfirmant. 3. Cum

---

[1] *In tertium annum,* lit. 'into the third year'; render *for* or *upon the third year.*   [2] See 78, Rule XXV.

FIRST CONJUGATION. 121

multīs cīvitātibus pācem et amīcitiam cōnfirmāverant. 4. Caesar Aeduōrum prīncipēs, quōrum māgnam cōpiam in castrīs habēbat, graviter accūsāvit. 5. Fugitīvī hostibus eam rem nūntiāvērunt. 6. Omnēs auxilium ā populō Rōmānō implōrābant. 7. Divitiacus Aeduus māximē plēbī acceptus erat. 8. Belgae prōximī sunt Germānīs quī trāns Rhēnum incolunt. 9. Trēverī prōximī flūminī Rhēnō fuērunt. 10. Caesar trēs legiōnēs quae circum Aquilēiam hiemābant ex hībernīs ēdūxit.[1] 11. Tum in Galliā hiemābāmus. 12. Auxilium ā Caesare implōrāverāmus. 13. Num nostra cōnsilia hostibus nūntiāvistī? Nōn vestra cōnsilia hostibus nūntiāvī. 14. Prīncipēs Aeduōrum graviter accūsāvistis. 15. Prō patriā fortiter pūgnābimus. 16. Nōnne timōris suspīciōnem vītābis? In reliquum tempus omnēs suspīciōnēs vītābō. 17. Helvētiī frūmentum sēcum[2] portābunt. 18. Helvētiī jam agrōs vāstāverant et oppida expūgnābant.

148. *Translate into Latin.*

1. Will this judge be acceptable to you? He will be acceptable to me and to all the citizens. 2. Have you announced this battle to the consul?[3] I have announced it to the consul and to the senate. 3. Shall you pass the winter in Italy? We shall pass the winter in Greece. 4. The commander will place his whole army in winter quarters in Gaul, and pass the the winter himself in Italy.

5. We hastened to establish peace and friendship with the neighboring states. 6. Did you not implore aid from your friends? We implored aid from all our friends. 7. You have severely censured the commander himself. 8. The Remi were friendly to the Romans. 9. Of all the Gauls the Helvetii were the nearest to the Germans, with whom[4] they were continually waging war.

---

[1] For *edūc-sit*, the perfect of *edūcit*.   [2] See 102, 181, 6.
[3] For the proper construction, see 54, Rule XII.
[4] *With whom.* See 106, 187, 2.

LESSON L.

FIRST CONJUGATION. — INDICATIVE ACTIVE. — REVIEW OF DECLENSIONS I. AND II. — RULE XXXI.

149. *Vocabulary.*

Absum, abesse, āfuī,	*to be absent, distant.*
Collis, is, m, like ignis.	*hill.*
Convocō, āre, āvī, ātum,	*to call together, assemble.*
Fuga, ae, f.	*flight.*
Movet,	*he moves.*
Nox, noctis, f.	*night.*
Occultō, āre, āvī, ātum,	*to hide.*
Praesidium, ii, n.	*garrison.*
Septimus, a, um,	*seventh.*
Subdūcit,	*he withdraws, leads off.*
Tentō, āre, āvī, atum,	*to try.*

150. *Translate into English.*

1. Rōmānī Helvētiōs superābunt. 2. Eō tempore[1] Helvētiī adventum Caesaris exspectābant. 3. Aeduī bellī fortūnam tentāvērunt. 4. Nox fugam hostium nōn occultāvit. 5. Ariovistus eās omnēs cōpiās ūnō proeliō superāvit. 6. Prōximō diē Caesar ē castrīs cōpiās ēdūxit. 7. Nōnne hōc proelium imperātōrī nūntiāvistī? 8. Hōc proelium imperātōrī nūntiābō. 9. Num bellum renovābitis? Multīs dē causīs[2] bellum renovābimus.

10. Caesar prīncipēs Aeduōrum convocāvit et graviter eōs accūsāvit. 11. Septimō diē Ariovistī cōpiae ā nōbīs nōn longē aberant. 12. Prōximā nocte castra movēbāmus. 13. Imperātor castra movet ut intellegat[3] utrum apud mīlitēs pudor atque officium an timor valeat.[3] 14. Caesar hōc

---

[1] For construction, see 93, Rule XXXI.
[2] Literally, *from* or *out of many causes*; render *for many reasons*.
[3] Explain Mood; 119 and 127, Rules XLII. and LV.

oppidum occupāvit et ibī praesidium collocāvit. 15. Suās cōpiās in prōximum collem subdūcit.

151. *Translate into Latin.*

1. Caesar was at that time praising the soldiers of the tenth legion. 2. He had often praised the valor of that legion. 3. On what day did you renew the war? We renewed the war on the tenth day. 4. On which day did the ambassadors announce to you the flight of the enemy? They announced it to us on the same day. 5. Caesar had called together the chiefs of the Aedui, that he might upbraid[1] them. 6. Have you called us together at this time, that you may upbraid us? I have called you together that I may praise your valor, and that I may announce to you the approach of the enemy.

7. For what reason[2] did you renew the war at that time? We renewed the war that we might conquer the enemy. 8. At that time we were awaiting the arrival of the general. 9. On the next night the Gauls seized the town. 10. We shall conquer in a single battle[3] all the forces of the enemy. 11. On the seventh day we shall have placed a garrison in the town, and on the next day we shall try the fortune of war.

LESSON LI.

FIRST CONJUGATION. — ACTIVE VOICE IN FULL. — REVIEW OF DECLENSION III.

152. *Lesson from the Grammar.*

In the verb *Amō*, learn the Active voice in full. See the following page.

---

[1] For Mood and Tense, see 119, Rules XLI. and XLII.
[2] *For what reason;* see note on *multīs dē causīs*, 150.
[3] *In a single battle;* Latin idiom, BY *a single battle.*

FIRST CONJUGATION: A VERBS.

205. ACTIVE VOICE.—Amŏ, *I love.*

Verb Stem and Present Stem, *amā*.[1]

PRINCIPAL PARTS.

Pres. Ind.	Pres. Inf.	Perf. Ind.	Supine
amŏ,	amāre,	amāvī,	amātum.

INDICATIVE MOOD.

Present Tense.

Singular		Plural	
amŏ,[1]	*I love,*[2]	amāmus,	*we love,*
amās,	*you love,*[3]	amātis,	*you love,*
amat,	*he loves;*	amant,	*they love.*

Imperfect.

amābam,	*I was loving,*	amābāmus,	*we were loving,*
amābās,	*you were loving,*	amābātis,	*you were loving,*
amābat,	*he was loving;*	amābant,	*they were loving.*

Future.

amābŏ,	*I shall love,*[4]	amābimus,	*we shall love,*
amābis,	*you will love,*	amābitis,	*you will love,*
amābit,	*he will love;*	amābunt,	*they will love.*

Perfect.

amāvī,	*I have loved,*[5]	amāvimus,	*we have loved,*
amāvistī,	*you have loved,*	amāvistis,	*you have loved,*
amāvit,	*he has loved;*	amāvērunt, *&c.*,	*they have loved.*

Pluperfect.

amāveram,	*I had loved,*	amāverāmus,	*we had loved,*
amāverās,	*you had loved,*	amāverātis,	*you had loved,*
amāverat,	*he had loved;*	amāverant,	*they had loved.*

Future Perfect.

amāverŏ,	*I shall have loved,*[4]	amāverimus,	*we shall have loved,*
amāveris,	*you will have loved,*	amāveritis,	*you will have loved,*
amāverit,	*he will have loved;*	amāverint,	*they will have loved.*

---

[1] The final ā of the stem disappears in *amŏ* for *ama-ŏ, amem, amis*, etc., for *ama-im, ama-is,* etc. Also in the Pass. in *amor* for *ama-or, amer*, etc., for *ama-ir*, etc. Final a, marked ā, is generally long.

[2] Or *I am loving, I do love.* So in the Imperfect, *I loved, I was loving, I did love.*

[3] Or *thou lovest.* So in the other tenses, *thou wast loving, thou wilt love*, etc.

[4] Or *I will love.* So in the Future Perfect, *I shall have loved* or *I will have loved.*

[5] Or *I loved.*

ACTIVE VOICE.

SUBJUNCTIVE.

PRESENT.

SINGULAR.		PLURAL.	
amem,	may I love,[1]	amēmus,	let us love,
amēs,	may you love,	amētis,	may you love,
amet,	let him love;	ament,	let them love.

IMPERFECT.

amārem,	I should love,	amārēmus,	we should love,
amārēs,	you would love,	amārētis,	you would love,
amāret,	he would love;	amārent,	they would love.

PERFECT.

amāverim,	I may have loved,[2]	amāverīmus,	we may have loved,
amāveris,	you may have loved,	amāverītis,	you may have loved,
amāverit,	he may have loved;	amāverint,	they may have loved.

PLUPERFECT.

amāvissem,	I should have loved,	amāvissēmus,	we should have loved,
amāvissēs,	you would have loved,	amāvissētis,	you would have loved,
amāvisset,	he would have loved;	amāvissent,	they would have loved.

IMPERATIVE.

Pres.	amā,	love thou;	amāte,	love ye.
Fut.	amātō,	thou shalt love,	amātōte,	ye shall love,
	amātō,	he shall love;	amantō,	they shall love.

INFINITIVE.

Pres. amāre, to love.
Perf. amāvisse, to have loved.
Fut. amātūrus[3] esse, to be about to love.

PARTICIPLE.

Pres. amāns,[4] loving.
Fut. amātūrus,[3] about to love.

GERUND.

Gen. amandī, of loving,
Dat. amandō, for loving,
Acc. amandum, loving,
Abl. amandō, by loving.

SUPINE.

Acc. amātum, to love,
Abl. amātū, to love, be loved.

---

[1] On the translation of the Subjunctive, see 111, 196.
[2] Often best rendered I have loved. So in the Pluperfect, I had loved.
[3] Decline like bonus, 39, 148.
[4] For declension, see 86, 157.

LESSON LII.

FIRST CONJUGATION. — ACTIVE VOICE. — REVIEW OF DECLENSION III. — RULE VI. — EXERCISES.

153. *Examples.* — *Two Accusatives.*

1. Platōnem Homērum philo-   *They call* PLATO THE HOMER *of*
sophōrum appellant.   *philosophers.*
2. Urbem Rōmam vocāvit.   *He called* THE CITY ROME.

NOTE. — In these examples observe that *appellant,* 'they call,' takes *two* Accusatives, *Platōnem* and *Homērum,* both referring to the same *person,* and that *vocāvit,* 'he called,' also takes *two* Accusatives, *urbem* and *Rōmam,* both referring to the same city. This Latin usage is expressed in the following

RULE VI. — Two Accusatives — Same Person.

373. Verbs of MAKING, CHOOSING, CALLING, REGARDING, SHOWING, and the like, admit two Accusatives of the same person or thing:

Hamilcarem *imperātōrem* fēcērunt, *they made Hamilcar* COMMANDER. Nep. Ancum *rēgem* populus creāvit, *the people elected Ancus* KING. Liv. Summum cōnsilium appellārunt *Senātum, they called their highest council* SENATE. Cic.

1. PREDICATE ACCUSATIVE. — One of the two Accusatives is the *Direct Object,* and the other an essential part of the Predicate. The latter may be called a *Predicate Accusative;* see 59, Rule I.

154. *Vocabulary.*

Allobrogēs, um, *m. pl.*   the *Allobroges,* a tribe of southeastern Gaul; *sing.* Allobrox, ogis.
Appellō, āre, āvī, ātum,   *to call.*
Boiī, ōrum, *m. pl.*   the *Boii,* a tribe of central Gaul.
Conjūnx, conjugis, *m. and f.*   *spouse, husband, wife.*
Cōnservō, āre, āvī, ātum,   *to preserve.*
Fīlius, iī,[1] *m.*   *son.*   [army.
Galba, ae, *m.*   *Galba,* a lieutenant in Caesar's

---

[1] In the singular, the *Genitive* and *Vocative* are generally contracted to *fīlī.* See 32, 51, 5.

FIRST CONJUGATION. 127

Gēns, gentis, *f*, like *cliēns*.	race, tribe, nation.
Līberī, ōrum, *m*. *pl.*[1]	children.
Mārcus, ī, *m*.	Marcus, a Roman name.
Nōmen, ĭnis, *n*.	name.
Nōmĭnō, āre, āvī, ātum,	to name, call.
Nūtrīx, īcis, *f*.	nurse.
Octōdūrus, ī, *m*.	Octodurus, a town of the Veragri,
Prōpulsō, āre, āvī, ātum,	to repulse. [now *Martigny*.
Recūsō, āre, āvī, ātum,	to reject.
Rōma, ae, *f*.	Rome.
Sicilia, ae, *f*.	Sicily. [Gaul.
Veragrī, ōrum, *m. pl.*	the Veragri, a tribe of eastern
Vergobretus, ī, *m*.	Vergobretus, the title of the chief magistrate of the Aeduī.

155. *Translate into English.*

1. Senātus Rōmānus Aeduōs frātrēs appellāvit. 2. Senātus Ariovistum rēgem et amīcum appellāverat. 3. Senātus patrem Casticī populī[2] Rōmānī amīcum appellat. 4. Galba in vīcō Veragrōrum hiemābat. 5. Gallī hunc vīcum Octōdūrum appellant. 6. Mārcus Catō nūtrīcem plēbis Rōmānae Sīciliam nōminābat. 7. Gallī omnēs auxilium ā populō Rōmānō implōrent. 8. Allobrogēs, quī trāns Rhodanum incolunt, auxilium ā Caesare implōrāre cōnstituērunt. 9. Boiī, quī trāns Rhēnum incolunt, hanc urbem oppūgnāre cōnstituērunt. 10. Cōnservāte vōs, conjugēs, līberōs, fortūnāsque vestrās. 11. Ariovistus cum Rōmānīs dēcertāre parātus erat. 12. Nē[3] timor exercitum Rōmānum occupet. 13. Utinam[4] timor omnem hostium exercitum occupāvisset.[4] 14. Nē populī Rōmānī amīcitiam recūsēmus. 15. Prō patriā fortiter pūgnēmus et hostēs prōpulsēmus. 16. Ariovistus partem suārum copiārum quae castra Rōmāna oppūgnāret[5] mīsit.

---
[1] Not used in the singular.
[2] Construe with *amicum*.
[3] Why is *nē* rather than *nōn* used? See 114, 483, 3.
[4] For *utinam* and for the force of the *Pluperfect*, see 114, 483, 1 and 2.
[5] For the use of *Mood*, see Rule XLII.

156. *Translate into Latin.*

1. They called the city Rome. 2. The Aedui called their chief Vergobretus. 3. Will you call us brothers? We shall call you all brothers. 4. The Romans call us Gauls. 5. At that time we called Ariovistus king. 6. Did not the consul name his son Marcus? Cicero the consul named his son Marcus. 7. The citizens called Marcus Cato wise. 8. The enemy had determined to call the bravest of their leaders general.

9. Galba determined to winter with the legion in a village which the Gauls call Octodurus. 10. Do you call Ariovistus a friend or an enemy?[1] I call him the enemy of the Roman people. 11. He inquired[2] whether you called him a friend or an enemy.[3] 12. Ariovistus, whom the Germans called king, was prepared to try the fortune of war. 13. The Gauls implored aid of the Romans, in order that they might repulse the enemy.

LESSON LIII.

FIRST CONJUGATION. — INDICATIVE PASSIVE. — REVIEW OF DECLENSIONS IV. AND V. — RULE XXII.

157. *Lesson from the Grammar.*

In the verb *Amō*, learn the Indicative Mood of the Passive voice. See page 136.

158. *Examples. — Ablative.*

1. Caedem ā vōbīs dēpellit. He wards off slaughter FROM YOU.
2. Statua *ex aere* facta. A statue made OF BRONZE.
3. Expulsus est *patriā*. He was banished FROM HIS COUNTRY.
4. Ars *ūtilitāte* laudātur. An art is praised BECAUSE OF ITS USEFULNESS.

---

[1] For the construction of *Double* or *Disjunctive Questions*, see 106, 353.

[2] Or *was inquiring*, imperfect.

[3] For the construction, see 127, 520, 3.

NOTE. — In these examples *vōbīs* (ā *vōbīs*), 'from you,' *aere* (*ex aere*), 'of bronze,' *patriā*, 'from his country,' and *ūtilitāte*, 'because of its usefulness,' are all in the *Ablative*, in accordance with the Latin usage expressed in the following

RULE XXII. — Separation, Source, Cause.

413. Separation, Source, and Cause are denoted by the *Ablative with* or *without a preposition*:

SEPARATION. — Caedem ā vōbīs dēpellō, *I ward off slaughter* FROM YOU. Cic. Expulsus est patriā, *he was banished from his country*. Cic. Urbem commeātū prīvāvit, *he deprived the city of supplies*. Nep. Cōnātū dēstitērunt, *they desisted from the attempt*. Caes.

SOURCE. — Hōc audīvī dē parente meō, *I heard this* FROM MY FATHER. Cic. Oriundi ab Sabīnīs, *descended* FROM THE SABINES. Liv. Statua ex aere facta, *a statue made of bronze*. Cic.

CAUSE. — Ars ūtilitāte laudātur, *an art is praised* BECAUSE OF ITS USEFULNESS. Cic. Rogātū vēneram, *I had come by request*. Cic. Ex vulnere aeger, *ill in consequence of his wound*. Cic.

415. The ABLATIVE OF SOURCE more commonly takes a preposition; see examples under 413. It includes *agency, parentage, material,* etc.

I. The *agent* or *author* of an action is designated by the *Ablative* with ā or ab:

Occīsus est ā Thēbānīs, *he was slain by the Thebans*. Nep.

NOTE 1. — The Accusative with *per* may be used of the *person through whose agency* the action is effected:

Ab Oppianicō per Fabriciōs factum est, *it was accomplished by Oppianicus* THROUGH THE AGENCY OF THE FABRICII. Cic.

LESSON LIV.

FIRST CONJUGATION. — INDICATIVE PASSIVE. — RULE XXII. — EXERCISES.

159. *Vocabulary.*

Conventus, ūs, *m.*   *assembly, meeting, council, convention.*
Ēnūntiō, āre, āvī, ātum,   *to report, disclose, announce.*
Etiam, *adv.*   *also, even.*

FIRST CONJUGATION.

Lingua, ae, f.   tongue, language.
Liscus, ī, m.   Liscus, the chief magistrate of the
Meritō, adv.   deservedly. [Aedui.
Paulātim, adv.   little by little, by degrees, gradually.
Per, prep. w. acc.   through, by, over.
Prōvincia, ae, f.   province. [of northwestern Gaul.
Santonēs, um, m. pl.   the Santoni or Santones, a tribe
Sed, conj.   but.

160. *Translate into English.*

1. Mīlitēs legiōnis decimae omnēs ā Caesare[1] laudantur.
2. Eōdem tempore multae legiōnēs meritō laudābantur.
3. Semper laudāberis. 4. Ab omnibus meritō laudāminī.
5. Ab omnibus laudātus es. 6. Divitiacus ad Caesarem vocātus erat. 7. Haec omnia Ariovistō ēnūntiāta sunt. 8. Pater Casticī ā senātū amīcus[2] appellātus erat. 9. Ea rēs per fugitīvōs[3] hostibus nūntiātur. 10. Aeduī frātrēs ab senātū appellātī sunt.

11. Timor eōs, quī nōn māgnum in eō mīlitārī[4] ūsum habēbant, occupāvit; hōrum timōre, paulātim etiam iī, quī māgnum in castrīs ūsum habēbant, perturbābantur. 12. Prīncipēs Helvētiōrum ā Caesare convocātī sunt. 13. Fīnēs Santonum ā prōvinciā Rōmānā nōn longē absunt. 14. Liscus multās rēs illō diē in conventū dīxit. 15. Iī quī tertiam Galliae partem incolunt nostrā linguā[5] Gallī appellantur. 16. Galba in vīcō quī appellātur Octōdūrus hiemābat.

161. *Translate into Latin.*

1. The brave soldiers will be praised by the general. 2. You have been deservedly praised by Caesar himself. 3.

---

[1] See 158, 415, I., and observe that in the *Active* construction the *Author* or *Agent* of the action is denoted by the *Nominative*; in the Passive by the *Ablative* with *ā* or *ab*. Thus in this sentence the Active construction would be: *Caesar mīlitēs . . . laudat.*

[2] *Predicate Nominative;* see 59, Rule I.

[3] See 158, 415, note 1.

[4] Lit. *in the military thing;* render, *in military affairs.*

[5] Ablative of Means; see 78, Rule XXV.

FIRST CONJUGATION. 131

Was not Cicero the consul praised by the senate? He was deservedly praised by the Roman people. 4. Has not this citizen been accused by you? He has not been accused by me, but by the magistrate. 5. Will not all these things be announced to the commander?

6. By whom were our plans announced to the enemy? They have not been announced to the enemy. 7. What has been announced to Caesar? All these things have been announced to him. 8. The consul, with a large army, is not far from the city. 9. At that time the enemy were not far from the village which is called Octodurus. 10. The Aedui, who had been called brothers by the senate, implored aid from Caesar.

LESSON LV.

FIRST CONJUGATION. — INDICATIVE PASSIVE. — REVIEW OF ADJECTIVES OF DECLENSIONS I. AND II.

162. *Vocabulary.*

Āc, *conj.*	and.
Alpēs, ium, *f. pl.*	the Alps.
Arverni, ōrum, *m. pl.*	the Arverni, a tribe of southern Gaul.
Celeriter, *adv.*	quickly.
Centuriō, ōnis, *m.*	centurion.
Excitō, āre, āvī, ātum,	to excite, arouse.
Fabius, iī, *m.*	Fabius, a celebrated Roman general.
Harūdēs, um, *m. pl.*	the Harudes, a tribe of southwestern [Germany.
Nūper, *adv.*	recently, of late.
Obsignō, āre, āvī, ātum,	to seal, sign and seal.
Paene, *adv.*	almost, well nigh, nearly.
Parō, āre, āvī, ātum,	to prepare.
Quintus, i, *m.*	Quintus, a Roman praenōmen.
Sēdēs, is, *f*, like *nūbēs.*	seat, abode; locus ac sēdēs, place of will. [abode.
Testāmentum, i, *n.*	
Trānsportō, āre, āvī, ātum,	to transport, carry over, take over, bring over. [universally.
Vulgō, *adv.*	commonly, as a general thing,

FIRST CONJUGATION.

163. *Translate into English.*

1. Oppida Aeduōrum paene in cōnspectū exercitūs nostrī expūgnāta sunt. 2. Rēs frūmentāria¹ māgnō cum perīculō comparāta erat. 3. Eōdem tempore agrī Aeduōrum vastābantur. 4. Ariovistus, rēx Germānōrum, amīcus ā senātū appellātus erat. 5. Māgnae Gallōrum cōpiae ab Ariovistō ūnō proeliō² superātae sunt. 6. Timor exercitum populī Rōmānī occupāvit; etiam centuriōnēs quī māgnum in rē mīlitārī ūsum habēbant perturbābantur; vulgō in castrīs testāmenta obsīgnābantur. 7. Omnēs ferē Gallī ad bellum celeriter excitantur. 8. Aeduī bellī fortūnam tentāvērunt et superātī sunt. 9. Harūdēs nūper in Galliam trānsportātī sunt.³ Hīs locus āc sēdēs parābuntur. 10. Imperātor in ulteriōrem Galliam per Alpēs cum quīnque legiōnibus contendit.⁴ 11. Multae gentēs ūnō nōmine Germānī appellantur. 12. Arvernī ab Quīntō Fabiō bellō superātī sunt.

164. *Translate into Latin.*

1. Our fields have been devastated by the enemy. 2. Many towns had been taken by storm.⁵ 3. Large forces of the enemy will be conquered by our commander. 4. The Gauls had been conquered by Caesar in many battles.⁶ 5. Many chiefs had been called together by Caesar. 6. The chiefs who had been called together said many things in the council. 7. Many Germans were carried over into Gaul by Ariovistus. For these Germans places of abode had been

---

¹ *Rēs frūmentāria*, lit. *the thing relating to corn* or *grain, the affair of the grain;* render 'grain' or 'supplies.'
² Observe the difference of construction between expressions of AGENCY, AUTHORSHIP, *ab Ariovistō*, and MEANS, *proeliō*.
³ That is, *across the Rhine.* ⁴ See 134, foot-note 2.
⁵ *By storm* is not to be rendered by a separate word, but is involved in the meaning of the Latin verb.
⁶ *In many battles;* Latin idiom, BY *many battles.*

prepared in Gaul. 8. These legions were wintering in Gaul with great peril. 9. We are not quickly aroused to war. 10. Many nations had already been aroused to war. 11. The fortune of war has been tried by the Gauls, and they will all be conquered. 12. Those who have large experience in military affairs, will not be quickly aroused to war. 13. Were all kings called friends of the Roman people? Many kings were called friends by the senate. 14. The lands of the Gauls were often devastated by the Germans. 15. The town in which our army wintered was not attacked by the Gauls.

LESSON LVI.

FIRST CONJUGATION. — SUBJUNCTIVE PASSIVE. — REVIEW OF ADJECTIVES. — RULE LIX.

165. *Lesson from the Grammar.*

In the verb *Amō*, learn the Subjunctive Mood of the Passive voice. See page 137.

166. *Examples. — Supine.*

1. Ad Caesarem *congrătulātum* convēnērunt.   They came to Caesar TO CONGRATULATE *him*.
2. Vēnērunt rēs *repetītum*.   They came TO DEMAND *restitution*.

NOTE. — In these examples the supines *congrătulātum* and *repetītum* are employed to denote the purpose of the leading action, in accordance with the Latin usage expressed in the following

RULE LIX. — Supine in Um.

546. The Supine in *um* is used with verbs of motion to express PURPOSE:

Lēgāti vēnērunt rēs repetītum, *deputies came to demand restitution*. Liv. Ad Caesarem congrătulātum convēnērunt, *they came to Caesar to congratulate him*. Caes.

LESSON LVII.

FIRST CONJUGATION. — SUBJUNCTIVE PASSIVE. — RULE LIX. — EXERCISES.

167. *Vocabulary.*

Cāsus, ūs, *m.*   *accident, occurrence, emergency.*
Commeātus, ūs, *m.*   *supplies.*
Dēdĭtĭō, ōnis, *f.*   *surrender.*
Iter, itineris, *n.*   *march, journey;* māgna itinera, *forced*
Jūdicium, iī, *n.*   *judgment, decision.*   [*marches.*
Observō, āre, āvī, ātum,   *to observe, keep, comply with.*
Sōcratēs, is, *m.*   *Socrates,* the celebrated Greek philosopher.
Sublevō, āre, āvī, ātum,   *to assist, support.*

168. *Translate into English.*

1. Adventus hostium Caesarī nūntiētur. 2. Utinam ea rēs imperātōrī nūntiāta esset.[1] 3. Utinam haec cōnsilia Helvētiīs nūntientur.[1] 4. Nē nostra cōnsilia per fugitīvōs hostibus nūntientur. 5. Jūdicium senātūs observētur. 6. Utinam omnia senātūs jūdicia observāta essent. 7. Ab hīs lēgātīs quaerit quantae Galliae cīvitātēs superātae sint.[2] 8. Ab hīs quaerēbat quae urbēs expūgnātae essent. 9. Quaerunt quam ob rem commeātūs nōn ad Caesarem portātī sint. 10. Eōdem tempore ille mōns ā Labiēnō occupētur.

11. Ab prīncipibus Aeduōrum quaerēbat quam ob rem exercitus populī Rōmānī ab iīs nōn sublevārētur. 12. Caesar ad omnēs cāsūs subsidia comparābat. 13. Sōcratēs omnium[3] sapientissimus fuit. 14. Imperātor in citeriōrem Galliam māgnīs itineribus[4] contendit. 15. Hae nāvēs lātiōrēs erant quam reliquae. 16. Prīncipēs Gallōrum lēgātōs ad senātum Rōmānum mittēbant. 17. Hostēs lēgātōs ad Caesarem dē

---
[1] Show the force of *Tenses* ; see 114, 483, 2.
[2] See 127, Rule LV., and Suggestion XVII., 2.
[3] *Partitive Genitive.*
[4] Lit. *with large journeys* ; render *with forced marches.*

FIRST CONJUGATION.

169. *Translate into Latin.*

dēditiōne¹ mittunt. 18. Aeduī lēgātos ad Caesarem mittunt rogātum² auxilium.

1. What towns have been taken by storm? 2. Let us ascertain what towns have been taken by storm. 3. Let not our fields be devastated in sight of your army. 4. Let us inquire for what reason these Germans have been brought over into Gaul. 5. May the laws be observed by us and by all the citizens. 6. May you all be wise. 7. Would that these boys were wiser. 8. Would that this mountain had been occupied by our army.

9. Let supplies be brought to our army by the Aedui. 10. Caesar was hastening with forced marches into Gaul. 11. Would that all the forces of the enemy had been conquered.³ 12. May our towns never be stormed by the enemy. 13. What towns of the Gauls were stormed by the Germans? 14. Let us inquire of the ambassadors what towns have been stormed and what fields have been devastated. 15. Let not these things be announced to the Germans. 16. Would that these towns were all occupied by our friends. Let us send ambassadors to the senate to ask⁴ aid.

LESSON LVIII.

FIRST CONJUGATION. — PASSIVE VOICE IN FULL. — REVIEW OF PRONOUNS. — RULES LVII. AND LVIII.

170. *Lesson from the Grammar.*

In the verb *Amō*, learn the Passive voice in full. See the following page.

---

¹ Lit. *concerning a surrender;* render *to treat for a capitulation,* or *to capitulate.*
² *To ask;* see 166, Rule LIX.
³ See 114, 483, 2.
⁴ See 166, Rule LIX.

FIRST CONJUGATION: A VERBS.

206. PASSIVE VOICE.—Amor, *I am loved.*

VERB STEM AND PRESENT STEM, *amā*.

PRINCIPAL PARTS.

PRES. IND.	PRES. INF.	PERF. IND.
amor,	amārī,	amātus sum.

INDICATIVE MOOD.

PRESENT TENSE.
I am loved.

SINGULAR.	PLURAL.
amor	amāmur
amāris, *or* re	amāmini
amātur	amantur

IMPERFECT.
I was loved.

amābar	amābāmur
amābāris, *or* re	amābāmini
amābātur	amābantur

FUTURE.
I shall or will be loved.

amābor	amābimur
amāberis, *or* re	amābimini
amābitur	amābuntur

PERFECT.
I have been loved or *I was loved.*

amātus sum[1]	amātī sumus
amātus es	amātī estis
amātus est	amātī sunt

PLUPERFECT.
I had been loved.

amātus eram[1]	amātī erāmus
amātus erās	amātī erātis
amātus erat	amātī erant

FUTURE PERFECT.
I shall or will have been loved.

amātus erō[1]	amātī erimus
amātus eris	amātī eritis
amātus erit	amātī erunt

---

[1] *Fuī, fuistī,* etc., are sometimes used for *sum, es,* etc.: *amātus fuī* for *amātus sum.* So *fueram, fuerās,* etc., for *eram,* etc.: also *fuerō,* etc., for *erō,* etc.

PASSIVE VOICE.

SUBJUNCTIVE.

PRESENT.
May I be loved, let him be loved.[1]

SINGULAR.	PLURAL.
amer	amēmur
amēris, *or* re	amēmini
amētur	amentur

IMPERFECT.
I should be loved, he would be loved.[1]

amārer	amārēmur
amārēris, *or* re	amārēmini
amārētur	amārentur

PERFECT.
I may have been loved, or I have been loved.[1]

amātus sim[2]	amāti sīmus
amātus sis	amāti sītis
amātus sit	amāti sint

PLUPERFECT.
I should have been loved, he would have been loved.[1]

amātus essem[2]	amāti essēmus
amātus essēs	amāti essētis
amātus esset	amāti essent

IMPERATIVE.

Pres. amāre, *be thou loved;*	amāmini, *be ye loved.*
Fut. amātor, *thou shalt be loved,* amātor, *he shall be loved;*	amantor, *they shall be loved.*

INFINITIVE.
Pres. amāri, *to be loved.*
Perf. amātus esse,[1] *to have been loved.*
Fut. amātum iri, *to be about to be loved.*

PARTICIPLE.
Perf. amātus, *having been loved.*
Ger.[3] amandus, *to be loved, deserving to be loved.*

---

[1] But on the translation of the Subjunctive, see 111, 196.
[2] *Fuerim, fueris,* etc., are sometimes used for *sim, sis,* etc.—So also *fuissem, fuisses,* etc., for *essem, esses,* etc.: rarely *fuisse* for *esse.*
[3] *Ger.* = Gerundive; see p. 14, 200, IV., note.

FIRST CONJUGATION.

171. *Examples.* — *Infinitive with Subject.*

1. *Pontem* jubet *rescindi.*   *He orders* THE BRIDGE TO BE BROKEN DOWN.
2. Sentimus *calēre ignem.*   *We perceive* THAT FIRE IS HOT.

NOTE 1. — The Latin usage illustrated in these examples by the Accusative and the Infinitive is expressed in the following

RULE LVII. — Accusative and Infinitive.

534. Many transitive verbs admit both an Accusative and an Infinitive:

Tĕ sapere docet, *he teaches you to be wise.* Cic. Eŏs suum adventum exspectāre jussit, *he ordered them to await his approach.* Caes. Pontem jubet rescindi, *he orders the bridge to be broken down.* Caes.

NOTE 2. — In the second of the above examples, the Accusative *ignem* may be regarded as the Subject of the Infinitive *calēre*, in accordance with the Latin usage expressed in the following

RULE LVIII. — Subject of Infinitive.

536. The Infinitive sometimes takes an Accusative as its subject:

Sentimus calēre ignem, *we perceive that fire is hot.* Cic. Platōnem Tarentum vēnisse reperiō, *I find that Plato came to Tarentum.* Cic.

172. *Vocabulary.*

Accommodātus, a, um,	*fitted, adapted.*
Carīna, ae, *f.*	*keel, bottom* (of a vessel).
Concursus, ūs, *m.*	*running together; running about, running to and fro, agitation.*
Extrā, *prep. w. acc.*	*beyond, outside of.*
Flūctus, ūs, *m.*	*wave.*
Fremitus, ūs, *m.*	*din, noise.*
Jubet,	*he orders, commands.*
Māgnitūdō, inis, *f.*	*size.*
Modus, ī, *m.*	*measure, manner.*
Nātiō, ōnis, *f.*	*nation.*
Nūdō, āre, āvī, ātum,	*to bare, expose.*
Paulum, *adv.*	*a little, somewhat.*
Plānus, a, um,	*flat, level.*

FIRST CONJUGATION. 139

Prior, us, *sup.* primus, a,
   um, 86, 100,   *former, first.*
Prōra, ae, *f.*   *prow.*
Scientia, ae, *f.*   *knowledge.*
Segusiāni, ōrum, *m. pl.*   *the Segusiani,* a tribe of southeastern
Sīgnĭfĭcō, āre, āvī, ātum,   *to signify, indicate.*   [Gaul.
Superus, a, um, *comp.* superior, us, *sup.* suprēmus
   and summus, a, um,   *upper;* summus, *highest, greatest.*
Tardō, āre, āvī, ātum,   *to retard, check, hinder, impede.*

173. *Translate into English.*

1. Castra ab ūnā parte[1] nūdāta sunt. 2. Nō tōta castra nūdentur. 3. Caesaris adventū paulum hostium impetus tardātus est. 4. Omnēs in cōnspectū imperātōris etiam in summō perīculō fortiter pūgnābant. 5. Agrī nostrī vastārī[2] nōn dēbent. 6. Oppida Aeduōrum paene in cōnspectū exercitūs nostrī expūgnārī nōn dēbent. 7. Timor hostium fremitū et concursū sīgnificābātur. 8. Māximae nātiōnēs ā Rōmānīs superātae sunt. 9. Intellegunt māximās nātiōnēs superātās esse.[3]

10. Ducēs hostium summam scientiam rēī mīlitāris habēre exīstimābantur. 11. Caesar duās legiōnēs in prōximō monte collocārī jubet. 12. Fugitīvī dīcunt montem ā Labiēnō occupārī.[3] 13. Segusiānī sunt extrā prōvinciam Rōmānam trāns Rhodanum prīmī. 14. Nāvēs hostium ad hunc modum aedificātae sunt; carīnae plāniōrēs sunt quam nostrārum nāvium,[4] prōrae ad māgnitūdinem flūctuum accommodātae.

174. *Translate into Latin.*

1. They say that supplies[5] have not been brought to Caesar by the Aedui. 2. He says that our fields have been devastated by the Gauls. 3. How many vessels have been

---

[1] *Ab ūnā parte;* Latin idiom, *from one part;* render, *on one side.*
[2] See 132, Rule LVI.   [3] See Suggestion XVIII., 1.
[4] *Nāvium* depends upon *carīnae* understood.
[5] See 171, Rule LVIII.

built by the Gauls? Let us ascertain how many vessels have been built by them. 4. Deserters say that ten vessels have been built by the Gauls. 5. They say that many cities were stormed by the Romans. 6. Deserters say that the camp of the enemy is exposed on (*from*) one side. 7. Let not our camp be exposed. 8. Our camp ought not to be exposed. 9. Will you not fight bravely in sight of your general? 10. We ought to fight bravely for our country. 11. Caesar orders this city to be occupied by our army. 12. An ambassador announced that the cities of our friends were occupied by the enemy. 13. The Germans ought not to lay waste the fields of the Gauls. 14. The arrival of Caesar checked the attack of the enemy. 15. They say that one legion was stationed in the city. 16. In what part of Gaul were the legions wintering? 17. Let us ask in what part of Gaul the legions are wintering. 18. Caesar said that the legions were wintering among the Belgae.

LESSON LIX.

FIRST CONJUGATION IN FULL. — EXERCISE IN READING AT SIGHT.

175. *Read at Sight, examine carefully, and Translate into English.*[1]

Helvētiī per agrum Aeduōrum in Santonum fīnēs contendēbant, quī nōn longē ā prōvinciā Rōmānā absunt. Ob eas causās Caesar in Italiam māgnīs itineribus contendit, duāsque ibi legiōnēs cōnscrīpsit, et trēs quae circum Aquilēiam hiemābant ex hībernīs ēdūxit, et in ulteriōrem Galliam per Alpēs cum hīs quīnque legiōnibus contendit. Ab citeriōre prōvinciā[2] in Segusiānōs exercitum dūxit. Hī sunt extrā prō-

---

[1] See Directions for Reading at Sight, 137.

[2] *Citerior prōvincia* is the Roman province of *Citerior* or *Cisalpine Gaul*, while *ulterior prōvincia* is the province of *Ulterior* or *Transalpine Gaul*.

vinciam trāns Rhodanum prīmī. Helvētiī jam Aeduōrum agrōs vastābant et oppida expūgnābant. Tum vērō tantus timor Aeduōs occupāvit ut omnium mentēs animōsque perturbāret. Lēgātōs igitur ad Caesarem mīsērunt. Eōdem tempore multae Galliae cīvitātēs auxilium ā Caesare implōrāvērunt.

176. *Translate into Latin.*

1. Caesar says that nearly all the Belgae conspired against the Roman people. The Gauls, whom Caesar had commanded to ascertain[1] what the Belgae were doing, announced that the enemy were collecting large forces (*bands of men*),[2] and bringing them together in (*into*) one place.[3] 2. How many legions did Caesar enrol in Italy? At that time he enrolled two legions there. How many legions will winter in the vicinity of this town (*around this town*)? The general says that three legions will winter in the vicinity of this town.

3. By whom have the lands of the Aedui been devastated? He inquired by whom the lands of the Aedui had been devastated. Ambassadors announced that the lands of the Aedui had been devastated by the Helvetii. 4. The general ought to lead all his forces out of winter quarters.

LESSON LX.

SECOND CONJUGATION. — INDICATIVE ACTIVE.

177. *Lesson from the Grammar.*

In the verb *Moneō*, learn the Indicative Mood of the Active voice. See page 144.

---

[1] Literally *to whom Caesar had given orders that they should ascertain;* see 120 and 119, 498.

[2] See 135, 10.

[3] Use *condŭcit* as in 135, 14, not *comportat*, which Caesar employs in speaking of bringing together *things* but not *men;* see 135, 9.

SECOND CONJUGATION.

178. Vocabulary.

Āgmen, ĭnis, n. — army on the march, *line of march.* line ; extrēmum āgmen, *the extremity of the line, the rear.*
Aliquamdiū, *adv.* — *for a time.*
Armŏ, āre, āvi, ātum, — *to arm.*
Dēbeō, ēre, uī, ĭtum, — *to owe ; ought.*
Exterus, a, um, *comp.* exterior, us, *sup.* extrēmus and extĭmus, a, um, — [*the extremity of.* outward ; extrēmus, *the outermost,*
Habeō, ēre, uī, ĭtum, — *to have, hold; to regard, regard as.*
Inermus, a, um, — *unarmed.*
Moneō, ēre, uī, ĭtum, — *to advise, warn.*
Nōnne, *interrog. part.*, — *not ?* 106, 351, 1, note 2.
Sĭne, *prep. w. abl.* — *without.*
Sustĭneō, ēre, tĭnuī, tentum, — *to sustain, withstand, resist.*
Tĭmeō, ēre, uī, — *to fear.*

179. Translate into English.

1. Num hostēs timētis? Nōn hostēs timēmus. 2. Timōris suspīciōnem vītāre dēbētis. 3. Nōnne omnēs suspīciōnēs vītāre dēbēmus? 4. Nōn sine causā hostēs timuimus. 5. Vōbīs omnia dēbeō. 6. Aeduī populō Rōmānō multum dēbēbant. 7. Id Caesarī nūntiāre dēbēmus. 8. Nostra oppida expūgnāre nōn dēbētis. 9. Centuriōnēs māgnum in castrīs ūsum habēbant. 10. Nōnne māgnum in rē mīlitārī ūsum habēbās? Nōn māgnum in rē mīlitārī ūsum habēbam. 11. Caesar Divitiacum fīdum semper habēbat. 12. Vōs fīdōs semper habēbimus. 13. Nōnne mē fīdum habēs? Tē fīdum habeō.

14. Caesar Dumnorigem ad sē vocāvit; monuit ut in reliquum tempus omnēs suspīciōnēs vītāret. 15. Vōs moneō ut in reliquum tempus hās suspīciōnēs vītētis. 16. Ariovistus Caesarem nōn prō amīcō,[1] sed prō hoste habēbit. 17. Tē prō amīcō semper habuī. 18. Num mē prō hoste habētis? Tē nōn prō hoste sed prō amīcō habēmus. 19. Impetum

---
[1] Render prō as, 'it. *for.*

hostium fortiter sustinuerāmus. 20. Hostēs ab extrēmō agmine[1] fortiter impetum nostrōrum mīlitum sustinēbant. 21. Quōs aliquamdiū inermōs sine causā timuerāmus, hōs posteā armātōs superāvimus.

180. *Translate into Latin.*

1. At that time the Gauls feared the Germans, who dwelt beyond (*across*) the Rhine. 2. Nearly all the Gauls feared Ariovistus, the king of the Germans. 3. Shall you, who have large experience in military affairs, fear the Gauls? We have not large experience in military affairs, but we do not fear this army. 4. These boys owe much to their father. 5. We all owe much to our fathers. 6. Ought we not to attack that town? We ought to take it by storm. 7. Our soldiers always withstand the attacks of the enemy.

8. We shall always regard you all as our friends.[3] 9. Caesar regarded the Germans not as friends, but as enemies. 10. Do you not regard your general as faithful? We all regard him as faithful. 11. Whom do these boys regard as faithful? They regard you as faithful. 12. Did I not warn you not to announce these things to the Germans?[2] You warned us not to announce your plans to the enemy. 13. Did you not fear Ariovistus at that time? I feared him, and regarded him as an enemy.

LESSON LXI.

SECOND CONJUGATION. — ACTIVE VOICE IN FULL.

181. *Lesson from the Grammar.*

In the verb *Moneō*, learn the Active voice in full. See the following page.

---

[1] Render *ab*, ON, lit. *from*. See note on *ab ūnā parte*, 173.

[2] Not to announce = that you should not announce, *nē* with Subjunctive; 119, 497. [3] *As our friends;* Latin idiom, FOR *our friends.*

SECOND CONJUGATION: E VERBS.

207. ACTIVE VOICE.—Moneŏ, *I advise.*

VERB STEM, mon, moni; PRESENT STEM, monē.

PRINCIPAL PARTS.

PRES. IND.	PRES. INF.	PERF. IND.	SUPINE.
moneō,	monēre,	monuī,	monitum.

INDICATIVE MOOD.

PRESENT TENSE.
I advise.

SINGULAR.	PLURAL.
moneō	monēmus
monēs	monētis
monet	monent

IMPERFECT.
I was advising, or *I advised.*

monēbam	monēbāmus
monēbās	monēbātis
monēbat	monēbant

FUTURE.
I shall or *will advise.*

monēbō	monēbimus
monēbis	monēbitis
monēbit	monēbunt

PERFECT.
I have advised, or *I advised.*

monuī	monuimus
monuistī	monuistis
monuit	monuērunt, *or* ēre

PLUPERFECT.
I had advised.

monueram	monuerāmus
monuerās	monuerātis
monuerat	monuerant

FUTURE PERFECT.
I shall or *will have advised.*

monuerō	monuerimus
monueris	monueritis
monuerit	monuerint

ACTIVE VOICE.

SUBJUNCTIVE.

PRESENT.
May I advise, let him advise.[1]

SINGULAR.	PLURAL.
moneam	moneāmus
moneās	moneātis
moneat	moneant

IMPERFECT.
I should advise, he would advise.

monērem	monērēmus
monērēs	monērētis
monēret	monērent

PERFECT.
I may have advised, or *I have advised.*[1]

monuerim	monuerīmus
monueris	monuerītis
monuerit	monuerint

PLUPERFECT.
I should have advised, he would have advised.[2]

monuissem	monuissēmus
monuissēs	monuissētis
monuisset	monuissent

IMPERATIVE.

Pres.	monē,	*advise thou;*	monēte,	*advise ye.*
Fut.	monētō,	*thou shalt advise,*	monētōte,	*ye shall advise,*
	monētō,	*he shall advise;*	monentō,	*they shall advise.*

INFINITIVE.
Pres.	monēre,	*to advise.*
Perf.	monuisse,	*to have advised.*
Fut.	monitūrus esse,	*to be about to advise.*

PARTICIPLE.
Pres.	monēns,	*advising.*
Fut.	monitūrus,	*about to advise.*

GERUND.
Gen.	monendī,	*of advising,*
Dat.	monendō,	*for advising,*
Acc.	monendum,	*advising,*
Abl.	monendō,	*by advising.*

SUPINE.
Acc.	monitum,	*to advise,*
Abl.	monitū,	*to advise, be advised.*

---

[1] But on the translation of the Subjunctive, see 111, 196.
[2] The Pluperfect, like the Perfect, is often rendered by the Indicative: *I had advised, you had advised,* etc.

LESSON LXII.

SECOND CONJUGATION. — ACTIVE VOICE. — EXERCISES.

182. *Vocabulary.*

Memoria, ae, *f.*	*memory, recollection.*
Novus, a, um,	*new;* novae res, *new things, a change*
Pareō, ēre, uī, itum,	*to obey.* [*of affairs, revolution.*
Pristinus, a, um,	*ancient, pristine.*
Retineō, ēre, tinuī, tentum,	*to retain, keep.*
Studeō, ēre, uī,	*to desire.*
Studium, iī, *n.*	*desire.*
Taceō, ēre, ui, itum,	*to be silent, keep silent, remain silent.*
Teneō, ēre, uī, tentum,	*to hold, keep.*

183. *Translate into English.*

1. Nē hostēs sine causā timeāmus. 2. Germānōs timēre nōn dēbēmus. 3. Hōs agrōs armīs teneāmus. 4. Mīlitēs dīcēbant sē hostēs nōn timēre.[1] 5. Hic centuriō dīcit sē hostēs nōn timuisse.[1] 6. Hostium impetum fortiter sustineāmus. 7. Eās rēs memoriā[2] teneāmus. 8. Nōnne eās rēs memoriā tenēre dēbēmus? 9. Mīlitēs suae pristinae virtūtis memoriam retineant. 10. Nostrae pristinae virtūtis memoriam retineāmus. 11. Tuae pristinae virtūtis memoriam retinēre dēbēs.

12. Vestrae pristinae virtūtis memoriam retinēte, hostiumque impetum fortiter sustinēte. 13. Dīcunt Caesarem ūnam legiōnem sēcum[3] habuisse.[1] 14. Dīcunt tē magnum amīcōrum numerum habuisse.[1] 15. Dīcunt tē magnum amīcōrum numerum habitūrum esse.[1] 16. Dīcunt vōs magnum amīcōrum numerum habitūrōs esse.[1] 17. Amīcōs habēns; cōnsul amīcōs habēns; amīcōs habitūrus; cōnsulēs amīcōs habitūrī. 18. Ob eās causās Dumnorix novīs rēbus[4] studēbat. 19. Monendō, timendō, tenendī, causa tenendī, studium habendī.

---

[1] See Suggestion XVIII., 1.
[2] *Memoriā*, literally, BY *the memory*, Ablative of *Means*; render IN *memory*.
[3] See 102, 134, 6.   [4] See 54, Rule XII.

20. Omnēs ferē Gallī novīs rēbus student et ad bellum celeriter excitantur; omnēs autem hominēs lībertātī student.

184. *Translate into Latin.*

1. We shall always retain the recollection of these things. 2. May you ever retain the recollection of this day. 3. The consul says that he shall always retain the recollection of your friendship. 4. For what reason did the Gauls desire a revolution at that time? 5. Does not Caesar say that the Gauls always desire a revolution? He says that all men desire liberty. 6. Let us obey all the laws, and let us not desire a revolution. 7. Obeying, about to obey; obeying the laws, about to obey the laws; by obeying[1] the laws,[2] of obeying the laws, the desire of obeying the laws.

8. By being silent[1] you avoided suspicion of fear. 9. Let us not fear the Germans without cause. 10. We ought not to regard them as enemies without cause. 11. Would that they had not feared[3] us without cause. 12. How many legions will our commander have with him in Italy? They say that he will have five legions with him. 13. The general says that he shall always regard us as his friends. 14. So great fear took possession of the Romans, that they did not retain[4] the recollection of their ancient courage.

LESSON LXIII.

FIRST AND SECOND CONJUGATIONS. — ACTIVE VOICE. — RULE XXX.

185. *Examples.* — *Place in which.*

1. In nostrīs *castrīs* fuit.	*He was in our* CAMP.
2. *Rōmae* fuit.	*He was* AT ROME.

---

[1] Use the Ablative of the Gerund, as *Ablative of Means.*
[2] Remember that the Gerund governs the same case as other parts of the verb.
[3] For Mood and Tense, see 114, 483, 2.   [4] See 123, 500, II.

PLACE IN WHICH.

NOTE.—The Latin usage illustrated in the Locative Ablative *castris*, and in the Locative *Rōmae*, is expressed in the following

RULE XXX.—Place in which.

425. The PLACE IN WHICH is denoted —

I. Generally by the *Locative Ablative*[1] *with the preposition* in:

Hannibal *in* Italiā fuit, *Hannibal was* IN ITALY. Nep. In nostris castris, *in our camp.* Caes. In Appiā viā, *on the Appian way.* Cic.

II. In NAMES OF TOWNS by the *Locative*,[2] if such a form exists, otherwise by the *Locative Ablative:*

Rōmae fuit, *he was* AT ROME. Cic. Corinthī puerōs docēbat, *he taught boys* AT CORINTH. Cic. Athēnis fuit, *he was* AT ATHENS. Cic.

1. In the names of places which are not towns, the LOCATIVE ABLATIVE is often used without a preposition, when the idea of *means, manner,* or *cause* is combined with that of *place*:

Castris sē tenuit, *he kept himself* IN CAMP. Caes. Aliquem *tectō* recipere, *to receive any one* IN ONE'S OWN HOUSE. Cic. Proeliō cadere, *to fall* IN BATTLE. Caes.

2. The Ablatives *locō, locīs, parte, partibus, dextrā, laevā, sinistrā, terrā,* and *mari,* especially when qualified by an adjective, and other Ablatives, when qualified by *tōtus*, are generally used without the preposition:

Aliquid *locō* pōnere, *to put anything* IN ITS PLACE. Cic. Terrā marīque, *on land and sea.* Liv. Tōtā Graeciā, *in all Greece.* Nep.

426. LIKE NAMES OF TOWNS are used —

1. Many NAMES OF ISLANDS :

Lesbī vixit, *he lived in Lesbos.* Nep. Conōn Cyprī vixit, *Conon lived in Cyprus.* Nep.

2. The LOCATIVES **domī, rūrī, humī, militiae,** and **bellī**:

Domī militiaeque, *at home and in the field.* Cic. Rūrī agere vitam, *to spend life in the country.* Liv.

---

[1] The *Locative Ablative* does not differ in *form* from any other Ablative. It is simply the *Ablative* used with the force of the original *Locative*, i.e. to designate the *place* of the action.

[2] See 11, 48, 4; 32, 51, 8; 63, 66, 4. The Locative was the original construction in all names of places.

186. Vocabulary.

Agedincum, i, n.	*Agedincum*, a town of the Senones in central Gaul.
Alesia, ae, f.	*Alesia*, a town in central Gaul.
Apertus, a, um,	*open.*
Avus, i, m.	*grandfather.*
Bibrax, actis, n.	*Bibrax*, a town of the Remi.
Contineō, ēre, tinui, tentum,	*to retain, keep, confine, restrain; to enclose, surround.*
Dēsignō, āre, avī, ātum,	*to designate, indicate.*
Dēterreō, ēre, ui, itum,	*to deter.*
Difficultās, ātis, f.	*difficulty.*
Domus, ūs, f.	*house, home;* domī, *at home.*
Genāva, ae, f.	*Geneva.*
Improbus, a, um,	*wicked, unprincipled.*
Karthāgō, inis, f.	*Carthage.*
Largiter, adv.	*largely, widely, extensively;* largiter potest, *he has extensive influence.*
Mare, is, n.	*sea.*
Multitūdō, inis, f.	*multitude; the multitude, common people.*
Obtineō, ēre, tinuī, tentum,	*to obtain, hold.*
Sēditiōsus, a, um,	*seditious.*
Servitūs, ūtis, f.	*servitude, slavery.*
Sōlum, adv.	*only.*
Vir, virī, m.	*man.*

187. *Translate into English.*

1. Caesar eō tempore in citeriōre Galliā erat. 2. Eōdem tempore exercitus noster in Galliā hiemābat. 3. Dīcunt imperātōrem in Galliā in hībernīs fuisse. 4. Germānī Aeduōs in servitūte tenēre nōn dēbent. 5. Ariovistus, rēx Germānōrum, eō diē exercitum castrīs[1] continuit. 6. Apertō marī[2] tempestātēs timēbāmus. 7. Summa erat apertō marī difficultās nāvigandī.[3] 8. Allobrogēs lēgātōs ad senātum mīsērunt rogātum auxilium. 9. Dumnorix māgnum numerum equitātūs habēbat.

---

[1] *Ablative of Place*, involving the idea of *Means*.
[2] See 185, 425, II., 2.
[3] *Nāvigandī*, Genitive of the Gerund, depending upon *difficultās*. Observe that the Genitive of the Gerund is here treated as any other Genitive would be treated in the same situation. See 28, Rule XVI.

10. Liscus dīcit Dumnorigem, Divitiacī frātrem, māgnum numerum equitātūs semper circum sē habēre. Is nōn sōlum domī,¹ sed etiam apud fīnitimās cīvitātēs largiter poterat.²
11. Caesar duās legiōnēs Agedincī¹ collocāverat. Ipse Bibracte hiemāre cōnstituit. 12. Cōnsul eō tempore Rōmae¹ erat. 13. Timor hostēs Alesiae occupāvit. 14. Avus hūjus Gallī, virī fortissimī, amīcus ab senātū nostrō appellātus erat. 15. Avus hūjus Gallī in cīvitāte suā rēgnum obtinuerat, amīcus ab senātū nostrō appellātus. 16. Dīcunt hāc ōrātiōne Dumnorigem dēsīgnātum esse. 17. Sēditiōsā atque improbā ōrātiōne multitūdinem dēterrētis nē frūmentum comportent.³

188. *Translate into Latin.*

1. They say that you have been in Italy. We were in winter quarters in Italy. 2. Ought we not to place our army in winter quarters in Gaul? The army ought to be placed in winter quarters in the vicinity of (*around*) Geneva. The general has already decided to station three legions at Geneva.⁴ 3. Ariovistus, the king of the Germans, was not at home,⁴ but was laying waste the lands of the Gauls. 4. Messengers announced that the consul at that time was at Carthage.

5. You ought not to hold the deserters in servitude. We shall keep them in camp.⁵ 6. How many Gauls did Ariovistus hold in servitude? They announced that Ariovistus always held a very large number of Gauls in servitude. 7. Was Caesar at that time in Italy, or in Gaul?⁶ He was at Rome, and he had with him a large number of friends. 8. Was there not at Geneva a bridge across the Rhone?⁷ Caesar says that at Geneva there was a bridge across the Rhone.

---

¹ See 185, 425, 426, II.
² *Largiter poterat*, literally, *was largely able;* render, *was very powerful*, or *had great influence.* ³ See 119, 497, II.
⁴ What *Case* will you use in rendering *at Geneva, at home?* See 185, 425; 426, 2.
⁵ In camp; see 185, 425, 1.   ⁶ For Double Question, see 106, 353.
⁷ *Across the Rhone;* Latin idiom, IN the Rhone.

LESSON LXIV.

SECOND CONJUGATION. — INDICATIVE PASSIVE. — RULE IV. — REVIEW OF RULES I., II., AND III.

189. *Lesson from the Grammar.*

In the verb *Moneō*, learn the Indicative Mood of the Passive voice. See page 154.

190. *Examples. — Vocative.*

1. Tuum est, *Servi,* regnum.   *The kingdom is yours,* SERVIUS.
2. Quid est, *Catilina?*   *Why is it,* CATILINE?

NOTE. — In these examples the names of the persons addressed, *Servi* and *Catilina,* are in the Vocative, in accordance with the Latin usage expressed in the following

RULE IV. — Case of Address.

369. The name of the person or thing addressed is put in the Vocative:

Perge, *Laeli, proceed,* LAELIUS. Cic.   Quid est, *Catilina? Why is it,* CATILINE? Cic.   Ō *dii* immortālēs, *O immortal* GODS. Cic.

LESSON LXV.

SECOND CONJUGATION. — INDICATIVE PASSIVE. — RULE IV. — REVIEW OF RULES I., II., AND III. — EXERCISES.

191. *Vocabulary.*

Alter, era, erum, 45, 151.	*other (of two), second.*
Anteā, *adv.*	*before.*
Ascendit,	*he ascends.*
Bellicōsus, a, um,	*warlike.*
Clāmor, ōris, *m.*	*shout.*
Cōnsultō, āre, āvī, ātum,	*to consult.*
Dēmum, *adv.*	*at length.*
Dētineō, ēre, tinuī, tentum,	*to detain.*
Ferus, a, um,	*fierce, savage.*

SECOND CONJUGATION.

Impendeō, ēre,	to overhang.
Inter, prep. w. acc.	among.
Jubeō, ēre, jussi, jussum,	to order. [Gaul.
Jūra, ae, m.	Jura, a mountain range in eastern
Lūx, lūcis, f.	light; prima lūx, the beginning of light, daybreak, early dawn.[1]
Mūnītiō, ōnis, f.	fortification.
Nervii, ōrum, m. pl.	the Nervii, a tribe of northern Gaul.
Obsideō, ēre, sēdi, sessum,	to besiege.
Salūs, ūtis, f.	safety.
Sapienter, adv.	wisely. [powerful German tribe.
Suēbi, ōrum, m. pl.	the Suebi, Suevi, or Suabians, a
Summus, a, um, sup. of superus,	highest; highest part of, top of.[1]
Terreō, ēre, ui, itum,	to terrify.

192. *Translate into English.*

1. Nōnne ab amīcīs monitī estis? Ā vōbīs, amīcī, monitī sumus. 2. Nunc, mīlitēs, sapienter monēmur. 3. Prīmā lūce summus mōns ā Labiēnō tenēbātur. 4. Nōnne hōc oppidum ab hostibus tenētur? Ab hostibus tenētur. 5. Vīcus quī appellātur Octōdūrus altissimīs montibus[2] continētur. 6. Montēs quī impendēbant ā maximā multitūdine hostium tenēbantur. 7. Nerviī maximē ferī inter Belgās habentur. 8. Helvētiī undique locī nātūrā continentur, ūnā ex parte flūmine Rhēnō, alterā ex parte monte[2] Jūrā. 9. Omnēs hostium impetūs fortiter sustinēbantur.

10. Hostēs quī Alesiae obsidēbantur dē salūte cōnsultābant. 11. Iī quī mūnītiōnibus continentur clāmōre suōrum animōs cōnfirmābant. 12. Suēbōrum gēns est longē maxima et bellicōsissima Germānōrum omnium. 13. Rōmānae nāvēs tempestātibus dētinēbantur. 14. Caesar Labiēnum cum duābus legiōnibus montem ascendere jubet. 15. Caesar prīncipēs convocāvit, in hīs Liscum,[3] magistrātum quī Ver-

---

[1] Certain adjectives often designate a PARTICULAR PART of an object: *prima nox*, 'the first part of the night;' *mediā aestāte*, 'in the middle of summer:' *summus mōns*, 'the top (highest part) of the mountain.' The adjectives thus used are *primus, medius, ultimus, extrēmus, postrēmus, intimus, summus, infimus, imus, suprēmus, reliquus, cētera*, etc.

[2] Ablative of *Means*. [3] Object of *convocāvit*.

gobretus appellātur. 16. Tum dēmum, quod anteā tacueram, ēnūntiāvī.

193. *Translate into Latin.*

1. Many Gauls were held in slavery by Ariovistus, the king of the Germans. 2. On that day the Germans were kept in camp by their commander. 3. Brave soldiers, you have been kept in camp by your commander. 4. Judges, you have been regarded by Caesar as friends.[1] 5. Galba, the lieutenant, was ordered to winter in a village which is called Octodurus. 6. You will always be regarded by us as friends. 7. This mountain was held on that day by the Romans. 8. Was not Labienus, the lieutenant, commanded by Caesar to ascend this mountain? He was commanded to ascend this mountain, and to hold it.

9. The difficulty of navigation[2] on the open sea is great, and our vessels will be detained by the storms. 10. Was not Dumnorix, the brother of Divitiacus, warned by Caesar? He was warned by Caesar to avoid all suspicion in future. 11. We have been warned not to attack this town, on account of the width of the moat and the height of the wall. 12. We have been ordered to fortify our camp with a rampart. 13. The Suebi were regarded by the Romans as very warlike.

LESSON LXVI.

SECOND CONJUGATION. — PASSIVE VOICE IN FULL. — REVIEW OF RULES XXXVII., XXXVIII, AND XL.

194. *Lesson from the Grammar.*

In the verb *Moneō*, learn the Passive voice in full. See the following page.

---

[1] Remember the Latin idiom, FOR *friends*.
[2] Use the *Gerund*.

SECOND CONJUGATION: E VERBS.

208. PASSIVE VOICE.—Moneor, *I am advised.*

VERB STEM, *mon, moni;* PRESENT STEM, *monē.*

PRINCIPAL PARTS.

PRES. IND.	PRES. INF.	PERF. IND.
moneor,	monērī,	monitus sum.

INDICATIVE MOOD.

PRESENT TENSE.
I am advised.

SINGULAR.	PLURAL.
moneor	monēmur
monēris, *or* re	monēminī
monētur	monentur

IMPERFECT.
I was advised.

monēbar	monēbāmur
monēbāris, *or* re	monēbāminī
monēbātur	monēbantur

FUTURE.
I shall or will be advised.

monēbor	monēbimur
monēberis, *or* re	monēbiminī
monēbitur	monēbuntur

PERFECT.
I have been advised, I was advised.

monitus sum[1]	monitī sumus
monitus es	monitī estis
monitus est	monitī sunt

PLUPERFECT.
I had been advised.

monitus eram[1]	monitī erāmus
monitus erās	monitī erātis
monitus erat	monitī erant

FUTURE PERFECT.
I shall or will have been advised.

monitus erō[1]	monitī erimus
monitus eris	monitī eritis
monitus erit	monitī erunt

---

[1] See 170, 206, foot-notes.

PASSIVE VOICE.

SUBJUNCTIVE.

PRESENT.
May I be advised, let him be advised.

SINGULAR.	PLURAL.
monear	moneāmur
moneāris, *or* re	moneāminī
moneātur	moneantur

IMPERFECT.
I should be advised, he would be advised.

monērer	monērēmur
monērēris, *or* re	monērēminī
monērētur	monērentur

PERFECT.
I may have been advised, or *I have been advised.*

monitus sim[1]	monitī sīmus
monitus sīs	monitī sītis
monitus sit	monitī sint

PLUPERFECT.
I should have been advised, he would have been advised.[2]

monitus essem[1]	monitī essēmus
monitus essēs	monitī essētis
monitus esset	monitī essent

IMPERATIVE.

Pres. monēre, *be thou advised;* | monēminī, *be ye advised.*
Fut. monētor, *thou shalt be advised,*
monētor, *he shall be advised;* | monentor, *they shall be advised.*

INFINITIVE.	PARTICIPLE.
Pres. monērī, *to be advised.*	
Perf. monitus esse,[1] *to have been advised.*	*Perf.* monitus, *advised.*
Fut. monitum īrī, *to be about to be advised.*	*Ger.* monendus, *to be advised, deserving to be advised.*

---

[1] See 177, 206, foot-notes.
[2] Or *I had been advised, you had been advised,* etc.

LESSON LXVII.

SECOND CONJUGATION. — PASSIVE VOICE. — REVIEW OF RULES XXXVII., XXXVIII., AND XL. — EXERCISES.

195. *Vocabulary.*

Amor, ōris, *m.*	love.
Annuus, a, um,	annual, annually, for a year.
Auctōritās, ātis, *f.*	authority, influence.
Cōnsidius, ii, *m.*	Considius, an officer in Caesar's
Creō, āre, āvi, ātum,	to create, appoint, elect. [army.
Falsus, a, um,	false.
Imperitus, a, um,	unskilful, ignorant.
Mors, mortis, *f.*	death.
Nex, necis, *f.*	death, putting to death.
Nōnnūllī, ae, a, *pl.*	some.
Perterreō, ēre, ui, itum,	to terrify greatly, terrify, frighten.
Plūs, *comp. adv., pos.* multum,	more.
Potestās, ātis, *f.*	power.
Pūblius, ii, *m.*	Publius, a Roman praenōmen.
Renūntiō, āre, āvi, ātum,	to report.
Rūmor, ōris, *m.*	rumor, report.
Sēsē,	reduplicated form of sē. See
Temerārius, a, um,	rash. [102, 184, 4.
Valeō, ēre, ui, itum,	to avail, prevail.

196. *Translate into English.*

1. Omnēs collēs ā nōbīs tenentur. 2. Omnia loca superiōra ā nōbīs tenēbuntur. 3. Omnēs collēs ac loca superiōra ab exercitū tenēbantur. 4. Nē falsīs rūmōribus terreāmur. 5. Nē hīs rūmōribus terreantur. 6. Utinam omnēs hostēs hōc rūmōre terreantur. 7. Dīcunt vōs hīs rūmōribus terrērī. 8. Hominēs temerāriī atque imperītī saepe falsīs rūmōribus terrentur. 9. Imperātor dīcit hominēs temerāriōs atque imperītōs saepe falsīs rūmōribus terrērī. 10. Pūblius Cōnsidius timōre perterritus renūntiāvit montem ab hostibus tenērī. 11. Sunt nōnnūllī quī multitūdinem dēterrent nē frūmentum comportent.

12. Nōnnūllī prīncipēs adventū nostrī exercitūs perterritī erant. Iī prīncipēs, adventū nostrī exercitūs perterritī, lēgātōs ad Caesarem mittēbant. 13. Liscus in conventū dīxit sēsē ob eam causam diū tacuisse. 14. Nōn is sum quī gravissimē mortis perīculō terrear.¹ 15. Mīlitēs mortis perīculō terrērī nōn dēbent. 16. Vergobretus, quī creātur annuus, vītae necisque in suōs² habet potestātem. 17. Auctōritās Dumnorigis apud plēbem plūs valēbat quam ipsīus magistrātūs.³

197. *Translate into Latin.*

1. Have not your vessels been detained by storms? Messengers have announced to us that our vessels have been detained by storms. 2. May we always be regarded by you as friends. 3. They say that the Aedui were always regarded by Caesar as friends. 4. Many towns were besieged by the Germans. 5. Messengers announce that many towns have been besieged by the Germans. Let us ascertain which towns have been besieged by them. 6. We are advised by our friends, who have large experience in military affairs, to remain (*keep ourselves*)⁴ in camp. 7. The ambassadors were so terrified that they remained silent for a long time.

8. You ought not to be terrified by these rumors. 9. Would that we had not been terrified by false rumors. 10. Were not the Gauls often terrified by false rumors? Caesar said that the Gauls were often terrified by false rumors. 11. By what rumors, my brave soldiers, have you been terrified? 12. With (*among*) you, Romans, the love of country ought to avail more than the fear of death. 13. Announce to the

---

¹ Subjunctive in a clause denoting Result. See 123, 500, I.; Suggestion XVII., 3.

² In *suōs*, literally *into* or *against his own*, render OVER or AMONG *his subjects*, or *his countrymen*. Adjectives in the plural are often used substantively in Latin, as in English. *Suōs* is thus used.

³ Governed by *auctōritās* understood.

⁴ For Mood, see 119, Rule XLII.

general that this mountain is held by us. 14. Let us hold the mountain which we were ordered to occupy.

LESSON LXVIII.

FIRST AND SECOND CONJUGATIONS. — PASSIVE VOICE IN FULL. — REVIEW OF RULES XLI., XLII., AND XLIII.

198. *Vocabulary.*

Adequitō, āre, āvī, ātum,	*to ride toward, ride.*
Alius, a, ud, 45, 151,	*other, another.*
Cōnservō, āre, āvī, ātum,	*to save, preserve, spare.*
Gubernātor, ōris, *m.*	*pilot.*
Impetrō, āre, āvī, ātum,	*to obtain one's request.*
Liger, is, *m.*	*the Liger, now the Loire, a river in southwestern Gaul.*
Lingonēs, um, *m. pl.*	*the Lingones, a tribe of central Gaul.*
Nauta, ae, *m.*	*sailor.*
Nāvis longa,	*a long ship, ship of war.*
Nēve, *conj.*	*nor, and not.*
Sed, *conj.*	*but.*
Triplex, icis,	*triple.*
Undique, *adv.*	*on every side.*

199. *Translate into English.*

1. Vīcus appellābātur Octōdūrus. 2. Dīcunt vīcum appellātum esse Octōdūrum. 3. Dīcēbant hunc vīcum altissimīs montibus undique continērī. 4. Nē ad bellum celeriter excitēmur. 5. Caesar dīcit omnēs ferē Gallōs novīs rēbus studēre et ad bellum celeriter excitārī. 6. Dīxērunt sē tibī rem ēnūntiāsse,[1] sed intellegere quantō cum perīculō eam rem ēnūntiāssent.[1] 7. Caesar ad Lingonēs litterās nūntiōsque mīsit nē Helvētiōs frūmentō nēve aliā rē juvārent. 8. Dīcunt eam rem per fugitīvōs hostibus nūntiātam esse. 9. Tum dēmum Caesar partem suārum cōpiārum quae castra

---

[1] Contracted from *ēnūntiāvisse* and *ēnūntiāvissent.*

FIRST AND SECOND CONJUGATIONS. 159

hostium oppūgnāret¹ mīsit. 10. Triplicem aciem prō castrīs īnstruēbat.

11. Gallī lēgātōs ad Caesarem dē dēditiōne mīsērunt, et impetrāvērunt ut cōnservārentur.² 12. Nē montēs quī vīcō Octōdūrō impendent ab hostibus teneantur. 13. Nāvēs longae in flūmine Ligere aedificentur. 14. Caesar nāvēs longās in flūmine Ligere aedificārī jubet. 15. Nautae gubernātōrēsque ex prōvinciā nostrā comparentur. 16. Caesar nautās gubernātōrēsque ex prōvinciā nostrā comparārī jubet. 17. Caesarī nūntiātum est³ equitēs Ariovistī ad nostrōs adequitāre.

200. *Translate into Latin.*

1. The village in which Galba wintered was surrounded by very high mountains. Did he understand with how great peril he was wintering in that village? He understood that he was wintering there with great peril. 2. Horsemen rode toward us to announce the words of the king. 3. The Aedui were so terrified, that they sent messengers to Caesar to implore help. 4. The general sent a part of his forces to fortify the town. 5. Caesar sent a lieutenant to order ships of war to be built. 6. Ten ships of war have been built on the Rhine. 7. The deserters obtained their request, not to be regarded (*that they might not be regarded*) as enemies.

8. Those who were ordered to withstand the attack of the enemy were so terrified, that they implored help from Caesar. 9. May our authority avail more with you than that⁴ of our enemies. 10. The messengers said that their towns had been besieged by the enemy. 11. Brave soldiers will not be terrified by the fear of death. 12. The general says that his

---

¹ For *Mood*, see 119, 497, I.; see also Suggestion XVII., 3.

² *Ut cōnservārentur.* This is an *Object Clause*, depending upon *impetrārērunt*, but it was developed out of a *Clause of Result*, and accordingly has the *Subjunctive*.

³ The *Subject* of *nūntiātum est* is the clause *equitēs . . . adequitāre.* See Suggestion XVIII., 1.

⁴ Omit the pronoun in rendering into Latin.

soldiers are so brave that they are not terrified by the fear of death. 13. May that city always be held by our friends. 14. Would that these towns were held by our friends.

LESSON LXIX.

FIRST AND SECOND CONJUGATIONS IN FULL. — EXERCISE IN READING AT SIGHT.

201. *Read at Sight, examine carefully, and translate into English.*[1]

Caesar convocāvit prīncipēs, quōrum māgnam cōpiam in castrīs habēbat, in hīs Liscum, magistrātum Aeduōrum. Hīc magistrātus, quī Vergobretus appellātur, creātur annuus, et vītae necisque in suōs habet potestātem.

Caesar prīncipēs Aeduōrum graviter accusāvit. Tum dēmum Liscus, quod anteā tacuerat, ēnūntiāvit. Haec sunt verba: "Sunt nōnnūllī, quōrum auctōritās apud plēbem plūs valet quam ipsōrum magistrātuum. Hī sēditiōsā atque improbā ōrātiōne multitūdinem dēterrent nē frūmentum comportent. Ab iīsdem vestra cōnsilia hostibus ēnūntiantur." Posteā dīxit intellegere sēsē quantō cum perīculō Caesarī rem ēnūntiāsset, et ob eam causam diū tacuisse.

Hāc ōrātiōne Dumnorix, Divitiacī frāter, dēsīgnātus est. Is māgnum numerum equitātūs semper circum sē habēbat, et nōn sōlum domī, sed etiam apud fīnitimās cīvitātēs, largiter poterat.

202. *Translate into Latin.*

1. Liscus said that with the populace the authority of these citizens availed more, than that of the magistrate himself, and that they deterred the multitude from bringing (*that they should not bring*) grain. He also said that they announced to the enemy nearly all the plans of the Romans.

---

[1] See Directions for Reading at Sight, 137.

2. Who was Dumnorix? He was an Aeduan chief, the brother of Divitiacus, who was called the friend of Caesar and the Roman people.

3. So great fear took possession of the Aedui, whose lands the Helvetii were devastating, that they sent ambassadors to Caesar to implore aid from him. 4. The general ought to lead his army through the lands (*fields*) of the Aedui into the territory of the Santones, who are not far from our province. 5. The general is hastening with forced marches into Italy; he will there enrol three legions, and lead out of winter quarters the five that are now wintering in the vicinity of Rome.

LESSON LXX.

THIRD CONJUGATION. — INDICATIVE ACTIVE. — REVIEW OF RULES V., VI., AND IX.

203. *Lesson from the Grammar.*

In the verb *Regō*, learn the Indicative Mood of the Active Voice. See page 164.

204. *Vocabulary.*

Auxilia, ōrum, n. pl.	*auxiliaries.*
Conscrībō, ere, scripsi, scriptum,	*to enrol, enlist.* [decide.
Constĭtuō, ere, stĭtui, stĭtūtum,	*to station, place; to determine,*
Continuus, a, um,	*continuous, successive.*
Dēlīberō, āre, āvī, ātum,	*to deliberate.*
Dīcō, ere, dīxī, dictum,	*to say, speak.*
Ēdūcō, ere, dūxī, ductum,	*to lead out.*
Hiems, emis, f.	*winter.*
Instruō, ere, strūxī, strūctum,	*to draw up, arrange, array.*
Interim, adv.	*meanwhile, in the meantime.*
Item, adv.	*also, likewise.*
Jugum, i, n.	*ridge, height.*
Mănĕō, ēre, mānsī, mānsum,	*to remain.*
Medius, a, um,	*middle; the middle of.*[1]

---

[1] See foot-note on *summus*, 191.

Mittō, ere, misi, missum,	to send.
Prōdūcō, ere, dūxi, ductum,	to lead forth.
Proximē, sup. adv.	nearest, most recently, last.
Quattuor, indeclinable,	four.
Redūcō, ere, dūxi, ductum,	to lead back.
Sextus, a, um,	sixth.
Subdūcō, ere, dūxi, ductum,	to withdraw, lead off.
Sūmō, ere, sūmpsi, sūmptum,	to take.
Veterānus, a, um,	veteran.

205. *Translate into English.*

1. Caesar diem ad dēlīberandum¹ sūmpsit. 2. Nōnne diem ad dēlīberandum sūmētis? Diem ad dēlīberandum sūmpsimus. 3. Hostēs diem ad dēlīberandum sūmpserant. 4. Quīnque legiōnēs quae sustineant² hostium impetum mittōmus. 5. Caesar copiās suās in prŏximum collem subdūxerat, equitātumque quī sustinēret² hostium impetum mīserat. Ipse interim in colle mediō³ aciem instrūxit legiōnum quattuor veterānārum, sed in summō³ jugō duās legiōnēs, quās in Galliā citeriōre prŏximē cōnscrīpserat, et omnia auxilia collocāvit. 6. Nōnne haec in conventū dīxistī? Ea quae in conventū dīxī sunt vēra. 7. Quid Liscus dīxerat? Liscus in conventū dīxerat Dumnorigem, Divitiaci frātrem, novīs rēbus studēre.

8. Imperātor sōlis occāsū⁴ suās cōpiās in castra redūcet. 9. Caesar ex eō diē diēs⁵ continuōs quīnque prō castrīs suās cōpiās prōdūxit et aciem instrūxit. 10. Ipse cōnstituerat in Galliā hiemāre et tōtam hiemem ad⁶ exercitum manēre. 11. Caesar sex legiōnēs prō castrīs in aciē cōnstituit. Hostēs item suās cōpiās ex castrīs ēdūxerant. 12. Nōnne dīxistī

---

¹ *Ad dēliberandum,* 'for deliberation,' or 'to deliberate.' *Dēliberandum* is a *Gerund* in the *Accusative* depending upon *ad.* In Gerunds the *Accusative* always depends upon a *preposition.*

² See Suggestion XVII., 3

³ See foot-note on *summus,* 191.

⁴ *Ablative of Time.* See 93. Rule XXXI.

⁵ *Duration of Time.* See 98, Rule IX.

⁶ *Near, in the vicinity of.*

Aeduōs ā senātū populī Rōmānī amīcōs appellātōs esse?
Dīxī eōs ā senātū frātrēs appellātōs esse.

206. *Translate into Latin.*

1. What did you say in the convention? I said that nearly all the Gauls at that time desired a revolution. 2. Shall you not send ambassadors to the neighboring states to implore aid from them? We have already sent ambassadors to these states, and have established peace and friendship with them. 3. How many legions shall you enrol in Italy? We shall enrol five legions in Italy, and three in Gaul. 4. The general had placed his legions in line of battle before the camp. 5. Have you taken time for[1] deliberation? We have taken time for deliberation, and have decided to send ambassadors to the Belgae.

6. The enemy kept themselves in camp for five days,[2] but on the sixth day they led their forces out of the camp, and placed them in line of battle. 7. Caesar placed in winter quarters the legions that he had enrolled in Italy. 8. Have you decided to pass the winter in Italy? We have decided to remain in Gaul during the whole winter. 9. For many days the Romans had formed the line of battle in front of the camp. 10. Caesar says that he remained near the army the whole winter.

LESSON LXXI.

THIRD CONJUGATION. — ACTIVE VOICE IN FULL.

207. *Lesson from the Grammar.*

In the verb *Regō*, learn the Active Voice in full. See the following page.

---

[1] *For;* render by *ad.*
[2] For the Latin construction, see 98, Rule IX.

THIRD CONJUGATION: CONSONANT VERBS.

209. ACTIVE VOICE.—Regŏ, *I rule.*

VERB STEM, *reg;* PRESENT STEM, *rege.*[1]

PRINCIPAL PARTS.

PRES. IND.	PRES. INF.	PERF. IND.	SUPINE.
regŏ,	regere,	rēxī,[2]	rēctum.[2]

INDICATIVE MOOD.
PRESENT TENSE.
I rule.

SINGULAR.	PLURAL.
regŏ	regĭmus
regĭs	regĭtis
regĭt	regunt

IMPERFECT.
I was ruling, or *I ruled.*

regēbam	regēbāmus
regēbās	regēbātis
regēbat	regēbant

FUTURE.
I shall or *will rule.*

regam	regēmus
regēs	regētis
reget	regent

PERFECT.
I have ruled, or *I ruled.*

rēxī	rēxĭmus
rēxistī	rēxistis
rēxit	rēxērunt, *or* ēre

PLUPERFECT.
I had ruled.

rēxeram	rēxerāmus
rēxerās	rēxerātis
rēxerat	rēxerant

FUTURE PERFECT.
I shall or *will have ruled.*

rēxerō	rēxerĭmus
rēxeris	rēxerĭtis
rēxerit	rēxerint

---

[1] The characteristic is a variable vowel—ŏ, u, e, ĭ: regŏ, regunt, regere, regis; Curtius calls it the *thematic vowel;* see Curtius, I., p. 199, but on ŏ, see also Meyer, 441.

[2] See p. 3, 30, 33.

ACTIVE VOICE.

SUBJUNCTIVE.

PRESENT.
May I rule, let him rule.[1]

SINGULAR.	PLURAL.
regam	regāmus
regās	regātis
regat	regant

IMPERFECT.
I should rule, he would rule.

regerem	regerēmus
regerēs	regerētis
regeret	regerent

PERFECT.
I may have ruled, or *I have ruled.*

rēxerim	rēxerīmus
rēxeris	rēxerītis
rēxerit	rēxerint

PLUPERFECT.
I should have ruled, he would have ruled.

rēxissem	rēxissēmus
rēxissēs	rēxissētis
rēxisset	rēxissent

IMPERATIVE.

Pres. rege, *rule thou;*	regĭte, *rule ye.*
Fut. regĭtō, *thou shalt rule,*	regĭtōte, *ye shall rule,*
regĭtō, *he shall rule;*	reguntō, *they shall rule.*

INFINITIVE.   PARTICIPLE.

Pres. regere, *to rule.*	*Pres.* regēns, *ruling.*
Perf. rēxisse, *to have ruled.*	
Fut. rēctūrus esse, *to be about to rule.*	*Fut.* rēctūrus, *about to rule.*

GERUND.   SUPINE.

Gen. regendī, *of ruling,*	
Dat. regendō, *for ruling,*	
Acc. regendum, *ruling,*	*Acc.* rēctum, *to rule,*
Abl. regendō, *by ruling.*	*Abl.* rēctū, *to rule, be ruled.*

---

[1] But on the translation of the Subjunctive, see 111, 196.

THIRD CONJUGATION.

208. *Vocabulary.*

Addūcŏ, ere, dūxī, ductum,	to lead to, lead, bring. [Gaul.
Arvernī, ōrum, *m. pl.*	the Arverni, a tribe of southern
Cōgnōscō, ere, nōvi, nitum,	to ascertain.
Conjungŏ, ere, jūnxi, jūnctum,	to join, unite.
Cōnsulō, ere, sului, sultum,	to consult.
Contendō, ere, tendi, tentum,	to contend, strive; to hasten.
Dēfendō, ere, fendi, fēnsum,	to defend.
Deinde, *adv.*	then, in the next place.
Genus, eris, *n.*	kind, class.
Inter sē,	among themselves; with each other, with one another, to-
Nōndum, *adv.*	not yet. [gether.
Nunc, *adv.*	now.
Perīculōsus, a, um,	perilous, dangerous.
Portus, ūs, *m.*	port, harbor.
Potentātus, ūs, *m.*	power, dominion, control.
Prīmum, *sup. adv.*	first.
Tenuis, e,	thin; feeble.
Tribūnus, ī, *m.*	tribune, one of the six principal officers of the legion.
Unquam, *adv.*	ever, at any time.

209. *Translate into English.*

1. Nunc dē hōc perīculōsō bellō dīcam. 2. Prīmum dē genere bellī, deinde dē māgnitūdine[1] dīcāmus. 3. Dē salūte civium dīcere dēbētis. 4. Patriam dēfendere dēbēmus. 5. Quae cīvitās unquam anteā tam tenuis fuit quae nōn portūs suōs et agrōs dēfenderet?[2] 6. Cōnsulite vōbīs, cōnservāte vōs, conjugēs, līberōs, fortūnāsque vestrās, populī Rōmānī nōmen salūtemque dēfendite. 7. Ob eās causās quīnque legiōnēs in Galliā cōnscrībāmus.

8. Caesar dīcit sē in Italiam māgnīs itineribus contendisse, duāsque ibi legiōnēs cōnscrīpsisse. 9. Aeduī et Arvernī dē potentātū inter sē multōs annōs contendēbant. 10. Imperātor tribūnōs mīlitum monuit ut paulātim sēsē legiōnēs conjungerent. 11. Mīlitēs castra dēfendant. 12.

---

[1] That is, *dē māgnitūdine bellī.*   [2] For Mood, see 123, 500, I.

Nōnne castra dēfendētis? Castra dēfendēmus. 13. Caesar Labiēnum lēgātum in Trēverōs cum equitātū mīsit. 14. Dīcunt imperātōrem suās cōpiās in prōximum collem subdūxisse. 15. Postulāmus nē quem mīlitem ad colloquium addūcātis. 16. Utinam Ariovistus suās cōpiās in castra redūcat.

210. *Translate into Latin.*

1. The general has decided to lead back his forces into camp. 2. Caesar says that the enemy led back their forces into camp at sunset. 3. Let us lead our forces out of the camp, and place them in line of battle. 4. Did you not say that the general placed his whole army in line of battle in front of the camp? We said that he led out six legions, and placed them in line of battle in front of the camp. 5. Would that the enemy would lead back their forces into camp. 6. Would that the general had led us back into camp.

7. Let us speak first of the Romans, then of the Gauls. 8. You have spoken of the valor of the soldiers; speak now of the safety of the citizens. 9. Let us defend the safety of our country. 10. Caesar said that these tribes were at that time contending with each other (*among themselves*). 11. We ought to consult, not for ourselves, but for our country. 12. The general says that he shall consult, not for himself, but for his country. 13. How many legions has the general enrolled in Gaul?

LESSON LXXII.

FIRST, SECOND, AND THIRD CONJUGATIONS. — ACTIVE VOICE. — REVIEW OF RULES XII. AND XIV.

211. *Vocabulary.*

Commeō, āre, āvī, ātum,	*to go back and forth, resort.*
Dēdūcō, ere, dūxī, ductum,	*to lead from, conduct.*
Dūcō, ere, dūxī, ductum,	*to lead.*
Effēminō, āre, āvī, ātum,	*to effeminate, enervate.*
Excūsō, āre, āvī, ātum,	*to excuse.*

THIRD CONJUGATION.

Gerŏ, ĕre, gessī, gestum, — to carry on, wage, do.
Importŏ, āre, āvī, ātum, — to bring in, import.
Incolŏ, ĕre, colui, cultum, — to inhabit, dwell.
Levĭtās, ātis, f. — levity, fickleness, impulsiveness.
Mātrĭmōnĭum, iī, n. — marriage; in mātrĭmōnĭum dūcĕre, to marry.
Menapiī, ōrum, m. pl. — the Menapii, a tribe of northern
Mercātor, ōris, m. — merchant, trader. [Gaul.
Mātūrē, adv. — promptly, early.
Nocturnus, a, um, — nocturnal, by night.
Perfringŏ, ĕre, frēgi, frāctum, — to break through.
Pertĭneŏ, ēre, tinuī, tentum, — to pertain, tend.
Phalanx, phalangis, f. — phalanx, line.
Praepōnŏ, ĕre, posui, positum, — to place over or in command of.
Regiŏ, ōnis, f. — direction; region, district.
Ripa, ae, f. — bank of a river.
Sĕquani, ōrum, m. pl. — the Sequani or Sequanians, a tribe
Sub, prep. w. acc. and abl. — under; up to. [of eastern Gaul.
Succēdŏ, ĕre, cessī, cessum, — to come under, come up to, approach.
Uterque, utraque, utrumque,[1] — each; both. [proach.

212. *Translate into English.*

1. Gallī lēgātōs ad Caesarem mīsērunt quī sē excūsārent. 2. Mercātōrēs ad Belgās nōn saepe commeant. 3. Mercātōrēs ea, quae ad effēminandōs animōs[2] pertinent, saepe important. 4. Menapiī eās regiōnēs incolēbant, et ad utramque rīpam flūminis Rhēnī agrōs vīcōsque habēbant. 5. Caesar mātūrius quam tempus annī postulābat in hīberna in Sēquanōs exercitum dēdūxit; hībernīs[3] Labiēnum praeposuit. 6. Gallī levitāte animī novīs rēbus stūdēbant. 7. Belgae cum Germānīs, quī trāns Rhēnum incolunt, bellum gerunt. 8. Lēgātī dīxērunt reliquōs omnēs Belgās in armīs esse. 9. Rēmī, quī proximī Galliae sunt, lēgātōs ad Caesarem

---

[1] Declined like *uter.* See 45, 151.

[2] *Ad effēminandos animōs* = *ad effēminandum animōs*, which is a rare construction. In the second form *animōs* depends upon the gerund *effēminandum;* in the first form it depends upon *ad*, and *effēminandōs* agrees with it; 40, Rule XXXIV. Literally, *to the souls to be enervated;* render *to enervate the soul.* [3] For construction, see 54, 384, II.

misērunt, quī dīcerent,¹ rcliquōs Belgās in armīs esse. 10. Dumnorix Helvētiīs erat amīcus, quod ex eā cīvitāte Orgetorigis fīliam in mātrimōnium dūxerat. 11. Hostēs sub prīmam nostram aciem successērunt. 12. Hostium phalangem perfringāmus. 13. Galliae cīvitātēs nocturnōs conventūs habēbant.

213. *Translate into Latin.*

1. Who inhabit these regions? Deserters say that the Menapii inhabit these regions, and that they have many villages beyond the Rhine. 2. Were not these Gauls friendly to Caesar? They were not friendly to him; they feared the Romans and desired a revolution. 3. Will not the soldiers obey the lieutenant? He has ordered them to fortify the winter quarters. They will obey him, and they will fortify the winter quarters with a high rampart. 4. Let the citizens consult in regard to the war.

5. To whom was Dumnorix friendly? Caesar says that Dumnorix, the brother of Diviticus, was friendly to the Helvetii. 6. For this reason² the chiefs remained silent many days. 7. The Aedui were always friends to the Romans. 8. The general sent a lieutenant to lead the army out of winter quarters. 9. We advise you not to speak of this war. 10. We ought to ascertain how many legions Caesar enrolled in Gaul. 11. Let us lead back the soldiers into the camp that we may defend it.

LESSON LXXIII.

THIRD CONJUGATION. — PASSIVE VOICE IN FULL. — REVIEW OF RULES XVI., XXIII., AND XXV.

214. *Lesson from the Grammar.*

In the verb *Regō*, learn the Passive voice in full. See the following page.

---

¹ For *Mood*, see 119, 497, I.   ² Latin idiom, *on account of these causes.*

THIRD CONJUGATION: CONSONANT VERBS.

210. PASSIVE VOICE.—Regor, *I am ruled.*

Verb Stem, *reg;* Present Stem, *rege.*[1]

PRINCIPAL PARTS.

Pres. Ind.	Pres. Inf.	Perf. Ind.
regor,	regī,	rēctus[1] sum.

INDICATIVE MOOD.

Present Tense.
I am ruled.

Singular	Plural
regor	regimur
regeris, *or* re	regiminī
regitur	reguntur

Imperfect.
I was ruled.

regēbar	regēbāmur
regēbāris, *or* re	regēbāminī
regēbātur	regēbantur

Future.
I shall or *will be ruled.*

regar	regēmur
regēris, *or* re	regēminī
regētur	regentur

Perfect.
I have been ruled, or *I was ruled.*

rēctus sum[2]	rēctī sumus
rēctus es	rēctī estis
rēctus est	rēctī sunt

Pluperfect.
I had been ruled.

rēctus eram[2]	rēctī erāmus
rēctus erās	rēctī erātis
rēctus erat	rēctī erant

Future Perfect.
I shall or *will have been ruled.*

rēctus erō[2]	rēctī erimus
rēctus eris	rēctī eritis
rēctus erit	rēctī erunt

---

[1] See 207, 209, foot-notes.   [2] See 170, 206, foot-notes.

PASSIVE VOICE.

SUBJUNCTIVE.

PRESENT.

May I be ruled, let him be ruled.

SINGULAR.	PLURAL.
regar	regāmur
regāris, *or* re	regāmini
regātur	regantur

IMPERFECT.

I should be ruled, he would be ruled.

regerer	regerēmur
regerēris, *or* re	regerēmini
regerētur	regerentur

PERFECT.

I may have been ruled, or *I have been ruled.*

rēctus sim [1]	rēctī sīmus
rēctus sīs	rēctī sītis
rēctus sit	rēctī sint

PLUPERFECT.

I should have been ruled, he would have been ruled.

rēctus essem [1]	rēctī essēmus
rēctus essēs	rēctī essētis
rēctus esset	rēctī essent

IMPERATIVE.

Pres. regere, *be thou ruled;* | regiminī, *be ye ruled.*
Fut. regitor, *thou shalt be ruled,*
regitor, *he shall be ruled;* | reguntor, *they shall be ruled.*

INFINITIVE. | PARTICIPLE.

Pres. regī, *to be ruled.*
Perf. rēctus esse,[1] *to have been ruled.* | *Perf.* rēctus, *ruled.*
Fut. rēctum īrī, *to be about to be ruled.* | *Ger.* regendus, *to be ruled, deserving to be ruled.*

---

[1] See 170, 206, foot-notes.

LESSON LXXIV.

THIRD CONJUGATION. — PASSIVE VOICE IN FULL. — REVIEW OF RULES XVI., XXIII., AND XXV. — EXERCISES.

215. Vocabulary.

Aedificium, ii, n.	building, house.
Aquilifer, eri, m.	standard-bearer.
Cārus, a, um,	dear.
Centum, indeclinable,	hundred.
Claudō, ere, clausi, clausum,	to shut, close.
Germānia, ae, f.	Germany.
Germānus, a, um,	German.
Incendō, ere, cendi, cēnsum,	to set on fire, fire, burn.
Insula, ae, f.	island.
Irrumpō, ere, rūpi, ruptum,	to break in, rush in.
Nunquam, adv.	never.
Occīdō, ere, cīdi, cīsum,	to kill, slay.
Pāgus, i, m.	division, canton.
Porta, ae, f.	gate.
Premō, ere, pressi, pressum,	to press, press hard, distress.
Quoque, adv.	also.
Remaneō, ēre, mānsi, mānsum,	to remain.
Repellō, ere, reppuli, repulsum,	to repel, repulse.
Ubii, ōrum, m. pl.	the Ubii, a tribe of western Germany. [many.
Usipetēs, um, m. pl.	the Usipetes, a tribe of northwestern Germany.
Vercingetorix, igis, m.	Vercingetorix, a Gallic chieftain.

216. *Translate into English.*

1. Aquilifer ipse prō castrīs fortissimē pūgnāns[1] occīditur. 2. Multī mīlitēs fortissimē pūgnantēs occīsī sunt. 3. Nōnne omnēs māgnā multitūdine hostium premēmur? 4. Utinam hostēs omnēs nostrā virtūte repellantur. 5. Num ab hostibus eō tempore repulsī estis? Nūnquam ab hostibus repulsī sumus. 6. Quid apud Alesiam geritur? Gallī perterritī in oppidum irrumpunt; Vercingetorix imperātor jubet portās

---
[1] *While fighting.* See Suggestion XIII., 3.

claudī, nē castra nūdentur. 7. Omnia vīcī Octōdūrī aedificia incēnsa sunt. 8. Nōnne multa oppida ab Helvētiīs incēnsa sunt? Post Orgetorigis mortem Helvētiī oppida sua omnia incendērunt.
9. Magna Germāniae pars ā bellicōsissimīs nātiōnibus eō tempore incolēbātur. 10. Multae īnsulae ā ferīs barbarīsque nātiōnibus incoluntur. 11. Caesar obsidēs ad sē addūcī jubet. 12. Usīpetēs Germānī ab Suēbīs multōs annōs premēbantur. Ubiī quoque graviter ab Suēbīs pressī erant. 13. Suēbī centum pāgōs habēre dīcuntur. 14. Omnium[1] quī Galliam incolunt fortissimī sunt Belgae. 15. Suēbī, quī bellicōsissimī Germānōrum omnium esse dīcuntur, ūnō in locō nōn longius annō[2] remanent. 16. Caesar mīlitum vītam suā salūte[3] cāriōrem habēbat.

217. *Translate into Latin.*

1. Were not the Belgae braver than the other Gauls?[3] They are said to have been the bravest of all the Gauls. Did they not often wage war with the Germans who dwelt beyond the Rhine? They are said to have waged war continually with the neighboring states. 2. What is dearer than life? To brave soldiers liberty and country are dearer than life. Ought we not to hold (*regard*) liberty and country dearer than life itself? 3. This part of Gaul has always been inhabited by warlike nations. 4. Which part of Gaul was inhabited by the brave Belgae? 5. One part of Gaul is said to have been inhabited by the Celts.

6. The bravest and most warlike of the Gauls were conquered by the Romans. 7. By the valor of our soldiers the enemy have been repulsed. 8. The bravest of the soldiers were slain. 9. Let us not remain in this town longer than one day. 10. Did you not say that these islands were inhabited by fierce nations? These islands are said to have

---

[1] *Partitive Genitive.* See 28, 397. [2] For Case, see 88, Rule XXIII.
[3] Render first with *quam*, and secondly without it.

been inhabited by barbarous nations. 11. Were not many towns burned by the enemy? Many towns are said to have been burned by them. 12. The general has ordered the army to be led back into camp, and the gates to be closed.

LESSON LXXV.

FIRST, SECOND, AND THIRD CONJUGATIONS. — PASSIVE VOICE. — REVIEW OF RULES XXX., XXXI., AND XXXIII.

218. *Vocabulary.*

Aquitāni, ōrum, *m. pl.*	the *Aquitani* or *Aquitanians*, the inhabitants of the southwestern division of Gaul.
Cabillōnum, i, *n.*	*Cabillonum*, a town of Eastern Gaul.
Certus, a, um,	*certain, fixed, appointed.*
Compleō, ēre, ēvi, ētum,	*to fill, cover.*
Confestim, *adv.*	*hastily, speedily.*
Cotta, ae, *m.*	*Cotta*, a lieutenant under Caesar.
Divĭdō, ere, visi, visum,	*to divide.*
Funda, ae, *f.*	*sling.*
Indīcō, ere, dixi, dictum,	*to appoint.*
Inopia, ae, *f.*	*lack, want, need.*
Mandō, āre, āvi, ātum,	*to commission, order; to entrust, consign, commit, betake.*
Matiscō, ōnis, *m.*	*Matisco*, a town in southeastern Gaul.
Novus, a, um,	*new.*
Sulpicius, ii, *m.*	*Sulpicius*, a lieutenant under Caesar.
Supplicātĭō, ōnis, *f.*	*thanksgiving.*
Tigurīnus, i, *m.*	*Tigurinus*, one of the four cantons of the Helvetii.
Vesper, eri, *m.*	*evening.*
Vīgintī, *indeclinable,*	*twenty.*
Vulnerō, āre, āvi, ātum,	*to wound.*

219. *Translate into English.*

1. Omnis cīvĭtās Helvētiōrum in quattuor pāgōs dīvīsa est. Hōrum ūnus appellātur Tigurīnus. 2. Gallia est dīvīsa

CONJUGATIONS I., II., AND III. 175

in partēs trēs, quārum ūnam incolunt Belgae, aliam Aquītānī, tertiam Gallī. 3. Imperātor hōrā septimā vīcum hominibus[1] complērī jussit. 4. Cotta lēgātus fortissimē pūgnāns[2] fundā vulnerātus est. 5. Rōmae diērum vīgintī[3] supplicātiō indīcitur. 6. Caesar Cicerōnem et Sulpicium Cabillōnī et Matiscōne in Aeduīs collocāvit. 7. Hostēs ad vesperum fortiter pūgnāvērunt; tum dēmum fugae sēsē mandāvērunt. 8. Litterae ad Caesarem cōnfestim ab Cicerōne mittuntur. 9. Ariovistus dīxit eās omnēs cōpiās ā sē ūnō proeliō superātās esse. 10. Multī omnium rērum inopiā adductī auxilium ā Caesare implōrābant. Itaque obsidēs imperāvit, eōsque ad certam[4] diem addūcī jussit. 11. Multa ab Caesare in colloquiō dicta sunt. 12. Duae legiōnēs, quae in Galliā prōximē cōnscrīptae erant, fugae sēsē mandābant.

220. *Translate into Latin.*

1. The lands of the Gauls were often seized by the Germans. 2. Many Gauls, distressed with want at home, implored aid from the neighboring towns. 3. At that time Caesar was enrolling new legions in Italy. 4. Many legions had already been enrolled in Gaul and Italy. 5. At Rome[5] Caesar is said to have been advised to hasten into Gaul. On the same day he was advised by Labienus to enlist a new legion. 6. A part of a legion had been placed in winter quarters at Octodurus. 7. At that time he is said to have ordered all the legions to be led out of winter quarters.

8. On that day the camp of the Romans was assaulted by the Gauls. 9. These brave soldiers were wounded while fighting[6] for their country. 10. Let us order them to remain

---

[1] For *Case*, see 78, Rule XVIII.
[2] See Suggestion XIII., 3.
[3] Literally, *of twenty days;* render, *for twenty days.* The *Accusative of Duration of Time* could have been used.
[4] See foot-note 1, page 234. [5] See 185, 425, II.
[6] In rendering into Latin, omit *while*. See Suggestion XIII., 3.

in the province during the winter.¹ 11. Into how many parts was Gaul divided? Caesar says that Gaul was divided into three parts. 12. Gaul is said to have been divided into three parts. 13. Into how many parts did you say that our country is divided? I said that it is divided into many parts. 14. He is said to have led his army back into camp about midday.

LESSON LXXVI.

FIRST, SECOND, AND THIRD CONJUGATIONS. — EXERCISE IN READING AT SIGHT.

221. *Read at Sight, examine carefully, and translate into English.*[2]

Caesar cōpiās suās in prōximum collem subdūxit, equitātumque quī sustinēret[3] hostium impetum mīsit. Ipse interim in colle mediō[4] triplicem aciem īnstrūxit legiōnum quattuor veterānārum, sed in summō jugō duās legiōnēs, quās in Galliā citeriōre prōximē cōnscrīpserat, et omnia auxilia collocārī, āc tōtum montem hominibus complērī jussit. Helvētiī sub prīmam nostram aciem successērunt, sed Rōmānī facile hostium phalangem perfrēgērunt. Hostēs ab hōrā septimā ad vesperum fortiter pūgnāvērunt. Diūtius nostrōrum impetūs sustinēre nōn poterant; multī vulnerātī erant; itaque timōre perterritī fugae sēsē mandāvērunt, atque in fīnēs Lingonum contendērunt. Caesar ad Lingonēs litterās nūntiōsque mīsit, nē eōs frūmentō nēve aliā rē juvārent. Tum dēmum Helvētiī, omnium rērum inopiā adductī, lēgātōs dē dēditiōne ad eum mīsērunt.

---

[1] *During the winter.* Use the Accusative of Duration of Time. See 98, 379.
[2] See Directions for Reading at Sight, 137.
[3] See Suggestion XVII., 3.
[4] See foot-note on *summus*, 141.

222. *Translate into Latin.*

1. About midday the general led out all his forces, and placed them in line of battle before the camp. The enemy in sight of their commander fought bravely for many hours, but at length, repulsed by the valor of our soldiers, and overcome (*terrified*) by fear, they betook themselves to flight. The general was wounded, and many soldiers were slain. 2. So great fear took possession of the Gauls, that they decided to fortify their cities, to bring grain into them from their lands, and to build a large number of ships. 3. The Gauls had filled this town with brave soldiers, and Caesar had been advised not to attack it on account of the valor of the men, the width of the moat, and the height of the wall. 4. At that time so great fear took possession of all the Aedui, whose lands the Helvetii were devastating, that they fortified their cities, and sent ambassadors to Caesar to ask aid.

LESSON LXXVII.

FOURTH CONJUGATION. — INDICATIVE ACTIVE. — REVIEW OF RULES XXXIV., XXXV. AND XXXVI.

223. *Lesson from the Grammar.*

In the verb *Audiō* learn the Indicative Mood of the Active Voice. See page 180.

224. *Vocabulary.*

Aduātucī, ōrum, m. pl.	the *Aduatuci*, a tribe of northern Gaul.
Ante, adv.	before.
Audiō, īre, īvī or iī, ītum,	to hear, hear of.
Clēmentia, ae, f.	clemency, forbearance, mercy.
Cōgō, ere, coēgī, coāctum,	to drive together, bring together, collect; to force, compel.

Convenĭō, ĭre, vēnī, ventum,	to come together, assemble, meet, [come.
Cotīdiānus, a, um,	daily.
Duplex, ĭcis,	double.
Helvĕtius, a, um,	Helvetian.
Latus, ĕris, n.	side.
Mūniō, ire, īvī or ĭi, ītum,	to fortify.
Neque, conj.	neither, nor; neque . . . neque,
Pĕs, pedis, m.	foot. [neither . . . nor.
Scrībō, ere, scrīpsī, scrīptum,	to write.
Venĭō, ire, vēnī, ventum,	to come.
Vĭdeō, ēre, vĭdī, vīsum,	to see.

225. *Translate into English.*

1. Nōnne vōcēs mīlitum audītis? Vōcēs omnium mīlitum audīmus. 2. Tum vērō nostrī clāmōrem ab eā parte audīvērunt. 3. Nōnne castra mūniētis? Castra vallō mūniēmus. 4. Caesar castra in altitūdinem pedum[1] duodecim vallō mūnīverat. 5. Legiōnēs sex, quae prīmae vēnerant, castra mūniēbant. 6. Aduātucī, dē quibus suprā scrīpsimus, ūnum oppidum duplicī altissimō mūrō mūnierant.[2] 7. Eō tempore castra vallō fossāque mūniēbāmus. 8. Ob eās rēs Galba ūnam partem vīcī, quī appellātur Octōdūrus, vallō fossāque cōnfestim mūnīvit.

9. Flūmen latus ūnum castrōrum mūniēbat. 10. Venetī oppida mūniēbant, frūmenta ex agrīs in oppida comportābant, nāvēs in Venetiam cōgēbant. 11. Rhēnus lātissimus atque altissimus agrum Helvētium ā Germānīs dīvidit. 12. Aduātucī Caesaris clēmentiam ab aliīs audiēbant. 13. Tanta opera neque vīderant ante[3] Gallī neque audierant.[2] 14. Eādem dē causā Helvētiī Celtārum omnium fortissimī sunt, quod ferē cotīdiānīs proeliīs cum Germānīs contendunt. 15. Totīus ferē Galliae lēgātī, prīncipēs cīvitātum, ad Caesarem convēnērunt.

---

[1] Construe with *vallō*.
[2] *Mūnierant*, contracted from *mūnīverant*; *audierant*, from *audīverant*.
[3] Observe that *ante* is sometimes an adverb, and sometimes a preposition.

FOURTH CONJUGATION.

226. *Translate into Latin.*

1. What did you hear at Rome? We heard that nearly all the Belgae had conspired against the Roman people. From whom did you hear this report? We heard it from many citizens and from the consuls themselves. 2. Judges, you have heard the words of many witnesses, and all these things which you have heard are true. 3. Have the enemy heard what we are doing? I hear that all our plans have been announced to them by deserters. 4. Have you heard what we have been doing at this time at Rome? We have heard of[1] the many good things which you have done in that city.

5. Have you not fortified all these towns with high walls? We fortify our towns, not by walls and ramparts, but by the valor of our citizens. 6. I have never seen the cities of which[2] you write, but I have heard of them from others. 7. The legions that had been enrolled in Gaul were at that time fortifying the camp. 8. Have you not often heard that the Belgae incessantly wage war with the Germans? I have often heard that[3] from you. 9. You have all heard that many states sent ambassadors to Caesar at that time to ask aid.

LESSON LXXVIII.

FOURTH CONJUGATION. — ACTIVE VOICE IN FULL. — REVIEW OF RULES LV., LVI., AND LXI.

227. *Lesson from the Grammar.*

In the verb *Audiō*, learn the Active Voice in full. See the following page.

---

[1] Omit *of* in rendering into Latin. See **225**, sentence 13.
[2] *Of which* = *concerning which*.
[3] When the antecedent is a *clause*, the pronoun must be *neuter*.

FOURTH CONJUGATION: I VERBS.

211. ACTIVE VOICE.—Audiŏ, *I hear.*

VERB STEM AND PRESENT STEM, *audī*.

PRINCIPAL PARTS.

PRES. IND.	PRES. INF.	PERF. IND.	SUPINE.
audiō,	audīre,	audīvī,	audītum.

INDICATIVE MOOD.

PRESENT TENSE.
I hear.

SINGULAR.	PLURAL.
audiō	audīmus
audīs	audītis
audit	audiunt

IMPERFECT.
I was hearing, or *I heard.*

audiēbam	audiēbāmus
audiēbās	audiēbātis
audiēbat	audiēbant

FUTURE.
I shall or *will hear.*

audiam	audiēmus
audiēs	audiētis
audiet	audient

PERFECT.
I have heard, or *I heard.*

audīvī	audīvimus
audīvistī	audīvistis
audīvit	audīvērunt, *or* ēre

PLUPERFECT.
I had heard.

audīveram	audīverāmus
audīverās	audīverātis
audīverat	audīverant

FUTURE PERFECT.
I shall or *will have heard.*

audīverō	audīverimus
audīveris	audīveritis
audīverit	audīverint

ACTIVE VOICE.

SUBJUNCTIVE.

PRESENT.
May I hear, let him hear.[1]

SINGULAR.	PLURAL.
audiam	audiāmus
audiās	audiātis
audiat	audiant

IMPERFECT.
I should hear, he would hear.

audīrem	audīrēmus
audīrēs	audīrētis
audīret	audīrent

PERFECT.
I may have heard, or I have heard.

audīverim	audīverīmus
audīveris	audīverītis
audīverit	audīverint

PLUPERFECT.
I should have heard, he would have heard.

audīvissem	audīvissēmus
audīvissēs	audīvissētis
audīvisset	audīvissent

IMPERATIVE.

Pres. audī, *hear thou;*	audīte, *hear ye.*
Fut. audītō, *thou shalt hear,*	audītōte, *ye shall hear,*
audītō, *he shall hear;*	audiuntō, *they shall hear.*

INFINITIVE.
Pres. audīre, *to hear.*
Perf. audīvisse, *to have heard.*
Fut. audītūrus esse, *to be about to hear.*

PARTICIPLE.
Pres. audiēns, *hearing.*
Fut. audītūrus, *about to hear.*

GERUND.
Gen. audiendī, *of hearing,*
Dat. audiendō, *for hearing,*
Acc. audiendum, *hearing,*
Abl. audiendō, *by hearing.*

SUPINE.
Acc. audītum, *to hear,*
Abl. audītū, *to hear, be heard.*

---

[1] But on the translation of the Subjunctive, see 111, 190, II.

228. Vocabulary.

Alō, ere, alui, alĭtum *and* altum,	*to nourish, support, sustain.*
Intellĕgō, ere, lēxi, lĕctum,	*to understand, know.*
Prōnūntĭō, āre, āvī, ātum,	*to proclaim, declare.*
Propterĕā, *adv.*	*for this reason;* propterea quod, *for the reason that, because.*
Quaerō, ere, quaesivi *or* ii, ītum,	*to seek, inquire, ask.*
Quisque, quaeque, quidque *and* quodque,	*every, every one, each, each one.*
Quod, *conj.*	*that; because.*
Sabīnus, i, *m.*	*Sabinus,* a lieutenant under
Scĭō, īre, īvī *or* ii, ītum,	*to know.* [Caesar.
Secundus, a, um,	*second.* [devote oneself to.
Servĭō, īre, īvī *or* ii, ītum,	*to serve, subserve; to promote,*
Sincērē, *adv.*	*truthfully.*
Sūmptus, ūs, *m.*	*expense.*
Titūrĭus, ĭi, *m.*	*Titurius,* a Roman name.
Ūllus, a, um, 45, 151,	*any.*
Ūtĭlĭtās, ātis, *f.*	*usefulness; interest, advantage.*
Vestĭō, īre, īvī *or* ii, ītum,	*to clothe.*
Vĭātor, ōris, *m.*	*traveller.*

229. *Translate into English.*

1. Hŏc oppidum duplicī mūrō mūniāmus. 2. Hostēs suam urbem altissĭmō mūrō mūnīre parābant. 3. Imperātor nōs castra vallō mūnīre jubet. 4. Caesar Quīntum Titūrium Sabīnum lēgātum castra in altitūdĭnem pedum duodecim vallō mūnīre jussit. 5. Utĭnam Caesar castra vallō fossāque mūnīvisset.[1] 6. Audĭāmus Rōmānōs mīlĭtēs. 7. Haec ut intellegātis ā mē sincērē prōnūntiārī, audīte Rōmānōs mīlĭtēs. 8. Caesar prīmam et secundam aciem in armīs esse, tertiam castra mūnīre jussit.

9. Siciliam nūtrīcem plēbis Rōmānae nōminō, proptereā quod sine ūllō sūmptū nostrō[2] māxĭmōs exercĭtūs nostrōs vestīvit, aluit, armāvit. 10. Cōnsŭlēs ūtilitātī salūtīque serviunt. 11. Salūtī cīvium omnium servīre dēbētis. 12. Dīcit

---
[1] For the force of the *Tense*, see 114, 483, 2.
[2] *Sūmptū nostrō,* literally, *our expense;* render, *expense* TO US.

sē hōc ab aliīs audīvisse. 13. Dīcunt sex legiōnēs castra mūnītūrās esse. 14. Studium audiendī; mūniendō; mīles vōcem audiēns; nostrī clāmōrem audientēs; mīlitēs castra munītūrī. 15. Gallī ab viātōribus quaerunt quid dē quāque rē audierint.

230. *Translate into Latin.*

1. Which legion was at that time fortifying the camp? The lieutenant said that the sixth legion was fortifying the camp. 2. The general says that he shall fortify the winter quarters with a high rampart. 3. We all know what you heard at Rome. 4. Let us now hear what you are doing and what you are seeing. 5. Lieutenants, fortify this city with a double wall; let not the enemy take it by storm.

6. Judges, hear now the words of these witnesses. 7. Would that you had all heard the words of these witnesses. 8. Hearing the shouts of the soldiers, the general ordered the lieutenants to lead out the whole army, and to place it in line of battle. 9. Have you heard which legions have been sent to sustain[1] the attack of the enemy? We have heard that five legions have been sent to sustain the attack of the enemy, and that two remain in camp.

LESSON LXXIX.

THE FOUR CONJUGATIONS. — ACTIVE VOICE. — RULE XXIX. — REVIEW OF RULES LVII. AND LVIII.

231. *Examples.* — *Ablative of Specification.*

1. *Nōmine* fuit rēx.   *He was king* IN NAME.
2. Claudus alterō *pede.*   *Lame* IN *one* FOOT.

NOTE. — The Latin usage illustrated in the Ablatives *nōmine* and *pede* is expressed in the following

---

[1] *To sustain;* render by a *Relative Clause* denoting *Purpose.*

FOUR CONJUGATIONS.

RULE XXIX.—Specification.

424. A noun, adjective, or verb may take an Ablative to define its application:

Nōmine, nōn potestāte fuit rēx, *He was king* IN NAME, *not* IN POWER. Nep. Claudus alterō pede, *lame* IN ONE FOOT. Nep. Reliquōs Gallōs virtūte praecēdunt, *they surpass the other Gauls in courage.* Caes.

232. *Vocabulary.*

Accurrō, ere, cucurrī *or* currī, cursum, — *to run to, hasten to, run.* [much.
Adamō, āre, āvī, ātum, — *to be greatly pleased with, like very*
Administrō, āre, āvī, ātum, — *to administer, manage, direct.*
Angustus, a, um, — *narrow, limited.* [Gaul.
Bellovaci, ōrum, *m. pl.* — *the Bellovaci, a tribe of northwestern*
Cultus, ūs, *m.* — *culture, refinement, civilization.*
Dēfēnsor, ōris, *m.* — *defender.*
Fīniō, īre, īvī *or* iī, ītum, — *to end; to bound, limit.*
Fluō, ere, flūxī, flūxum, — *to flow.*
Imperium, ī, *n.* — *empire, government.*
Influō, ere, flūxī, flūxum, — *to flow into, empty, flow.*
Instituō, ere, uī, ūtum, — *to begin, proceed.*
Lacus, ūs, *m.* — *lake.* [Lake of Geneva.
Lemannus, ī, *m.* — *Lemannus, Leman;* lacus Lemannus,
Minus, *comp. adv.* — *less;* minimē, *sup., least, very little, not at all, by no means.*

Noviodūnum, ī, *n.* — *Noviodunum,* a town in northwestern
Praecēdō, ere, cessī, cessum, — *to surpass.* [Gaul.
Superior, us, *comp. of* superus, *superior.*
Vacuus, a, um, — *vacant, empty, deserted, abandoned.*

233. *Translate into English.*

1. Eō tempore Rhēnus populī Rōmānī imperium ūnā ex parte fīniēbat. 2. Minimē ad Belgās mercātōrēs saepe commeant. 3. Helvētiī angustōs fīnēs habent, et ob eam rem minus facile cum fīnitimīs bellum gerere possunt. 4. Rhodanus inter fīnēs Helvētiōrum et Allobrogum fluit. 5. Lacus Lemannus in flūmen Rhodanum influit. 6. Ducēs hostium castra mūnīre instituunt. 7. Caesar in fīnēs Suessiōnum exercitum dūxit, et māgnīs itineribus ad oppidum Noviodū-

FOURTH CONJUGATION. 185

num contendit; id vacuum ab dēfēnsōribus esse audierat. 8. Helvētiī reliquōs Gallōs virtūte praecēdunt. 9. Imperātor hostēs equitātū superiōrēs esse intellegēbat. 10. Germānī, hominēs ferī āc barbarī, agrōs et cultum et cōpiās Gallōrum adamābant. 11. Cōnsĭdius ad Caesarem accurrit, et dīcit montem ab hostibus tenērī. 12. Bellovacī sē cum Rōmānīs bellum gestūrōs¹ dīxērunt. 13. Vercingetorix bellum administrāre parābat.

234. *Translate into Latin.*

1. Caesar says that the warlike Germans were greatly pleased with (*liked very much*) the refinement of the Gauls. 2. We all know that the river Rhone separated the territory of the Helvetii from the Roman province. 3. The Romans are said to have surpassed the Gauls in valor. 4. I have often heard that the Gauls at that time surpassed the Germans in refinement. 5. I have heard from deserters that a brave lieutenant was slain in that battle.

6. They say that the enemy have fortified their towns, and that they will fight bravely for their country. 7. We have heard that you will remain in Italy the whole winter. 8. Have you not heard that many Gauls were held in servitude by Ariovistus. We have often heard that from the Gauls themselves. 9. The Aedui ought not to be held in servitude by barbarians. 10. At Geneva many friends were awaiting our arrival from Italy.

LESSON LXXX.

FOURTH CONJUGATION. — PASSIVE VOICE IN FULL.

235. *Lesson from the Grammar.*

In the verb *Audiō*, learn the Passive Voice in full.

---

¹ In the compound forms of the Infinitive, *esse* is often thus omitted.

FOURTH CONJUGATION: I VERBS.

212. PASSIVE VOICE.—Audior, *I am heard.*

VERB STEM AND PRESENT STEM, *audī.*

PRINCIPAL PARTS.

PRES. IND.	PRES. INF.	PERF. IND.
audior,	audīrī,	audītus sum.

INDICATIVE MOOD.

PRESENT TENSE.
I am heard.

SINGULAR.	PLURAL.
audior	audīmur
audīris, *or* re	audīminī
audītur	audiuntur

IMPERFECT.
I was heard.

audiēbar	audiēbāmur
audiēbāris, *or* re	audiēbāminī
audiēbātur	audiēbantur

FUTURE.
I shall or will be heard.

audiar	audiēmur
audiēris, *or* re	audiēminī
audiētur	audientur

PERFECT.
I have been heard, or *I was heard.*

audītus sum[1]	audītī sumus
audītus es	audītī estis
audītus est	audītī sunt

PLUPERFECT.
I had been heard.

audītus eram[1]	audītī erāmus
audītus erās	audītī erātis
audītus erat	audītī erant

FUTURE PERFECT.
I shall or will have been heard.

audītus erō[1]	audītī erimus
audītus eris	audītī eritis
audītus erit	audītī erunt

---

[1] See 170, 206, foot-notes.

PASSIVE VOICE.

SUBJUNCTIVE.

PRESENT.
May I be heard, let him be heard.

SINGULAR.	PLURAL.
audiar	audiāmur
audiāris, *or* re	audiāminī
audiātur	audiantur

IMPERFECT.
I should be heard, he would be heard.

audīrer	audīrēmur
audīrēris, *or* re	audīrēminī
audīrētur	audīrentur

PERFECT.
I may have been heard, or *I have been heard.*

audītus sim [1]	audītī sīmus
audītus sīs	audītī sītis
audītus sit	audītī sint

PLUPERFECT.
I should have been heard, he would have been heard.

audītus essem [1]	audītī essēmus
audītus essēs	audītī essētis
audītus esset	audītī essent

IMPERATIVE.

Pres.	audīre, *be thou heard;*	audīminī, *be ye heard.*
Fut.	audītor, *thou shalt be heard,* audītor, *he shall be heard;*	audiuntor, *they shall be heard.*

INFINITIVE.

Pres. audīrī, *to be heard.*
Perf. audītus esse,[1] *to have been heard.*
Fut. audītum īrī, *to be about to be heard.*

PARTICIPLE.

Perf. audītus, *heard.*
Ger. audiendus, *to be heard, deserving to be heard.*

---

[1] See 170, 200, foot-notes.

LESSON LXXXI.

FOURTH CONJUGATION. — PASSIVE VOICE IN FULL. — RULE XXVIII. — REVIEW OF RULE XXII. — EXERCISES.

236. *Examples. — Ablative of Difference.*

1. Ūnō diē longior mēnsis. A month one DAY longer (longer BY one DAY).
2. Biduō mē antecessit. He preceded me BY TWO DAYS.

NOTE. — The Latin usage illustrated in the Ablatives *diē* and *biduō* is expressed in the following

RULE XXVIII. — Ablative of Difference.

423. The MEASURE OF DIFFERENCE is denoted by the Ablative:

Ūnō diē longiōrem mēnsem faciunt, *they make the month* ONE DAY *longer* (longer BY ONE DAY). Cic. Biduō mē antecessit, *he preceded me* BY TWO DAYS. Cic. Sōl multīs partibus major est quam terra, *the sun is very much* (literally BY MANY PARTS) *larger than the earth.* Cic.

237. *Vocabulary.*

Britannī, ōrum, m. pl.	the Britons.
Cantium, iī, n.	Kent.
Cevenna, ae, f.	Cevenna, a mountain range in southern Gaul, now the Cévennes.
Ēgregiē, adv.	excellently.
Existimō, āre, āvī, ātum,	to think.
Hūmānus, a, um,	civilized.
Impediō, īre, ivi or ii, itum,	to impede, hinder, embarrass.
Impedītus, a, um,	entangled.
Mēnsis, is, m.	month.
Oppūgnātiō, ōnis, f.	assault, attack.
Paucī, ae, a,	few.
Pellis, is, f.	skin.
Plērusque, raque, rumque,	the larger or greater part, the most.
Praesēns, entis, like prūdēns,	present; in praesentia (neut. plur.) for the present.

FOURTH CONJUGATION. 189

Prohĭbeō, ēre, uī, ĭtum, — *to prohibit, check, prevent, keep.*
Rapīna, ae, *f.* — *robbery, plundering, pillaging.*
Reperĭō, īre, repperī, repertum, — *to find.*
Satis, *adv.* — *enough;* satis habēre, *to consider*
Tamen, *adv.* — *yet, nevertheless.* [*it sufficient.*
Vesontĭō, ōnis, *m.* — Vesontio, a town of eastern Gaul,
Vincō, ere, vīcī, victum, — *to conquer.* [now *Besançon.*

238. *Translate into English.*

1. Vesontĭŏ, oppidum māximum Sēquanōrum, nātūrā locī mūniēbātur. 2. Nostrum oppidum altissimō mūrō mūnīrī dēbet. 3. Nostra oppida ēgregiō mūniantur. 4. Ille locus ēgregiō nātūrā atque opere mūnītus est. 5. Britannī silvam impedītam, vallō atque fossā mūnītam, oppidum vocant. 6. Caesar oppidum ēgregiō nātūrā atque opere mūnītum repperit; tamen hōc duābus ex partibus oppūgnāre contendit. 7. Iter agminis nostrī multīs rēbus impediēbātur. 8. Aduātucī, dē quibus suprā scrīpsimus, sua omnia in ūnum oppidum ēgregiō nātūrā mūnītum comportābant.

9. Ex Britannīs[1] omnibus longē sunt hūmānissimī quī Cantium incolunt; interiōrēs plērīque pellibus sunt vestītī. 10. Oppidōrum oppūgnātiō duābus rēbus impediēbātur. 11. Arvernī sē monte Cevennā mūnītōs esse exīstimābant. 12. Ex captīvīs quaerāmus quam ob rem hostēs castra nōn mūniant. 13. Caesar suōs ā proeliō continēbat, āc satis habēbat[2] in praesentia[3] hostem rapīnīs prohibēre. 14. Ariovistus paucīs mēnsibus[3] ante Gallōrum cōpiās proeliō vīcerat.

239. *Translate into Latin.*

1. These cities are all excellently fortified by nature and art. 2. You will find that city excellently fortified with a double wall. 3. Did you say that the winter quarters of the

---

[1] Literally, *out of the Britons*; render, or *the Britons.* It has the force of a *Partitive Genitive.*
[2] See *Vocabulary.*
[3] See **236**, Rule XXVIII.

enemy are not fortified? I have heard from captives that the winter quarters of the Gauls are not fortified by art, but that they are enclosed on all sides¹ by high mountains. 4. Those who inhabited a large part of this island were barbarians, and were clothed in skins. 5. Many islands were then inhabited by barbarians, who were clothed in skins.

6. Among barbarians an entangled forest, fortified with a rampart and a moat, is often called a town. 7. Our cities will all be fortified many days² before the arrival of the enemy. 8. From whom did you hear that the camp of the Britons is already fortified with a high rampart? I have heard that report from the captives, of whom I have written above. 9. Did you not say that this tower is higher than that? It is higher than that by many feet. 10. The deserters said that the town had been fortified two years before. 11. Would that your towns had been fortified before the arrival of the enemy.

LESSON LXXXII.

FOUR CONJUGATIONS IN FULL. — PASSIVE VOICE. — REVIEW OF RULE IV. — RULE XXXII.

240. *Lesson from the Grammar.*

RULE XXXII.³ — Ablative Absolute.⁴

431. A noun and a participle may be put in the Ablative to add to the predicate an attendant circumstance:

---

¹ *On all sides;* Latin idiom, FROM *all sides;* or render by a single adverb.
² Use the *Ablative of Difference.*
³ It seems to be no longer necessary to introduce Rules, as in previous lessons, by means of examples. The pupil has already learned the fact that a *Grammatical Rule* is nothing more than a *statement of the general usage of the language.* The introductory examples were intended chiefly to show him this fact.
⁴ This Ablative is called *absolute*, because it is not directly dependent for its construction upon any other word in the sentence.

ABLATIVE ABSOLUTE.

Serviō rēgnante viguērunt, *they flourished in the reign of Servius (Servius reigning)*.[1] Cic. Rēgibus exāctis, cōnsulēs creāti sunt, *after the banishment of the kings*,[2] *consuls were appointed*. Liv. Equitātū praemissō, subsequēbātur, *having sent forward his cavalry, he followed*. Caes. Rēgnum haud satis prōsperum neglēctā rēligiōne, *a reign not sufficiently prosperous because religion was neglected*. Liv. Perditīs rēbus omnibus tamen virtūs sē sustentāre potest, *though all things are lost, still virtue is able to sustain itself*. Cic.

1. The Ablative Absolute, much more common than the English Nominative Absolute, generally expresses the *time, cause*, or some *attendant circumstance* of an action.

2. This Ablative is generally best rendered — (1) by a *noun* with a *preposition — in, during, after, by, with, through*, etc.; (2) by an *active participle* with its *object*; or (3) by a *clause* with *when, while, because, if, though*, etc.;[3] see examples above.

3. A connective sometimes accompanies the Ablative:
Nisi mūnitīs castrīs, *unless the camp should be fortified*. Caes.

4. A *noun* and an *adjective*, or even *two nouns*, may be in the Ablative Absolute:[4]
Serēnō caelō, *when the sky is clear*. Sen. Caniniō cōnsule, *in the consulship of Caninius*. Cic.

241. *Vocabulary.*

Abstineō, ēre, tinuī, tentum,	*to abstain, refrain.*
Acūtus, a, um,	*sharpened, sharp.*
Adhūc, *adv.*	*hitherto, thus far, as yet.*
Catēna, ae, *f.*	*chain.*
Culpa, ae, *f.*	*fault, blame.*
Dēligō, ere, lēgi, lēctum,	*to choose, select, elect.*
Latīnus, a, um,	*Latin.*
Līberō, āre, āvī, ātum,	*to free, liberate.*
Ligārius, iī, *m.*	*Ligarius*, a prominent Roman in whose behalf Cicero pleaded before Caesar.
Nāvigium, iī, *n.*	*vessel, ship.*

---

[1] Or, *while Servius was reigning* or *was king*.
[2] Or, *after the kings were banished*.
[3] The first method of translation comes nearer the original Latin conception, but the other methods generally accord better with the English idiom.
[4] This construction is peculiar to the Latin. In the corresponding constructions in Sanskrit, Greek, and English, the present participle of the verb *to be* is used.

Nōbilitās, ātis, *f.*	*nobility; the nobility, nobles.*
Probō, āre, āvī, ātum,	*to approve; to prove.*
Quārē, *adv.*	*wherefore.*
Relinquō, ere, līquī, lictum,	*to leave.*
Spoliō, āre, āvī, ātum,	*to despoil, rob, deprive.*
Sudēs, is, *f.*	*stake.*
Tamesis, is, *m.*	*the Thames.*
Trīnī, ae, a,	*three-fold, triple.*
Vacō, āre, āvī, ātum,	*to be without, be free from.*
Vinciō, īre, vīnxī, vīnctum,	*to bind.*

242. *Translate into English.*

1. Labiēnus monte occupātō nostrōs exspectābat, proeliōque abstinēbat. 2. Mūnītīs castrīs, Caesar duās ibī legiōnēs relīquit, quattuor reliquās in castra redūxit. 3. Ducēs iī[1] dēliguntur, quī summam scientiam reī mīlitāris habēre exīstimantur. 4. Caesar ad[2] flūmen Tamesim exercitum dūxit; ad[2] alteram flūminis rīpam māgnae cōpiae hostium erant īnstrūctae; rīpa autem erat acūtīs sudibus mūnīta. 5. Captīvī trīnīs catēnīs vinctī sunt. 6. Celtae Latīnā linguā Gallī appellantur.

7. Dumnorix, Divitiacī frāter, dīxit Galliam omnī nōbilitāte spoliātam esse. 8. Helvētiī tertiā ex parte lacū Lemannō et flūmine Rhodanō continentur. 9. Imperātor fortīs servitūte Graeciam līberāvit. 10. Mūrus dēfēnsōribus nūdātus est. 11. Tuum, Brūte,[3] jūdicium probō. 12. Adhūc, Caesar,[3] Quīntus Ligārius omnī culpā vacat. 13. Quārē cōnservāte, jūdicēs,[3] hunc hominem nōbilissimum. 14. Caesar nāvigia, quae sēcum habēbat, mīlitibus complērī jussit, et lēgātōs tribūnōsque mīlitum monuit, ut ad[2] tempus omnēs rēs ab iīs administrārentur.

---

[1] Observe that *iī* is the *subject*, and *ducēs* a *Predicate Noun.*

[2] Observe that different English words must be used in rendering this preposition, according to the connection in which it occurs. Thus *to the river, on* or *near the bank, at the* (proper) *time,* or *in time.*

[3] The Vocative rarely stands at the beginning of a sentence. It usually follows an emphatic word.

243. *Translate into Latin.*

1. As the general had freed the citizens from servitude,[1] he was called the father of his country. 2. May our country always be protected (*fortified*) by the valor of its citizens. 3. Having filled the ships with soldiers,[1] Caesar prepared to hasten into Britain. 4. Soldiers,[2] may you be called true friends of your country.
5. Having led his army to the Thames,[1] Caesar was told[3] that the enemy were on the other bank of the river. 6. General,[2] we ask that your army be led back into camp. 7. On hearing our words,[1] the general ordered his army to be led back into camp. 8. Citizens,[2] this man is free from blame; let him be selected as leader. 9. The general, leaving one legion in camp,[1] led the others toward the enemy.

LESSON LXXXIII.

FOUR CONJUGATIONS IN FULL. — EXERCISE IN READING AT SIGHT.

244. *Read at Sight, examine carefully, and translate into English.*

Gallia est dīvīsa in partēs trēs, quārum ūnam incolunt Belgae, aliam Aquītānī, tertiam Celtae, quī Latīnā linguā Gallī appellantur. Hōrum omnium fortissimī sunt Belgae, proptereā quod minimē ad eōs mercātōrēs saepe commeant, atque ea quae ad effēminandōs animōs pertinent important, prōximīque sunt Germānīs, quī trāns Rhēnum incolunt, qui-

---

[1] Be careful here and elsewhere not to render the English *words* by the corresponding Latin *words*, but consider by what *idiom* the *thought* should be expressed in Latin. Here the Ablative Absolute should be used, as if the English were *the citizens having been freed*, etc. In the first sentence, *the general* will become the subject of the principal verb.

[2] On the position of the Vocative, see page 192, foot-note 3.

[3] Latin idiom, *it was told to Caesar.*

buscum continenter bellum gerunt. Eādem dē causā Helvētiī reliquōs Celtās virtūte praecēdunt, quod ferē cotīdiānīs proeliīs cum Germānīs contendunt.

Helvētiī undique locī nātūrā continentur; ūnā ex parte flūmine Rhēnō, lātissimō atque altissimō, quī agrum Helvētium ā Germānīs dīvidit; alterā ex parte monte Jūrā, quī est inter Sēquanōs et Helvētiōs; tertiā lacū Lemannō et flūmine Rhodanō, quī prōvinciam Rōmānam ab Helvētiīs dīvidit. Ob eās rēs minus facile cum fīnitimīs bellum gerere possunt.

245. *Translate into Latin.*

1. War could not readily be waged[1] by the Helvetii with their neighbors. 2. Lake Lemannus and the river Rhone, by which the Helvetii are separated from the Roman province, shut in the Helvetii on one side. 3. The rest of the Celts are surpassed in valor by the Helvetii. 4. Wars were incessantly waged by the Germans with the Helvetii.

5. The things which are imported by merchants frequently weaken the spirit of the Gauls. 6. Caesar says that Gaul is divided into three parts. By whom are these parts of Gaul inhabited? 7. Those whom the Romans named Gauls, called themselves Celts. 8. Who were the bravest of all those who inhabited Gaul?

LESSON LXXXIV.

THIRD CONJUGATION. — VERBS IN IŌ. — ACTIVE VOICE. — REVIEW OF RULE LIX. — RULE LX.

246. *Lesson from the Grammar.*

217. A few verbs of the Third Conjugation form the Present Indicative in **iō, ior**, like verbs of the Fourth Conjugation. They are inflected with the endings of the Fourth, wherever those endings have two successive vowels.

---

[1] Render *was not able to be waged.*

VERBS IN IŌ.

218. Active Voice. — Capiō, *I take*.

Verb Stem, *cap;* **Present Stem,** *cape.*

PRINCIPAL PARTS.

Pres. Ind.	Pres. Inf.	Perf. Ind.	Supine.
capiō,	capere,	cēpi,	captum.

Indicative Mood.

PRESENT TENSE.

SINGULAR.   PLURAL.
capiō, capis, capit; | capimus, capitis, capiunt.

IMPERFECT.
capiēbam, -iēbās, -iēbat; | capiēbāmus, -iēbātis, -iēbant.

FUTURE.
capiam, -iēs, -iet; | capiēmus, -iētis, -ient.

PERFECT.
cēpī, -istī, -it; | cēpimus, -istis, -ērunt, *or* ēre.

PLUPERFECT.
cēperam, -erās, -erat; | cēperāmus, -erātis, -erant.

FUTURE PERFECT.
cēperō, -eris, -erit; | cēperimus, -eritis, -erint.

Subjunctive.

PRESENT.
capiam, -iās, -iat; | capiāmus, -iātis, -iant.

IMPERFECT.
caperem, -erēs, -eret; | caperēmus, -erētis, -erent.

PERFECT.
cēperim, -eris, -erit; | cēperimus, -eritis, -erint.

PLUPERFECT.
cēpissem, -issēs, -isset; | cēpissēmus, -issētis, -issent.

Imperative.

SINGULAR.   PLURAL.
Pres. cape; | capite.
Fut. capitō, | capitōte,
      capitō; | capiuntō.

VERBS IN IŌ.

INFINITIVE.	PARTICIPLE.
Pres. capere.	*Pres.* capiens.
Perf. cēpisse.	
Fut. captūrus esse.	*Fut.* captūrus.

GERUND.	SUPINE.
Gen. capiendī,	
Dat. capiendō,	
Acc. capiendum,	*Acc.* captum,
Abl. capiendō.	*Abl.* captū.

RULE LX. — Supine in ū.

547. The Supine in *ū* is generally used as an Ablative of Specification (231, 424):

Quid est tam jūcundum audītū, *what is so agreeable to hear (in hearing)?* Cic. Difficile dictū est, *it is difficult to tell.* Cic. Dē genere mortis difficile dictū est, *it is difficult to speak of the kind of death.* Cic. Cīvitās incrēdibile memorātū est quantum crēverit, *it is incredible to relate how much the state increased.* Sall.

247. *Vocabulary.*

Carrus, ī, *m.*	cart, wagon.
Certus, a, um,	certain; certiōrem facere, *to make more certain, to inform.*
Coëmō, ere, ēmī, ēmptum,	to buy up, obtain by purchase.
Cōnātum, ī, *n.*	undertaking, attempt, purpose.
Conjūrātiō, ōnis, *f.*	conspiracy.
Cupidītās, ātis, *f.*	desire.
Dō, dare, dedī, datum,	to give.
Facilis, e, *comp.* facilior, *sup.* facillimus,	easy.
Faciō, ere, fēcī, factum,	to do, make.
Fidēs, ēī, *f.*	faith, confidence; assurance,
Indūcō, ere, dūxī, ductum,	to induce, lead on. [pledge.
Jumentum, ī, *n.*	draught animal, beast of burden.
Mille,[1] *indeclinable,*	a thousand.

---

[1] *Mille* as an adjective is indeclinable; as a substantive it is used in the Nominative and Accusative singular, but in the plural it is declined like the plural of *mare* (63, 63): *milia, milium, milibus.* With the *substan-*

Parcō, ere, pepercī, parsum,	to spare. (Followed by the Dative.)
Perficiō, ere, fēci, fectum,	to accomplish.
Permoveō, ēre, mōvī, mōtum,	to move, induce, influence.
Quam, adv.	how; with a superlative, as . . . as possible; quam māximus, the largest possible, as large as possible.
Recipiō, ere, cēpi, ceptum,	to retake, betake.
Sementis, is, f.	sowing, planting.
Suscipiō, ere, cēpī, ceptum,	to take up, undertake.

248. *Translate into English.*

1. Caesar pācem cum Helvētiīs fēcit. 2. Pācem cum hostibus faciāmus. 3. Nōnne pācem cum Gallīs faciētis? Pācem cum iīs faciēmus. 4. Orgetorix sibī lēgātiōnem ad cīvitātēs suscēpit. Is rēgnī cupiditāte inductus conjūrātiōnem nōbilitātis Helvētiōrum fēcit. 5. Orgetorix facile esse factū Casticō et Dumnorigī probāvit cōnāta perficere. Iī hāc ōrātiōne adductī inter sē fidem dedērunt.[1] 6. Nostrī mīlitēs sub occāsum sōlis sē in castra recēpērunt. 7. Helvētiī, auctōritāte Orgetorīgis permōtī, cōnstituērunt jūmentōrum et carrōrum quam māximum numerum coëmere, et sēmentēs quam māximās facere.

8. Hostēs posterō diē castra ex eō locō movent: idem facit Caesar, equitātumque omnem ad numerum quattuor mīlium mittit, quī videant[2] quās in partēs hostēs iter faciant. 9. Omnēs ūnō tempore in hostēs impetum faciēmus. 10. Utinam eō tempore in hostēs impetum fēcissētis. 11. Nūntiī Caesarem dē hīs rēbus certiōrem faciēbant. 12. Dux Gallōrum māgnā manū ad castra nostra oppūgnātum venit. Hīs rēbus permōtus Quīntus Titūrius lēgātum ad Gallōs mittit rogātum ut sibī mīlitibusque[3] parcant.

---

tre mille, milia, the name of the objects enumerated is generally in the Genitive.

[1] *Inter sē dare,* 'to give each other,' 'to exchange.'
[2] See Suggestion XVII., 3.
[3] Indirect object; see 54, Rule XII.

249. *Translate into Latin.*

1. The Helvetii sent ambassadors to Caesar to ask peace. 2. As hostages had been sent by the Helvetii,[1] Caesar said that he would make peace with them. 3. The Gauls hastened to the winter quarters of the legion to attack it. 4. Caesar understood that to conquer the Helvetii was not an easy thing to do. 5. An hour[2] before sunset we shall betake ourselves into our camp.

6. Which is the easier thing to do, to march into the forest or to remain in the camp? 7. Who will inform us in which direction the enemy marched?[3] 8. The chiefs of the Gauls did not accomplish their purposes. 9. To accomplish[4] the purposes of the Helvetii, Orgetorix had undertaken an embassy to the other states of Gaul.

LESSON LXXXV.

THIRD CONJUGATION. — VERBS IN IO. — PASSIVE VOICE. RULE XLIV.

250. *Lesson from the Grammar.*

219. PASSIVE VOICE. — Capior, *I am taken.*

PRINCIPAL PARTS.

PRES. IND.	PRES. INF.	PERF. IND.
capior,	capi,	captus sum.

INDICATIVE MOOD.

PRESENT TENSE.

SINGULAR.	PLURAL.
capior, caperis, capitur;	capimur, capimini, capiuntur.

IMPERFECT.

capiëbar, -iëbāris, -iëbātur;	capiëbāmur, -iëbāmini, iëbantur.

---

[1] Use the Ablative Absolute.   [2] Ablative of Difference.
[3] An Indirect Question. What mood must be used?
[4] Remember that it is only after *verbs of motion* that the Supine is used to express purpose. Here a clause with *ut* should be used.

	FUTURE.
capiar, -iĕris, -iĕtur;	capiĕmur, -iĕminī, -ientur.
	PERFECT.
captus sum, es, est;	capti sumus, estis, sunt.
	PLUPERFECT.
captus eram, eras, erat;	capti eramus, eratis, erant.
	FUTURE PERFECT.
captus erō, eris, erit;	capti erimus, eritis, erunt.

SUBJUNCTIVE.

PRESENT.

SINGULAR.	PLURAL.
capiar, -iaris, iatur;	capiāmur, -iamini, -iantur.
	IMPERFECT.
caperer, ereris, -eretur;	caperemur, -eremini, -erentur.
	PERFECT.
captus sim, sis, sit;	capti simus, sitis, sint.
	PLUPERFECT.
captus essem, esses, esset;	capti essemus, essetis, essent.

IMPERATIVE.

Pres. capere;	capimini.
Fut. capitor, capitor;	capiuntor.

INFINITIVE.	PARTICIPLE.
Pres. capi.	
Perf. captus esse.	*Perf.* captus.
Fut. captum iri.	*Ger.* capiendus.

506. Every conditional sentence consists of two distinct parts, expressed or understood — the *Condition* and the *Conclusion:*

Si negem, mentiar, *if I should deny it, I should speak falsely.*[1] Cic.

---

[1] Here *si negem* is the condition, and *mentiar*, the conclusion.

CONDITIONAL SENTENCES.

RULE XLIV.— Conditional Sentences with si, nisi, ni, sin.

507. Conditional sentences with **si, nisi, ni, sin,** take —

I. The INDICATIVE in both clauses *to assume* the supposed case:

Sī spīrĭtum dūcit, vīvit, *if he breathes, he is alive.* Cic. Sī tot exempla virtūtis nōn movent, nihil unquam movēbit, *if so many examples of valor do not move (you), nothing will ever move (you).* Liv.

II. The PRESENT or PERFECT SUBJUNCTIVE in both clauses to represent the supposed case as *possible:*

Diēs dēficiat, si velim causam dēfendere, *the day would fail me, if I should wish to defend the cause.* Cic. Improbē fēcĕris, nisi monueris, *you would do wrong, if you should not give warning.* Cic.

III. The IMPERFECT or PLUPERFECT SUBJUNCTIVE in both clauses to represent the supposed case as *contrary to fact:*

Plūribus verbis ad tē scrīberem, si rēs verba dēsiderāret, *I should write to you more fully (with more words), if the case required words.* Cic. Si voluisset, dīmicāsset, *if he had wished, he would have fought.* Nep.

251. *Vocabulary.*

Admittō, ere, misi, missum,	*to admit, commit.*
Biennium, ii, *n.*	*two years, space of two years.*
Cōnficiō, ere, fēci, fectum,	*to accomplish, complete, finish, bring to a close.*
Contrōversia, ae, *f.*	*controversy, dispute.*
Dēcernō, ere, crēvī, crētum,	*to decide, decree.*
Dēfessus, a, um,	*tired, exhausted, weary.*
Dēleō, ēre, ēvī, ētum,	*to destroy.*
Druidēs, um, *m. pl.*	*Druids,* the priests of the Gauls.
Facinus, facinoris, *n.*	*misdeed, crime.*
Hērēditās, ātis, *f.*	*inheritance.*
Interficiō, ere, fēci, fectum,	*to kill, slay, put to death.*
Jaciō, ere, jēci, jactum,	*to throw.*
Labor, ōris, *m.*	*labor, toil, effort, exertion.*
Mōs, mōris, *m.*	*usage, custom.*
Poena, ae, *f.*	*penalty, punishment.*
Praecipitō, āre, āvī, ātum,	*to precipitate, throw, hurl.*

Prīvātus, a, um, — *private, personal.*
Prōdĭtor, ōris, m. — *traitor.*
Prōĭcĭō,[1] ere, prōjēcī, jectum, — *to throw forward, throw down.*
Pūblĭcus, a, um, — *public.*
Sī, *conj.* — *if.*
Vĭnculum, ī, n. — *fetter, bond, chain.*

252. *Translate into English.*

1. Germānōrum[2] bellum celeriter cōnficiētur. 2. Bellum Helvētiōrum[2] jam cōnfectum erat. 3. Bellō Helvētiōrum cōnfectō,[3] totīus ferē Galliae lēgātī, prīncipēs cīvitātum, ad Caesarem convēnērunt. 4. Germānī suōs interficī vīdērunt; māgnō numerō interfectō,[3] reliquī sē in flūmen praecipitāvērunt. 5. Quid cōnficiētur? Eae rēs cōnficī dēbent. Ad eās rēs cōnficiendās[4] biennium nōbīs satis dūcimus. Quis ad eās rēs cōnficiendās[4] dēligētur? Jam tū dēlēctus es. 6. Lapidēs undique in mūrum jaciuntur, mūrusque dēfēnsōribus nūdātur. 7. In Galliā Druidēs ferē dē omnibus contrōversiīs pūblicīs prīvātīsque cōnstituunt; sī quod est admissum facinus, poenās cōnstituunt; sī dē hērēditāte contrōversia est, iīdem dēcernunt. 8. Sī quod sit admissum facinus, poenās cōnstituāmus. 9. Sī quod esset admissum facinus, poenās cōnstituissēmus.

10. Ego hōc cōnsilium probārem, sī nūllum perīculum vidērem. 11. Ego hōc cōnsilium probāvissem, sī nūllum perīculum vīdissem. 12. Helvētiī, sī pācem populus Rōmānus cum iīs fēcisset, arma prōjēcissent. 13. Nisi tōtīus diēī labōre mīlitēs essent dēfessī, omnēs hostium cōpiae dēlētae essent. 14. Helvētiī mōribus suīs[5] prōditōrem ex vinculīs[6] dīcere[7] coēgērunt.

---

[1] Pronounced as though spelled *prōjĭcĭō*.
[2] English idiom, *war with the Germans*, etc.
[3] See Suggestion XVI., (1).
[4] See Suggestion XIII., 4.
[5] *In accordance with*, etc. See 158, Rule XXII.
[6] English idiom, IN *chains*.
[7] In this connection *dicere* may be rendered *plead*.

253. *Translate into Latin.*

1. If stones had been thrown against the wall, it would have been stripped of soldiers. 2. Should stones be thrown against the wall, the town would be taken. 3. If the general were in the camp, the soldiers would not be daunted by fear. 4. If the general is in the camp, we ought not to fear danger. 5. If the war with the Helvetii should be finished, ambassadors would assemble from the rest of Gaul.

6. If any crime has been committed by these men, let the penalty be determined by the judge. 7. If our city had been fortified, we should not see these perils.[1] 8. If we approved your plan, we should not have accomplished these things so successfully.[1] 9. After these things were accomplished,[2] peace was made with the enemy.

LESSON LXXXVI.

FOUR CONJUGATIONS IN FULL, INCLUDING VERBS IN
IŎ. — RULE XLVI.

254. *Lesson from the Grammar.*

514. A concessive clause is one that concedes or admits something, generally introduced in English by *though* or *although:*[3]

Quamquam itinere fessi erant, tamen prōcēdunt, *although they were weary with the journey, they still* (yet) *advanced.* Sall.

---

[1] Observe that in 7, the condition refers to past time, and the conclusion to present time, while in 8 the condition refers to present time, and the conclusion to past time.

[2] Use the Ablative Absolute.

[3] *Concessive* clauses bear a close resemblance to *conditional* clauses both in form and in use. *Sī optimum est,* 'if it is best,' is a condition; *etsī optimum est,* 'even if (or though) it is best,' is a concession; the one *assumes* a supposed case, the other *admits* it.

CONCESSIVE CLAUSES.

RULE XLVI.— Moods in Concessive Clauses.

515. Concessive clauses take —

I. Generally the *Indicative* in the best prose, when introduced by *quamquam :*

Quamquam intellegunt, tamen nunquam dicunt, *though they understand, they never speak.* Cic. Quamquam festinās, nōn est mora longa, *though you are in haste, the delay is not long.* Hor.

II. The *Indicative* or *Subjunctive*, when introduced by *etsī, etiamsī, tametsī,* or *sī,* like conditional clauses with *sī.* Thus —

1. The *Indicative* is used to represent the supposed case as a *fact:*

Gaudeō, etsī nihil sciō quod gaudeam, *I rejoice, though I know no reason why I should rejoice.* Plaut.

2. The *Present* or *Perfect Subjunctive,* to represent the supposed case as *possible:*

Etsī nihil habeat in sē glōria, tamen virtūtem sequitur, *though glory may not possess anything in itself, yet it follows virtue.* Cic.

3. The *Imperfect* or *Pluperfect Subjunctive,* to represent the supposed case as *contrary to fact:*

Etiamsī mors oppetenda esset, domī māllem, *even if death ought to be met, I should prefer to meet it at home.* Cic.

III. The *Subjunctive,* when introduced by *licet, quamvīs, ut, nē, cum,* or the relative *quī :*

Licet irrideat, plūs tamen ratiō valēbit, *though he may deride, reason will yet avail more.* Cic. Nōn tū possis, quamvīs excellās, *you would not be able, although you excel.* Cic. Ut dēsint virēs, tamen est laudanda voluntās, *though the strength fails, still the will should be approved.* Ovid. Nē sit summum malum dolor, malum certē est, *though pain may not be the greatest evil, it is certainly an evil.* Cic. Cum domī dīvitiae adfluerent, fuēre tamen cīvēs, etc., *though wealth abounded at home, there were yet citizens,* etc. Sall.

255. *Vocabulary.*

Aestās, ātis, *f.*	*summer.*
Circummūniō, īre, īvī, ītum,	*to wall around, encompass, surround.*
Conciliō, āre, āvī, ātum,	*to win, secure.*
Crēber, bra, brum,	*frequent.*

CONCESSIVE CLAUSES.

Cupiō, ere, īvī *or* iī, ītum, — to desire.
Cūrō, āre, āvī, ātum, — to care, care for; aliquid faciendum cūrāre, to have anything done.
Etsi, conj. — although.
Excursiō, ōnis, f. — sally, sortie.
Exigō, ere, ēgī, āctum, — to complete, finish, end.
Exiguus, a, um, — restricted, limited, scanty, small.
Graecus, a, um, — Greek, Grecian. [brief.
Ignōrō, āre, āvī, ātum, — not to know, to be ignorant of.
Indicium, iī, n. — testimony, evidence.
Juvō, āre, jūvī, jūtum, — to aid.
Mātūrus, a, um, — early.
Orbis, is, m. — circle, circuit; orbis terrārum, the
Ōrdō, inis, m. — rank. [earth, world.
Perpetuus, a, um, — perpetual, endless, uninterrupted.
Respiciō, ere, spēxī, spectum, — to regard, look upon.
Tabula, ae, f. — table, tablet; document, record.
Terra, ae, f. — earth, land.
Trānsdūcō, ere, dūxī, ductum, to lead across.

256. *Translate into English.*

1. Ea rēs Helvētiīs per indicium ēnūntiātur. 2. Caesar pontem in[1] Ararē faciendum cūrāvit[2] atque ita exercitum trānsdūxit. 3. In castrīs Helvētiōrum tabulae repertae sunt, litterīs Graecīs cōnfectae. 4. Orgetorix dīxit sē suae cīvitātis imperium obtentūrum esse. Is sē suīs cōpiīs suōque exercitū Casticō Dumnorigīque rēgna conciliātūrum esse cōnfirmābat. 5. Sī Lingonēs Helvētiōs frūmentō jūvissent, Caesar eōs prō hostibus habuisset. 6. Hostēs prīmō adventū exercitūs nostrī crēbrās ex oppidō excursiōnēs faciēbant; posteā vallō circummūnītī[3] oppidō sēsē continēbant. 7. Eōdem ferē tempore Caesar, etsī prope exācta jam aestās erat, tamen in aliam gentem exercitum addūxit.

8. Exiguā parte aestātis reliquā, Caesar, etsī in Galliā mātūrae sunt hiemēs, tamen in Britanniam contendit. 9.

---

[1] English idiom, OVER.
[2] Literally, *cared for a bridge to be made*, i.e. *attended to the making of a bridge;* render, *had a bridge made.*
[3] That is, *by our works.*

Etsī nōndum Britannōrum cōnsilia cōgnōverat, tamen perīculum vidēbat. 10. Cum ea ita sint, tamen vōbīscum pācem faciēmus. 11. Cum prīmī ōrdinēs hostium interfectī essent, tamen reliquī fortiter pūgnābant. 12. Caesar sē prīncipem nōn sōlum urbis Rōmae, sed orbis terrārum esse cupiēbat. 13. Sī ea quae in aliīs nātiōnibus geruntur īgnōrātis, respicite fīnitimam Galliam, quae perpetuā premitur servitūte.

257. *Translate into Latin.*

1. Although we see other lands distressed by slavery, our country is free. 2. Although these things have been announced to the enemy,[1] they do not know what is done in our camp. 3. Although many very brave soldiers have been slain,[1] we desire to make peace with the enemy. 4. Although a bridge has been made over the river,[1] the army has not yet been led across.

5. What was found in the camp of the Helvetii? Caesar tells us what was found in their camp.[2] 6. Caesar regarded them as enemies, in order that other nations might not assist the Helvetii. 7. If a bridge had been made,[1] the army could have been[3] led over. 8. Although they had made peace[1] a few days before, they made frequent attacks upon the Roman camp.

LESSON LXXXVII.

FOUR CONJUGATIONS. — DEPONENT VERBS. —
RULE XXVI.

258. *Lesson from the Grammar.*

DEPONENT VERBS.

231. Deponent Verbs have in general the forms of the Passive Voice with the signification of the Active. But —

---

[1] In all these sentences we may use the Ablative Absolute, but a finite verb with a conjunction expresses more clearly the *concessive* or *conditional* force of the clause.

[2] An *Indirect Question*. [3] Render, *would have been able to be led.*

DEPONENT VERBS.

1. They have also in the Active, the future Infinitive, the participles, gerund, and supine.

2. The gerundive generally has the passive signification; sometimes also the perfect participle: *hortandus*, to be exhorted; *expertus*, tried.

3. The Future Infinitive of the Passive form is rare, as the Active form is generally used.

NOTE.—The synopsis of a single example will sufficiently illustrate the peculiarities of Deponent Verbs.

232. Hortor, *I exhort*.

1. PRINCIPAL PARTS.

hortor,   hortāri,   hortātus sum.

2. PRESENT SYSTEM; STEM, *hortā*.

INDICATIVE.	SUBJUNCTIVE.	IMPER.	INFINITIVE.	PARTICIPLE.
Pres. hortor[1]	horter		hortāre, hortāri	hortāns
Imp. hortābar	hortārer			
Fut. hortābor			hortātor	

Gerund, hortandī.   Gerundive, hortandus.

3. SUPINE SYSTEM; STEM, *hortāt*.

Perf. hortātus sum	hortātus sim		hortātus esse	hortātus
Plup. hortātus eram	hortātus essem			
F. P. hortātus erō				
Fut.			hortātūrus esse	hortātūrus

Supine, hortātum, hortātū.

RULE XXVI.—Ablative in Special Constructions.[2]

421. The Ablative is used—

I. With **ūtor, fruor, fungor, potior, vescor**, and their compounds:

---

[1] The tenses are inflected regularly throughout: *hortor, hortāris, hortātur; hortāmur, hortāmini, hortantur.* All the forms in this synopsis have the active meaning, *I exhort, I was exhorting*, etc., except the Gerundive, which has the passive force, *deserving to be exhorted, to be exhorted*. The Gerundive, as it is passive in meaning, cannot be used in intransitive Deponent Verbs, except in an impersonal sense; see 281, 301, 1.

[2] This Ablative is readily explained as the Ablative of *means:* thus, *ūtor*, 'I use,' 'I serve myself *by means of*'; *fruor*, 'I enjoy,' 'I delight myself *with*'; *vescor*, 'I feed upon,' 'I feed myself *with*,' etc.

DEPONENT VERBS. 207

Plūrimīs rēbus fruimur et ūtimur, we enjoy and use VERY MANY THINGS. Cic. *Māgnā est praedā potītus,* he obtained GREAT BOOTY. Nep. *Lacte et carne vescēbantur,* they lived upon milk and flesh. Sall.

II. With VERBS and ADJECTIVES OF PLENTY:

Villa abundat *lacte, cāseō, melle,* the villa abounds IN MILK, CHEESE, and HONEY. Cic. Urbs referta *copiīs,* a city filled WITH SUPPLIES. Cic. Virtūte praeditus, *endowed with virtue.* Cic. Deus bonis explēvit mundum, *God has filled the world with blessings.* Cic.

III. With dignus, indignus,[1] and contentus:

Dignī sunt *amīcitiā,* they are worthy OF FRIENDSHIP. Cic. Vir patre dignus, *a man worthy* OF HIS FATHER. Cic. Honōre indignissimus, *most unworthy of honor.* Cic. Nātūrā parvō contenta, *nature content with little.* Cic.

NOTE 1. — Transitive verbs of Plenty[2] take the Accusative and Ablative:

Armīs nāvēs onerat, *he loads the ships with arms.* Sall.

259. *Vocabulary.*

Abundō, āre, āvī, ātum,	*to abound, to be well supplied*
Arbitror, ārī, ātus sum,	*to think.* [*with.*
Cōnfīdō, ere, fīsus sum,[3]	*to trust, have confidence in, rely*
Cōnor, ārī, ātus sum,	*to try, attempt.* [*upon.*
Contentus, a, um,	*content, satisfied.*
Indignus, a, um,	*unworthy.*
Interclūdō, ere, clūsī, clūsum,	*to cut off.*
Nūllus, a, um, 45, 151,	*not any, no, none.*
Persuādeō, ēre, suāsī, suāsum,	*to persuade.*
Potior, īrī, ītus sum,	*to gain possession of, take possession of, obtain possession of.*
Prīvō, āre, āvī, ātum,	*to deprive.*
Proficīscor, ī, profectus sum,	*to start, set out.*

---

[1] The nature of the Ablative with *dignus* and *indignus* is somewhat uncertain. On etymological grounds it is explained as *instrumental;* see Delbrück, p. 72; Corssen, 'Krit. Beitr.,' p. 47.

[2] Transitive verbs of *plenty* mean 'to fill,' 'to furnish with,' etc., as *cumulō, compleō, impleō, imbuō, instruō, onerō, ornō,* etc.

[3] *Cōnfīdō* is a *semi-deponent,* i.e. in the tenses for completed action it has the forms of the passive voice, with the meaning of the active.

DEPONENT VERBS.

Trānō, āre, āvī, ātum,   *to swim across.*
Tūtō, *adv.*   *safely.*
Tūtus, a, um,   *safe.*
Ūllus, a, um, 45, 131,   *any, any one.*
Ūtor, ī, ūsus sum,   *to use.*
Versus, ūs, *m.*   *verse.*
Vīs, vīs, *f.*   *force, violence; pl.* vīrēs, vīrium,
Vulnus, eris, *n.*   *wound.*   [*strength.*

260. *Translate into English.*

1. Helvētiī dē fīnibus suīs cum omnibus cōpiīs proficīscōantur. 2. Orgetorix Casticō[1] persuādet ut rēgnum in cīviāte suā occupet, itemque[2] Dumnorigī ut idem cōnētur. 3. Prōditōrēs hanc urbem dēlēre cōnantur. 4. Prōditor nōs omnēs vītā prīvāre cōnātus est. 5. Tibī, Caesar, bonī virī grātiās agunt. 6. Bellō cōnfectō, omnēs Galliae cīvitātēs ēgātōs ad Caesarem mīsērunt. 7. Eō tempore Druidēs Graecīs litterīs ūtēbantur. 8. Druidēs versūs suōs litterīs ōn mandant, cum in reliquīs ferē rēbus Graecīs litterīs itantur.

9. Aeduī prō Bellovacīs rogābant ut Caesar suā clementiā n eōs ūterētur. 10. Labiēnus castrīs hostium potītus est. 1. Hostēs, commeātū interclūsō, sine ūllō vulnere vīctōriā otīrī cupiunt. Illī, etsī sē tūtō pūgnātūrōs exīstimābant, amen tūtius[3] esse arbitrābantur, commeātū interclūsō, sine illō vulnere vīctōriā potīrī. 12. Hostēs ad flūmen Rhēnum 'ēnērunt; ibī paucī vīribus cōnfīsī trānāre contendērunt. 13. Vercingetorix equitātū abundābat. Is mīlitibus quōs anteā iabuerat sē esse contentum dīxit. 14. Mīlitēs extrēmam 'amem sustinēbant, nūlla tamen vōx est ab[4] iīs audīta, populī Rōmānī glōriā et superiōribus vīctōriīs indīgna. 15. Gallī uperiōrem partem collis castrīs suīs complēvērunt.

---

[1] *Indirect Object;* the clause with *ut* is the *Direct Object.*
[2] *Item* modifies *persuādet.*
[3] What determines the gender of this predicate adjective?
[4] The context here shows that *ab* should be rendered *from*, not *by.*

261. *Translate into Latin.*

1. Although the Gauls were well supplied with grain, Caesar was cut off from supplies. 2. Gaul was filled with very warlike nations. 3. We shall not obtain possession of the camp of the enemy without receiving[1] many wounds. 4. Many words which we hear are unworthy of wise men. 5. The Helvetii were not contented with their territory, but desired to obtain possession of the lands of their neighbors. 6. The general, relying on[2] the valor of his soldiers, has determined to assault the town. 7. We shall attempt to set out to-night.[3] 8. Caesar thought that he should use the supplies of grain which were sent by the Aedui. 9. Do you understand for what reason the Druids used Greek letters?[4]

LESSON LXXXVIII.

FOUR CONJUGATIONS IN FULL. — RULES LIII. AND LIV.

262. *Lesson from the Grammar.*

INDIRECT DISCOURSE. — *Ōrātiŏ Oblīqua.*

522. When a writer or speaker expresses thoughts, whether his own or those of another, in any other form than in the original words of the author, he is said to use the Indirect Discourse — *Ōrātiŏ Oblīqua :*[5]

Platōnem ferunt in Ītaliam vēnisse, *they say that Plato came into Italy.* Cic. Respondeō tē dolōrem ferre moderātē, *I reply that you bear the affliction with moderation.* Cic. Ūtilem arbitror esse scientiam, *I think that knowledge is useful.* Cic.

---

[1] In rendering, omit *receiving.*
[2] See 260, sentence 12.
[3] Render on *this night.*
[4] What kind of a clause? See 127, 529.
[5] Thus, in the first example, *Platōnem in Ītaliam vēnisse* is in the indirect discourse; in the direct, i e. in the original words of those who made the statement, it would be *Platō in Ītaliam vēnit.*

1. In distinction from the INDIRECT DISCOURSE — *Ōrātiō Obliqua*, the original words of the author are said to be in the DIRECT DISCOURSE — *Ōrātiō Rēcta*.

2. Words quoted without change belong to the DIRECT DISCOURSE: Rēx 'duumvirōs' inquit 'secundum lēgem faciō,' *the king said, 'I appoint duumvirs according to law.'* Liv.

RULE LIII.— Moods in Principal Clauses.

523. The principal clauses of the DIRECT DISCOURSE on becoming INDIRECT take the *Infinitive* or *Subjunctive* as follows:

I. When DECLARATIVE, they take the *Infinitive with a Subject Accusative*.

Dicēbat animōs esse divinōs, *he was wont to say that souls are divine.* Cic. Platōnem Tarentum vēnisse reperiō, *I find that Plato came to Tarentum.* Cic. Catō mirāri sē aiēbat, *Cato was wont to say that he wondered.* Cic. Hippiās glōriātus est, ānulum sē suā manū cōnfēcisse,[1] *Hippias boasted that he had made the ring with his own hand.* Cic.

II. When INTERROGATIVE, they take —

1. Generally the *Subjunctive:*

Ad postulāta Caesaris respondit, quid sibi vellet, cūr veniret,[2] *to the demands of Caesar he replied, what did he wish, why did he come?* Caes.

2. Sometimes the *Infinitive with a Subject Accusative*, as in rhetorical questions:[3]

---

[1] In the direct discourse these examples would read — (1) *animi sunt divini*, (2) *Platō Tarentum rēnit*, (3) *miror*, and (4) *ānulum meā manū cōnfēci*. Observe that the pronominal subjects implied in *miror* and *cōnfēci* are expressed with the Infinitive, as *mirāri sē, sē cōnfēcisse*. But the subject is sometimes omitted when it can be readily supplied; see second example under II., 2, below.

[2] In the direct discourse this example would read — *quid tibi vis? cūr venis?*

[3] A question used for rhetorical effect in place of an assertion is called a *Rhetorical Question*, as *num potest*, 'can he?' = *nōn potest*, 'he can not'; *quid est turpius*, 'what is baser?' = *nihil est turpius*, 'nothing is baser.'

Docēbant rem esse testimōniō, etc.; quid esse levius, etc., *they showed that the fact was a proof* (for a proof), etc.; *what was more inconsiderate*, etc. ? Caes. Respondit, num memoriam dēpōnere posse,[1] *he replied, could he lay aside the recollection ?* Caes.

III. When IMPERATIVE,[2] they take the *Subjunctive:*

Scribit Labiēnō cum legiōne veniat, *he writes to Labienus to come (that he should come) with a legion.* Caes. Redditur respōnsum, castris sē tenērent, *the reply was returned, that they should keep themselves in camp.* Liv. Mīlitēs certiōrēs facit, sē reficerent, *he directed the soldiers to refresh themselves.* Caes. Ōrābant ut sibi auxilium ferret, *they prayed that he would bring them help.* Caes. Nūntius vēnit, nē dubitāret,[3] *a message came that he should not hesitate.* Nep.

RULE LIV.— Moods in Subordinate Clauses.

524. The subordinate clauses of the DIRECT DISCOURSE on becoming INDIRECT take the *Subjunctive:*

Respondit sē id quod in Nerviīs fēcisset factūrum,[4] *he replied that he would do what he had done in the case of the Nervii.* Caes. Hippiās glōriātus est, ānulum quem habēret sē suā manū cōnfēcisse,[5] *Hippias boasted that he had made with his own hand the ring which he wore.* Cic.

526. In passing from the DIRECT DISCOURSE to the INDIRECT, pronouns of the first and second persons are generally changed to pronouns of the third person,[6] and the first and

---

Here belong many questions which in the direct form have the verb in the first or in the third person. As such questions are equivalent to declarative sentences, they take the same construction, the Infinitive with its subject.

[1] Direct discourse — (1) *quid est levius* = *nihil est levius*, and (2) *num memoriam dēpōnere possum* = *memoriam dēpōnere nōn possum*.
[2] Imperative sentences include those sentences which take the Subjunctive *of Desire;* see 114, 483.
[3] In the direct discourse these examples would read — (1) *cum legiōne venī*, (2) *castrīs vōs tenēte*, (3) *vōs reficite*, (4) *nōbīs auxilium fer*, (5) *nōlī dubitāre*.
[4] Direct, *faciam id quod in Nerviīs fēcī.*
[5] Direct, *ānulum quem habeō meā manū cōnfēcī.*
[6] Thus — (1) *ego* is changed to *suī, sibī,* etc., or to *ipse; meus* and *noster to suus;* (2) *tū* to *is* or *ille*, sometimes to *suī,* etc.; *tuus* and *vester* to *suus* or to the Genitive of *is;* and (3) *hīc* and *iste* to *ille.*

INDIRECT DISCOURSE.

second persons of verbs are generally changed to the third person:

Gloriātus est, ānulum sē suā manū cōnfēcisse,[1] *he boasted that he had made the ring with his own hand.* Cic. Redditur respōnsum, castris sē tenērent,[2] *the reply was returned that they should keep themselves in camp.* Liv. Respondit, sī obsidēs ab iīs sibi dentur, sēsē cum iīs pācem esse factūrum,[3] *he replied that if hostages were given to him by them, he would make peace with them.* Caes.

263. *Vocabulary.*

Appetō, ere, petīvī *or* iī, ītum,	*to seek after, seek.*
Artificium, iī, *n.*	*artifice.*
Concilium, iī, *n.*	*council, meeting.*
Creō, āre, āvī, ātum,	*to create, elect, appoint.*
Discēdō, ere, cessī, cessum,	*to depart, withdraw, swerve.*
Polliceor, ērī, itus sum,	*to promise.*
Prius, *adv. comp.*, *sup.* prīmum,	*before, sooner;* prius quam, *sooner than, before.*
Quisquam, quaequam, quicquam,	*anyone, anything.*
Respondeō, ēre, spondī, spōnsum,	*to answer.*

264. *Translate into English.*

1. Ariovistus respondit sē prius in Galliam vēnisse, quam populum Rōmānum.[4] Dīxit omnēs Galliae cīvitātēs contrā sē castra habuisse,[5] eās omnēs cōpiās ā sē ūnō proeliō superātās esse.[4] 2. Posterō diē, conciliō convocātō, Vercingetorix dīxit nōn virtūte neque in aciē vīcisse Rōmānōs,[4] sed artificiō quōdam et scientiā oppūgnātiōnis.[6] 3. Aeduī summō in perīculō sunt. Aeduī dīcunt sē summō in perīculō esse.[4] Dīxērunt sē summō esse in perīculō. 4. Aeduī summō in

---

[1] Direct, *ānulum ego meā manū cōnfēcī. Ego* becomes *sē*, and *meā, suā.*
[2] Direct, *castris vōs tenēte. Vōs* becomes *sē*, and *tenēte, tenērent.*
[3] Direct, *si obsidēs ā vōbīs mihī dabuntur, vōbīscum pācem faciam. A vōbīs* becomes *ab iīs; mihī* becomes *sibī; vōbīscum, cum iīs;* and the implied subject of *faciam* becomes *sēsē*, the subject of *esse factūrum*.
[4] Give the Direct form corresponding to this Indirect Discourse.
[5] *Castra habēre*, literally, *to have camp*, may be rendered *to encamp, to take the field.*
[6] English idiom, *skill in assault*.

periculō erant. Aeduī dīcunt sē summō fuisse in periculō.¹ Dīxērunt sē summō fuisse in periculō.

5. Liscus magistrātum gerēbat. Hōc tempore duo magistrātum gerunt. Aeduī summō in periculō sunt quod duo magistrātum gerunt. Aeduī dīcunt sē summō esse in periculō, quod duo magistrātum gerant, et sē uterque eōrum lēgibus creātum esse dīcat.¹ Dīxērunt sē summō esse in periculō, quod duo magistrātum gererent, et sē uterque eōrum lēgibus creātum esse dīceret.

6. Nōnne Orgetorix suae cīvitātis imperium obtinēbit? Dīcit sē suae cīvitātis imperium obtentūrum esse.¹ 7. Imperātor cum hostibus pācem faciet. Dīcit sī² obsidēs ab hostibus sibī dentur, utī eōs ea quae polliceantur factūrōs intellegat, sēsē cum iīs pācem esse factūrum.¹ 8. Caesar dīxit Ariovistum sē cōnsule³ populī Rōmānī amīcitiam appetisse;¹ cūr hunc quisquam ab officiō discessūrum jūdicāret?

265. *Translate into Latin.*

1. Caesar says that Gaul was divided into three parts; that the Belgae inhabited one of these, the Aquitani another, and the Celts the third.⁴ 2. He said that a third part of Gaul was inhabited by those who called themselves Celts, but whom the Romans named Gauls.⁴ He said that the Helvetii were the bravest of the Gauls, and that they were nearest to the Germans, with whom they were continually waging war.⁴ 3. The Helvetii said that if the Romans made peace with them, they would remain where Caesar desired; but that if peace was not made, the Romans would be regarded by them as enemies.⁴ Although they had attempted to march through the province, they said that they wished to make peace.⁴

---

¹ Give the corresponding Direct form.
² What form of condition in Direct Discourse?
³ Ablative Absolute, *he being consul;* render, *in his consulship.*
⁴ Give the corresponding Direct form in English and in Latin.

LESSON LXXXIX.

PERIPHRASTIC CONJUGATIONS. — EXERCISE IN READING AT SIGHT.

266. *Lesson from the Grammar.*

233. The ACTIVE PERIPHRASTIC CONJUGATION, formed by combining the Future Active Participle with *sum*, denotes an intended or future action:

Amātūrus sum, *I am about to love.*

	INDICATIVE.	SUBJUNCTIVE.	INFINITIVE.
Pres.	amātūrus sum[1]	amātūrus sim	amātūrus esse
Imp.	amātūrus eram	amātūrus essem	
Fut.	amātūrus erō		
Perf.	amātūrus fui	amātūrus fuerim	amātūrus fuisse
Plup.	amātūrus fueram	amātūrus fuissem	
F. P.	amātūrus fuerō[1]		

234. The PASSIVE PERIPHRASTIC CONJUGATION, formed by combining the Gerundive with *sum*, denotes *necessity* or *duty*.

Amandus sum, *I must be loved.*[2]

Pres.	amandus sum	amandus sim	amandus esse
Imp.	amandus eram	amandus essem	
Fut.	amandus erō		
Perf.	amandus fui	amandus fuerim	amandus fuisse
Plup.	amandus fueram	amandus fuissem	
F. P.	amandus fuerō		

267. *Read at Sight, examine carefully, and translate into English.*

Helvētiī, auctōritāte Orgetorigis permōtī, cōnstituērunt dē fīnibus suīs cum omnibus cōpiīs proficīscī, jūmentōrum et carrōrum quam māximum numerum coëmere, sēmentēs quam māximās facere, cum prōximīs cīvitātibus pācem et amīcitiam cōnfirmāre. Ad eās rēs cōnficiendās biennium sibī satis esse

---

[1] The periphrastic forms are inflected regularly. The Future Perfect is exceedingly rare.   [2] Or, *I deserve* (ought) *to be loved.*

dūxĕrunt; in tertium annum profectiōnem lēge cōnfirmāvērunt. Ad eās rēs cōnficiendās Orgetorix dēlēctus est. Is sibī lēgātiōnem ad cīvitātēs suscēpit. In eō itinere persuāsit Casticō Sēquanō, ut rēgnum in cīvitāte suā occupāret; itemque Dumnorigī Aeduō, ut idem cōnārētur persuāsit. Facile esse factū illīs probāvit cōnātūs perficere; sē suae cīvitātis imperium obtentūrum esse, et suīs cōpiīs suōque exercitū illīs rēgna conciliātūrum cōnfirmāvit. Hāc ōrātiōne adductī inter sē fidem dedērunt. Ea rēs est Helvētiīs per indicium ēnūntiāta. Mōribus suīs Orgetorigem ex vinculīs causam dīcere coēgērunt.

268. *Translate into Latin.*

1. Orgetorix was intending to secure[1] regal power in his state. 2. There were many things to be accomplished[2] by the Helvetii, if they wished to set out from their territory. 3. In accordance with the customs[3] of the Helvetii, Orgetorix, who was regarded by them as a traitor, was forced to plead his cause in chains.[4] 4. It was announced to the Helvetii what Orgetorix was attempting to accomplish. 5. He had said that he would secure for these chieftains regal power in their states. To accomplish his attempt was not an easy thing to do. He had persuaded the Helvetii to set out from their territory with all their forces.

LESSON XC.

IRREGULAR VERBS.—*Possum* AND *Ferō*.

269. *Lesson from the Grammar.*

289. A few verbs which have special irregularities are called, by way of preëminence, *Irregular* or *Anomalous Verbs*.

---

[1] See 266, 233. [2] See 266, 234.
[3] *In accordance with*, etc., use the Ablative, under 158, 413.
[4] See 252, sentence 14.

POSSUM AND FERŌ.

290. **Possum,**[1] posse, potuī, *to be able.*

INDICATIVE.
SINGULAR.   **PLURAL.**

Pres. possum, potes, potest; possumus, potestis, possunt.
Imp. poteram;[2] poterāmus.
Fut. poterō; poterimus.
Perf. potuī; potuimus.
Plup. potueram; potuerāmus.
F. P. potuerō; potuerĭmus.

SUBJUNCTIVE.

Pres. possim, possis, possit; possīmus, possītis, possint.
Imp. possem; possēmus.
Perf. potuerim; potuerĭmus.
Plup. potuissem; potuissēmus.

INFINITIVE.   PARTICIPLE.

Pres. posse.   *Pres.* potēns (*as an adjective*).
Perf. potuisse.

292. **Ferō,**[3] ferre, tulī, lātum, *to bear.*

ACTIVE VOICE.
INDICATIVE.
SINGULAR.   **PLURAL.**

Pres. ferō, fers, fert; ferimus, fertis,[4] ferunt.
Imp. ferēbam;[5] ferēbāmus.
Fut. feram; ferēmus.
Perf. tulī; tulimus.
Plup. tuleram; tulerāmus.
F. P. tulerō; tulerĭmus.

---

[1] *Possum* is compounded of *potis*, 'able,' and *sum*, 'to be.' In *possum* observe —

1) That *potis* drops *is*, and that *t* is assimilated before *s*; *possum* for *potsum.*
2) That the Perfect is *potuī*, not *potfuī.*
3) That the Infinitive *posse* and Subjunctive *possem* are shortened forms for *potesse* and *potessem.*

[2] Inflected regularly through the different persons: *poteram, poterās, poterat,* etc. So also in the other tenses: *potuī, potuisti,* etc.

[3] *Ferō* has forms derived from three independent stems, seen in *ferō, tulī, lātum.*

[4] *Fer-s, fer-t, fer-tis,* instead of *feris, ferit, feritis.*

[5] Inflect the several tenses in full: *ferēbam, ferēbās,* etc.

FERO.

SUBJUNCTIVE.

Pres. feram;	ferāmus.
Imp. ferrem;	ferrēmus.[1]
Perf. tulerim;	tulerĭmus.
Plup. tulissem;	tulissēmus.

IMPERATIVE.

Pres. fer;[2]	ferte.
Fut. fertō,	fertōte,
fertō;	feruntō.

INFINITIVE.	PARTICIPLE.
Pres. ferre.[1]	*Pres.* ferĕns.
Perf. tulisse.	
Fut. lātūrus esse.	*Fut.* lātūrus.

GERUND.	SUPINE.
Gen. ferendī,	
Dat. ferendō,	
Acc. ferendum,	*Acc.* lātum,
Abl. ferendō.	*Abl.* lātū.

PASSIVE VOICE.

feror,   ferri,   lātus sum,   *to be borne.*

INDICATIVE.

SINGULAR.	PLURAL.
Pres. feror, ferris, fertur;	ferimur, ferimĭnī, feruntur.
Imp. ferēbar;	ferēbāmur.
Fut. ferar;	ferēmur.
Perf. lātus sum;	lātī sumus.
Plup. lātus eram;	lātī erāmus.
F. P. lātus erō;	lātī erĭmus.

SUBJUNCTIVE.

Pres. ferar;	ferāmur.
Imp. ferrer;	ferrēmur.
Perf. lātus sim;	lātī sīmus.
Plup. lātūs essem;	lātī essēmus.

---

[1] *Ferrem*, etc., for *fererem*, etc.; *ferre* for *ferere* (e dropped).
[2] *Fer* for *fere*; *fertō, ferte, fertōte*, for *feritō, ferite, feritōte*.

IRREGULAR VERBS.

IMPERATIVE.

Pres. ferre; feriminī.
Fut. fertor,
fertor; feruntor.

INFINITIVE.   PARTICIPLE.
Pres. ferrī.
Perf. lātus esse.   *Perf.* lātus.
Fut. lātum īrī.   *Ger.* ferendus.

LESSON XCI.

IRREGULAR VERBS. — *Possum* AND *Ferō.* — EXERCISES.

270. *Vocabulary.*

Arrogantia, ae, *f.*	*arrogance.*
Avāritia, ae, *f.*	*avarice.*
Classis, is, *f.*	*fleet.*
Coërceō, ēre, uī, itum,	*to restrain, control.*
Dolor, ōris, *m.*	*pain.* [ferre, *to propose a law.*
Ferō, ferre, tulī, lātum,	*to bear, carry; to endure;* lēgem
Juvenis, is, *m.*	*youth, a youth.*
Nihil, *n. indeclinable,*	*nothing.*
Patienter, *adv.*	*patiently.*
Praetor, ōris, *m.*	*praetor,* a Roman magistrate.
Prīvātim, *adv.*	*privately, in a private capacity.*
Sententia, ae, *f.*	*thought, plan, opinion.*
Statuō, ere, uī, ūtum,	*to determine, decide.*

271. *Translate into English.*

1. Hī cīvēs plūs possunt quam ipsī magistrātūs.[1] Liscus dīcit esse nōnnūllōs, quī prīvātim plūs possint quam ipsī magistrātūs; hōs ā sē coërcērī nōn posse. 2. Nōnne hī juvenēs arma ferre possunt? In Galliā arma ferunt. 3. In exercitū Caesaris erant multī quī arma in Italiā tulerant. 4.

---

[1] After a comparative, *quam* is followed by the same construction as that which precedes it. *Magistrātūs* is here the subject of *possunt* to be supplied.

IRREGULAR VERBS.

Cīvēs Rōmānī avāritiam praetōris ferre nōn potuērunt. 5. Ea quae ferrī possunt ferenda sunt. 6. Ferimus ea quae sunt ferenda. 7. Nōnne imperātor fīnitimīs cīvitātibus auxilium feret? Iīs auxilium ferre nōn poterit. 8. Rhēnus per fīnēs Helvētiōrum fertur. 9. Haec lēx ferētur. 10. Bonae lēgēs ferantur. 11. Multae lēgēs lātae sunt. 12. Gallī nostrōrum mīlitum impetum sustinēre nōn potuērunt. 13. Liscus dīcit sē quam diū potuerit tacuisse.[1] 14. Dolōrem patienter ferāmus. 15. Dolor patienter ferendus est. 16. Ariovistus tantam arrogantiam sūmpserat, ut ferendus nōn vidērētur. 17. Nihil dē eōrum sententiā dictūrus sum quī hostēs timent. 18. Classis est exspectanda. Caesar statuit exspectandam esse classem. 19. Cum fīnitimīs cīvitātibus pācem factūrī sumus. 20. Hostēs suam urbem altissimō mūrō mūnītūrī sunt.

272. *Translate into Latin.*

1. We can fortify all our cities with walls and with moats. 2. If we are intending to bear[2] aid to our friends, our cities must be fortified.[3] 3. We have decided that we must await, in this place, the arrival[4] of our friends. 4. If you cannot endure pain, you must make peace[4] with your enemies.

5. If you had to endure the arrogance[4] of this general, you would not be silent. 6. They are intending to set out[2] for Gaul, to carry[5] arms against the Romans. 7. Good laws should be proposed[3] by those who are regarded as the friends of all the citizens. 8. To endure pain patiently is not an easy thing to do.[6] 9. The soldiers must be warned[3] not to fear the enemy. 10. In our state no citizens have greater

---

[1] *Tacuisse* must here be rendered, *that he has kept silent*, not *that he kept silent*.

[2] See 266, 233.   [3] See 266, 234.

[4] Render as if the English were, *the arrival must be awaited, peace must be made, arrogance had to be endured.*

[5] See 119, 497.   [6] See 248, sentence 5.

power than the magistrates. 11. All of us can carry arms in defence of[1] our country.

LESSON XCII.

IRREGULAR VERBS. — *Volŏ, Nōlō,* AND *Mālō.* —
RULE VII.

273. *Lesson from the Grammar.*

293. Volŏ,[2]   velle,   voluī,   *to be willing.*
Nōlō,[3]   nōlle,   nōluī,   *to be unwilling.*
Mālō,[3]   mālle,   māluī,   *to prefer.*

INDICATIVE.

Pres. volŏ,	nōlō,	mālō,
vīs,	nōn vīs,	māvīs,
vult;	nōn vult;	māvult;
volumus,	nōlumus,	mālumus,
vultis,	nōn vultis,	māvultis,
volunt.	nōlunt.	mālunt.
Imp. volēbam.[4]	nōlēbam.	mālēbam.
Fut. volam.	nōlam.	mālam.
Perf. voluī.	nōluī.	māluī.
Plup. volueram.	nōlueram.	mālueram.
F. P. voluerō.	nōluerō.	māluerō.

SUBJUNCTIVE.

Pres. velim.[5]	nōlim.	mālim.
Imp. vellem.[6]	nōllem.	māllem.
Perf. voluerim.	nōluerim.	māluerim.
Plup. voluissem.	nōluissem.	māluissem.

---

[1] 'In defence of,' *prō.*
[2] The stem of *volō* is *vol,* with variable stem vowel, o, e, u.
[3] NŌLŌ is compounded of *ne* or *nōn* and *volō* ; MĀLŌ, of *magis* and *volō.*
[4] Inflect the several tenses in full.
[5] *Velim* is inflected like *sim,* and *vellem* like *essem.*
[6] *Vellem* and *velle* are syncopated forms for *velerem, velere* ; *e* is dropped and *r* assimilated ; *velerem, velrem, vellem* ; *velere, velre, velle.* So *nōllem* and *nōlle,* for *nōlerem* and *nōlere* ; *māllem* and *mālle,* for *mālerem* and *mālere.*

IRREGULAR VERBS.

IMPERATIVE.

Pres. nōli, nōlīte.
Fut. nōlĭtō, nōlĭtōte,
nōlĭtō, nōluntō.

INFINITIVE.

Pres. velle. nōlle. mālle.
Perf. voluisse. nōluisse. māluisse.

PARTICIPLE.

Pres. volens. nōlens.

RULE VII.— Two Accusatives — Person and Thing.

374. Some verbs of ASKING, DEMANDING, TEACHING, and CONCEALING, admit two Accusatives — one of the *person* and the other of the *thing:*

Mē sententiam rogāvit, *he asked me* MY OPINION. Cic. Philosophia nōs rēs omnēs docuit, *philosophy has taught us all* THINGS. Cic. Auxilia rēgem ōrābant, *they asked* AUXILIARIES *from the king.* Liv. Pācem tē poscimus, *we demand* PEACE *of you.* Verg. Nōn tē cēlāvī sermōnem, *I did not conceal from you* THE CONVERSATION. Cic.

1. In the PASSIVE the PERSON becomes the subject, and the Accusative of the thing is retained:

Mē sententiam rogāvit, *he asked me* MY OPINION. Cic. Ego sententiam rogātus sum, *I was asked* MY OPINION. Cic. Artēs ēdoctus fuerat, *he had been taught* THE ARTS. Liv.

LESSON XCIII.

IRREGULAR VERBS. — *Volŏ, Nōlŏ,* AND *Mālŏ.* — RULE VII. — EXERCISES.

274. *Vocabulary.*

Auctor, ōris, *m.* author, advocate.
Crēdō, ere, dĭdī, dĭtum, *to believe.* (Followed by the Dative
Cūr, *adv.* *why ?* [of the person believed).
Exūrō, ere, ussī, ūstum, *to burn up, burn.*

IRREGULAR VERBS.

Flāgĭtō, āre, āvī, ātum,	to demand.
Lĭbenter, adv.	willingly, gladly.
Malefĭcĭum, ĭī, n.	mischief, harm.
Mālō, mālle, māluī,	to prefer.
Nōlō, nōlle, nōluī,	to be unwilling, not to be willing.
Perfĕrō, ferre, tulī, lātum,	to endure. [not to wish.
Permăneō, ēre, mānsī, mānsum,	to continue to remain, to remain.
Ūnā, adv.	together.
Unde, adv.	whence, from which place.
Vĭdeor,[1] ērī, vīsus sum,	to seem, appear.
Vŏlŏ, velle, voluī,	to wish, to be willing.

275. *Translate into English.*

1. Caesar dē summīs rēbus cum Ariovistō, rēge Germānōrum, agere volēbat. 2. Num bellī fortūnam tentāre vultis? Patriam dēfendere volumus. Nōlīte dubitāre[2] lībertātem dēfendere. 3. Galba saepius[3] fortūnam tentāre nōlēbat. 4. Faciam id quod vultis. 5. Catō esse bonus[4] volēbat. 6. Hī cīvēs vidērī bonī volunt. 7. Catō esse quam[5] vidērī bonus mālēbat. 8. Libenter hominēs id quod volunt crēdunt. 9. Auctōrēs[6] bellī esse nōlēbāmus. 10. Auctōrēs[6] bellī esse nōlēmus. 11. Caesar montem ā Labiēnō occupārī voluit. 12. Cōnsīdius timōre perterritus dīcit montem, quem Caesar ā Labiēnō occupārī voluerit, ab hostibus tenērī.

13. Per prōvinciam nostram iter facere cōnābuntur, proptereā quod aliud iter habent nūllum. 14. Imperātor nōluit eum locum, unde Helvētiī discesserant, vacāre. 15. Dīxērunt sibī esse in animō sine ūllō maleficiō iter facere. 16. Gallī servitūtem perferre nōlēbant. In lībertāte permanēre

---

[1] *Videor* is the passive of *videō*, 'to see,' but it is also used as a deponent verb with a special meaning.

[2] Literally, *be unwilling to hesitate*; render, *do not hesitate*,—a common circumlocution in prohibitions instead of *nē dubitā*, a form used in poetry only; as in English, *do not hesitate*, instead of *hesitate not*.

[3] The comparative sometimes has the force of TOO.

[4] A *predicate adjective* after *esse*, agreeing with *Catō*.

[5] *Quam* after *mālō* may be rendered *rather than*.

[6] See 59, 362.

IRREGULAR VERBS.

quam servitūtem perferre mālēbant. Reliquīs cīvitātibus persuāsērunt ut in lībertāte permanēre quam servitūtem perferre māllent. 17. Jūdicem sententiam rogābunt. 18. Cotīdiē Caesar Aeduōs frūmentum flāgitābat. 19. Helvētiī trēs cōpiārum partēs flūmen Ararim[1] trānsdūxerant. 20. Rhodanus inter fīnēs Helvētiōrum et Allobrogum fluit. 21. Allobrogibus sēsē persūasūrōs esse existimābant utī, oppidīs suīs vīcīsque exūstīs,[2] ūnā cum iīs proficīscerentur.

276. *Translate into Latin.*

1. You were unwilling to ask us our opinion.[3] 2. I do not understand why you wish to ask this man his opinion.[3] Will you tell me why you wish to ask this man his opinion? 3. How large an army is the general willing to lead across the river?[4] 4. He prefers to remain in camp rather than to lead his soldiers across this river,[4] although a bridge has been built[5] over it.

5. If the Aedui had not told Caesar that they would assist him, he would not have demanded grain of them.[3] 6. Are you not willing to do that which I demand of you?[6] 7. You preferred to ask his opinion,[6] in order that he might believe you to be his friend. 8. If you should persuade us to remain, what should you wish us to do? 9. Do not wish[7] that which cannot be done. 10. Those who are willing to try the fortune of war must not fear danger. 11. All of us[8] ought to be willing to defend our country.

---

[1] A few compounds of *trāns, circum*, and *ad*, admit two Accusatives, dependent, the one upon the verb, the other upon the preposition.
[2] See Suggestion XVI., (3).
[3] See 273, 374.
[4] See 275, sentence 19.
[5] Use the Ablative Absolute.
[6] To ask his opinion = to ask him his opinion. 273, 374.
[7] See 275, sentence 2.
[8] In Latin, *nōs omnēs*, ' we all,' or simply *omnēs*, agreeing with the subject implied in the ending of the verb.

LESSON XCIV.

IRREGULAR VERBS.—*Fīō* AND *Eō*.—RULES X. AND XXI.

277. *Lesson from the Grammar.*

294. Fīŏ, fĭerī, factus sum, *to become, be made.*

INDICATIVE.

SINGULAR.	PLURAL.
Pres. fīŏ, fīs, fĭt;	fīmus, fītis, fīunt.
Imp. fīĕbam;[1]	fīĕbāmus.
Fut. fīam;	fīĕmus.
Perf. factus sum;	factī sumus.
Plup. factus eram;	factī erāmus.
F. P. factus erŏ;	factī erĭmus.

SUBJUNCTIVE.

Pres. fīam;	fīāmus.
Imp. fĭerem;	fĭerēmus.
Perf. factus sim;	factī sīmus.
Plup. factus essem;	factī essēmus.

IMPERATIVE.

Pres. fī;   fīte.

INFINITIVE.   PARTICIPLE.

Pres. fĭerī.
Perf. factus esse.   *Perf.* factus.
Fut. factum irī.   *Ger.* faciendus.

295. Eō, īre, īvī, itum, *to go.*

INDICATIVE.

Pres. eō, īs, ĭt;	īmus, ītis, eunt.
Imp. ībam;[1]	ībāmus.
Fut. ībŏ;	ībimus.
Perf. īvī;	īvimus.
Plup. īveram;	īverāmus.
F. P. īverŏ;	īverĭmus.

---

[1] Inflect the several tenses in full.

IRREGULAR VERBS. 225

SUBJUNCTIVE.

Pres. eam; cūmus.
Imp. irem; irēmus.
Perf. iverim; iverīmus.
Plup. ivissem; ivissēmus.

IMPERATIVE.

Pres. ī; īte.
Fut. ītŏ, ītōte,
     ītŏ; euntō.

INFINITIVE.   PARTICIPLE.

Pres. ire.   *Pres.* iens,   *Gen.* euntis.
Perf. ivisse.
Fut. itūrus esse.   *Fut.* itūrus.

GERUND.   SUPINE.

Gen. eundi,
Dat. eundŏ,
Acc. eundum,   *Acc.* Itum,
Abl. eundŏ.   *Abl.* itū.

RULE X. — Accusative of Limit.

380. The PLACE TO WHICH is designated by the Accusative:[1]

I. Generally with a preposition — **ad** or **in**:

Legiōnes *ad urbem* addūcit, *he is leading the legions* TO *or* TOWARD THE CITY. Cic. *In Asiam* redit, *he returns* INTO ASIA. Nep.

II. In names of towns without a preposition:

Nūntius *Rōmam* redit, *the messenger returns* TO ROME. Liv. Fūgit *Tarquiniōs, he fled* TO TARQUINII. Cic.

NOTE.—Verbs meaning *to collect, to come together*, etc.,—*conveniō, cōgō, convocō*, etc. — are usually treated as verbs of *motion*, and thus take the Accusative, generally with a preposition; but verbs meaning *to place* —*locō, collocō, pōnō*, etc., — are usually treated as verbs of *rest*, and thus take the Ablative (185, 425), generally with a preposition:

---

[1] Originally the *place to which* was uniformly designated by the Accusative *without* a preposition. Names of towns have retained the original construction, while most other names of places have assumed a preposition.

Ūnum *in locum* convenīre, *to meet* IN one PLACE. Caes. *In alterīus manū vītam pōnere, to place one's life* IN THE HAND *of an)ther.* Cic.

1. In the NAMES OF TOWNS the *Accusative* with **ad** occurs — (1) to denote *to, toward, in the direction of, into the vicinity of,* and (2) in contrast with *ā* or *ab:*

Ad Zamam pervēnit, *he came* TO THE VICINITY OF ZAMA. Sall. A *Diānio ad Sinōpēn, from Dianium* TO SINOPE. Cic.

2. Like NAMES OF TOWNS are used —

1) The Accusatives **domum, domōs, rūs**:

Domum reductus est, *He was conducted* HOME. Cic. *Domōs* abducti, *led* TO THEIR HOMES. Liv. *Rūs* ēvolāre, *to hasten* INTO THE COUNTRY. Cic.

RULE XXI. — Place from which.

412. The PLACE FROM WHICH is denoted by the Ablative:

I. Generally *with a preposition* — **ā, ab, dē,** or **ex**:

Ab urbe profīcīscitur, *he sets out* FROM THE CITY. Caes. *Dē forō, from the forum.* Cic. *Ex Africā, from* (out of) *Africa.* Liv.

II. In NAMES OF TOWNS *without a preposition:*[1]

Platōnem Athēnis arcēssīvit, *he summoned Plato* FROM ATHENS. Nep. *Fūgit Corinthō, he fled from Corinth.* Cic.

1. Many names of *islands,* and the Ablatives, *domō* and *rūre,* are used like names of towns:

Domō profūgit, *he fled* FROM HOME. Cic. *Dēlō* profīcīscitur, *he proceeds* FROM DELOS. Cic.

LESSON XCV.

IRREGULAR VERBS. — *Fīō* AND *Eō.* — RULES X. AND XXI. — EXERCISES.

278. *Vocabulary.*

Caedēs, is, *f.*   *slaughter.*
Cibāria, ōrum, *n. pl.*   *food, provisions.*
Combūrō, ere, bussī, būstum,   *to burn up, burn.*
Efferō, ferre, extulī, ēlātum,   *to carry forth.*

---

[1] This was the original construction for all places alike.

IRREGULAR VERBS.

Ēgredior, ī, gressus sum,	to go out, go forth, depart.
Eō, īre, īvī or iī, itum,	to go.
Equester, tris, tre,	equestrian; equestre proelium, a cavalry engagement.
Excō, īre, iī, itum,[1]	to go out, go forth, depart.
Fīō, fierī, factus sum,	to be made; to happen.
Lutetia, ae, f.	Lutetia, a city in Gaul, now Paris.
Melodūnum, ī, n.	Melodunum, a town of the Senones.
Narbō, ōnis, m.	Narbo, a town in southern Gaul.
Nihilum, ī, n.	nothing.
Patior, ī, passus sum,	to suffer, permit.
Peditātus, ūs, m.	infantry.
Plānitiēs, ēī, f.	plain.
Praeterquam, adv.	except.
Tolōsa, ae, f.	Tolosa, a town in southern Gaul.
Trānseō, īre, iī,[1] itum,	to go over, cross.
Vigilia, ae, f.	watch.[2]

279. *Translate into English.*

1. Helvētiī ē fīnibus suīs exībant. Ē fīnibus suīs exīre cōnābantur. Post Orgetorigis mortem nihilō[3] minus ē fīnibus suīs exīre cōnābantur. 2. Id quod cōnstituērunt facere cōnantur, ut ē fīnibus suīs exeant. 3. Haec omnia contrā lēgem facta sunt. 4. Illud quod faciendum prīmum fuit factum est. 5. Id quod vultis nūllō modō fierī potest. 6. Nōlīte id velle, quod fierī nōn potest. 7. Caesar suum equitātum contrā hostem īre jubet. 8. Omnēs legiōnēs contrā hostem ībant. 9. Fit equestre proelium in plānitiē; Caesar legiōnēs prō castrīs cōnstituit, nē qua irruptiō ab hostium peditātū fīat; hostēs fugae sēsē mandant; fit magna caedēs; nōnnūllī fossam trānsīre cōnantur.
10. Divitiacus auxiliī rogandī causā Rōmam[4] ad senātum profectus est. 11. Labiēnus cum quattuor legiōnibus Lu-

---
[1] The compounds of *eō* take the contracted form *iī* in the perfect.
[2] Among the Romans, the night, from sunset to sunrise, was divided into four *watches* of equal length.
[3] Ablative of Difference: *less by nothing.* Render, *none the less.*
[4] See 277, 380.

tetiam proficīscitur. 12. Ē castrīs tertiā vigiliā ēgressus Melodūnum vēnit. 13. Gallī per suōs fīnēs nōs īre patientur. 14. Imperātōrem dē hīs rēbus certiōrem faciāmus. 15. Ubī dē hīs rēbus certiōrēs factī sunt, prīvāta aedificia incendērunt. 16. Lēgātōs, nōbilissimōs cīvitātis, ad rēgem mīsērunt. 17. Frūmentum omne, praeterquam[1] quod sēcum portātūrī erant, combussērunt. 18. Suēbī, quī ad rīpās Rhēnī vēnerant, domum revertērunt. 19. Dux Rōmānus multōs virōs fortēs Tolōsā et Narbōne[2] ēvocāvit. 20. Helvētiī trium mēnsium cibāria sibī quemque domō[3] efferre jussērunt.

280. *Translate into Latin.*

1. Orgetorix persuaded the Helvetii to go forth from their territory. 2. We shall be informed what they carried from home with them. 3. We shall go to Rome, and remain there the whole winter. 4. We shall send you letters often, that you may be informed in what direction we are going.[3] We have heard that you say that you have not been informed by us in what direction we are going. Do you know in what direction we have gone?

5. Caesar was intending to go from Italy to Geneva with five legions. 6. Having accomplished[4] this, Caesar orders the Helvetii to return to their homes. 7. Do you prefer to go home rather than to remain at Rome?[5] 8. The Helvetii thought that they should persuade the Sequani to suffer them to go through their territory. 9. Caesar thought that peace should not be made with the Helvetii, unless they returned home. 10. What did the Helvetii attempt to do after the death of Orgetorix? They attempted to persuade their neighbors to burn all their towns.

---

[1] The construction with *praeterquam* is elliptical; we may supply after it *id frūmentum nōn combussērunt*. Of course the ellipsis need not be supplied in translation.   [2] See 277, 412.

[3] What mood must be used in an Indirect Question?

[4] Use the Ablative Absolute.

[5] See 185, 425.

LESSON XCVI.

IMPERSONAL VERBS. — REVIEW OF RULE XLIII. — RULE XIII.

281. *Lesson from the Grammar.*

298. Impersonal Verbs correspond to the English Impersonal with *it : licet*, it is lawful; *oportet*, it behooves.[1] They are conjugated like other verbs, but are used only in the third person singular of the Indicative and Subjunctive, and in the Present and Perfect Infinitive:

Decet, decuit, *it becomes.* Oportet, oportuit, *it behooves.*
Miseret, miseritum est, *it excites pity.*[2] Paenitet, paenituit, *it causes regret.*[2]

300. Generally Impersonal are several verbs which designate the changes of the weather, or the operations of nature:

Fulminat, it lightens; *grandinat*, it hails; *lūcēscit*, it grows light; *pluit*, it rains; *rōrat*, dew falls; *tonat*, it thunders.

301. Many other verbs are often used impersonally:

Accidit, it happens; *appāret*, it appears; *cōnstat*, it is evident; *contigit*, it happens; *dēlectat*, it delights; *dolet*, it grieves; *interest*, it concerns; *juvat*, it delights; *patet*, it is plain; *placet*, it pleases; *praestat*, it is better; *rēfert*, it concerns.

1. In the PASSIVE VOICE intransitive verbs can be used only impersonally. The participle is then neuter:

Mihĭ crēditur, it is credited to me, I am believed; *tibĭ crēditur*, you are believed; *crēditum est*, it was believed; *certātur*, it is contended; *currĭtur*, there is running, people run; *pūgnātur*, it is fought, they, we, etc., fight; *vīvĭtur*, we, you, they live.

2. The PASSIVE PERIPHRASTIC CONJUGATION (266, 234) is often used impersonally. The participle is then neuter:

Mihĭ scrībendum est, I must write; *tibĭ scrībendum est*, you must write; *illi scrībendum est*, he must write.

---

[1] The subject is generally an infinitive or clause, but may be a noun or pronoun denoting a *thing*, but not a *person: hŏc fĭeri oportet*, that this should be done is necessary.

[2] *Mē miseret*, I pity; *mē paenitet*, I repent.

RULE XIII.—Two Datives—To which and For which.

390. Two Datives — the OBJECT TO WHICH and the OBJECT or END FOR WHICH — occur with a few verbs:

I. With INTRANSITIVE and PASSIVE verbs:

Malō est hominibus avāritia, avarice is AN EVIL TO MEN (literally is TO MEN FOR AN EVIL). Cic. Est mihi cūrae, it is A CARE TO ME. Cic. Domus dēdecori dominō fit, *the house becomes* A DISGRACE TO ITS OWNER. Cic. Vēnit Atticis auxiliō, *he came to the assistance of the Athenians.* Nep. Hōc illi tribuēbātur ignāviae, *this was imputed to him as cowardice (for cowardice).* Cic. Eis subsidiō missus est, *he was sent to them as aid.* Nep.

II. With TRANSITIVE verbs in connection with the ACCUSATIVE:

Quinque cohortēs *castris praesidiō* reliquit, *he left five cohorts* FOR THE DEFENCE OF THE CAMP (literally TO THE CAMP FOR A DEFENCE). Caes. Periclēs agrōs suōs dōnō rēi pūblicae dedit, *Pericles gave his lands to the republic as a present* (literally, *for a present*). Just.

282. *Vocabulary.*

Accidō, ere, 1,	*to fall to, befall;* accidit, *it happens, Athens.* [*comes to pass.*
Athēnae, ārum, *f. pl.*	
Athēniēnsis, is, *m. and f.*	*an Athenian.*
Atticus, ī, *m.*	*Atticus,* a Roman name.
Cōiciō,[1] ere, cōjēci, jectum,	*to cast, hurl, throw.*
Difficilis, e,	*difficult.*
Impedimentum, ī, *n.*	*hinderance, embarrassment;* impedimenta, *pl., hinderances; baggage (of an army).* [*against.*
Inferō, ferre, intulī, illātum,	*to bear into, bear against, wage*
Instō, āre, stitī,	*to be near, be at hand.*
Lūna, ae, *f.*	*moon.*
Mētior, īrī, mēnsus sum,	*to measure, allot.*
Multō,[2] *adv.*	*much, far.*
Novissimus, a, um, *sup. of* novus,	*newest;* novissimum āgmen, *the rear.*
Oportet, ēre, uit,	*it behooves, is proper; one ought.*

---

[1] Pronounced as if spelled *cōjiciō*.
[2] Originally an Ablative of Difference; literally, *by much.*

IMPERSONAL VERBS.

Ōrnāmentum, ī, n.   ornament, honor.
Plēnus, a, um,   full.
Subsidium, iī, n.   aid, support, reënforcement.
Tēlum, ī, n.   dart; weapon.
Titus, ī, m.   Titus, a Roman name.

283. *Translate into English.*

1. Caesarī nūntiātum est, equitēs Ariovistī lapidēs tēlaque in nostrōs cōicere. 2. Helvētiīs est in animō per agrum Aeduōrum iter facere. Caesarī nūntiātur, Helvētiīs esse in animō per agrum Aeduōrum iter facere. 3. Germānōs trāns Rhēnum incolere dictum est. 4. Eā nocte accidit ut esset lūna plēna. 5. Helvētiī undique locī nātūrā continēbantur. Hāc rē fīēbat ut minus facile fīnitimīs bellum īnferre possent. 6. Frūmentum mīlitibus mētīrī oportet. Diēs īnstat, quō diē¹ frūmentum mīlitibus mētīrī oportēbit. 7. Ea rēs Gallīs² māgnō ad pūgnam erat impedīmentō.² 8. Legiōnēs duae in novissimō āgmine praesidiō² impedīmentīs² erant.

9. Erant itinera duo, quibus Helvētiī domō exīre possent; ūnum³ angustum et difficile; mōns autem altissimus impendēbat; alterum,³ multō facilius. 10. Atticus Athēnīs ita vīxit, ut Athēniēnsibus esset cārissimus. 11. Amīcitia populī Rōmānī mihī² ōrnāmentō² est. 12. Amīcitiam populī Rōmānī mihī² ōrnāmentō² et praesidiō² esse oportet. 13. Ariovistus dīxit amīcitiam populī Rōmānī sibī² ōrnāmentō² et praesidiō² esse oportēre. 14. Lēgātīs respondeāmus nōs diem ad dēlīberandum sūmptūrōs esse. 15. Titus Labiēnus decimam legiōnem subsidiō² nostrīs² mīsit. 16. Gallī oppidum Noviodūnum, nō cui⁴ esset ūsuī² Rōmānīs,² incendērunt.

---

¹ *Quō* is here an adjective agreeing with *diē*. The antecedent is usually expressed but once; here *diē* may be omitted in rendering.
² See 281, 3º0.
³ Supply *erat*.
⁴ *Cui* is here the indefinite pronoun, agreeing with *ūsuī*.

284. *Translate into Latin.*

1. In the towns of the Gauls were many things which were of great use to the Romans.[1] 2. The friendship of the general ought to be a safeguard to us.[1] 3. We should all live in such a way, as not to be a grief to our friends.[1] 4. It often happens, that what ought to be done is not easy to do. 5. It is our intention to go to Geneva and to Rome[2] this summer. 6. The friendship of the good is always an honor to us.[1] 7. It was announced to Caesar that the Helvetii had set out from their territory, and that they were attempting to march through the province. 8. It is stated by Caesar that the Helvetii were the bravest of the Gauls. 9. It was the intention of Orgetorix to obtain possession of the sovereignty[3] of all Gaul. 10. Let soldiers remain, to be a garrison to the city. 11. The horsemen of Ariovistus hurled stones and darts upon the Romans. 12. Your friendship ought to be a safeguard to me.[1]

LESSON XCVII.

IMPERSONAL VERBS. — RULE XX.

285. *Lesson from the Grammar.*

RULE XX. — Accusative and Genitive.

409. The ACCUSATIVE of the PERSON and the GENITIVE of the THING are used with a few transitive verbs:

I. With verbs of *reminding, admonishing:*

Tē amīcitiae commonefacit, *he reminds you* OF FRIENDSHIP. Cic. Milītēs necessitātis monet, *he reminds the soldiers of the necessity.* Ter.

II. With verbs of *accusing, convicting, acquitting:*

Virōs sceleris arguis, *you accuse men* OF CRIME. Cic. Levitātis eum convincere, *to convict him of levity.* Cic. Absolvere injūriae eum, *to acquit him of injustice.* Cic.

---

[1] See 282, 390.   [2] See 277, 380.   [3] See 258, 421.

III. With *miseret, paenitet, pudet, taedet,* and *piget:*
Eōrum nōs miseret, *we pity* THEM (It moves our pity OF THEM).
Cic. Cōnsilii mē paenitet, *I repent of my purpose.* Cic. Mē stultitiae meae pudet, *I am ashamed of my folly.* Cic.

NOTE 1. — The *Genitive of the Thing* designates, with verbs of *reminding*, etc., that to which the attention is called; with verbs of *accusing*, etc., the crime, charge; and with *miseret, paenitet*, etc., the object which produces the feeling; see examples.

NOTE 2. — The personal verbs included under this rule retain the *Genitive* in the *Passive:*
Accūsātus est *prōditiōnis, he was accused* OF TREASON. Nep.

286. *Vocabulary.*

Ācriter, *adv.*	*sharply, severely.*
Anceps, cipitis,	*double, twofold; undecided.*
Beneficium, iī, *n.*	*benefit, favor.*
Celeritās, ātis, *f.*	*celerity, speed.*
Commūnis, e,	*common;* commūnis rēs, *the common interest.*
Incrēdibilis, e,	*incredible.* [mon interest.
Ineō, īre, iī, itum,	*to go into, enter upon, begin, undertake.*
Īnsimulō, āre, āvī, ātum,	*to accuse.* [take.
Lēnitās, ātis, *f.*	*smoothness, gentleness.*
Licet, ēre, uit,	*it is lawful, is permitted; one may.*
Necesse,[1]	*necessary.*
Paenitet, ēre, uit,	*it causes regret;* mē paenitet, *I*
Petō, ere, īvī *or* iī, ītum,	*to seek, request, ask.* [repent.
Prōditiō, ōnis, *f.*	*treason.*
Prōsequor, ī, secūtus sum,	*to follow up, pursue.*
Prōspiciō, ere, spēxī, spectum,	*to look forward; to look out for.* (In the latter sense followed by the Dative.)

287. *Translate into English.*

1. Ancipitī proeliō diū pūgnātum est.[2] Ab hōrā septimā ad vesperum fortiter pūgnātum est. Ad multam noctem etiam

---

[1] *Necesse* is an adjective used only in the Nominative and Accusative Neuter Singular.

[2] Observe in this sentence and the others in this Lesson, that an impersonal verb can not be rendered literally. Thus, *diū pūgnātum est* would become in English, *a long battle was fought, the fighting went on for a long time.*

ACCUSATIVE AND GENITIVE.

ad impedimenta pūgnātum est. 2. Proeliō equestrī inter duās aciēs contendēbātur. 3. Caesar Titum Labiēnum cum legiōnibus tribus hostēs prōsequī jussit: ad novissimum agmen ventum est. Eī ad quōs ventum erat fortiter impetum Rōmānōrum sustinuērunt. 4. Rēī frūmentāriae prōspiciendum est. 5. Caesar rēī frūmentāriae prōspiciendum esse existimābat. 6. Dē commūnī rē in colloquiō dīcendum est. 7. Vercingetorix prōditiōnis īnsimulātus est. 8. "Haec," dīxit Vercingetorix, "ā mē beneficia habētis, quem prōditiōnis īnsimulātis."

9. Flūmen est Arar, quod in Rhodanum īnfluit incrēdibilī lēnitāte, ita ut oculīs in utram partem fluat jūdicārī nōn possit. Caesar per explōrātōrēs certior factus est, trēs jam cōpiārum partēs Helvētiōs id flūmen trānsdūxisse. 10. Gallōs hūjus cōnsiliī paenitēbat. 11. Gallī saepe cōnsilia ineunt quōrum eōs paenitet. 12. Saepe cōnsilia inīmus quōrum nōs paenitēre necesse est. 13. Nōbīs concilium in diem certam[1] indīcere licet. 14. Vōbīs concilium in diem certam indīcere liceat. 15. Gallī petiērunt utī sibī concilium totīus Galliae in diem certam indīcere licēret. 16. Mīlitēs eā[2] celeritāte iērunt ut hostēs impetum legiōnum sustinēre nōn possent.

288. *Translate into Latin.*

1. The town was reached[3] by us an hour before sunset. 2. A long and severe battle took place[3] near the camp. 3. I have to speak[3] of things which you ought to wish to hear. 4. It should be stated[3] that the Gauls already repented of their plan. 5. Caesar told the Gauls that they might[3] appoint a council.

6. You cannot bring the war to an end, but you may[3] repent of your plans. 7. It cannot be ascertained what the enemy intend to do. 8. It was necessary to provide[3] for

---
[1] Diēs, usually *masculine*, is *feminine* when it signifies a day *fixed* or *appointed*.   [2] Literally, *that;* render, such.
[3] In all these cases express the thought impersonally in Latin.

IMPERSONAL VERBS. 235

the protection of the camp. 9. Orgetorix (when) accused of treason, was compelled to plead his cause in chains. 10. Crimes should be repented of. 11. The rear of the enemy was reached, and a severe battle took place. 12. Fighting will go on from midday to sunset. 13. As so many have been slain, we may judge how severe a battle has been fought.

LESSON XCVIII.

REVIEW OF RULES LIII., LIV., AND LV. — EXERCISE IN READING AT SIGHT.

289. *Read at Sight, examine carefully, and translate into English.*

Post Orgetorigis mortem nihilō minus Helvētiī id quod cōnstituerant facere cōnābantur, ut ē fīnibus suīs[1] exīrent. Ubī sē[1] ad eam rem parātōs esse arbitrātī sunt, oppida sua omnia, vīcōs, prīvāta aedificia incendērunt; frūmentum omne, praeterquam quod sēcum portātūrī erant, combussērunt. ut parātiōrēs ad omnia perīcula essent; trium mēnsium cibāria sibī quemque domō efferre jussērunt. Persuāsērunt fīnitimīs utī, oppidīs suīs vīcīsque exūstīs, ūnā cum iīs proficīscerentur.

Erant itinera duo, quibus ē fīnibus suīs exīre possent: ūnum per Sēquanōs, angustum et difficile, inter montem Jūram et flūmen Rhodanum, mōns autem altissimus impendēbat; alterum per prōvinciam nostram, multō facilius. Allobrogibus sēsē persuāsūrōs esse exīstimābant, ut per suōs fīnēs eōs īre paterentur. Ob eās causās per prōvinciam nostram iter facere cōnātī sunt.

Caesar, hīs rēbus audītīs, mātūrāvit ab urbe proficīscī et māximīs itineribus in Galliam contendit. Ubī dē ējus ad-

---

[1] The pupil should exercise especial care in this Exercise to determine the *antecedents* of the pronouns which occur in it, particularly of *suus* and *sui*.

ventū Helvētiī certiōrēs factī sunt, lēgātōs ad eum misērunt, quī dīcerent, sibī esse in animō iter per prōvinciam facere. Caesar lēgātīs respondit, diem sē ad dēlīberandum sūmptūrum.

290. *Translate into Latin.*

1. I shall take time for deliberation. 2. I wish to inform you of my arrival. 3. I send you a messenger to inform you of my arrival. 4. We intend to march through your country without (doing) any harm. 5. I intend to march through the province, because I have no other route. 6. Ambassadors were sent to Caesar to say what the Helvetii intended to do. 7. After hearing the words[1] of our friends, we shall set out from this city, and hasten home. 8. We attempted to set out before. 9. I wish you to try to tell me what you intend to do.[2] 10. Do you think that you will persuade me to tell you what I intended to do?[2] 11. Burn your towns and villages, and set out together with us. 12. You will never persuade us to set fire to our towns. 13. Let us always be prepared for danger. 14. We have burned all our grain, except what we carried with us. 15. Let each one take with him from home provisions for six months. 16. How many routes are there by which we can go?

LESSON XCIX.

GERUNDS, GERUNDIVES, AND PARTICIPLES. — REVIEW OF RULES LIX., LX., AND XXXII.

291. *Lesson from the Grammar.*

I. GERUNDS.

541. The GERUND is a verbal noun which shares so largely the character of a verb that it governs oblique cases, and takes adverbial modifiers:

---

[1] Use the Ablative Absolute.
[2] Observe that this is an Indirect Question.

Jūs vocandi[1] senātum, *the right of summoning the senate.* Liv.
Beātē vivendi[1] cupiditās, *the desire of living happily.* Cic.

542. The GERUND has four cases — the *Genitive, Dative, Accusative,* and *Ablative* — used in general like the same cases of nouns. Thus —

I. The GENITIVE OF THE GERUND is used with nouns and adjectives:

Ars vivendi, *the art of living.* Cic. Studiōsus erat audiendi, *he was desirous of hearing.* Nep. Cupidus tē audiendi, *desirous of hearing you.* Cic. Artem vēra āc falsa dijūdicandi, *the art of distinguishing true things from false.* Cic.

II. The DATIVE OF THE GERUND is used with a few verbs and adjectives which regularly govern the Dative:

Cum solvendō nōn essent, *since they were not able to pay.* Cic. Aqua ūtilis est bibendō, *water is useful for drinking.* Plin.

III. The ACCUSATIVE OF THE GERUND is used after a few prepositions:[2]

Ad discendum prōpēnsi sumus, *we are inclined to learn* (to learning). Cic. Inter lūdendum, *in* or *during play.* Quint.

IV. The ABLATIVE OF THE GERUND is used (1) as *Ablative of Means,* and (2) with *prepositions:*

Mēns discendō alitur, *the mind is nourished by learning.* Cic. Salūtem hominibus dandō, *by giving safety to men.* Cic. Virtūtēs cernuntur in agendō, *virtues are seen in action.* Cic. Dēterrēre ā scribendo, *to deter from writing.* Cic.

II. GERUNDIVES.

543. The GERUNDIVE, like other participles, agrees with nouns and pronouns:

Inita sunt cōnsilia urbis dēlendae, *plans have been formed for destroying the city* (of the city to be destroyed). Cic. Numa sacerdōtibus creandis animum adjēcit, *Numa gave his attention to the appointment of priests.* Liv.

---

[1] *Vocandi* as a Genitive is governed by *jūs*, and yet it governs the Accusative *senātum; vivendi* is governed by *cupiditās*, and yet it takes the adverbial modifier *beātē.*

[2] Most frequently after *ad;* sometimes after *inter* and *ob;* very rarely after *ante, circā,* and *in.*

544. The GERUNDIVE CONSTRUCTION may be used —

1. In place of a *Gerund with a direct object.* It then takes the case of the Gerund whose place it supplies:

Libīdō ējus vidēndī (= libīdō eum vidēndī), *the desire of seeing him* (literally, *of him to be seen*). Cic. Platōnis audiendī (= Platōnem audiendī) studiōsus, *fond of hearing Plato.* Cic. Legendīs ōrātōribus (= legendō ōrātōrēs), *by reading the orators.* Cic.

2. In the *Dative* and in the *Ablative with a preposition:*

Locum oppidō condendō cēpērunt, *they selected a place for founding a city.* Liv. Tempora dēmetendīs frūctibus accommodāta, *seasons suitable for gathering fruits.* Cic. Brūtus in līberandā patriā est interfectus, *Brutus was slain in liberating his country.* Cic.

III. PARTICIPLES.

548. The PARTICIPLE is a verbal adjective which governs the same cases as the verb:

Animus sē nōn vidēns alia cernit, *the mind, though it does not see itself* (literally, *not seeing itself*), *discerns other things.* Cic.

549. PARTICIPLES are often used —

1. To denote, TIME, CAUSE, MANNER, MEANS:

Platō scrībēns mortuus est, *Plato died while writing.* Cic. Itūri in proelium canunt, *they sing when about to go into battle.* Tac. Sōl oriēns diem cōnficit, *the sun by its rising causes the day.* Cic. Mīlitēs renūntiant sē perfidiam veritōs revertisse, *the soldiers report that they returned because they feared perfidy* (having feared). Caes.

2. To denote CONDITION or CONCESSION:

Mendācī hominī nē vērum quidem dīcentī crēdere nōn solēmus, *we are not wont to believe a liar, even if he speaks the truth.* Cic. Scrīpta tua jam diū exspectāns, nōn audeō tamen flāgitāre, *though I have been long expecting your work, yet I do not dare to ask for it.* Cic.

3. To denote PURPOSE:

Perseus rediit, bellī cāsum tentātūrus, *Perseus returned to try* (about to try) *the fortune of war.* Liv. Attribuit nōs trucīdandōs Cethēgō, *he assigned us to Cethegus to slaughter.* Cic.

4. To supply the place of RELATIVE CLAUSES:

Omnēs aliud agentēs aliud simulantēs, improbī sunt, *all who do one thing and pretend another are dishonest.* Cic.

GERUNDS, PARTICIPLES. 239

5. To supply the place of PRINCIPAL CLAUSES:
Clāssem dēvictam cēpit, *he conquered and took the fleet* (took the fleet conquered). Nep.

550. The TENSES OF THE PARTICIPLE — *Present, Perfect,* and *Future* — denote only *relative* time. They accordingly represent the time respectively as *present, past,* and *future* relatively to that of the principal verb:

Oculus sē nōn vidēns alia cernit, *the eye, though it does not see itself* (not seeing itself), *discerns other things.* Cic. Platō scrībēns mortuus est, *Plato died while writing.* Cic. Ūva mātūrāta dulcēscit, *the grape, when it has ripened* (having ripened), *becomes sweet.* Cic. Sapiēns bona semper placitūra laudat, *the wise man praises blessings which will always please* (being about to please). Sen.

LESSON C.

GERUNDS, GERUNDIVES, AND PARTICIPLES. — REVIEW OF RULES LIX., LX., XXXII. — EXERCISES.

292. *Vocabulary.*

Accipiō, ere, cēpī, ceptum,	*to receive.*
Aggredior, ī, gressus sum,	*to attack.*
Ārdeō, ēre, ārsi, ārsum,	*to burn, to be ardent, be eager.*
Concidō, ere, ī,	*to fall.*
Concīdō, ere, cīdī, cīsum,	*to cut down, destroy, slay.*
Cōnsīdō, ere, sēdī, sessum,	*to settle, post one's self, encamp.*
Crūdēliter, *adv.*	*cruelly.*
Dēpopulor, ārī, ātus sum,	*to ravage, lay waste.*
Excruciō, āre, āvī, ātum,	*to torture.*
Frūmentātiō, ōnis, *f.*	*foraging, provisioning.*
Grātulor, ārī, ātus sum,	*to congratulate; to thank.* (Followed by the Dative.)
Initium, iī, *n.*	*beginning.*
Īnsequor, ī, secūtus sum,	*to pursue, follow.*
Moror, ārī, ātus sum,	*to delay, tarry.*
Perfacilis, e,	*very easy.*
Perveniō, īre, vēnī, ventum,	*to arrive, come.*
Sepultūra, ae, *f.*	*burial, interment.*

GERUNDS, PARTICIPLES.

Subveniō, īre, vēnī, ventum, *to come to the help of, succor, aid.*
(Followed by the Dative.)
Triduum, ī, n. *space of three days, three days.*
Ulcīscor, ī, ultus sum, *to avenge one's self on, punish; to take vengeance.*

293. *Translate into English.*

1. Divitiacus auxiliī petendī causā Rōmam ad senātum profectus est. 2. Animī Rōmānōrum ad ulcīscendum ārdēbant. 3. Titūrius in illō locō hiemandī causā cōnsēderat. 4. Reperiēbat in quaerendō Caesar initium fugae factum esse ā Dumnorige. 5. Caesar equitātum ad eam regiōnem dēpopulandam mittit. 6. Fīnitimī lēgātōs ad Aeduōs mittunt subsidium rogātum. 7. Prīncipēs Aeduōrum ad Caesarem veniunt ōrātum ut cīvitātī subveniat. 8. Tōtīus ferē Galliae lēgātī,[1] prīncipēs cīvitātum, ad Caesarem grātulātum[2] convēnērunt.

9. Caesar ē castrīs profectus ad eam partem pervēnit, quae nōndum flūmen trānsierat. 10. Caesar Helvētiōs aggressus[3] māgnam eōrum partem concīdit. 11. Gallī dīcunt perfacile esse factū frūmentātiōnibus Rōmānōs prohibēre. 12. Centuriō, multīs vulneribus acceptīs,[4] pūgnāns[5] concidit. 13. Legiō decima Gallōs īnsequentēs[6] tardāvit. 14. Cīvēs Rōmānōs crūdēliter excruciātōs[3] interfēcērunt. 15. Caesar, hōc proeliō factō, pontem in Arare faciendum cūrat. 16. Rōmānī, propter sepultūram occīsōrum trīduum morātī, hostēs sequī nōn potuerant.

294. *Translate into Latin.*

1. One legion of Caesar's army retarded for three hours the enemy (who were) pursuing. 2. After a beginning of

---

[1] Literally, 'ambassadors *of* Gaul'; render, 'FROM Gaul.'
[2] Supply in English the object, *him.*
[3] See Suggestion XIII., 5.   [4] See Suggestion XVI., (3).
[5] In English the present participle in such a connection is usually accompanied by *while.*   [6] See Suggestion XIII., 2.

flight had been made[1] by one division of the enemy, the rest were easily conquered. 3. The Romans defeated the enemy (who were) not informed of their approach. 4. Let us send to our friends, to ask aid against those who have come for the purpose of ravaging our lands. 5. To conquer the brave and the free is not an easy thing to do.

6. For the sake of crossing the river more easily, Caesar had a bridge built over the Rhine. 7. Our soldiers ought to be prepared for setting out from camp, and for fighting with the enemy. 8. In asking aid, the Aedui said that they were eager to take vengeance.[2] 9. For defending the bridge which had been made, Caesar stationed soldiers on each bank of the river. 10. The Gallic chieftains said to Caesar: "We have been sent to you by our states to congratulate you."[3]

---

[1] Use the Ablative Absolute.
[2] Render, 'for (ad) taking vengeance.'
[3] See 166, 546.

NARRATIVES FROM CAESAR.

THE EMIGRATION OF THE HELVETII, THEIR DEFEAT BY THE ROMANS, AND THEIR RETURN TO THEIR COUNTRY.[1]

The Inhabitants of Gaul. The Valor of the Helvetii.

I. Gallia est dīvīsa in partēs trēs, quārum[2] ūnam[3] incolunt Belgae, aliam[3] Aquītānī,[4] tertiam[3] Gallī.[4] Helvētiī reliquōs Gallōs virtūte[5] praecēdunt, quod ferē cotīdiānīs proeliīs[6] cum Germānīs contendunt.

Orgetorix and His Project of Emigration.

II. Apud Helvētiōs nōbilissimus et dītissimus fuit Orgetorix. Is,[7] Messāllā et Pīsōne cōnsulibus,[8] cīvitātī[9] persuāsit ut dē fīnibus suīs exīrent.[10] Helvētiī continentur ūnā ex parte[11] flūmine Rhēnō, lātissimō atque altissimō, quī agrum Helvētium ā Germānīs dīvidit; alterā ex parte monte Jūrā

---

[1] From Caesar's "Commentaries on the Gallic War," I., 1-29. For Suggestions on Exercises in Latin Composition, see page 300.
[2] Partitive Genitive. 28, 397. [3] Supply *partem* as object of *incolunt*.
[4] Subject of *incolunt*. Observe that the term *Gallī* is used in two senses. It properly denotes the inhabitants of all Gaul, but it is often used, as in this instance, to designate the inhabitants of the third division of the country, i.e. of Celtic Gaul. [5] 231, 424. [6] 78, 420.
[7] *Is* would not be expressed unless it were emphatic, as in English, 'it was *he* who,' etc., i.e. it was Orgetorix who originated the project of emigration. [8] 240, 431. This was in the year 61 B. C.
[9] 54, 384. *Cīvitātī* is here used as a collective noun: 'the citizens;' observe that this is shown by the number of *exīrent*.
[10] 119, 497; 491. [11] 'On one side.'

quī est inter Sēquanōs et Helvētiōs; tertiā¹ lacū Lemannō et flūmine Rhodanō quī prōvinciam ab Helvētiīs dīvidit. Hīs rēbus² fīēbat ut minus facile fīnitimīs³ bellum inferre possent.⁴ Prō⁵ multitūdine autem hominum et prō glōriā fortitūdinis angustōs sē fīnēs habēre arbitrābantur.

The Helvetii Prepare to Leave their Country.

III. Hīs rēbus adductī et auctōritāte ⁶ Orgetorigis⁷ permōtī, cōnstituērunt ea quae ad proficīscendum pertinērent⁸ comparāre. Ubī jam sē ad eam rem parātōs esse arbitrātī sunt,⁹ oppida sua omnia, vīcōs, reliquaque prīvāta aedificia incendērunt; frūmentum omne, praeterquam¹⁰ quod sēcum portātūrī erant, combussērunt, ut domum reditiōnis spē sublātā parātiōrēs ad omnia perīcula subeunda¹¹ essent.¹²

The Route Selected and the Day Appointed.

IV. Erant omnīnō itinera duo quibus⁶ domō¹³ exīre possent; ūnum¹⁴ per Sēquanōs, angustum et difficile, alterum per prōvinciam, multō facilius, quod inter fīnēs Helvētiōrum et Allobrogum Rhodanus fluit, isque nōnnūllīs locīs¹⁵ vadō⁶ trānsītur.¹⁶ Extrēmum oppidum Allobrogum est prōximum-

---

¹ Supply *ex parte*. ² 158, 413. ³ 54, 394.
⁴ 123, 500. ⁵ *Prō*, 'in proportion to.' ⁶ 78, 420.
⁷ The secret purpose of Orgetorix was to possess himself of sovereign power among the Helvetii, and then to use this valiant and warlike nation, with the aid of a few other tribes, whose chieftains he had won to his purposes, in bringing the whole of Gaul under his control. His treasonable plot was detected; but just before the time appointed for his trial by the Helvetian authorities, he suddenly died, as it was suspected, by his own hand. The Helvetians did not, however, give up their project of emigration.
⁸ *Quae ... pertinērent*, 'which would be requisite for their departure.' 123, 503.
⁹ 258, 231. ¹⁰ See 279, sentence 17. ¹¹ 291, 544. ¹² 110, 497.
¹³ 277, 412. ¹⁴ *Ūnum*, in apposition with *itinera*. 28, 363.
¹⁵ 185, 425, 2.
¹⁶ *Vadō trānsītur*, 'is crossed by means of a ford,' i.e. 'is fordable.'

que Helvētiōrum fīnibus[1] Genāva. Ex eō oppidō pōns ad Helvētiōs pertinet.[2] Allobrogibus sēsē vel persuāsūrōs[3] existimābant vel vī coāctūrōs,[3] ut per suōs fīnēs eōs īre paterentur.[4] Omnibus rēbus[5] ad profectiōnem comparātīs, diem dīxērunt quā diē[6] ad rīpam Rhodanī omnēs convenīrent.[7] Is diēs erat ante diem quīntum Kalendās Aprīlēs,[8] Pīsōne, Gabīniō[9] cōnsulibus.

Caesar Hastens into Gaul, and Receives an Embassy from the Helvetii.

V. Caesarī cum nūntiātum esset[9] eōs per prōvinciam iter facere cōnārī,[10] mātūrāvit ab urbe[11] proficīscī, et ad Genāvam[12] pervēnit. Ubī dē ējus adventū Helvētiī certiōrēs factī sunt, lēgātōs ad eum mīsērunt quī dīcerent,[13] sibī esse in animō iter per prōvinciam facere, proptereā quod aliud iter habērent nūllum; rogāre, ut ējus voluntāte id sibī facere licēret.[14] Caesar, quod memoriā tenēbat[15] Lūcium

---

[1] 141, 391.   [2] *Ad . . . pertinet,* 'leads over to the Helvetii.'
[3] 171, 534.   [4] 119, 498.   [5] Ablative Absolute.
[6] 93, 429.   [7] 123, 500.
[8] *Ante . . . Aprilēs;* this whole expression may be regarded as an indeclinable noun, in this instance a *predicate nominative* after *erat;* 59, 362. It means 'the fifth day before the Calends (*the first*) of April,' which according to the Roman reckoning was not the 27th but the 28th day of March. This was in the year 58 B. C.   [9] 119, 491.
[10] *Eōs . . . cōnārī:* subject of *nūntiātum esset.*
[11] *Ab urbe,* i.e. from Rome.
[12] *Ad Genāvam,* 'into the vicinity of Geneva;' 'to Geneva' would be simply *Genāvam;* 277, 380.   [13] *Qui dicerent, to say;* 119, 497.
[14] *Sibī . . . licēret,* Indirect Discourse. In Direct Discourse, thus: *Nōbis est in . . . facere, proptereā . . . habēmus nūllum; rogāmus ut tuā voluntāte id nōbis facere liceat.* Explain the changes of Mood, etc. 262, 523, 524. Observe that *esse* and *rogāre* are the leading verbs in the principal clauses, and that the subject of *esse* is the clause *iter . . . facere.*— *Rogāre,* 'that they asked;' the subject, if expressed, would be *sē.*— *Ut . . . licēret;* 119, 498. *Licēret* has *id facere* as its subject, and *sibī* as its indirect object; 54, 384.—*Ējus voluntāte,* 'with his (Caesar's) consent,' 158, 413.
[15] *Memoriā tenēbat:* retained in (by means of) *memory.*

Cassium cōnsulem occīsum, exercitumque ējus ab Helvētiis pulsum et sub jugum missum,¹ concēdendum² nōn putābat. Tamen, ut spatium intercēdere posset,³ dum mīlitēs, quōs imperāverat, convenīrent, lēgātīs respondit, diem⁴ sē ad dēlīberandum sūmptūrum; sī quid vellent, ad Īdūs Aprīlēs⁵ reverterentur.⁶

Caesar takes Measures to prevent the March of the Helvetii.

VI. Intereā eū legiōne,⁷ quam sēcum habēbat, mīlitibusque,⁷ quī ex prōvinciā convēnerant, ā lacū Lemannō ad montem Jūram, quī fīnēs Sēquanōrum ab Helvētiīs dīvidit, mīlia⁸ passuum decem novem mūrum fossamque perdūxit. Ubī ea diēs, quam cōnstituerat cum lēgātīs, vēnit, et lēgātī ad eum revertērunt, negāvit sē posse iter ūllī per prōvinciam dare,⁹ et, sī vim facere cōnārentur,¹⁰ prohibitūrum¹¹ ostendit. Helvētiī perrumpere cōnātī, operis mūnītiōne et mīlitum tēlīs repulsī, hōc cōnātū¹² dēstitērunt.

The Helvetii decide to March by a different Route.

VII. Relinquēbātur ūna per Sēquanōs via,¹³ quā, Sēquanīs invītīs, propter angustiās īre nōn poterant. Illīs cum suā

---

1 This defeat of the Roman army under Cassius occurred near the Lake of Geneva, 107 B. C.   2 *Concēdendum*, i.e. the request of the Helvetii.
3 119, 497.   4 *Diem*, render *time*.
5 *Ad Īdūs Aprīlēs*, on the Ides of April, i.e. on the 13th of April.
6 *Sī . . . reverterentur:* in Direct Discourse, *si quid vultis . . . revertimini*, 262, 523, 524.   7 Ablative of Means with *perdūxit*.
8 *Milia*, 98, 397. These defences extended along the southern side of the Rhone, from the Lake of Geneva to Mount Jura, and commanded all the fords of the Rhone by which the Helvetii could enter the Roman province.
9 *Negāvit . . . dare: said that he could not grant;* literally, *denied that he was able to give.*   10 262, 524.
11 *Prohibitūrum*, i.e. *sē prohibitūrum esse.*   12 158, 413.
13 *Ūna . . . via: only the way through the Sequani*, i.e. the narrow pass along the north bank of the Rhone, between the mountains and the river.

17

sponte¹ persuādēre nōn possent,² lēgātōs ad Dumnorigem
Aeduum mīsērunt, ut eō dēprecātōre³ ā Sēquanīs impetrā-
rent.⁴ Dumnorix apud Sēquanōs plūrimum poterat,⁵ et
Helvētiīs erat amīcus, quod ex eā cīvitāte Orgetorigis fīliam
in mātrimōnium dūxerat.⁶ Itaque rem suscēpit⁷ et ā Sēquanīs impetrāvit, ut per fīnēs suōs Helvētiōs īre paterentur.

*Caesar Marches Five Legions of Roman Soldiers into
Gaul.*

VIII. Caesarī renūntiātum est, Helvētiīs esse in animō per
agrum Sēquanōrum et Aeduōrum iter in Santonum fīnēs
facere.⁸ Id sī fieret, intellegēbat māgnō cum perīculō prōvinciae futūrum.⁹ Ob eās causās eī mūnītiōnī, quam fēcerat,
Titum Labiēnum lēgātum praefēcit; ipse in Italiam contendit duāsque ibī legiōnēs cōnscrīpsit, et trēs, quae circum
Aquilēiam hiemābant, ex hībernīs ēdūxit, et in ulteriōrem
Galliam cum hīs quīnque legiōnibus īre contendit.

*Caesar Surprises and Routs One Canton of the Helvetii
at the River Arar.*

IX. Helvētiī jam per angustiās¹⁰ et fīnēs Sēquanōrum suās
cōpiās trānsdūxerant, et in Aeduōrum fīnēs pervēnerant.¹¹
Flūmen est Arar, quod¹² per fīnēs Aeduōrum et Sēquanōrum
in Rhodanum īnfluit. Id Helvētiī trānsībant.¹³ Ubī Caesar
certior factus est, trēs jam cōpiārum partēs¹⁴ Helvētiōs id
flūmen¹⁴ trānsdūxisse, quartam vērō partem citrā flūmen¹⁵

---

¹ *Suā sponte, of themselves.* ² See suggestion xvii, 2.
³ *Eō dēprecātōre, by his intercession;* literally, *he being an intercessor.*
⁴ 119, 497. ⁵ *Plūrimum poterat: had very great influence.*
⁶ *In mātrimōnium dūxerat: had married.*
⁷ *Rem suscēpit: he undertook the service.*
⁸ *Facere:* subject of *esse.* ⁹ Supply *esse.*
¹⁰ The *narrow pass* between the Jura and the Rhone.
¹¹ 'Had come,' i. e. during Caesar's absence.
¹² The antecedent is *flūmen.*
¹³ Observe the force of the tense: 'were crossing.'
¹⁴ See 275, sentence 19.
¹⁵ *Citrā flūmen: on this side of the river,* i.e. on the east side.

Ararim reliquam esse, cum legiōnibus tribus ē castrīs profectus, ad eam partem pervēnit, quae nōndum flūmen trānsierat. Eōs aggressus māgnam eōrum partem concīdit; reliquī fugae sēsē mandārunt. Is pāgus appellābātur Tigurīnus; nam omnis cīvitās Helvētia in quattuor pāgōs dīvīsa est. Ille pāgus ūnus, patrum nostrōrum memoriā,[1] Lūcium Cassium cōnsulem interfēcerat, et ējus exercitum sub jugum mīserat. Ita quae pars cīvitātis Helvētiae īnsīgnem calamitātem populō Rōmānō intulerat, ea[2] prīnceps poenās persolvit.[3]

Caesar Crosses the Arar, and Receives a Second Embassy from the Helvetii.

X. Hōc proeliō factō, reliquās cōpiās Helvētiōrum ut cōnsequī posset, pontem in Arare faciendum cūrāvit, atque ita exercitum trānsdūxit. Helvētiī ējus adventū commōtī, lēgātōs ad eum misērunt, cūjus lēgātiōnis Divicō prīnceps fuit. Is ita cum Caesare ēgit:[4] Sī pācem populus Rōmānus cum Helvētiīs faceret, in eam partem itūrōs atque ibī futūrōs[5] Helvētiōs, ubi eōs Caesar esse voluisset; sīn bellō persequī[6] persevērāret,[7] reminīscerētur et veteris incommodī[8] populī Rōmānī et prīstinae virtūtis Helvētiōrum. Caesar respondit: Sī[9] obsidēs ab iīs sibī darentur, utī ea,[10] quae pollicērentur, factūrōs intellegeret, sēsē cum iīs pācem esse factūrum. Divicō

---

[1] *Patrum . . . memoriā: within the memory of our fathers;* 93, 429.
[2] Render as if it read, *ea pars cīvitātis Helvētiae quae . . . intulerat.*
[3] *Princeps persolvit: was the first to pay.*
[4] *Ita ēgit: discoursed as follows.* The words following, *Sī . . . Helvētiōrum,* are in Indirect Discourse. The Direct Discourse would be: *Sī . . . faciet, . . . ībunt . . . erunt Helvētiī, ubi eōs esse volueris; sin . . . perseverābis, reminīscere,* etc. Explain the changes; 262, 523, 524.
[5] *Ibī futūrōs: would remain there.* Supply *esse.*
[6] *Persequī;* supply *eōs.*   [7] The subject is Caesar.
[8] *Incommodī populī,* etc. This refers to the defeat of Cassius.
[9] *Sī . . . factūrum* is in Indirect Discourse. The Direct Discourse would be: *Sī . . . mihī dabuntur . . . polliceantur, . . . intellegam,* (ego) *. . . faciam;* 262, 523, 524.
[10] *Ea:* object of *factūrōs* (*esse*), the subject of which is (*eōs*), referring to the Helvetii.

respondit: Helvētiōs ā mājōribus suīs īnstitūtōs esse, utī obsidēs accipere, nōn dare, cōnsuēssent;[1] ējus rēī populum Rōmānum esse testem.[2] Hōc respōnsō [3] datō discessit.

The Helvetii proceed on their March, followed by the Roman Army. A Cavalry Skirmish, in which the Helvetii are Successful.

XI. Posterō diē castra ex eō locō movērunt.[4] Idem fēcit Caesar, equitātumque omnem praemīsit, quī vidērent,[5] quās in partēs hostēs iter facerent.[6] Quī cupidius [7] novissimum āgmen īnsecūtī, aliēnō locō [8] cum equitātū Helvētiōrum proelium commīsērunt, et paucī dē nostrīs [9] cecidērunt. Quō proeliō [10] sublātī Helvētiī, quod quīngentīs equitibus [10] tantam multitūdinem equitum prōpulerant,[11] audācius subsistere, nōnnūnquam ex novissimō āgmine proeliō nostrōs lacēssere coepērunt. Caesar suōs ā proeliō continēbat, ac satis habēbat [12] in praesentiā hostem rapīnīs,[13] pābulātiōnibus, populātiōnibusque prohibēre. Ita diēs [14] circiter quīndecim iter fēcērunt, utī inter novissimum hostium āgmen et nostrum prīmum [15] nōn amplius [16] quīnīs aut sēnīs mīlibus [17] passuum interesset.[18]

---

[1] *Cōnsuēssent,* contracted from *cōnsuēvissent.* In this verb the Perfect has the sense of a Present, and therefore the Pluperfect of an Imperfect.

[2] *Ējus . . . testem: that the Roman people were witnesses of this,* alluding to the hostages given by the survivors after the defeat and death of Cassius.

[3] Ablative Absolute. [4] The subject is *Helvētiī* to be supplied.
[5] 119, 497. [6] 127, 529. [7] See 275, sentence 3.
[8] 185, 425, 2.
[9] *Paucī dē nostrīs: a few of our men;* see 125, sentence 8.
[10] 78, 420.
[11] Is this the reason of Caesar, or of the Helvetii?
[12] The object is the clause *hostem . . . prohibēre.* [13] 158, 413.
[14] 98, 379. [15] *Primum:* supply *āgmen,* our van.
[16] *Amplius:* subject of *interesset.*
[17] *Quīnīs mīlibus;* 88, 417. The Distributive implies that the statement is true for each of the fifteen days; 97, 172.
[18] 123, 500.

Caesar Plans an Attack upon the Camp of the Helvetii.

XII. Caesar ab explōrātōribus certior factus,[1] hostēs sub monte cōnsēdisse mīlia [2] passuum ab ipsīus castrīs octo, dē tertiā vigiliā Titum Labiēnum, lēgātum, cum duābus legiōnibus summum jugum montis ascendere jussit. Ipse dē quartā vigiliā eōdem itinere, quō hostēs ierant, ad eōs contendit. Pūblius Cōnsīdius, quī reī mīlitāris [3] perītissimus habēbātur, cum explōrātōribus praemissus est.

Caesar's Plan Defeated by the Mistake of Consĭdius.

XIII. Prīmā lūce,[4] cum summus mōns ā Titō Labiēnō tenērētur, ipse ab hostium castrīs nōn longius mīlle et quīngentīs passibus abesset,[5] neque aut ipsīus adventus aut Labiēnī cōgnitus esset,[6] Cōnsīdius equō admissō ad eum accurrit, dīxit montem, quem ā Labiēnō occupārī voluisset,[6] ab hostibus tenērī; id sē ā Gallicīs armīs cōgnōvisse. Caesar suās cōpiās in prōximum collem subdūxit, aciem īnstrūxit. Labiēnus, ut erat eī praeceptum [7] ā Caesare, nē proelium committeret, nisi ipsīus cōpiae [8] prope hostium castra vīsae essent,[6] ut undique ūnō tempore in hostēs impetus fieret, monte occupātō nostrōs exspectābat proeliōque abstinēbat. Multō dēnique diē [9] per explōrātōrēs Caesar cōgnōvit, et montem ā suīs tenērī, et Helvētiōs castra mōvisse, et Cōnsīdium timōre perterritum, quod nōn vīdisset, prō vīsō sibi renūntiāsse.[10] Eō diē, quō cōnsuērat intervallō,[11] hos-

---

[1] See *certus*, vocabulary. [2] 98, 379. [3] See vocabulary. [4] 93, 420.

[5] *Abesset* and *cōgnitus esset*, as well as *tenērētur*, depend upon *cum*.

[6] 127, 529, II.

[7] The subject of *erat praeceptum* is the clause *nē ... committeret*, which also expresses purpose; 119, 497.

[8] *Ipsīus cōpiae: his own* (Caesar's) *forces.*

[9] *Multō diē: late in the day,* though only relatively to *prīmā lūce.*

[10] *Quod ... renūntiāsse: had reported to him what he had not seen, as if seen,* literally, *for seen.* The antecedent of *quod* is the omitted object of *renūntiāsse.*

[11] *Quō ... intervallō = intervallō quō cōnsuērat: at the usual distance.* See above, XI., last line.

tūs secūtus est, et mīlia passuum tria ab eōrum castrīs castra sua posuit.

To secure Supplies, Caesar turns aside from the Pursuit of the Helvetii. The Helvetii change their Route and follow the Roman Army.

XIV. Postrīdiē, quod ā Bibracte, oppidō Aeduōrum cōpiōsissimō, nōn amplius mīlibus passuum octōdecim aberat, reī frūmentāriae prōspiciendum exīstimāvit,[1] iter ab Helvētiīs āvertit, āc Bibracte[2] īre contendit.[3] Ea rēs per fugitīvōs hostibus nūntiātum est. Helvētiī, seu[4] quod timōre perterritōs Rōmānōs discēdere ā sē exīstimārent, sīve quod rē[5] frūmentāriā interclūdī posse[6] cōnfīderent, itinere conversō, nostrōs[7] ā novissimō āgmine[8] īnsequī āc lacēssere coepērunt.

Caesar Prepares for a General Engagement.

XV. Postquam id animadvertit, cōpiās suās Caesar in prōximum collem subdūxit, equitātumque, quī sustinēret[9] hostium impetum, mīsit. Ipse interim in colle mediō[10] triplicem aciem īnstrūxit legiōnum quattuor veterānārum; sed in summō jugō duās legiōnēs, quās in Galliā citeriōre cōnscrīpserat, et omnia auxilia collocārī jussit. Helvētiī, cum omnibus suīs carrīs secūtī, impedīmenta in ūnum locum contulērunt; ipsī cōnfertissimā aciē, rejectō nostrō equitātū, phalange factā, sub prīmam nostram aciem successērunt.

---

[1] *Rēi . . . exīstimāvit:* he thought that he ought to provide supplies. With *prōspiciendum* supply *esse*; 281, 301; 54, 384.

[2] 277, 380.

[3] *Āvertit āc contendit:* no conjunction is expressed, connecting these verbs with *exīstimāvit*; we may supply *and accordingly*.

[4] *Seu . . . cōnfīderent:* either because they thought, etc., or because they trusted, etc.

[5] 158, 413.

[6] *Posse:* supply *eōs*, referring to the Romans.

[7] See 125, sentence 8.   [8] *Ā . . . āgmine:* on the rear.

[9] 119, 497.   [10] *In . . . mediō:* midway up the hill.

THE HELVETII.

In a fierce Battle the Helvetii are totally Defeated and put to Flight.

XVI. Caesar cohortātus suōs proelium commīsit. Mīlitēs, ē locō superiōre pīlīs missīs, facile hostium phalangem perfrēgērunt. Eā¹ disjectā, gladiīs dēstrictīs in eōs² impetum fēcērunt. Diū atque ācriter pūgnātum est.³ Nam hōc tōtō proeliō,⁴ cum⁵ ab hōrā septimā⁶ ad vesperum pūgnātum esset, āversum hostem vidēre nēmō potuit. Ad multam noctem⁷ etiam ad impedīmenta pūgnātum est, proptereā quod prō vallō carrōs objēcerant, et ē locō superiōre in nostrōs venientēs⁸ tēla cōiciēbant, et nōnnūllī inter carrōs rotāsque matarās āc tragulās subiciēbant, nostrōsque vulnerābant. Diū cum esset pūgnātum,⁹ impedīmentīs¹⁰ castrīsque nostrī potītī sunt. Ex eō proeliō circiter mīlia hominum centum et trīgintā superfuērunt, eāque tōtā nocte continenter iērunt; nūllam partem¹¹ noctis itinere intermissō, in fīnēs Lingonum diē quartō pervēnērunt, cum, et propter vulnera mīlitum et propter sepultūram occīsōrum nostrī trīduum¹¹ morātī, eōs sequī nōn potuissent.¹² Caesar ad Lingonēs litterās nūntiōsque mīsit, nē eōs frūmentō nēve aliā rē juvārent; quī sī jūvissent,¹³ sē eōdem locō, quō Helvētiōs, habitūrum.¹⁴ Ipse, trīduō intermissō, cum omnibus cōpiīs eōs sequī coepit.

¹ *Ea* refers to *phalangem*.   ² *Eōs* refers to *hostium*.
³ *Pūgnātum est: they fought*, 281, 301.
⁴ 185, 425, 1.   ⁵ 254, 515.
⁶ As the Romans divided the day from sunrise to sunset into twelve hours, the *seventh hour* would be about one o'clock.
⁷ *Ad . . . noctem: far into the night.*
⁸ *In . . . venientēs: against our men who were advancing.*
⁹ 281, 301.   ¹⁰ 258, 421.
¹¹ 98, 379.   ¹² With *cum*, denoting cause.
¹³ *Quī sī jūvissent: if they should aid;* 127, 529, II.
¹⁴ *Sē . . . habitūrum:* 'that he should regard them as in the same situation as the Helvetii.' *Sē habitūrum* (*esse*) depends upon the verb implied in *litterās . . . mīsit.* Supply, as the object of *habitūrum, eōs*, referring to *Lingonēs. Helvētiōs* is the object of *habēret*, to be supplied.

NARRATIVES FROM CAESAR.

The Helvetii submit to Caesar's Terms, and return to their Country. One Canton unsuccessfully Attempts to take Refuge in Germany.

XVII. Helvētiī, omnium rērum inopiā adductī, lēgātōs dē dēditiōne ad eum mīsērunt. Caesar obsidēs, arma, servōs, quī ad eōs perfūgissent,[1] poposcit. Dum ea[2] conquīruntur et cōnferuntur, nocte intermissā,[3] circiter[4] hominum mīlia sex ējus pāgī, quī Verbigēnus appellātur, sīve timōre perterritī,[5] nē armīs trāditīs suppliciō adficerentur,[6] sīve spē salūtis inductī, prīmā nocte[7] ex castrīs Helvētiōrum ēgressī, ad Rhēnum fīnēsque Germānōrum contendērunt. Quod ubi Caesar resciit,[8] quōrum[9] per fīnēs ierant, hīs[10] utī conquīrerent et redūcerent imperāvit; reductōs in hostium numerō habuit;[11] reliquōs omnēs, obsidibus, armīs, perfugīs trāditīs, in dēditiōnem accēpit. Helvētiōs in fīnēs suōs, unde erant profectī, revertī jussit, et Allobrogibus imperāvit, ut iīs frūmentī cōpiam facerent;[12] ipsōs[13] oppida vīcōsque, quōs incenderant, restituere jussit. Id eā māximē ratiōne[14] fēcit, quod nōluit eum locum, unde Helvētiī discesserant, vacūre, nē propter bonitātem agrōrum Germānī, quī trāns Rhēnum incolunt, ē suīs fīnibus in Helvētiōrum fīnēs trānsīrent, et fīnitimī Galliae prōvinciae essent.

---

[1] 123, 503.   [2] *Ea: these,* — literally, *these things.*
[3] 240, 431.   [4] *Circiter :* an adverb, modifying *sex.*
[5] *Perterriti* agrees with *milia* by a construction *according to sense.*
[6] *Nē . . . adficerentur* depends upon *timōre.* '*with fear lest,*' etc.; 119, 497.
[7] See 191, foot-note.   [8] *When Caesar ascertained this.*
[9] *Quōrum :* the antecedent is *his.*
[10] *His* depends on *imperāvit ;* 54, 384.
[11] *Reductōs . . . habuit : when they were brought back, he treated them as enemies:* literally, *had them in the number of enemies.* They were probably sold as slaves.
[12] *Ut . . . facerent. to furnish a supply,* etc.; 119, 498.
[13] *Ipsōs : them,* emphatic, in distinction from *Allobrogibus.*
[14] *Eā . . . ratiōne : principally for this reason,* explained by *quod nōluit,* etc.

The Numbers of the Helvetii before and after their Disastrous Enterprise.

XVIII. In castrīs Helvētiōrum tabulae repertae sunt quibus in tabulīs ratiŏ cōnfecta erat, quī numerus[1] domō[2] exīsset.[3] Summa erat Helvētiōrum mīlia ducenta et sexāgintā tria. Eōrum, quī domum rediērunt, cēnsū habitō, repertus est numerus mīlium centum et decem.

CAESAR'S FIRST INVASION OF BRITAIN, 55 B. C.[4]

Caesar's Reasons for the Expedition.

I. Caesar in Britanniam proficīscī contendit, quod omnibus ferē Gallicīs bellīs[5] hostibus nostrīs inde subministrāta[6] auxilia intellegēbat; et sī tempus annī ad bellum gerendum[7] dēficeret,[8] tamen māgnō sibī ūsuī[9] fore[10] arbitrābātur, sī modo īnsulam adīsset[9] et genus hominum perspēxisset, loca, portūs, aditūs cōgnōvisset; quae omnia ferē Gallīs erant incōgnita. Neque enim temere praeter mercātōrēs illō adit quisquam, neque hīs ipsīs[11] quicquam, praeter ōram maritimam atque eās regiōnēs, quae sunt contrā Galliās, nōtum est. Itaque vocātīs ad sē undique mercātōribus,[12] neque quanta esset[13] īnsulae māgnitūdō, neque quae aut quantae nātiōnēs incolerent, neque quem ūsum bellī habērent, neque quī essent ad nāvium multitūdinem idōneī portūs, reperīre poterat.

Preparations for the Expedition.

II. Ad haec cōgnōscenda[7] Gāium Volusēnum cum nāvī longā praemīsit. Huic mandāvit, utī explōrātīs omnibus

---
[1] *Ratiŏ, qui numerus: an account showing what number.*
[2] 212, 412, 1.
[3] *Qui ... exisset* is in apposition with *ratiŏ;* 127, 529, I.
[4] From Caesar's "Commentaries on the Gallic War," IV., 20–36.
[5] 93, 429.   [6] Supply *esse*.   [7] 291, 543.   [8] 127, 529, II.
[9] 281, 390.   [10] 140, 204, 2.   [11] *Hīs ipsis*, i.e. *mercātōribus*.
[12] *Vocātis ... mercātōribus*, Ablative Absolute; *although he summoned*, etc.   [13] *Quanta esset:* object of *reperire;* 127, 529, I.

rēbus¹ ad sē quam prīmum² reverterētur.³ Ipse cum omnibus cōpiīs in Morinōs profectus est, quod inde erat brevissimus in Britanniam trājectus. Hūc nāvēs undique ex fīnitimīs regiōnibus et, quam⁴ superiōre aestāte effēcerat, classem jussit convenīre. Volusēnus, perspectīs regiōnibus¹ omnibus, quīntō diē ād Caesarem revertit, quaeque ibī perspēxisset⁵ renūntiāvit.

Caesar crosses the Channel.

III. Caesar nactus idōneam ad nāvigandum⁶ tempestātem, tertiā ferē vigiliā⁷ solvit, et hōrā diēī circiter quartā⁸ cum prīmīs nāvibus Britanniam attigit, atque ibī in omnibus collibus expositās hostium cōpiās armātās cōnspēxit. Cūjus locī haec erat nātūra, utī ex locīs superiōribus in lītus tēlum adigī posset.⁹ Hunc ad ēgrediendum⁶ nēquāquam idōneum locum arbitrātus, circiter mīlia¹⁰ passuum septem ab eō locō prōgressus, apertō āc plānō lītore nāvēs cōnstituit.¹¹

The Britons Oppose the Landing of the Romans.

IV. At barbarī, praemissō equitātū¹ et essedāriīs, reliquīs cōpiīs subsecūtī, nostrōs nāvibus ēgredī prohibēbant. Quod ubī Caesar animadvertit, nāvēs longās, quārum speciēs erat barbarīs inūsitātior, paulum removērī ab onerāriīs nāvibus, et rēmīs incitārī, et ad latus apertum¹² hostium cōnstituī, atque inde fundīs,¹³ sagittīs, tormentīs, hostēs prōpellī āc submovērī

---

¹ Ablative Absolute.   ² *Quam prīmum: as soon as possible.*
³ 119, 497.   ⁴ *Quam:* the antecedent is *classem.*
⁵ 127, 529, I.   ⁶ 291, 542.   ⁷ 93, 429.
⁸ About ten o'clock in the morning, probably on the 26th of August. See page 291, foot-note 6.
⁹ 123, 500.   ¹⁰ 98, 379.
¹¹ *Apertō . . . cōnstituit: he anchored off an open and level shore;* probably on the coast of Deal; 185, 425, 1.
¹² The *exposed flank* was the right flank, as the shield was carried on the left arm.
¹³ 78, 420.

jussit: quae rēs māgnō ūsuī nostrīs¹ fuit. Nam et nāvium figūrā² et rēmōrum mōtū et inūsitātō genere tormentōrum permōtī, barbarī cōnstitērunt āc paulum pedem rettulērunt. Atque nostrīs mīlitibus³ cunctantibus, māximē propter altitūdinem maris, quī⁴ decimae legiōnis aquilam⁵ ferēbat : " Dēsilīte," inquit, "commīlitōnēs, nisi vultis aquilam hostibus prōdere:⁶ ego certē meum reī pūblicae atque imperātōrī officium praestiterō." Hōc cum māgnā vōce dīxisset,⁷ sē ex nāvī prōjēcit atque in hostēs aquilam ferre coepit. Tum nostrī ūniversī ex nāvī dēsiluērunt. Hōs item ex proximīs nāvibus cum cōnspēxissent,⁷ subsecūtī hostibus appropīnquārunt.

The Romans Effect a Landing, and put the Britons to Flight.

V. Pūgnātum est ab utrīsque ācriter. Nostrī tamen, quod neque ōrdinēs servāre neque firmiter īnsistere poterant,⁸ māgnō opere perturbābantur. Hostēs vērō, nōtīs omnibus vadīs,⁹ ubi aliquōs singulārēs ex nāvī ēgredientēs cōnspēxerant,⁹ incitātīs equīs,⁸ adoriēbantur; plūrēs¹⁰ paucōs circumsistēbant; aliī in ūniversōs¹¹ tēla cōiciēbant. Quod cum animadvertisset⁷ Caesar, scaphās longārum nāvium mīlitibus complērī jussit, et quōs labōrantēs cōnspēxerat, hīs subsidia submittēbat. Nostrī simul⁹ in āridō cōnstitērunt, in hostēs impetum fēcērunt atque eōs in fugam dedērunt.

The Britons Sue for Peace.

VI. Hostēs, proeliō¹² superātī, statim ad Caesarem lēgātōs dē pāce mīsērunt. Caesar obsidēs imperāvit, quōrum illī

---

¹ 281, 390. ² 158, 413. ³ Ablative Absolute.
⁴ *Quī, he who.* ⁵ The eagle was the standard of the legion.
⁶ The loss of the eagle was regarded as a great disgrace.
⁷ Temporal clause. ⁸ Caesar's reason. ⁹ Temporal clause.
¹⁰ *Plūrēs: several,* i. e. of the enemy.
¹¹ *In ūniversōs: against our assembled forces,* opposed to *aliquōs singulārēs.* ¹² 185, 425, 1.

partem statim dedērunt, partem paucīs diēbus¹ sēsē datūrōs
dīxērunt.

The Roman Fleet seriously Damaged by a high Tide and a Storm.

VII. Hīs rēbus pāce² cōnfirmātā, post diem quartum, quam³ est in Britanniam ventum,⁴ accidit, ut esset lūna plēna,⁵ quī diēs⁶ maritimōs aestūs māximōs in Ōceanō efficere cōnsuēvit; nostrīsque id⁷ erat incōgnitum. Ita ūnō tempore¹ et longās nāvēs, quās Caesar in āridum subdūxerat, aestus complēbat, et onerāriās, quae ad ancorās erant dēligātae, tempestās afflīctābat. Complūribus nāvibus³ frāctīs, māgna tōtīus exercitūs perturbātiō facta est. Neque enim nāvēs erant aliae, quibus reportārī possent,⁸ et, quod omnibus cōnstābat hiemārī in Galliā oportēre,⁹ frūmentum hīs in locīs in hiemem prōvīsum nōn erat.

The British Chieftains plot a Renewal of Hostilities.

VIII. Quibus rēbus³ cōgnitīs, prīncipēs¹⁰ Britanniae, cum equitēs et nāvēs et frūmentum Rōmānīs deesse intellegerent,¹¹ et paucitātem mīlitum ex castrōrum exiguitāte cōgnōscerent, optimum factū¹² esse dūxērunt, rebelliōne² factā, frūmentō¹³ commeātūque nostrōs prohibēre, et rem in hiemem prōdūcere,¹⁴ quod, hīs² superātīs aut reditū¹³ interclūsīs, nēminem

---

¹ 93, 429. ² Ablative Absolute.

³ *Post . . . quam: on the fourth day after;* diem is in the Accusative with the preposition *post*, and *quam* is here used as a conjunction with the force of *postquam*; literally, *after the fourth day, after,* etc.

⁴ 281, 301. ⁵ This was on the 30th of August.

⁶ *Qui diēs: which period,* or *a period which.*

⁷ *Id: that = this fact,* i.e. the fact expressed in *qui . . . cōnsuēvit.*

⁸ 123, 500, I.

⁹ *Cōnstābat . . . oportēre: hiemārī,* used impersonally, is the subject of *oportēre;* 281, 301; *oportēre* is the subject of *cōnstābat.*

¹⁰ Subject of *dūxērunt.*

¹¹ Observe mood. ¹² 246, 547. ¹³ 158, 413.

¹⁴ *Rem . . . prōdūcere: to protract the war.*

posteā bellī īnferendī¹ causā in Britanniam trānsitūrum² cōnfīdēbant.

Caesar Suspects the Plot of the Britons, and Prepares to Meet it.

IX. At Caesar, etsī nōndum eōrum cōnsilia cōgnōverat, tamen fore³ id, quod accidit, suspicābātur. Itaque ad omnēs cāsūs subsidia comparābat. Nam et frūmentum ex agrīs cotīdiē in castra cōnferēbat, et quae gravissimē adflīctae erant nāvēs, eārum⁴ māteriā⁵ atque aere ad reliquās reficiendās¹ ūtēbātur, et quae ad eās rēs erant ūsuī,⁶ ex continentī comportārī jubēbat. Itaque, duodecim nāvibus āmissīs, reliquīs ut nāvigārī posset,⁷ effēcit.

The Britons Surprise a Roman Foraging Party. Caesar Hastens to the Rescue.

X. Dum ea geruntur,⁸ legiōne ūnā frūmentātum⁹ missā, neque ūllā ad id tempus bellī suspīciōne interpositā, iī, quī prō portīs castrōrum in statiōne erant, Caesarī nūntiāvērunt pulverem mājōrem, quam cōnsuētūdō ferret,¹⁰ in eā parte vidērī, quam in partem¹¹ legiō iter fēcisset. Caesar suspicātus aliquid novī ā barbarīs initum cōnsiliī,¹² cohortēs, quae in statiōnibus erant,¹³ sēcum in eam partem proficīscī, ex reliquīs duās in statiōnem cohortēs succēdere,¹⁴ reliquās ar-

---

1 291, 543.   2 Supply *esse*.   3 See 140, 204, 2.
4 *Quae nārēs, cārum* = *eārum nāvium, quae.*   5 258, 421.
6 281, 300; one of the two Datives, as here, is often omitted, when it would be some word like *alicui, to any one.*
7 *Ut . . . posset* is the object of *effēcit,* 'he made it possible to sail with the rest'; 123, 501. *Nāvigārī,* used impersonally, is the subject of *posset;* 281, 301.   8 Render by imperfect.   9 166, 546.
10 *Quam cōnsuētūdō ferret: than usual; literally, than custom bore.*
11 *Quam in partem;* render as if it were *in quam.*
12 *Aliquid . . . cōnsiliī; aliquid* is subject of *initum* (*esse*); *cōnsiliī* is Partitive Genitive after *aliquid;* 28, 397.
13 One cohort guarded each of the four gates of a Roman camp.
14 *Ex . . . succēdere: two of the other (six) cohorts to take their place on guard.* He could spare only two, instead of four, to guard the gates.

mūrī et cōnfestim sēsē subsequī jussit. Cum paulō longius ā castrīs prōcessisset,[1] suōs[2] ab hostibus premī, atque aegrē sustinēre animadvertit. Nam quod, omnī ex reliquīs partibus dēmessō frūmentō,[3] pars ūna[4] erat reliqua, suspicātī hostēs hūc nostrōs esse ventūrōs, noctū in silvīs dēlituerant; tum dispersōs,[5] dēpositīs armīs,[6] in metendō[6] occupātōs subitō adortī, paucīs interfectīs, reliquōs perturbāverant; simul equitātū atque essedīs circumdederant.

The Use of War-chariots by the Britons.

XI. Genus hōc est[7] ex essedīs pūgnae: prīmō per omnēs partēs perequitant et tēla cōiciunt, atque ipsō terrōre equōrum[8] et strepitū rotārum ōrdinēs plērumque perturbant, et cum sē inter equitum turmās īnsinuāvērunt,[9] ex essedīs dēsiliunt et pedibus proeliantur. Aurīgae interim paulātim ex proeliō excēdunt, atque ita currūs collocant, ut, sī illī[10] ā multitūdine hostium premantur,[11] expedītum ad suōs[2] receptum habeant.[12] Ita mōbilitātem equitum, stabilitātem peditum in proeliīs praestant.

Caesar Rescues his Foraging Party. Storms interfere with Military Operations.

XII. Quibus rēbus[13] perturbātīs nostrīs[2] tempore[14] opportūnissimō Caesar auxilium tulit; namque ējus adventū[15] nostrī[2] sē ex timōre recēpērunt. Quō[3] factō, ad committendum

---

[1] Temporal clause.   [2] See 125, sentence 8.   [3] Ablative Absolute.

[4] *Pars ūna: only one part*, i.e. only one place from which grain could be obtained.

[5] *Dispersōs*; this participle, like *occupātōs*, agrees with *nostrōs*, to be supplied as the object of *adortī*; *while scattered*, etc.

[6] 291, 542.   [7] *Hōc est: is as follows.*

[8] *Ipsō . . . equōrum: by the very terror caused by their horses.*

[9] Temporal clause.

[10] *Illī*, i.e. the warriors, in distinction from the drivers, *aurīgae*.

[11] 127, 529, II.   [12] 123, 500, II.

[13] 78, 420.   [14] 93, 429.

[15] 185, 425, 1.

proelium¹ aliēnum esse tempus arbitrātus, brevī tempore² intermissō in castra legiōnēs redūxit. Secūtae sunt continuōs complūrēs diēs³ tempestātēs, quae et nostrōs in castrīs continērent,⁴ et hostem ā pūgnā prohibērent.

The Britons Combine, and March upon the Roman Camp, but Suffer a total Defeat.

XIII. Interim barbarī nūntiōs in omnēs partēs dīmisērunt, paucitātemque nostrōrum mīlitum suīs praedicāvērunt, et quanta in perpetuum suī līberandī⁵ facultās darētur,⁶ sī Rōmānōs castrīs⁷ expulissent,⁸ dēmōnstrāvērunt. Hīs rēbus⁹ celeriter māgnā multitūdine² peditātūs equitātūsque coāctā, ad castra vēnērunt. Caesar legiōnēs in aciē prō castrīs cōnstituit. Commissō proeliō,² nostrōrum mīlitum impetum hostēs ferre nōn potuērunt, āc terga vertērunt. Quōs secūtī, complūrēs ex iīs occīdērunt; deinde omnibus longē lātēque aedificiīs² incēnsīs, sē in castra recēpērunt.

The Britons Sue for Peace. Caesar Returns to the Continent.

XIV. Eōdem diē¹⁰ lēgātī ab hostibus missī ad Caesarem dē pāce vēnērunt. Hīs¹¹ Caesar numerum obsidum, quem anteā imperāverat, duplicāvit eōsque in continentem addūcī jussit. Ipse idōneam tempestātem nactus nāvēs solvit, quae omnēs incolumēs ad continentem pervēnērunt.

---

¹ 291, 513. ² Ablative Absolute.
³ 98, 379. ⁴ 123, 500, I.
⁵ *Sui liberandi: of freeing themselves;* literally, *of the freeing of themselves. Sui* is in the Genitive plural after *liberandi*, according to Rule XVI., 28, 395. The Gerund usually governs the same case as the verb, but sometimes, by virtue of its *substantive nature*, it governs the Genitive, especially the Genitive of personal pronouns, *mei, nostri, tui, vestri,* and *sui*.
⁶ 127, 529, I. ⁷ 153, 413. ⁸ 127, 529, II.
⁹ 78, 420. ¹⁰ 93, 429. ¹¹ 54, 384, II.

LATIN COMPOSITION.

SUGGESTIONS ON EXERCISES IN LATIN COMPOSITION.

No exercises for Translation into Latin are given in connection with these passages of connected narrative, but it is not intended that this important subject should be neglected. The pupil may now begin Part II. of the "Introduction to Latin Composition"; but an exercise as often as once a week or once a fortnight is recommended, to be prepared *by the teacher*, and based upon some passage of the Latin which the pupils have read. At first the pupils may be permitted to make their translation with the aid of the Latin, but the plan should be adopted early, of assigning the passage to be *committed to memory* by the pupil, and then requiring the translation into Latin within the hour assigned for the exercise, with no aid but the pupil's memory and the knowledge that he has acquired of the language. The following exercise, based upon paragraph II., page 282, is given simply as an illustration.

Translate into Latin.

Caesar says that in the consulship of Messala, Orgetorix, a chieftain (*prīnceps*[1]) of very high birth and of great wealth, persuaded the Helvetii to emigrate from their country. The territory of this tribe (*gēns*) was very limited for its population, and it was separated from the adjacent countries (*terra*) by high mountains and deep rivers. The Rhine hemmed them in on one side, Mount Jura on another, and on a third the Lake of Geneva and the Rhone. Thus (*itaque*) the warlike (*bellicōsus*) Helvetii were not able readily to carry on war against their neighbors.

---

[1] Words not occurring in the Latin passage may be furnished to the pupil, but in general he should be expected to give familiar words without aid.

SUGGESTIONS TO THE LEARNER.

I. The preparation of a reading lesson in Latin involves:
1. An exact comprehension of the thought expressed in the original.
2. An appropriate expression of that thought in an English translation.

MEANING OF THE LATIN.

II. In preparing your lessons take special note, from the outset, of the more obvious difference between the Latin and the English.

III. The Latin gives new names to persons and things already familiar to you. Therefore store your memory as rapidly as possible with these new names. Learn the vocabularies so thoroughly that you will be able, not only to give with promptness either the English for the Latin or the Latin for the English, but also, what is of supreme importance, to recognize the full meaning in the Latin word itself, without any thought of the English. It is not enough to find English equivalents for Latin words. In your vocabulary, Latin nouns must represent not *mere words*, but *real persons* and *things;* AGRICOLA, not the English word *husbandman*, but the *husbandman himself*, not the *name*, but the *man*.

IV. Remember that the full meaning of an inflected word can seldom be ascertained from the dictionary alone. Every word of this kind has a significant ending, which gives it an important part of its meaning. Therefore make yourself so familiar with all the endings of inflection, whether in declension or conjugation, that you will readily distinguish not only the different parts of speech, but also the different forms of the same word.

V. But these endings of inflection should not only enable you to distinguish the parts of speech, should not only tell you the *cases* of *nouns*, and the *voices*, *moods*, *tenses*, *numbers*, and *persons* of *verbs*, but they should also give you the exact *meaning* of all these forms. The meaning is what you must have. It will be of little use to you to know that a verb is in the Imperfect tense, for instance, unless you also know what that tense really means, what it really tells you about the action of the verb.

VI. Again, the dictionary and the grammar combined often fail to meet the needs of the student. If I tell you that *rēgēs* is the first word in a sentence, and then ask you to give me its full and exact meaning, I require an absolute impossibility. The most learned Roman that ever lived could not answer the question. The dictionary can only tell you that the general idea is that designated by our word *king*, while the grammar informs you that *rēgēs* is in the plural number, and that the form may be found in the Nominative, Accusative or Vocative. It will also tell you that, *if* it is in the Nominative, it may be the subject of an action, an appositive, or a predicate Nominative; that *if* it is in the Accusative, it may be the object of an action, an appostive, a predicate Accusative, or the subject of an infinitive; and that, *if* it is in the Vocative, it is used as a form of address; but neither the dictionary nor the grammar can tell you which case it is, or which one of these numerous meanings it actually has. How, then, can you ever ascertain what it really means? Simply by the light which the subsequent words in the sentence will cast upon it.

I now give you the second word in the sentence, *sententiam*, and you have *rēgēs sententiam*. Can you tell the meaning of these words, or of either of them? *Sententiam* must be an Accusative, but as that case may be variously used, its special force in this sentence is still uncertain. The Accusative *sententiam*, however, makes it probable that *rēgēs* is not an Accusative, but either a Nominative or a Vocative. I add *probant* and thus complete the thought: *Rēgēs sententiam probant*. Notice now the *effect* of this last word upon the meaning of the sentence. It shows that the Accusative *sententiam*, which of itself might have various meanings, is here simply the object of the action and that *rēgēs*, which at first covered such a variety of cases is simply the subject of the action. We are now prepared to translate: *The kings approve the opinion.*

VII. From the example just given, observe to what an extent the meaning of a word is determined by the connection in which it is used. Standing alone it may perhaps be any one of three or four cases but as soon as it is combined with other words in a sentence, it stands revealed in the clearest light as a single case with a definite and distinct meaning. Accordingly, in all your reading, as each successive word meets your eye, let it be your unfailing rule to study its *effect* upon the meaning of the sentence, to observe the light which it throws upon the words that precede it and the light which it in turn will derive from those which are to follow; to observe, in fine, how the thought is gradually unfolded.

VIII. In taking up a Latin sentence remember that your object is not primarily to translate it, but *to understand* and *appreciate the thought in the original.* This should be done, not only without translating it, but even without thinking of the corresponding English words. To this end, you will find it helpful to read over your Latin exercises, especially the longer passages, somewhat frequently, with the special purpose of appreciating and enjoying the thought in its original form. Under this treatment, the Latin constructions so strange to the beginner, will soon be found to be entirely simple and natural, and the language will in time become a second vernacular, and you will then enjoy fine thoughts in Latin as you enjoy them in English.

IX. But if you would fully appreciate the thoughts of a Latin writer, you must take his words in the order in which he wrote them. The arrangement of the words is an essential part of a Latin sentence and one of the means by which its meaning may be most successfuly reached. The Latin order, more flexible than the English, allows a much larger scope for emphasis, and thus shows the relative importance of the several words. In general the subject and its verb, so essential to the thought, are assigned important places, the former at the beginning and the latter at the end of the sentence, yet other words when especially *emphatic* may occupy either of these positions.

X. Finally, never attempt to translate a Latin sentence until you clearly comprehend the exact thought in the original. The habit of starting off blindly to render separate words without any conception of the thought which they are intended to express is fatal to all high scholarship. Therefore, make it your first and chief object to ascertain the exact thought contained in the sentence. To accomplish this object, you will need to attend to the following particulars:

1. The general meaning of the several words as given in the vocabulary.

2. Their more definite meaning as determined by their endings.

3. The exact sense which they assume in consequence of the connection in which they are used.

XI. In the use of the Dictionary, remember that you are to look, not for the particular form which occurs in the sentence, but for the Nominative Singular of nouns, adjectives, and pronouns, and for the First Person Singular, Present Indicative Active of Verbs. Therefore

1. In Pronouns, make yourself so familiar with their declension that any oblique case will at once suggest the Nominative Singular.

2. In Nouns and Adjectives, make yourself so familiar with the case-endings, that you will be able to drop that of the given case, and substitute for it that of the Nominative Singular.

3. In verbs, change the ending of the given form into that of the First Person Singular of the Present Indicative Active.

Translation.

XII. In translating, render as literally as possible without doing violence to the English.

In many important idioms of the Latin, a literal translation not only would fail to do justice to the original, but also would be a gross perversion of the mother-tongue. The following suggestions are intended to aid the pupil in disposing of such cases; but even in these, it is earnestly recommended that he should first construe literally, in order that he may be made to feel the force of the Latin construction before attempting a translation.

Participles.

XIII. These are much more extensively used in Latin than in English; hence the frequent necessity, in translating them, of deviating from the Latin construction. They may generally be rendered in some one of the following ways[1] (**291**, 549).

---

[1] The pupil must early learn to determine from the context the appropriate rendering in each instance.

1. Literally:

Pyrrhus proeliō fūsus ā Tarentō recessit, *Pyrrhus having been defeated in battle withdrew from Tarentum.*

2. By a Relative Clause:

Omnēs aliud agentēs, aliud simulantēs improbī sunt, *all who do one thing and pretend another are dishonest.*

3. By a Clause with a Conjunction:

1) With a Conjunction of Time, — *while, when, after,* etc.

Ūva mātūrāta dulcēscit, *the grape when it has ripened* (having ripened), *becomes sweet.*

2) With a Conjunction of Cause, Reason, Manner, — *as, for, since,* etc.

Militēs perfidiam veritī revertērunt, *the soldiers returned, because they feared perfidy.*

3) With a Conjunction of Condition, — *if.*

Accūsātus damnābitur, *if he is accused he will be condemned.*

4) With a Conjunction of Concession, — *though, although.*

Urbem ācerrimē dēfēnsam cēpit, *he took the city, though it was valiantly defended,* or *though valiantly defended.*

4. By a Verbal Noun:

Ad Rōmam conditam, *to the founding of Rome;* literally, *to Rome founded.* Ab urbe conditā, *from the founding of the city.* Post rēgēs exāctōs, *after the expulsion of the kings.*

5. By a Verb:

Rēx ēi benignē receptō filiam dedit, *the king received him kindly and gave him his daughter;* literally, *gave his daughter to him kindly received.*

XIV. Participles with *nōn* or *nihil* are sometimes best rendered by *Participial* nouns dependent upon *without:*

Nōn ridēns, *without laughing.*

XV. Future Participles are sometimes best rendered by *Infinitives,* or by *Participial Nouns* with *for the purpose of:*

Rediit bellī cāsum tentātūrus, *he returned to try* (about to try) *the fortune of war.*

XVI. The Ablative Absolute is sometimes best rendered (1) by a *Clause with—when, while, after, for, since, if, though*, etc., (2) by a *Noun* with a *Preposition,—in, during, after, by, from, through*, etc., or (3) by an *Active Participle* with its *Object:*

Servió rēgnante, *while Servius reigned*, or *in the reign of Servius* (literally, *Servius reigning*). Duce Fabiō, *under the command of Fabius* (literally, *Fabius being commander*).

Sometimes, as in the last example, a word denoting the *doer* of an action can be best rendered by the word which denotes the *thing done*. Thus, instead of *commander, consul, king*, we have *command, consulship, reign*.

Subjunctive.

XVII. This may be rendered as follows:

1. With the *Potential* signs, *may, might, would, should*, or with *let*.

Forsitan quaerātis, *perhaps you may inquire*. Hōc nēmō dīxerit, *no one would say this*.

2. By the English Indicative. This is generally the best rendering

1) In clauses denoting Cause or Time, as after *cum, quod, quia, quoniam*, etc.

Cum vīta metūs plēna sit, *since life is full of fear*. Cum Rōmam vēnisset, *when he had come to Rome*.

2) In Indirect Questions (**127**, 529, I.):

Quaeritur, cūr dissentiant, *it is asked why they disagree*.

3) In the Subjunctive in Indirect Clauses (**127**, 529, II.):

Vereor, nē, dum minuere velim labōrem, augeam, *I fear I shall increase the labor, while I wish to diminish it*.

4) In the Subordinate Clauses of Indirect Discourse (**262**, 524):

Hippiās glōriātus est ānulum quem habēret sē suā manū cōnfēcisse, *Hippias boasted that he had made with his own hand the ring which he wore* (had).

5) In Relative Clauses defining indefinite antecedents, and sometimes in clauses denoting *result* (**123**, 503, 500, 501):

Sunt qui putent, *there are some who think.* Ita vixit ut Athēniēnsibus esset cārissimus, *he so lived, that he was very dear to the Athenians.*

6) Sometimes in Conditional and Concessive clauses, and in clauses with *Quin* and *Quōminus* (**250**, 560, **254**, 515, **123**, 500, II., **119**, 497, II.):

Dum metuant, *if only* (provided) *they fear.* Sī voluisset, dimicāsset, *if he had wished, he would have fought.* Ut dēsint vīrēs, tamen est laudanda voluntās, *though the strength fails, still the will should be approved.* Adest nēmō, quin videat, *there is no one present who does not see.*

3. By the Infinitive.[1] This is often the best rendering

1) In Clauses denoting Purpose (**119**, 497):

Contendit ut vincat, *he strives to conquer* (that he may conquer). Decemviri creāti sunt qui lēgēs scrīberent, *decemvirs were appointed to prepare the laws* (who should prepare).

2) In Clauses denoting Result: hence after *dignus, indignus, idōneus, aptus,* etc. (**123**, 500, 503):

Nōn is sum qui his ūtar, *I am not such a one as to use* (he who may use) *these things.* Fābulae dignae sunt quae legantur, *the fables are worthy to be read* (which, or that they, should be read).

Infinitive.

XVIII. The Infinitive has a much more extensive use in Latin than in English. The following points require notice.

1. The Infinitive with a Subject is rendered by a *Finite* verb with *that:*

Dīxit sē rēgem vīdisse, *he said that he had seen the king.*

2. The Historical Infinitive[2] is rendered by the Imperfect Indicative:

Iram pater dissimulāre, *the father concealed his anger.*

---

[1] Observe, however, that the Infinitive here is not the translation of the Subjunctive alone, but of the Subjunctive with its subject and connective; ut vincat, *to conquer* (literally, *that he may conquer*); qui ūtar, *as to use* (literally, *who should* or *may use*).

[2] In lively descriptions the Present Infinitive is sometimes used for the *Imperfect* or the *Perfect Indicative.* It is then called the Historical Infinitive, and, like a finite verb, has its subject in the Nominative.

3. The Infinitive is sometimes best rendered by a *Participial noun* with *of, with*, etc.

Insimulātur mystēria violāsse, *he is accused of having violated the mysteries*.

Miscellaneous Idioms.

XIX. The following Miscellaneous Idioms are added:

1. *Certiōrem facere* should be rendered, *to inform*, and *certior fieri*, *to be informed:*

Caesar certior factus est, *Caesar was informed.*

2. *Inter sē*, literally *between themselves*, is often best rendered, *from each other, from one another, to each other, to one another, together.*

Omnēs inter sē differunt, *they all differ from one another.*

3. *Nē — quidem*, with one or more words between the parts, should be rendered, *not even*, or *even — not:*

Nē nōmen quidem, *not even the name.*

4. When two or more verbs stand together in the same compound tense, the copula (*sum*) is generally expressed with the last only, but in rendering, the copula should be expressed with the first only:

Captus et in vincula cōjectus est, *he was taken and thrown into chains.*

5. *Quantō — tantō*, literally, *by as much as — by so much*, is often best rendered before comparatives, *the — the:*

Quantō diūtius cōnsiderō, tantō rēs vidētur obscūrior, *the longer* (by as much as the longer) *I consider the subject, the more obscure* (by so much the more obscure) *does it appear.*

6. A Clause with *quōminus*, 'by which the less,' or 'that the less,' may generally be rendered by a *Clause* with *that*, by the *Infinitive*, or by a *Participial noun* with *from.*

Per eum stetit quōminus dīmicārētur, *it was owing to him* (stood through him) *that the engagement was not made.* Nōn recūsāvit quōminus poenam subīret, *he did not refuse to submit to punishment.* Rēgem impediit quōminus pūgnāret, *he prevented the king from fighting.*

ABBREVIATIONS.

abl.	ablative.	m.	masculine.
acc.	accusative.	n.	neuter.
adj.	adjective.	nom.	nominative.
adv.	adverb.	p.	page.
comp.	comparative.	part.	participle.
conj.	conjunction.	pers.	personal.
f.	feminine.	pl.	plural.
gen.	genitive.	pos.	positive.
impers.	impersonal.	prep.	preposition.
indef.	indefinite.	pron.	pronoun.
interj.	interjection.	sing.	singular.
interrog.	interrogative.	sup.	superlative.
lit.	literally.	w.	with.

LATIN-ENGLISH VOCABULARY.

A.

Ā, ab. *prep. w. abl. From; by, in the direction of; on.*

Abeō, īre, iī, itum. *To go away, depart.*

Abstineō, ēre, uī, tentum. *To abstain, refrain.* ABSTAIN.[1]

Absum, esse, āfuī. *To be absent, distant.* ABSENT.

Abundō, āre, āvī, ātum. *To abound, to be well supplied with.* ABOUND.

Āc, *conj. And.*

Acceptus, a, um, *part and adj. Acceptable.* ACCEPT.

Accĭdō, ere, ī. *To fall to, befall, happen;* accidit, *it happens, comes to pass;* 281, 301. ACCIDENT.

Accĭpiō, ere, cēpī, ceptum. *To accept, receive, take, admit.* ACCEPT.

Accommodātus, a, um, *part. and adj. Fitted, adapted.* ACCOMMODATE.

Accurrō, ere, currī *and* cucurrī, cursum. *To run to, hasten to.*

Accūsātiō, ōnis, *f. Accusation.*

Accūsātor, ōris, *m. Accuser.* ACCUSATION.

Accūsō, āre, āvī, ātum. *To accuse, censure, upbraid.* ACCUSE.

Ācer, ācris, ācre. *Sharp, severe.*

Aciēs, ēī, *f. Edge, line; line of battle;* aciem instruere, *to form the line of battle.*

Ācriter, *adv. Sharply, briskly, severely, vigorously, violently, harshly;* ācriter pūgnātur, *a severe battle is fought;* 281, 301.

Acūtus, a, um, *part.* and *adj. Sharpened, sharp.*

Ad, *prep. w. acc. To, toward, for; at, on, near, in the vicinity of; according to.*

Adamō, āre, āvī, ātum. *To be greatly pleased with, to like very much.*

Addūcō, ere, dūxī, ductum. *To lead to, lead, bring, induce.* ADDUCE.

Adeō, īre, iī, itum. *To go to, arrive at, reach, visit.*

Adequitō, āre, āvī, ātum. *To ride toward, ride.*

Adficiō, ere, fēcī, fectum. *To affect, visit.* AFFECT.

---

[1] The words thus added to the definition in SMALL CAPITALS are such as from their form readily suggest the corresponding Latin word.

Adfinitās, ātis, *f.* Connection, relationship. AFFINITY.

Adflictō, āre, āvī, ātum. To trouble; to strand. AFFLICT.

Adflīgō, ere, flixī, flictum. To crush, damage. AFFLICT.

Adhūc, *adv.* Hitherto, as yet, thus far.

Adigō, ere, ēgī, āctum. To drive, impel, hurl, throw.

Aditus, ūs, *m.* Approach.

Adjungō, ere, jūnxī, jūnctum. To join, add, unite. ADJOIN.

Administrō, āre, āvī, ātum. To administer, manage, execute, direct, perform. ADMINISTER.

Admittō, ere, misī, missum. To send to, send on, let go, admit; to commit; equō admissō, with his horse at full speed. ADMIT.

Adorior, īrī; ortus sum. To rise upon, attack.

Aduātucī, ōrum, *m. pl.* The Aduatuci, a tribe of northern Gaul.

Adulēscēns, entis, *m.* and *f.* Youth, young man, young woman. ADOLESCENCE.

Adventus, ūs, *m.* Approach, arrival. ADVENT.

Aedificium, ii, *n.* Building, house. EDIFICE.

Aedificō, āre, āvī, ātum. To build. EDIFICE.

Aeduī, ōrum, *m. pl.* The Aedui or Aeduans, a tribe of central Gaul.

Aeduus, a, um. Aeduan; Aeduus, ī, *m.*, an Aeduan, one of the Aedui.

Aegrē, *adv.* With difficulty, hardly, scarcely.

Aequitās, ātis, ness, kindn

Aes, aeris, *n.*

Aestās, ātis,

Aestus, ūs, *m*

Actās, ātis, *f*

Agedincum, town in cer

Ager, agrī, *m* fields, land

Aggredior, ī, attack, ass

Āgmen, inis march, lin mum āgme the line, th āgmen, the men, the r

Agō, ere, ēg drive; to treat, plea grātiās age thank. A

Agricola, ae, farmer.

Alcēs, is, *f.*

Alesia, ae, *f.* central Ga

Aliēnus, a, u favorable,

Aliquamdiū,

Aliquis, qua, any one.

Alius, a, ud. other. AL

Allobrogēs, Allobrox, broges, a t Gaul.

Alō, ere, aluī To nourish

Alpēs, ium,

Alter, tera, terum. 45, 151. *The other of two, second.*
Altitūdŏ, inis, *f. Height, depth.*
Amicitĭa, ae, *f. Friendship.*
Amīcus, a, um. *Friendly;* amīcus, ī, *m., friend.* AMICABLE.
Āmittō, ere, mīsī, missum. *To lose.*
Amō, āre, āvī, ātum. *To love.*
Amor, ōris, *m. Love.*
Amplus, a, um. *Ample, much.* AMPLE.
An, *conj. Or.*
Anceps, ancipĭtis. *Double, twofold; doubtful, undecided.*
Ancora, ae, *f. Anchor.*
Angustiae, ārum, *f. pl. Narrowness; narrow pass, defile.*
Angustus, a, um. *Narrow; limited, contracted; steep.*
Animadvertō, ere, ī, sum. *To turn the attention to, observe, notice.* ANIMADVERT.
Animal, ālis, *n. Animal.*
Animus, ī, *m. Mind, heart, soul.*
Annus, ī, *m. Year.* ANNUAL.
Annuus, a, um. *Annual, yearly, annually, for a year.* ANNUAL.
Ante, *adv.,* and *prep. w. acc. Before;* ante diem quīntum Kalendās Aprilēs, *the 28th of March.*
Anteā, *adv. Before, formerly, previously.*
Antequam, *conj. Before.*
Antīquus, a, um. *Ancient, old, former.* ANTIQUE.
Ānulus, ī, *m. Ring.*
Apertus, a, um, *part.* and *adj. Open, exposed.*
Appellō, āre, āvī, ātum. *To call.* APPEAL.

Appetō, ere, īvī or iī, ītum. *To seek after, seek.* APPETITE.
Appropinquō, āre, āvī, ātum. *To approach.*
Aprīlis, e. *Of April;* ante diem quīntum Kalendās Aprilēs, *the 28th of March.*
Apud, *prep. w. acc. In the presence of, near, among, in, with, in the vicinity of; in the works of.*
Aquila, ae, *f. Eagle,* the standard of the legion.
Aquilēia, ae, *f. Aquileia,* a town in northern Italy.
Aquilĭfer, eri, *m. Standard-bearer.*
Aquitāni, ōrum, *m. pl. The Aquitani* or *Aquitanians,* the inhabitants of the southwestern division of Gaul.
Arar, aris, *m.* 128. *The Arar,* a river in southeastern Gaul, now the *Saône.*
Arbitror, ārī, ātus sum. *To think.* ARBITRATE.
Arcessō, ere, sīvī *or* siī, sītum. *To summon, invite.*
Ardeō, ēre, ārsī, ārsum. *To burn; to be ardent, be eager.* ARDOR.
Ārĭdum, ī, *n. Dry land.* ARID.
Ariovistus, ī, *m. Ariovistus,* a king of the Germans.
Arma, ōrum, *n. pl. Arms.*
Armō, āre, āvī, ātum. *To arm.*
Arō, āre, āvī, ātum. *To plough.*
Arrogantĭa, ae, *f. Arrogance.*
Artē, *adv. Closely; soundly.*
Artemisĭa, ae, *f. Artemisia,* queen of Caria.
Artificĭum, iī, *n. Artifice.*
Arverni, ōrum, *m. pl. The Arverni,* a tribe of southern Gaul.

Arx, arcis, *f.* Citadel.
Ascendō, ere, ī, cēnsum. *To as-
[cend.*
At, *conj.* But, yet.
Athēnae, ārum, *f. pl.* Athens.
Athēniēnsis, is, *m. and f.* Athenian.
Atque, *conj.* And.
Atticus, ī, *m.* Atticus, a Roman name.
Attingō, ere, tigī, tactum. *To touch, reach.*
Auctor, ōris, *m.* Author, advocate.
Auctōritās, ātis, *f.* Authority, influence, reputation.
Audācia, ae, *f.* Audacity, boldness. AUDACITY.
Audācter, *adv.* Boldly. AUDACITY.
Audeō, ēre, ausus sum. *To dare, venture.*
Audiō, īre, īvī *or* iī, ītum. *To hear, hear of.* AUDIENCE.
Augeō, ēre, auxī, auctum. *To augment, increase.*
Aureus, a, um. Golden, gold.
Auriga, ae, *m.* Charioteer, driver.
Aurum, ī, *n.* Gold.
Aut, *conj.* Either, or; aut . . . aut, *either . . . or.*
Autem,[1] *conj.* But.
Auxilium, iī, *n.* Aid, help; auxilia, *pl.,* auxiliaries.
Avāritia, ae, *f.* Avarice.
Āvertō, ere, ī, sum. *To turn aside, turn away;* āversus, *turned away, in retreat, retreating.* AVERT.
Avis, is, *f.* Bird.
Avus, ī, *m.* Grandfather.

B.

Barbarus, a, um. Barbarous, rude; barbarus, ī, *m.,* a barbarian. BARBAROUS.
Beātus, a, um. Blessed, happy, prosperous.
Belgae, ārum, *m. pl.* The Belgae *or* Belgians, the inhabitants of the northern division of Gaul.
Bellicōsus, a, um. Warlike.
Bellō, āre, āvī, ātum. *To wage war, carry on war.*
Bellovaci, ōrum, *m. pl.* The Bellovaci, a tribe of northwestern Gaul.
Bellum, ī, *n.* War.
Beneficium, iī, *n.* Benefit, favor. BENEFICE.
Bibracte, is, *n.* Bibracte, the chief town of the Aedui.
Bibrax, actis, *n.* Bibrax, a town of the Remi.
Biennium, iī, *n.* Two years, space of two years. BIENNIAL.
Biturigēs, um, *m. pl.* The Bituriges, a tribe of central Gaul.
Boiī, ōrum, *m. pl.* The Boii, tribe of central Gaul.
Bonitās, ātis, *f.* Goodness, excellence.
Bonus, a, um. 86, 105. Good.
Brevis, e. Short, brief.
Breviter, *adv.* Briefly.
Britannī, ōrum, *m. pl.* Britons.
Britannia, ae, *f.* Britain.
Brūtus, ī, *m.* Brutus, a Roman name.

---

[1] Autem is postpositive, i. e. it is placed after one or more words in its clause.

C.

Cabillōnum, ī, n. *Cabillonum*, a town in eastern Gaul.

Cadō, ere, cecidī, cāsum. *To fall.*

Caedēs, is, f. *Slaughter.*

Caesar, aris, m. *Caesar*, the celebrated general, statesman, and author.

Calamitās, ātis, f. *Calamity, disaster.* CALAMITY.

Cantium, iī, n. *Kent.*

Cantus, ūs, m. *Singing, song.*

Capillus, ī, m. *Hair.* CAPILLARY.

Capiō, ere, cēpī, captum. *To take;* cōnsilium capere, *to take counsel, form a plan.*

Captīvus, ī, m. *Captive.*

Caput, itis, n. *Head.* CAPITAL.

Cāria, ae, f. *Caria*, a country in Asia Minor.

Carīna, ae, f. *Keel, bottom of a vessel.*

Carō, carnis, f. *Flesh.* CARNAL.

Carrus, ī, m. *Cart, wagon.*

Cārus, a, um. *Dear.*

Cassius, iī, m. *Cassius*, a Roman name.

Castellum, ī, n. *Redoubt.* CASTLE.

Casticus, ī, m. *Casticus*, a Sequanian chieftain.

Castra, ōrum, n. pl. *Camp.*

Cāsus, ūs, m. *Accident, occurrence, emergency, vicissitude, fortune.*

Catēna, ae, f. *Chain.*

Catō, ōnis, m. *Cato*, a Roman name.

Causa, ae, f. *Cause, reason.* CAUSE.

Cecidī. *See* cadō.

Celeritās, ātis, f. *Celerity, speed.* CELERITY.

Celeriter, adv. *Quickly, speedily.* CELERITY.

Celtae, ārum, m. pl. *Celts*, the inhabitants of the central division of Gaul.

Cēnsus, ūs, m. *Census, enumeration.*

Centum, indeclinable. *Hundred.*

Centuriō, ōnis, m. *Centurion.*

Certē, adv. *Certainly, at least.* CERTAIN.

Certus, a, um. *Certain, fixed, appointed;* certiōrem facere, *to make more certain; to inform.* CERTAIN.

Cevenna, ae, m. *Cevenna*, a mountain range in southern Gaul, now the *Cévennes.*

Cicerō, ōnis, m. *Cicero;* (1) the celebrated orator; (2) a lieutenant under Caesar.

Circiter, adv., and prep. w. acc. *About.*

Circum, prep. w. acc. *Around, about, near, in the vicinity of.*

Circumdō, are, dedī, datum. *To place around; to surround.*

Circummūniō, īre, īvī, ītum. *To wall around, to surround.*

Circumsistō, ere, stitī. *To stand around, surround.*

Cis, prep. w. acc. *On this side of.*

Citerior, us, comp. adj., sup. citimus. *Nearer;* Gallia citerior, *the Roman province of Gaul, south of the Alps, Cisalpine Gaul.*

Citrā, prep. w. acc. *On this side of.*

Civis, is, m. and f. *Citizen.*

Cīvitās, ātis, *f.* State; citizens; citizenship.
Clāmitō, āre, āvī, ātum. To exclaim, cry out.
Clāmor, ōris, *m.* Shout.
Clārus, a, um. Clear; illustrious, renowned. CLEAR.
Classis, is, *f.* Fleet.
Claudō, ere, sī, sum. To close, shut. CLOSE.
Clēmentia, ae, *f.* Clemency, mercy. CLEMENCY.
Cliēns, entis, *m. and f.* Client, dependant. CLIENT.
Coēmō, ere, ēmī, ēmptum. To buy up, buy, purchase, obtain by purchase.
Coepī, isse.[1] To begin.
Coërceō, ēre, uī, itum. To restrain, control. COERCE.
Cognōscō, ere, nōvī, itum. To ascertain.
Cōgō, ere, ēgī, āctum. To drive together, bring together, collect; to force, compel.
Cohors, ortis, *f.* Cohort, a tenth of a legion.
Cohortātiō, ōnis, *f.* Exhortation, encouragement.
Cohortor, ārī, ātus sum. To exhort, encourage.
Cōiciō,[2] ere, jēcī, jectum. To throw, hurl, cast.
Collis, is, *m.* Hill.
Collocō, āre, āvī, ātum. To place, station. COLLOCATE.
Colloquium, ii, *n.* Conversation, conference, interview. COLLOQUY.

Colōnia, ae, *f.* Colony.
Combūrō, ere, ussi, ustum. To burn up, burn. COMBUSTION.
Comes, itis, *m. and f.* Companion.
Commeātus, ūs, *m.* Supplies, provisions.
Commemorātiō, ōnis, *f.* Mentioning, mention, remembrance. COMMEMORATION.
Commemorō, āre, āvī, ātum. To mention; to speak. COMMEMORATE.
Commeō, āre, āvī, ātum. To go back and forth, resort.
Commīlitō, ōnis, *m. and f.* Fellow-soldier.
Committō, ere, misī, missum. To commit; proelium committere, to engage in battle.
Commius, ii, *m.* Commius, a chieftain of the Atrebates.
Commoveō, ēre, mōvī, mōtum. to move, disturb, alarm. COMMOTION.
Commūniō, īre, īvī or ii, ītum. To wall around, encompass, surround.
Commūnis, e. Common, general; commūnis rēs, common interest.
Comparō, āre, āvī, ātum. To prepare, raise.
Compellō, ere, pulī, pulsum. To drive. COMPEL.
Compleō, ēre, ēvī, ētum. To fill, cover. COMPLETE.
Complūrēs, plūra or plūria. Very many, many, several.

---

[1] Not used in the Present system.
[2] Pronounced as if spelled *cōjiciō*.

VOCABULARY.

Comportō, āre, āvī, ātum. *To bring together, gather.*
Cōnātus, ūs, *m. Undertaking, attempt, purpose.*
Concēdō, ere, cessi, cessum. *To concede, grant, permit.* CONCEDE.
Concīdō, ere, ī. *To fall.*
Concīdō, ere, ī, sum. *To cut down, destroy, kill, slay.*
Conciliō, āre, āvī, ātum. *To win, secure.* CONCILIATE.
Concilium, lī, *n. Council, meeting.* COUNCIL.
Conclāmō, āre, āvī, ātum. *To shout, call out.*
Concursus, ūs, *m. Running together, running about, running to and fro, agitation.* CONCOURSE.
Condōnō, āre, āvī, ātum. *To condone, pardon, forgive.* CONDONE.
Condūcō, ere, dūxī, ductum. *To lead together.* CONDUCT.
Cōnferō, ferre, contulī, collātum. *To carry together, bring together, gather, collect.* CONFER.
Cōnfertus, a, um. *Dense, crowded, compact.*
Cōnfestim, *adv. Hastily, speedily.*
Cōnficiō, ere. fēcī, fectum. *To make out, make, complete, accomplish, finish, bring to a close.*
Cōnfīdō, ere, fīsus sum.[1] *To trust, be confident; to have confidence in, rely upon.* CONFIDE. (Followed by the Ablative or by the Dative.)
Cōnfīrmō, āre, āvī, ātum. *To confirm, strengthen, establish, assure, fix; to comfort.* CONFIRM.
Cōnflīgō, ere, flīxī, flictum. *To contend, fight.* CONFLICT.
Conjungō, ere, jūnxī, jūnctum. *To join, unite.* CONJOIN.
Conjūnx, ugis, *m.* and *f. Spouse; husband; wife.*
Conjūrātiō, ōnis, *f. Conspiracy.*
Conjūrō, āre, āvī, ātum. *To conspire.*
Cōnor, ārī, ātus sum. *To attempt, try.*
Conquīrō, ere, sīvī *or* sīī, sītum. *To search for, seek.*
Cōnscius, a, um. *Conscious, aware.* CONSCIOUS.
Cōnscrībō, ere, scripsī, scriptum. *To enrol, enlist.* CONSCRIPT.
Cōnsequor, ī, secūtus sum. *To pursue, follow, overtake.*
Cōnservō, āre, āvī, ātum. *To save, preserve, spare.* CONSERVE.
Cōnsidius, iī, *m. Considius*, an officer in Caesar's army.
Cōnsīdō, ere, sēdī, sessum. *To sit down, settle, post one's self, encamp.*
Cōnsilium, iī, *n. Counsel, plan.* COUNSEL.
Cōnsimilis, e. *Similar, like.*
Cōnsistō, ere, stitī, stitum. *To get a footing, stand firm.* CONSIST.
Cōnspectus, ūs, *m. Sight, view.* CONSPICUOUS.

---

[1] See 259.

19

Cōnspiciō, ere, spēxī, spectum. To behold. CONSPICUOUS.
Cōnstanter, adv. Consistently, uniformly. CONSTANT.
Cōnstantia, ae, f. Constancy, steadfastness. CONSTANCY.
Cōnstituō, ere, uī, ūtum. To station, place; to determine, decide. CONSTITUTE.
Cōnstō, āre, stitī, stātum. To stand firm; to be established, be evident, be plain, be manifest, be admitted. CONSTANT.
Cōnsuēscō, ere, suēvī, suētum. To become accustomed; cōnsuēvī, I have become accustomed, I am accustomed.
Cōnsuētūdō, inis, f. Custom, usage.
Cōnsul, ulis, m. Consul, one of the two presidents of the Roman commonwealth.
Cōnsulō, ere, uī, sultum. To consult.
Cōnsultō, āre, āvī, ātum. To consult.
Cōnsultum, ī, n. Decree.
Contendō, ere, ī, tentum. To contend; to hasten. CONTEND.
Contentus, a, um. Content, contented, satisfied. CONTENT.
Continēns, entis, f. Continent, mainland. CONTINENT.
Continenter, adv. Continually, incessantly.
Contineō, ēre, uī, tentum. To retain, restrain, confine, keep, enclose, surround. CONTAIN.
Continuus, a, um. Continuous, successive. CONTINUOUS.
Contrā, adv., and prep. w. acc. Against, contrary to, over against, opposite, in opposition. CONTRARY.
Contrahō, ere, traxī, tractum. To contract.
Contrōversia, ae, f. Controversy, dispute. CONTROVERSY.
Conveniō, īre, vēnī, ventum. To come together, meet, come. CONVENE.
Conventus, ūs, m. Convention, meeting, assembly, council. CONVENTION.
Convertō, ere, ī, sum. To turn, change. CONVERT.
Convocō, āre, āvī, ātum. To call together, assemble. CONVOKE.
Cōpia, ae, f. Abundance, supply, number; pl., supplies; forces, troops. COPIOUS.
Cōpiōsus, a, um. Well-supplied, wealthy. COPIOUS.
Corōna, ae, f. Crown, garland. CROWN.
Cotīdiānus, a, um. Daily.
Cotīdiē, adv. Daily.
Cotta, ae, m. Cotta, a lieutenant under Caesar.
Crassus, ī, m. Crassus, a Roman name.
Crēber, bra, brum. Frequent.
Crēdō, ere, didī, ditum. To believe. CREED. (Followed by the Dative.)
Creō, āre, āvī, ātum. To create, make, appoint, elect. CREATE.
Crūdēlis, e. Cruel.
Crūdēliter, adv. Cruelly.
Culpa, ae, f. Fault, blame. CULPABLE.
Cultus, ūs, m. Cultivation, refinement, civilization.
Cum, prep. w. abl. With.

VOCABULARY. 279

Cum, *conj.* *When, while; since, as; although.*

Cunctor, āri, ātus sum. *To hesitate.*

Cupĭdē, *adv.* *Eagerly.*

Cupĭdus, a, um. *Desirous.*

Cupĭō, ere, īvī or iī, ītum. *To desire.*

Cūr, *conj.* *Why.*

Cūra, ae, *f.* *Care.*

Cūrō, āre, āvī, ātum. *To care, care for;* aliquid faciendum cūrō, *to have a thing done.*

Currus, ūs, *m.* *Chariot.*

Cūstōdīō, īre, īvī or iī, ītum. *To guard.* CUSTODY.

Cȳrus, ī, *m.* *Cyrus,* king of Persia.

D.

Dē, *prep. w. abl.* *Of, from; about, in regard to, concerning; in the course of; for.*

Dēbeō, ēre, uī, ītum. *To owe; ought.* DEBT.

Decem, *indeclinable.* *Ten;* decem novem, *nineteen.*

Dēcernō, ere, crēvī, crētum. *To decide, decree.*

Dēcertō, āre, āvī, ātum. *To contend, struggle, fight.*

Decĭmus, a, um. *Tenth.* DECIMAL. |*sion.*

Dēcrētum, ī, *n.* *Decree,* decision.

Dēdĭtĭō, ōnis, *f.* *Surrender.*

Dēdūcō, ere, dūxī, ductum. *To l ad forth, conduct.* DEDUCE.

Dēfendō, ere, ī, fēnsum. *To defend.*

Dēfēnsor, ōris, *m.* *Defender.*

Dēfessus, a, um. *Tired, exhausted, weary.*

Dēfĭcĭō, ere, fēcī, fectum. *To fail, to be insufficient.* DEFICIENT.

Deinde, *adv.* *Then, in the next place.*

Dēlectō, āre, āvī, ātum. *To delight, please.*

Dēleō, ēre, ēvī, ētum. *To destroy.*

Dēlībero, āre, āvī, ātum. *To deliberate.*

Dēlĭgō, ere, lēgī, lēctum. *To choose, elect, select.*

Dēlĭgō, āre, āvī, ātum. *To fasten, moor.*

Dēlĭtēscō, ere, lituī. *To hide.*

Dēmetō, ere, messuī, messum. *To cut down, reap.*

Dēmĭnuō, ere, uī, ūtum. *To diminish, lessen.*

Dēmōnstrō, āre, āvī, ātum. *To demonstrate, show.* DEMONSTRATE.

Dēmum, *adv.* *At length.*

Dēnĭque, *adv.* *Finally, at length.*

Dēpōnō, ere, posuī, positum. *To lay down, lay aside.* DEPOSE.

Dēpopulor, āri, ātus sum. *To ravage, lay waste.* DEPOPULATE.

Dēprecātor, ōris, *m.* *Pleader, spokesman, agent;* eō dēprecātōre, *by his intercession.* DEPRECATE.

Dēsignō, āre, āvī, ātum. *To designate, indicate.* DESIGNATE.

Dēsĭlĭō, īre, uī, sultum. *To leap out, leap forth, leap down.*

Dēsistō, ere, stĭtī, stĭtum. *To desist, cease.* DESIST.

Dēstringō, ere, strinxī, strictum. *To unsheathe, draw.*

Dēsum, esse, fuī. *To be wanting, to fail.* (Followed by the Dative.)

Dēterreō, ēre, uī, itum. *To deter.*

Dētĭneō, ēre, uī, tentum. *To detain.*

Dētrĭmentum, ī, n. *Detriment, loss, disadvantage.* DETRIMENT.

Dīcō, ere, dīxī, dictum. *To say, speak, mention, state; to appoint;* causam dicere, *to plead a cause, make a defence.*

Dĭēs, ēī, m. *Day; time;* multō dĭē, *long after sunrise;* ante diem quintum Kalendās Aprīlēs, *the 28th of March.*

Difficilis, e. *Difficult.*

Difficultās, ātis, f. *Difficulty.*

Diligenter, adv. *Diligently, attentively.* DILIGENT.

Diligentia, ae, f. *Diligence, carefulness.* DILIGENCE.

Dionȳsius, iī, m. *Dionysius,* tyrant of Syracuse.

Discēdō, ere, cessī, cessum. *To withdraw, depart, swerve.*

Discipulus, ī, m. *Pupil.* DISCIPLE.

Disiciō,[1] ere, jēcī, jectum. *To break asunder, separate.*

Dispergō, ere, sī, sum. *To scatter, disperse.* DISPERSE.

Dissentiō, ōnis, f. *Dissension, disagreement.* DISSENSION.

Distineō, ēre, tinuī, tentum. *To keep apart, separate.*

Dĭū, adv., comp. diūtius, sup. diūtissimē. *Long, for a long time;* quam diū, *as long as.*

Dives, itis, comp. divitior *or* ditior, sup. divitissimus *or* ditissimus. *Rich, wealthy.*

Divīcō, ōnis, m. *Divico,* an Helvetian chieftain.

Divīdō, ere, visī, visum. *To divide, separate.* DIVIDE.

Divīnus, a, um. *Divine, religious.* DIVINE.

Divitiacus, ī, m. *Divitiacus,* an Aeduan chieftain.

Dō, dare, dedī, datum. *To give;* in fugam dare, *to put to flight.*

Doceō, ēre, uī, doctum. *To teach, inform.*

Doctrīna, ae, f. *Learning.* DOCTRINE.

Doctus, a, um, part. *and* adj. *Learned.*

Dolor, ōris, m. *Pain, grief.*

Domus, ūs, f. *House; home;* domī, *at home.*

Dōnō, āre, āvī, ātum. *To present.*

Dōnum, ī, n. *Gift, present.*

Dormiō, īre, īvī *or* iī, itum. *To sleep.* DORMANT.

Druīdēs, um, m. pl. *Druids,* the priests of the Gauls.

Dubĭtō, āre, āvī, ātum. *To doubt, hesitate.*

Ducenti, ae, a. *Two hundred.*

Dūcō, ere, dūxī, ductum. *To lead.* DUCT.

Dum, conj. *While; until.*

Dumnorix, igis, m. *Dumnorix,* an Aeduan chieftain.

Duo, ae, o. 97, 175. *Two.*

Duodecim, *indeclinable*. *Twelve.*

Duodēquadrāgintā, *indeclinable*. *Thirty-eight.*

---

[1] Pronounced as if spelled *disjiciō*.

Duplex, Icis. *Double.*
Duplicō, āre, āvī, ātum. *To double.* DUPLICATE.
Dux, ducis, *m.* and *f.* *Leader.*

E.

Ē, *prep. w. abl.* See *Ex.*
Ēdūcō, ere, dūxī, ductum. *To lead out.* EDUCE.
Effēminō, āre, āvī, ātum. *To effeminate, enervate.* EFFEMINATE.
Efficiō, ere, fēcī, fectum. *To make, construct, effect, produce, occasion, bring about.* EFFECT.
Ego, meī, *pers. pron.* 102, 184. *I, myself.*
Ēgredior, ī, gressus sum. *To go out, go forth, depart, disembark.* EGRESS.
Ēgregiē, *adv.* *Excellently.* EGREGIOUS.
Ēgregius, a, um. *Distinguished.* EGREGIOUS.
Ēiciō,[1] ere, jēcī, jectum. *To cast out, drive out, expel.* EJECT.
Enim,[2] *conj.* *For.*
Ēnūntiō, āre, āvī, ātum. *To announce, report, disclose.*
Eō, īre, īvī *or* iī, itum. 277, 205. *To go.*
Epistula, ae, *f.* *Letter, epistle.* EPISTLE.
Eques, itis, *m.* *Horseman;* pl., *horsemen, cavalry.*
Equester, tris, tre. *Equestrian;* equestre proelium, *cavalry engagement.*

Equitātus, ūs, *m.* *Cavalry.*
Equus, ī, *m.* *Horse.*
Eram. See *Sum.*
Ērigō, ere, rēxī, rēctum. *To erect, raise;* sē ērigere, *to lift one's self, rise.* ERECT.
Ērudiō, īre, īvī *or* iī, itum. *To instruct.* ERUDITE.
Esseda, ae, *f.* *War-chariot, chariot.*
Essedārius, iī, *m.* *Chariot-fighter,* a warrior who fought in a war-chariot.
Et, *conj.* *And;* et . . . et, *both . . . and.*
Etiam, *adv.* *Also, even.*
Etsī, *conj.* *Although.*
Ēvocō, āre, āvī, ātum. *To summon forth, call out.* EVOKE.
Ex, ē, *prep. w. abl.* *Out of, from, of.*
Excēdō, ere, cessī, cessum. *To withdraw.*
Excitō, āre, āvī, ātum. *To excite, arouse.* EXCITE.
Excruciō, āre, āvī, ātum. *To torture.* EXCRUCIATING.
Excursiō, ōnis, *f.* *Sally, sortie.* EXCURSION.
Excūsō, āre, āvī, ātum. *To excuse.*
Exemplum, ī, *n.* *Example.*
Exeō, īre, iī, itum. *To go out, go forth, depart.* EXIT.
Exercitus, ūs, *m.* *Army.*
Exigō, ere, ēgī, āctum. *To complete, finish, end.* EXACT.
Exiguitās, ātis, *f.* *Smallness, small size.*

---

[1] Pronounced as if spelled *ējiciō.*
[2] *Enim is postpositive;* see page 274, foot-note.

Exiguus, a, um. *Restricted, limited, scanty, small, brief.*
Existimo, āre, āvī, ātum. *To think.*
Expeditus, a, um, *part. and adj. Unembarrassed, ready, quick.* EXPEDITE.
Expello, ere, pulī, pulsum. *To expel, drive out.* EXPEL.
Explōrātor, ōris, *m. Scout.* EXPLORER.
Explōro, āre, āvī, ātum. *To explore, investigate.* EXPLORE.
Expōno, ere, posuī, positum. *To expose, arrange.* EXPOSE.
Expūgno, āre, āvī, ātum. *To take by storm, storm.*
Exspecto, āre, āvī, ātum. *To expect, await.* EXPECT.
Exspoliō, āre, āvī, ātum. *To rob, deprive.*
Exsul, ulis, *m. and f. Exile.*
Exterus, a, um, *comp.* exterior, *sup.* extrēmus *and* extimus. *Outer;* extrēmus, *extreme; outermost extremity of.*
Extrā, *prep. w. acc. Beyond, outside of.*
Exūro, ere, ussī, ūstum. *To burn up, burn.*

F.

Fabius, iī, *m. Fabius,* a celebrated general.
Fābula, ae, *f. Fable, story.* FABLE.
Facile, *adv. Easily.* FACILE.
Facilis, e, *comp.* facilior, *sup.* facillimus. *Easy.* FACILE.
Facinus, oris, *n. Misdeed, crime.*
Faciō, ere, fēcī, factum. *To do, make;* iter facere, *to march;* vim facere, *to use force.* FACT.

Facultās, ātis, *f. Ability, opportunity, means; pl., means, wealth.* FACULTY.
Falsus, a, um. *False.*
Famēs, is, *f. Hunger.*
Familiāris, e. *Domestic, private :* rēs familiāris, *private property.*
Faveō, ēre, fāvī, fautum. *To favor.* (Followed by the Dative.)
Fēliciter, *adv. Happily, successfully.* FELICITOUS.
Fēlix, īcis. *Happy, fortunate.*
Ferāx, ācis. *Productive, fertile.*
Ferē, *adv. Almost, nearly.*
Ferō, ferre, tulī, lātum. **269,** 292. *To bear, carry, present, bring; to endure;* lēgem ferre, *to propose a law.*
Fertilis, e. *Fertile.*
Fertilitās, ātis, *f. Fertility.*
Ferus, a, um. *Fierce, savage.*
Fidēlis, e. *Faithful.* FIDELITY.
Fidēs, ēī, *f. Faith, confidence, trust; pledge.*
Fidus, a, um. *Faithful.*
Figūra, ae, *f. Figure, form, shape.* FIGURE.
Filia, ae, *f. Daughter.* FILIAL.
Filius, iī, *m.* **32,** 51, 5. *Son.* FILIAL.
Fingō, ere, finxī, fictum. *To form, fashion;* vultum fingere, *to control the countenance.*
Finiō, ire, īvī or iī, ītum. *To bound, limit, end.* FINAL.
Finis, is, *m. and f. End, limit;* finēs, *m. pl., boundaries; territory.*
Finitimus, a, um. *Neighboring.*
Fīō, fierī, factus sum. **277,** 294. *To be made; to happen, come to pass.*

Firmĭter, *adv.* *Firmly.*
Flaccus, i, *m.* *Flaccus,* a Roman name.
Flăgĭtō, āre, ävī, ātum. *To demand.*
Flūctus, ûs, *m. Wave.* FLUCTUATE.
Flūmen, Inis, *n. Stream, river.*
Fluō, ere, flūxī, flūxum. *To flow.*
Fore. See 140, 204, 2.
Forsĭtan, *adv. Perhaps.*
Fortis, e. *Brave.*
Fortĭter, *comp.* fortĭus, *sup.* fortissĭmē, *adv. Bravely, valiantly.*
Fortĭtūdō, ĭnis, *f. Fortitude, courage.* FORTITUDE.
Fortūna, ae, *f. Fortune.*
Fossa, ae, *f. Ditch, moat.* Foss.
Frangō, ere, frēgī, frāctum. *To break, crush, wreck.* FRACTURE.
Frāter, tris, *m. Brother.* FRATERNAL.
Fremĭtus, ûs, *m. Din, noise.*
Frētus, a, um. *Relying on, trusting to.*
Frūmentārius, a, um. *Pertaining to grain;* rēs frūmentāria, *grain, supplies.*
Frūmentātĭō, ōnis, *f. Foraying, provisioning.*
Frūmentor, ārī, ātus sum. *To gather grain, forage.*
Frūmentum, ī, *n. Grain.*
Fuga, ae, *f. Flight;* in fugam dare, *to put to flight.*
Fugĭtīvus, ī, *m. Runaway, deserter.* FUGITIVE.
Funda, ae, *f. Sling.*
Futūrus, a, um. See *Sum.*

G.

Gabīnĭus, iī, *m. Gabinius,* a Roman name.
Gāĭus, iī, *m. Gaius,* a Roman name.
Galba, ae, *m. Galba,* a lieutenant under Caesar.
Gallĭa, ae, *f. Gaul.*
Gallĭcus, a, um. *Gallic.*
Gallus, ī, *m. Gaul, a Gaul.*
Gemma, ae, *f. Gem.*
Genāva, ae, *f. Geneva.*
Gener, erī, *m. Son-in-law.*
Gēns, gentis, *f. Race, tribe, nation.*
Genus, eris, *n. Kind, class.*
Germānia, ae, *f. Germany.*
Germānus, a, um. *German;* Germānus, ī, *m.,* a German.
Gerō, ere, gessī, gestum. *To bear, conduct, carry on, wage, do; to hold.*
Gladĭus, iī, *m. Sword.*
Glōrĭa, ae, *f. Glory.*
Gnaeus, i, *m. Gnaeus,* a Roman name.
Graecia, ae, *f. Greece.*
Graecus, a, um. *Greek, Grecian.*
Grātia, ae, *f. Gratitude, favor;* *pl.,* thanks. GRACE.
Grātŭlor, ārī, ātus sum. *To congratulate; to thank.* (Followed by the Dative.)
Grātus, a, um. *Acceptable, pleasing.*
Gravis, e. *Heavy, severe, grave.* GRAVE.
Gravĭter, *adv. Severely, grievously.*
Gubernātor, ōris, *m. Pilot.* GUBERNATORIAL.

H.

Habeō, ēre, uī, itum. *To have, hold, regard, regard as.*

Habitō, āre, āvī, ātum. *To reside, live, dwell.*

Hannibal, alis, *m*. *Hannibal, a celebrated Carthaginian general.*

Harūdēs, um, *m. pl.* *The Harudes, a tribe of southwestern Germany.*

Helvētiī, ōrum, *m. pl.* *The Helvetii or Helvetians, a people inhabiting Switzerland.*

Helvētius, a, um. *Helvetian.*

Hērēditās, ātis, *f*. *Inheritance.*

Hērodotus, ī, *m*. *Herodotus, a Greek historian.*

Hiberna, ōrum, *n. pl.* *Winter quarters.*

Hīc, haec, hōc. 102, 186. *This, this one, the latter, he, she, it.*

Hiemō, āre, āvī, ātum. *To winter, pass the winter.*

Hiems, emis, *f*. *Winter.*

Historia, ae, *f*. *History.*

Homō, inis, *m. and f*. *Man, human being, person.*

Honor, ōris, *m*. *Honor.*

Hōra, ae, *f*. *Hour.*

Hortor, ārī, ātus sum. *To exhort, urge.*

Hospes, itis, *m. and f*. *Guest; host.*

Hostis, is, *m. and f*. *Enemy.*

Hūc, *adv*. *Hither; to this place.*

Hūmānitās, ātis, *f*. *Culture, refinement.* HUMANITY.

Hūmānus, a, um. *Humane; civilized.* HUMANE.

I.

Ibī, *adv*. *There.*

Idem, eadem, idem. 102, 186. *Same, the same.*

Idōneus, a, um. *Suitable, fit, proper.*

Īdūs, uum, *f. pl*. *Ides, the 15th of March, May, July and October; in other months the 13th.*

Ieram, ii. See *Eō*.

Igitur, *conj*. *Therefore.*

Ignis, is, *m*. *Fire.*

Ignōrō, āre, āvī, ātum. *Not to know, to be ignorant of.*

Ignōsco, ere, nōvī, nōtum. *To pardon, forgive.*

Ille, a, ud. 102, 186. *That, that one, the former, he, she, it.*

Illō, *adv*. *Thither, to that place.*

Impedimentum, ī, *n*. *Hinderance, embarrassment; pl., hinderances; baggage.*

Impediō, īre, īvī or iī, ītum. *To impede, hinder, embarrass.* IMPEDE.

Impedītus, a, um, *part. and adj*. *Impeded, hindered, embarrassed; entangled.* IMPEDED.

Impendeō, ēre. *To overhang.* IMPEND. (Followed by the Dative.)

Imperātor, ōris, *m*. *General, commander.*

Imperātum, ī, *n*. *Order, bidding, command;* imperātum facere, *to do one's bidding, execute one's order.*

Imperītus, a, um. *Unskilful, ignorant.*

Imperium, iī, *n*. *Command, sway, government, empire.*

Impĕrō, āre, āvī, ātum. *To order, command.*
Impĕtrō, āre, āvī, ātum. *To obtain one's request.*
Impĕtus, ūs, *m. Attack, charge.* IMPETUOUS.
Importō, āre, āvī, ātum. *To bring in, import.* IMPORT.
Improbus, a, um. *Wicked, unprincipled.*
Imprōvisus, a, um. *Unforeseen, unexpected;* dē imprōvisō, *unexpectedly, suddenly.*
In, *prep. w. acc. and abl.; see page 58, foot-note 1. In, into, to; for; over, across.*
Incendium, ii, *n. Fire, burning, conflagration.* INCENDIARY.
Incendō, ere, ī, cēnsum. *To set on fire, fire, burn.* INCENSE.
Incitō, āre, āvī, ātum. *To impel, urge on, urge forward.* INCITE.
Incōgnĭtus, a, um. *Unknown.*
Incŏlō, ere, uī, cultum. *To inhabit, dwell.*
Incŏlumis, e. *Unharmed, safe.*
Incommŏdum, ī, *n. Misfortune, disaster, defeat.*
Incrēdĭbĭlis, e. *Incredible.*
Inde, *adv. Thence, from that place.*
Indīcō, ere, dīxī, dictum. *To appoint.*
Indignus, a, um. *Unworthy.*
Indūcō, ere, dūxī, ductum. *To lead into, lead on, induce.* INDUCE.

Incō, īre, iī, itum. *To go into, enter upon, begin, initiate, undertake.*
Inermus, a, um. *Unarmed.*
Infēlix, īcis. *Unhappy, unfortunate.*
Inferō, ferre, intuli, illātum. *To bear into, wage into, wage against, wage upon, wage; to inflict upon, inflict.*
Infĭcĭō, ere, fēcī, fectum. *To stain, color, dye.*
Influō, ere, fluxī, fluxum. *To flow into, empty, flow.*
Ingrātus, a, um. *Ungrateful, unpleasant, disagreeable.*
Inimīcus, ī, *m. Enemy, personal enemy.*
Inīquus, a, um. *Unequal; unfair, unjust; unfavorable, disadvantageous.*
Initium, iī, *n. Beginning.* INITIATE.
Injūria, ae, *f. Injury, wrong.* INJURY.
Inopia, ae, *f. Lack, want, need, scarcity.*
Inquam,[1] *I say;* inquit, *present: he says; perfect: he said, said he.*
Insequor, i, secūtus sum. *To follow close upon, follow up, follow, pursue.*
Insignis, e. *Marked, signal, remarkable.*
Insĭmŭlō, āre, āvī, ātum. *To accuse.*
Insinuō, āre, āvī, ātum. *To introduce, insinuate;* sē insin-

---

[1] *Inquam* is a *defective* verb. It is used in a few parts only of the active voice.

uáre, *to make one's way, force one's self.* INSINUATE.

Insistō, ere, stiti. *To stand, get a foothold.* INSIST.

Instituō, ere, uī, ūtum. *To begin, proceed; to train, instruct.* INSTITUTE.

Instō, āre, stiti, stătum. *To be near, be at hand.* INSTANT.

Instruō, ere, strŭxī, strŭctum. *To construct, draw up, array;* aciem instruere, *to form the line of battle.*

Insuētus, a, um. *Unaccustomed.*

Insŭla, ae, *f. Island.*

Integrĭtās, ātis, *f. Integrity, uprightness.* INTEGRITY.

Intellegō, ere, lēxī, lēctum. *To understand.* INTELLECT.

Inter, *prep. w. acc. Among;* inter sē, *among themselves; with each other, with one another, together;* inter sē dare, *to exchange.*

Intercēdō, ere, cessī, cessum. *To come between, intervene.* INTERCEDE.

Interclūdō, ere, sī, sum. *To cut off.*

Interdīcō, ere, dīxī, dictum. *To forbid, prohibit, exclude.* INTERDICT.

Intereā, *adv. Meantime, in the meanwhile.*

Intereō, īre, ii, itum. *To perish.*

Interficiō, ere, fēcī, fectum. *To kill, slay, put to death.*

Interim, *adv. Meanwhile, in the mean time.*

Interior, us, *comp. adj.* 86, 166. *Interior, inner.*

Intermittō, er To *send b* mit, *interru brought betu* INTERMIT.

Interpōnō, ere, *interpose, su* TERPOSE.

Intersum, esse tween, *inter personal, it* INTEREST.

Intervallum, I, *between.*

Inūsitātus, a, u *familiar, str*

Inūtilis, e. *U*

Invitus, a, um.

Ipse, a, um. *she, it;* ille

Īrācundus, a, *violent.*

Irrumpō, ere, *break in, ru*

Irruptiō, ōnis, *an attack.*

Is, ea, id. *this, that she, it.*

Iste, a, ud. *yours, that she, it.*

Ita, *adv. So, thus.*

Italia, ae, *f.*

Itaque, *conj. fore.*

Item, *adv. A*

Iter, itineris, ney; *way,* era, *forced m to march.*

J.

Jăcĭō, ere, jēcī, jactum. *To throw.*
Jam, adv. *Already, now.*
Jŭbeō, ēre, jussī, jussum. *To order, command.*
Jūdex, ĭcis, m. and f. *Judge.*
Jūdĭcĭum, ĭī, n. *Judgment, decision.*
Jūdĭcō, āre, āvī, ātum. *To judge.*
Jŭgum, ī, n. *Yoke; ridge, height.*
Jūmentum, ī, n. *Draught animal, beast of burden.*
Jūra, ae, m. *Jura, a mountain range in western Gaul.*
Jussi. See *Jubeō.*
Jūstĭtĭa, ae, f. *Justice.*
Jŭvĕnis, is, m. and f. *Youth, a youth.* JUVENILE.
Jŭvō, āre, jūvī, jūtum. *To aid, help, assist.*

K.

Kălendae, ārum, f. pl. *Calends, the first day of the month; ante diem quintum Kalendās Aprilēs, the 28th of March.* CALENDAR.
Karthāgō, ĭnis, f. *Carthage.*

L.

Lăbĭēnus, ī, m. *Labienus, a lliutenant under Caesar.*
Lăbor, ōris, m. *Labor, toil, effort, exertion.*
Lăbōrō, āre, āvī, ātum. *To labor, struggle, to be in trouble.* LABOR.
Lăcessō, ere, sīvī or sĭī, sītum. *To harass, provoke, assail, attack.*
Lăcrĭma, ae, f. *Tear.*
Lăcrĭmō, āre, āvī, ātum. *To weep.*
Lăcus, ūs, m. *Lake.*
Lăpis, ĭdis, m. *Stone.*
Largĭor, īrī, ītus sum. *To bestow, make gifts.*
Largĭter, adv. *Largely, widely, extensively;* largiter posse, *to have extensive influence.*
Lātē, adv. *Widely; longē lātēque, far and wide.*
Lătīnus, ī, m. *Latinus, king of the Laurentians in central Italy.*
Lătīnus, a, um. *Latin.*
Lătĭtūdō, ĭnis, f. *Width, breadth.* LATITUDE.
Lătrō, ōnis, m. *Robber, brigand.*
Lātus, a, um. *Broad, wide, extensive.*
Lătus, ĕris, n. *Side.*
Laudō, āre, āvī, ātum. *To praise.* LAUD.
Lāvĭnĭa, ae, f. *Lavinia, daughter of King Latinus.*
Lēgātĭō, ōnis, f. *Embassy.*
Lēgātus, ī, m. *Ambassador; lieutenant.* LEGATE.
Legĭō, ōnis, f. *Legion.*
Lĕgō, ere, lēgī, lēctum. *To read.*
Lĕmannus, ī, m. *Lemannus, Leman, Lake of Geneva.*
Lēnĭtās, ātis, f. *Smoothness, gentleness.*
Lĕō, ōnis, m. *Lion.*
Lĕvĭtās, ātis, f. *Levity, fickleness, impulsiveness.* LEVITY.
Lex, lēgis, f. *Law.*
Lĭbenter, adv. *Willingly, gladly.*
Lĭber, brī, m. *Book.*
Līber, era, erum. *Free.*
Līberālĭtās, ātis, f. *Liberality.*

Liberi, ōrum, m. pl. *Children.*
Liberō, āre, āvī, ātum. *To liberate, free.* LIBERATE.
Libertās, ātis, f. *Liberty, freedom.* LIBERTY.
Liceor, ēri, itus sum. *To bid at auction.*
Licet, ēre, licuit, impers. *It is lawful, is permitted, one may.*
Ligārius, ii, m. *Ligarius,* a prominent Roman in whose behalf Cicero pleaded before Caesar.
Liger, is, m. *The Liger,* a river in southwestern Gaul, now the *Loire.*
Lingonēs, um, m. pl. *The Lingones,* a tribe of central Gaul.
Lingua, ae, f. *Tongue, language.*
Liscus, i, m. *Liscus,* a chieftain of the Aedui.
Litavicus, i, m. *Litavicus,* an Aeduan chieftain.
Littera, ae, f. *Letter;* pl., *letters; a letter, epistle.*
Lītus, oris, n. *Shore.*
Locus, i, m., pl. loca, ōrum, n. *Place, position.* LOCAL.
Longē, adv. *Long, far, by far.* LONG.
Longinquus, a, um. *Distant, remote.*
Longus, a, um. *Long.*
Lūcius, ii, m. *Lucius,* a Roman name.
Lūna, ae, f. *Moon.* LUNAR.
Lutetia, ae, f. *Lutetia,* a town in central Gaul, now *Paris.*
Lūx, lūcis, f. *Light, daylight;* prima lūx, *daybreak.*

M.

Magistrātus, ūs, m. *Magistracy, magistrate.*
Magnitūdō, inis, f. *Size, magnitude, height.* MAGNITUDE.
Magnus, a, um, comp. major, su, maximus. *Great, large; numerous; loud;* mājōrēs, m. ar f. pl., *elders; ancestors, for fathers.*
Maleficium, ii, n. *Mischie, harm.*
Mālō, mālle, māluī. 273, 293. *prefer.*
Mandō, āre, āvī, ātum. *To commission, order, entrust, co, sign, commit, betake.* MAI DATE.
Maneō, ēre, mānsī, mānsum. *remain.* MANSE.
Manus, ūs, f. *Hand; band;* manibus, *in hand; at han, close at hand.*
Mārcus, i, m. *Marcus,* a Roma name.
Mare, is, n. *Sea.*
Maritimus, a, um. *Maritim, pertaining to the sea; o, maritima, sea-coast.* MAR TIME.
Matara, ae, f. *Javelin, pike.*
Māter, tris, f. *Mother.*
Māteria, ae, f. *Timber.* M, TERIAL.
Matiscō, ōnis, m. *Matisco,* town in southwestern Gaul.
Mātrimōnium, ii, n. *Marriage;* in mātrimōnium dūcere, *marry.* MATRIMONY.
Mātūrē, adv. *Early, promptl,* MATURE.

Mātūrō, āre, āvī, ātum. *To hasten.* MATURE.
Mātūrus, a, um. *Early.* MATURE.
Mausōlus, ī, *m. Mausolus,* king of Caria.
Māxĭmē, *sup. adv. Most, very greatly, chiefly, especially.*
Māxĭmus, a, um. *See magnus.*
Mĕdĭus, a, um. *Middle, middle of;* 191, foot-note.
Melodūnum, ī, *n. Melodunum,* a town in central Gaul.
Memōria, ae, *f. Memory, recollection.* MEMORY.
Menapĭī, ōrum, *m. pl. The Menapii,* a tribe of northern Gaul.
Mēns, mentis, *f. Mind, intellect.* MENTAL.
Mensis, is, *m. Month.*
Mercātor, ōris, *m. Merchant, trader.*
Merĭdĭēs, ēī, *m. Midday, noon.* MERIDIAN.
Merĭtō, *adv. Deservedly.* MERIT.
Messālla, ae, *m. Messala,* a Roman name.
Mētĭor, īrī, mēnsus sum. *To measure, allot.*
Mĕtō, ere, messuī, messum. *To reap, harvest, gather grain.*
Meus, a, um. 185. *My, mine.*
Mīles, itis, *m.* and *f. Soldier.* MILITIA.
Militāris, e. *Military; rēs militāris, military affairs.*
Mille, *pl.* milia, ium, *n.* 247, footnote. *Thousand;* mille passūs, *a thousand paces, a* (Roman) *mile.*
Mĭnus, *comp. adv. Less; sup.* minimē, *least, very little, by no means.*

Mittō, ere, mīsi, missum. *To send.* MISSION.
Mōbĭlĭtās, ātis, *f. Mobility, rapidity.* MOBILITY.
Modestē, *adv. Modestly.* MODEST.
Modo, *adv. Only.*
Modus, ī, *m. Measure; manner.*
Molestē, *adv. With trouble;* molestē ferre, *to be vexed at, annoyed at.*
Moneō, ēre, uī, ĭtum. *To advise, warn.*
Mōns, montis, *m. Mountain.* MOUNT.
Morīnī, ōrum, *m. pl. The Morini,* a tribe of northern Gaul.
Moror, ārī, ātus sum. *To tarry, delay, wait.*
Mors, mortis, *f. Death.* MORTAL.
Mōtus, ūs, *m. Movement, motion,* MOTION.
Moveō, ēre, mōvī, mōtum. *To move, remove.* MOVE.
Mulier, eris, *f. Woman.*
Multĭtūdō, ĭnis, *f. Multitude; the multitude, common people, populace.* MULTITUDE.
Multō, *adv. By much, by far.*
Multum, *adv., comp.* plūs, *sup.* plūrimum. *Much.*
Multus, a, um, *comp.* plūs, *n.* (*pl.* plūrēs, plūra), *sup.* plūrimus. *Much; many;* multō diē, *long after day break.*
Mūnĭō, īrĕ, īvī or iī, ītum. *To fortify.* MUNITION.
Mūnītĭō, ōnis, *f. Fortification;* opus mūnītiōnis, *fortified work* MUNITION.
Mūrus, ī, *m. Wall.*

N.

Nactus, a, um. See *nanciscor*.
Nam, namque, *conj.* *For; for indeed.*
Nanciscor, i, nactus sum. *To get, obtain, secure.*
Narbō, ōnis, *m.* *Narbo,* a town in southern Gaul.
Nātĭō, ōnis, *f.* *Nation.*
Nātūra, ae, *f.* *Nature.*
Nauta, ae, *m.* *Sailor.*
Nāvālis, e. *Naval.*
Nāvigium, li, *n.* *Vessel, ship.*
Nāvigō, āre, āvī, ātum. *To sail.* NAVIGATE.
Nāvis, is, *f.* *Ship, vessel;* nāvis longa, *ship of war;* nāvis onerāria, *transport vessel, transport.* NAVY.
-Ne, *conj.* Interrogative particle. See 106, 351, 1 and 2.
Nē, *adv. and conj.* With the Imperative or the Subjunctive of Desire, *not;* with the Subjunctive of Purpose, *that not, lest;* after words of *fearing, lest, that.*
Necesse, 286. *Necessary.*
Neglegō, ere, lēxī, lēctum. *To neglect, disregard.*
Negō, āre, āvī, ātum. *To deny, refuse; to say not.*
Negōtium, li, *n.* *Business, occupation;* negōtium dare, *to entrust a task or enterprise.*
Nēmō,[1] ĭnis, *m. and f.* *No one, nobody.*
Nepōs, ōtis, *m.* *Grandson.*

Nēquāquam, *adv.* *By no means.*
Neque, *conj.* *Neither, nor, and not;* neque . . . neque, *neither . . . nor.*
Nervii, ōrum, *m. pl.* *The Nervii,* a tribe of northern Gaul.
Nēve, *conj.* *Nor, and not.*
Nex, necis, *f.* *Death, putting to death.*
Nihil, *indeclinable,* nihilum, i, *n.* *Nothing.*
Nisi, *conj.* *Unless.*
Nōbilis, e. *Noble, of high birth.* NOBLE.
Nōbilitās, ātis, *f.* *Nobility; the nobility, nobles.* NOBILITY.
Noctū, *adv.* *By night.*
Nocturnus, a, um. *Nocturnal, by night.* NOCTURNAL.
Nōlō, nolle, nōlui, 273, 293. *To be unwilling, not to be willing, not to wish.*
Nōmen, ĭnis, *n.* *Name;* suo nomine, *on his own account.* NOMINAL.
Nōminō, āre, āvī, ātum. *To name.* NOMINATE.
Nōn, *adv.* *Not.*
Nōndum, *adv.* *Not yet.*
Nōnne, *conj.* Interrogative particle. *Not?* See 106, 351, note 2.
Nōnnūllī, ae, a. *Some.*
Nōnnūnquam, *adv.* *Sometimes.*
Nōnus, a, um. *Ninth.*
Nōscō, ere, nōvī, nōtum. *To become acquainted with;* nōvī, *I have become acquainted with* = *I know.*

---

[1] *Nēmō* generally wants the Genitive and Ablative; they are supplied by these cases of *nullus.*

Noster, tra, trum. **102, 185.** *Our, ours.*
Nōtus, a, um, *part. and adj.* *Known.*
Novem, *indeclinable.* *Nine;* decem novem, *nineteen.*
Noviodûnum, i, *n.* *Noviodunum,* a town of northwestern Gaul.
Novus, a, um. *New;* rēs novae, *change of affairs, revolution;* novissimum āgmen, *rear.*
Nox, noctis, *f.* *Night.*
Nūbēs, is, *f.* *Cloud.*
Nūbō, ere, nūpsi, nūptum. *To veil one's self; to assume the bridal veil for — to marry.* NUPTIAL. (Followed by the Dative.)
Nūdō, āre, āvī, ātum. *To bare, expose, strip.*
Nūllus, a, um. **45, 131.** *Not any, no, none.*
Num, *conj.* Interrogative particle. For meaning in direct questions, see **106, 351,** 1, note 3; in indirect questions, *whether.*
Numa, ae, *m.* *Numa,* the second of the legendary kings of Rome.
Numerus, i, *m.* *Number.*
Nunc, *adv.* *Now, at this time.*
Nūnquam, *adv.* *Never.*
Nūntiō, āre, āvī, ātum. *To announce.*
Nūntius, ii, *m.* *Messenger; tidings.*
Nūper, *adv.* *Recently, of late.*
Nūtrix, icis, *f.* *Nurse.*

O.

Ob, *prep. w. acc.* *On account of, for.*
Obiciō,[1] ere, jēci, jectum. *To throw against, throw up.* OBJECT.
Observō, āre, āvi, ātum. *To observe, keep, comply with.* OBSERVE.
Obses, idis, *m. and f.* *Hostage.*
Obsideō, ēre, sēdi, sessum. *To besiege.*
Obsidiō, ōnis, *f.* *Siege, blockade.*
Obsignō, āre, āvi, ātum. *To seal, sign and seal.*
Obtineō, ēre, ui, tentum. *To obtain, hold.* OBTAIN.
Occāsus, ūs, *m.* *Setting;* sōlis occāsus, *sun-set.*
Occīdō, ere, i, sum. *To kill, slay.*
Occultō, āre, āvi, ātum. *To hide.* OCCULT.
Occupō, āre, āvi, ātum. *To occupy, seize, take possession of; to busy.* OCCUPY.
Ōceanus, i, *m.* *Ocean, the Atlantic Ocean.*
Octāvus, a, um. *Eighth.* OCTAVE.
Octo, *indeclinable.* *Eight.*
Octōdecim, *indeclinable.* *Eighteen.*
Octōdūrus, i, *m.* *Octodurus,* a town in Gaul, now *Martigny.*
Oculus, i, *m.* *The eye, sight.*
Ōdi, isse. *To hate, detest.*
Officium, ii, *n.* *Duty, allegiance.* OFFICE.
Omnīnō, *adv.* *In all, only.*
Omnis, e. *All.*

---

[1] Pronounced as if spelled *objicio.*

Onerārius, a, um. *Pertaining to burdens, carrying cargoes;* onerāria nāvis, *a transport vessel, transport.*
Opera, ae, *f. Work;* operam dare, *to take pains, endeavor.*
Oportet, ēre, uit, *impers. It behooves, is proper. is necessary, is fitting; one ought.*
Oppidum, i, n. *Town.*
Opportūnus, a, um. *Opportune, appropriate.* OPPORTUNE.
Oppūgnātiō, ōnis, *f. Assault, attack.*
Oppūgnō, āre, āvi, ātum. *To assault, attack.*
Optimus, a, um. See *bonus.*
Opus, eris, n. *Work, task; art;* operis mūnītiō, *fortified work;* māgnō opere, *greatly.*
Ōra, ae, *f. Coast.*
Ōrātiō, ōnis, *f. Oration, speech.* ORATION.
Ōrātor, ōris, m. *Orator.*
Orbis, is, m. *Circle, circuit;* orbis terrae, orbis terrārum, *the world.* ORB.
Ōrdō, inis, m. *Rank.* ORDER.
Orgetorix, igis, m. *Orgetorix,* an Helvetian chieftain.
Ōrnāmentum, i, n. *Ornament, honor.* ORNAMENT.
Ōrō, āre, āvi, ātum. *To ask, beg, plead.*
Ostendō, ere, i, tentum *or* tēnsum. *To show, explain, make known, declare.*

P.

Pābulātiō, ōnis, *f. Foraging.*
Pābulum, i, n. *Fodder.*
Paene, adv. *Almost, nearly.*

Paenitet, ēre *causes regr repent.*
Pāgus, i, m.
Pār, paris. *i*
Parātus, a, u *Prepared,*
Parcō, ere, pe *spare.* (Fo tive.)
Pāreō, ēre, u (Followed b
Parō, āre, āvi
Pars, partis, *quarter, di*
Passus, ūs, m sūs, a (Rom passuum, *tu*
Pāstor, ōris, n
Pater, tris, m.
NAL.
Patienter, adi
Patior, i, pass *permit.*
Patria, ae, *f one's counti*
Pauci, ae, a.
Paucitās, ātis, *number.*
Paulātim, adi *by degrees,*
Paulō, adv.
Paulum, adv.
Pāx, pācis, *f.*
Pedes, itis, m. *foot-soldier*
Peditātus, ūs,
Pedius, ii, m. ant under C
Pellis, is, *f.*
Pellō, ere, p *drive, rout.*

Pendō, ere, pependi, pēnsum. *To weigh; to pay.*

Per, *prep. w. acc. Through, by, over, by means of; on account of.*

Perdūcō, ere, dūxi, ductum. *To lead through, extend, construct.*

Perequitō, āre, āvī, ātum. *To ride through, ride.*

Perfacīlis, e. *Very easy.*

Perferō, ferre, tuli, lātum. *To endure.*

Perficiō, ere, fēci, fectum. *To accomplish.* PERFECT.

Perfringō, ere, frēgi, frāctum. *To break through.*

Perfuga, ae, *m. Deserter, fugitive.*

Perfugiō, ere, fūgi. *To flee for refuge, flee, escape.*

Periculōsus, a, um. *Perilous, dangerous.* PERILOUS.

Periculum, i, *n. Peril, danger.* PERIL.

Peritus, a, um. *Skilful, skilled, expert;* with gen. *skilled in.*

Permaneō, ēre, mānsi, mānsum. *To continue to remain, to remain.* PERMANENT.

Permoveō, ēre, mōvi, mōtum. *To move, induce, influence; to disturb, daunt, alarm.*

Perpetuus, a, um. *Perpetual, endless, uninterrupted;* in perpetuum, *for ever.* PERPETUAL.

Perrumpō, ere, rūpi, ruptum. *To break through, force a passage, force one's way.*

Persequor, ī, secūtus sum. *To follow up, pursue, persecute; to avenge.* PERSECUTE.

Perseverō, āre, āvi, ātum. *To persevere, persist.* PERSEVERE.

Persolvō, ere, i, solūtum. *To pay.*

Perspiciō, ere, spēxi, spectum. *To examine, investigate, perceive.* PERSPICUOUS.

Persuādeō, ēre, si, sum. *To persuade.*

Perterreō, ēre, ui, itum. *To terrify greatly, terrify, frighten.*

Pertineō, ēre, ui, tentum. *To pertain, tend; to extend, reach.* PERTAIN.

Perturbātiō, ōnis, *f. Disturbance, agitation.* PERTURBATION.

Perturbō, āre, āvi, ātum. *To disturb, throw into confusion.* PERTURB.

Perveniō, ire, vēni, ventum. *To arrive, come, reach.*

Pēs, pedis, *m. Foot;* pedibus, on foot; pedem referre, *to retreat.* PEDAL.

Petō, ere, ivi or ii, ītum. *To seek, request, ask.*

Phalanx, angis, *f. Phalanx, line.*

Pilum, i, *n. Javelin, spear.*

Pisistratus, i, *m. Pisistratus,* tyrant of Athens.

Pīsō, ōnis, *m. Piso,* a Roman name.

Placeō, ere, ui, itum. *To please.* (Followed by the Dative.)

Plānitiēs, ēi, *f. Plain.*

Plānus, a, um. *Flat, level.* PLANE.

Platō, ōnis, *m. Plato,* a celebrated Greek philosopher.

Plēbs, ēbis, *f. The common people, populace.* PLEBEIAN.

Plēnus, a, um. *Full.*

Plērumque, *adv.* *As a general thing, generally.*

Plērusque, aque, umque. *The larger or greater part, the most.*

Plūs, plūris, *n.*, *pl.* plūrēs, plūra, *comp. of* multus. *More; several.* PLURAL.

Plūs, *adv.*, *comp. of* multum, *sup.* plūrimum. *More;* plūs posse, *to have greater power or influence;* plūrimum posse, *to have very great power or influence.*

Poena, ae, *f.* *Penalty, punishment, satisfaction.*

Poēta, ae, *m.* *Poet.* [*ive.*

Polliceor, ēri, Itus sum. *To prom-*

Pompēius, ii, *m.* *Pompey,* a celebrated general and statesman.

Pōnō, ere, posuī, positum. *To place;* castra pōnere, *to pitch a camp, encamp.*

Pōns, pontis, *m.* *Bridge.*

Populātiō, ōnis, *f.* *Ravaging, devastating, laying waste.*

Populus, i, *m.* *People, a people.*

Porta, ae, *f.* *Gate.* PORTAL.

Portō, āre, āvī, ātum. *To carry, bring, take.*

Portōrium, ii, *n.* *Tax, toll, duty* on imports or exports.

Portus, ūs, *m.* *Port, harbor.* PORT.

Poscō, ere, poposcī. *To demand.*

Possum, posse, potuī. 269, 290. *To be able; can;* multum posse, *to have great power or influence.*

Post, *adv.* *After, afterward.*

Post, *prep. w. acc.* *After, behind.*

Posteā, *adv.* *Afterward.*

Posteāquam, *conj.* *After.*

Posterus, a, um, *comp.* posterior *sup.* postrēmus *und* postumus *Subsequent, following, next.*

Postquam, *conj.* *After.*

Postridiē, *adv.* *On the following day.*

Postulō, āre, āvī, ātum. *To demand.*

Potēns, entis. *Powerful.* POTENT.

Potentātus, ūs, *m.* *Power, dominion, control.*

Potentia, ae, *f.* *Power, influence.* POTENCY.

Poteram. See *possum.*

Potestās, ātis, *f.* *Power.*

Potior, īrī, ītus sum. *To gain — take — obtain possession of, to obtain.*

Potuī. See *possum.*

Praecēdō, ere, cessī, cessum. *To surpass.* PRECEDE.

Praeceps, ipitis. *Precipitate, headlong.* PRECIPITATE.

Praecipiō, ere, cēpī, ceptum. *To enjoin upon, direct.* PRECEPT.

Praecipitō, āre, āvī, ātum. *To precipitate, throw, hurl.* PRECIPITATE.

Praedīcō, āre, āvī, ātum. *To assert, state.* PREDICATE.

Praeficiō, ere, fēcī, fectum. *To place in command of, in charge of, over.* (Followed by the Dative.)

Praemittō, ere, mīsī, missum. *To send on — ahead — forward — in advance.*

Praemium, ii, *n.* *Reward.* PREMIUM.

Praepōnō, ere, posuī, positum. *To place over* or *in command of.* (Followed by the Dative.)

Praesĕns, entis. *Present.*
Praesentia, ae, *f. Presence; in* praesentiā, *at present, for the present.*
Praesidium, ii, n. *Garrison, defence, guard, safeguard, protection.*
Praestō, āre, stĭtī, stĭtum or stătum. *To stand before, excel; to furnish, discharge, fulfil, present, manifest, show, put forth.*
Praesum, esse, fui. *To be in charge or command of, to superintend.* (Followed by the Dative.)
Praeter, *prep. w. acc. Except.*
Praeterquam, *adv. Except.*
Praetor, ōris, *m. Praetor,* a Roman magistrate.
Premō, ere, pressi, pressum. *To press, press hard, distress.* PRESS.
Pretiōsus, a, um. *Precious, valuable.* PRECIOUS.
Pretium, ii, *n. Price.*
Primō, *adv. First, at first.* PRIME.
Primum, *sup. adv., pos. wanting, comp. prius. First.* PRIME.
Primus, a, um, *sup., pos. wanting, comp. prior. First; the first part of;* primum āgmen, *the van;* prima lūx, *daybreak.* PRIME.
Princeps, ipis. *First;* princeps, ipis, *m., leader, chief, chieftain.* PRINCIPAL.
Principātus, ūs, *m. Sovereignty, dominion.*
Prior, us, *comp. adj., pos. wanting, sup.* primus. *Former.*

Pristĭnus, a, um. *Ancient, pristine.* PRISTINE.
Prius, *comp. adv., pos. wanting, sup.* primum. *Before, sooner;* prius quam, *sooner than, before.*
Priusquam, *conj. Before.*
Privātim, *adv. Privately, in a private capacity.* PRIVATE.
Privātus, a, um, *part and adj. Private;* privātus, i, *m., private citizen.* PRIVATE.
Privō, āre, āvi, ātum. *To deprive.*
Prō, *prep. w. abl. For; in proportion to, considering; before.*
Probō, āre, āvi, ātum. *To prove; to approve.* PROBATE.
Procēdō, ere, cessi, cessum. *To proceed, advance.* PROCEED.
Procillus, i, *m. Procillus,* a prominent Gaul.
Proditiō, ōnis, *f. Treason.*
Proditor, ōris, *m. Traitor.*
Prodō, ere, didi, ditum. *To betray.*
Prodūcō, ere, dūxi, ductum. *To lead forth, lead on; to protract.* PRODUCE.
Proelior, āri, ātus sum. *To fight.*
Proelium, ii, *n. Battle, engagement.*
Profectiō, ōnis, *f. Departure, starting, setting out.*
Proficiō, ere, fēci, fectum. *To accomplish, effect.*
Proficiscor, i, profectus sum. *To start, set out, depart, proceed.*
Profugiō, ere, fūgi. *To flee away, flee, escape.*
Progredior, i, gressus sum. *To go forward, advance.* PROGRESS.

Prohĭbeō, ēre, uī, ĭtum. *To prohibit, check, prevent, keep.* PROHIBIT.

Prŏĭcĭō,[1] ere, jēcī, jectum. *To cast forth, throw forward, throw down.* PROJECT.

Prōmissus, a, um, *part. and adj. Hanging down, long.*

Prōnūntĭō, āre, āvī, ātum. *To proclaim, state.* PRONOUNCE.

Prope, *adv., comp.* propius, *sup.* proxĭmē. *Near.*

Prope, *prep. w. acc. Near.*

Prŏpellō, ere, ulī, ulsum. *To drive forward, repulse, rout.* PROPEL.

Propĭor, us, *comp. adj., pos. wanting, sup.* proxĭmus. *Nearer.*

Prŏpōnō, ere, posuī, posĭtum. *To set forth.* PROPOSE.

Propter, *prep. w. acc. On account of.*

Proptereā, *adv. For this reason;* proptereā quod, *for this reason, that; because.*

Prōpulsō, āre, āvī, ātum. *To repulse.*

Prōra, ae, *f. Prow.*

Prōsequor, ī, secūtus sum. *To follow up, pursue.* PROSECUTE.

Prōspĭcĭō, ere, spexī, spectum. *To look forward; to look out for.* (Followed by the Dative.) PROSPECT.

Prōvĭdeō, ēre, vīdī, vīsum. *To look out for, provide.* (Followed by the Dative.) PROVIDE.

Prōvincia, ae, *f. Province.*

Proxĭmē, *sup. adv., pos.* prope. *Most recently, last.*

Proxĭmus, a, um, *sup. adj., pos. wanting, comp.* propĭor. *Nearest, next, adjacent.*

Pūblĭcus, a, um. *Public.*

Pūblĭus, ĭī, *m. Publius,* a Roman name.

Pudor, ōris, *m. Shame, respect.*

Puella, ae, *f. Girl.*

Puer, erī, *m. Boy.* PUERILE.

Pugna, ae, *f. Fight, fighting, battle.*

Pugnō, āre, āvī, ātum. *To fight.*

Pulcher, chra, chrum. *Beautiful.*

Pulsus, a, um. See *pellō.*

Pulvis, eris, *m. Dust.*

Putō, āre, āvī, ātum. *To think.*

Q.

Quaerō, ere, sīvī *or* sĭī, sītum. *To inquire, ask, seek.* QUEST.

Quam, *adv. How; w. sup., as* ... *as possible;* quam prīmum, *as soon as possible.*

Quam, *conj. Than.*

Quantus, a, um. *How great; as great.*

Quārē, *conj. Wherefore, why.*

Quārtus, a, um. *Fourth;* quartus decimus, *fourteenth.*

Quattuor, *indeclinable. Four.*

-Que, *conj. enclitic.* 103. *And.*

Queror, ī, questus sum. *To complain.*

Quī, quae, quod. 106, 187. *Who, that, which.*

Quīdam, quaedam, quiddam *or* quoddam. 106, 190. *A certain, a certain one, some.*

Quīn, *conj. That not, but, that.*

---

[1] Pronounced as if spelled *prōjĭcĭō.*

Quindecim, *indeclinable. Fifteen.*
Quingenti, ae, a. *Five hundred.*
Quini, ae, a. 97, 172, 3. *Five by five, five each, five.*
Quinque, *indeclinable. Five.*
Quintus, a, um. *Fifth;* ante diem quintum Kalendas Apriles, *the 28th day of March.*
Quintus, i, *m. Quintus,* a Roman name.
Quis, quae, quid, *interrog. pron.* 106, 188. *Who, what, which?*
Quis, quae, quid, *indef. pron.* 106, 190. *One, any one, anything.*
Quisquam, quaequam, quicquam, *indef. pron. Any, anyone.*
Quisque, quaeque, quodque *and* quidque, *indef. pron. Each, every, each one, every one.*
Quō, *adv. Whither, to which place, to what place.*
Quō, *conj. That;* quō minus, *that not, so that not.*
Quoad, *conj. Until.*
Quod, *conj. That; because.*
Quoque, *adv. Also.*
Quot, *indeclinable. How many.*

R.

Rapina, ae, *f. Robbery, pillaging.* RAPINE.
Ratio, ōnis, *f. Reasoning, reason; account, reckoning; method, way.*
Rebelliō, ōnis, *f. Rebellion.*
Receptus, ūs, *m. Retreat.*
Recipiō, ere, cēpī, ceptum. *To recover, retake, betake; to receive; sē recipere, to retire, return, betake one's self.*
Recūsō, āre, āvī, ātum. *To reject.*
Reddō, ere, didī, ditum. *To give back, restore, return.*
Redeō, ire, īi, itum. *To go back, return.*
Redimō, ere, ēmī, ēmptum. *To buy up, buy, purchase.* REDEEM.
Reditiō, ōnis, *f. Going back, return.*
Reditus, ūs, *m. Return.*
Redūcō, ere, dūxī, ductum. *To lead back.*
Referō, ferre, rettulī, relātum. *To draw back, bring back;* pedem referre, *to retreat.*
Reficiō, ere, fēcī, fectum. *To repair.*
Refugiō, ere, fūgī. *To flee back, flee.* REFUGE.
Regina, ae, *f. Queen.*
Regiō, ōnis, *f. Direction; region.* REGION.
Regnō, āre, āvī, ātum. *To reign, rule.* REIGN.
Regnum, i, *n. Kingdom, regal power.* REIGN.
Regō, ere, rēxī, rēctum. *To rule.*
Rēiciō,[1] ere, jēcī, jectum. *To drive back, repulse.* REJECT.
Relinquō, ere, liquī, lictum. *To leave.* RELINQUISH.
Reliquus, a, um. *Remaining, the rest of, the other, left.*
Remaneō, ēre, mānsī, mānsum. *To remain.*
Remi, ōrum, *m. pl. The Remi,* a tribe of northern Gaul.

---

[1] Pronounced as if spelled *rējiciō.*

Reminiscor, i. *To remember.* RE-
MINISCENCE.
Removeō, ēre, mōvi, mōtum. *To
remove.*
Rēmus, i, m. *Oar.*
Renovō, āre, āvi, ātum. *To renew.*
RENOVATE.
Renūntiō, āre, āvi, ātum. *To report.* RENOUNCE.
Repellō, ere, reppuli, repulsum.
To drive back, repel, repulse.
REPEL.
Reperiō, ire, repperi, repertum.
To find, discover.
Repetō, ere, ivi, or ii, itum. *To
seek, exact.* REPEAT.
Reportō, āre, āvi, ātum. *To carry
back.* REPORT.
Rēs, rĕi, f. *Thing, affair; reason; res militāris, military
affairs.*
Resciscō, ere, scivi *or* scii, scitum.
To learn, ascertain.
Respiciō, ere, spēxi, spectum.
To regard, look upon. RESPECT.
Respondeō, ēre, i. spōnsum. *To
answer.* RESPOND.
Restituō, ere, ui, ūtum. *To restore.* RESTITUTION.
Retineō, ēre, ui, tentum. *To retain, keep.* RETAIN.
Rettuli. See *referō.*
Revertor, i, reverti, reversum.[1]
To return. REVERT.
Rēx, rēgis, m. *King.* REGAL.
Rhēnus, i, m. *The Rhine.*
Rhodanus, i, m. *The Rhone.*
Ripa, ae, f. *Bank.* RIPARIAN.

Rōbur, oris, n. *Oak.*
Rogō, āre, āvi, ātum. *To ask.*
Rōma, ae, f. *Rome.*
Rōmānus, a, um. *Roman;* Rōmānus, i, m., *a Roman.*
Rōmulus, i, m. *Romulus,* the
legendary founder of Rome.
Rota, ae, f. *Wheel.* ROTATE.
Rūmor, ōris, m. *Rumor, report.*
Rūrsus, *adv. Again.*

S.

Sabīnus, i, m. *Sabinus,* a lieutenant under Caesar.
Sacrificium, ii, n. *Sacrifice.*
Saepe, *adv. Often.*
Sagitta, ae, f. *Arrow.*
Salūs, ūtis, f. *Safety, salvation,
escape.*
Santonēs, um, m. pl. *The Santones* or *Santoni,* a tribe of
central Gaul.
Sānus, a, um. *Sound, sane.*
SANE.
Sapiēns, entis. *Wise.*
Sapienter, *adv. Wisely.*
Sapientia, ae, f. *Wisdom.*
Satis, *adv. Enough;* satis habēre *or* dūcere, *to regard it as
sufficient.*
Scapha, ae, f. *Skiff, boat.*
Schola, ae, f. *School.*
Scientia, ae, f. *Knowledge, skill.*
SCIENCE.
Sciō, ire, ivi *or* ii, itum. *To
know.*
Scrībō, ere, scripsi, scriptum. *To
write.* SCRIBE.

---

[1] *Revertor* is deponent in the present system. The other forms are in
the active voice.

Secundus, a, um. *Second.*
Sed, *conj.* *But.*
Sēdēs, is, *f.* *Seat, abode;* locus ac sēdēs, *place of abode.* SEAT.
Sēditiōsus, a, um. *Seditious.*
Segusiāni, ōrum, *m. pl.* *The Segusiani,* a tribe of southeastern Gaul.
Sēmentis, is, *f.* *Sowing, planting.*
Semper, *adv.* *Always, ever.*
Senātus, ūs, *m.* *Senate.*
Sēni, ae, a. 97, 172, 3. *Six by six, six each, six.*
Senonēs, um, *m. pl.* *The Senones,* a tribe of central Gaul.
Sententia, ae, *f.* *Thought, opinion, plan.* SENTENCE.
Sentiō, ire, sēnsi, sēnsum. *To think.* SENSE.
Septem, *indeclinable.* *Seven.*
Septimus, a, um. *Seventh.*
Sepultūra, ae, *f.* *Burial.* SEPULTURE.
Sēquani, ōrum, *m. pl.* *The Sequani* or *Sequanians,* a tribe of eastern Gaul.
Sēquanus, a, um. *Sequanian;* Sēquanus, i, *m., a Sequanian, one of the Sequani.*
Sequor, i, secūtus sum. *To follow.* SEQUENCE.
Sermō, ōnis, *m.* *Discourse, conversation.* SERMON.
Serviō, ire, ivi or li, itum. *To serve, subserve, be devoted to.* SERVE.
Servitūs, ūtis, *f.* *Servitude, slavery.* SERVITUDE.
Servō, āre, āvi, ātum. *To keep, preserve.*
Servus, i, *m.* *Slave.* SERVE.
Sēsē. See 102, 184, 4.

Seu, *conj.* *Or if;* seu . . . sive, *either . . . or.*
Sevērus, a, um. *Severe.*
Sex, *indeclinable.* *Six.*
Sexāgintā, *indeclinable.* *Sixty.*
Sextus, a, um. *Sixth.*
Si, *conj.* *If.*
Sicilia, ae, *f.* *Sicily.*
Significō, āre, āvi, ātum. *To signify, indicate.* SIGNIFY.
Signum, i, *n.* *Standard;* signa ferre, *to carry the standards — to advance.* SIGN.
Silva, ae, *f.* *Wood, forest.* SYLVAN.
Similis, e. *Like.* SIMILAR.
Simpliciter, *adv.* *Simply.*
Simul, simul atque, *conj.* *As soon as.*
Sin, *conj.* *But if.*
Sincērē, *adv.* *Truthfully.* SINCERE.
Sine, *prep. w. abl.* *Without.*
Singulāris, e. *Single, singly, individual, separate; singular, remarkable.* SINGULAR.
Sive, *conj.* *Or if;* sive . . . sive, *either . . . or.*
Socer, eri, *m.* *Father-in-law.*
Sōcratēs, is, *m.* *Socrates,* a celebrated Greek philosopher.
Sōl, sōlis, *m.* *Sun.*
Sōlum, *adv.* *Only, alone.*
Solvō, ere, i, solūtum. *To loose; with* nāvēs *expressed or understood, to set sail.* SOLVE.
Spatium, ii, *n.* *Space, interval, distance; time.* SPACE.
Speciēs, ēi, *f.* *Look, appearance.*
Spēs, spēi, *f.* *Hope.*
Spiritus, ūs, *m.* *Breath; pl., airs, haughtiness.* SPIRIT.

Spollō, āre, āvī, ātum. *To despoil, rob, deprive.* SPOIL.

Spōns, spontis, *f.* *Used in gen. and abl. sing. only.* Sponte, suā sponte, *by one's own agency, by one's self, unassisted.*

Stabilitās, ātis, *f.* *Stability, firmness.* STABILITY.

Statim, *adv.* *Immediately.*

Statiō, ōnis, *f.* *Station, post, guard.* STATION.

Statuō, ere, ui, ūtum. *To determine, decide.*

Stipendium, ii, *n.* *Tax, tribute.* STIPEND.

Stō, āre, stetī, stătum. *To stand.*

Strepitus, ūs, *m.* *Din, noise.*

Studeō, ēre, ui. *To desire.* STUDY. (Followed by the Dative.)

Studium, ii, *n.* *Desire, zeal.* STUDY.

Sub, *prep. w. acc. and abl.* *Under, up to, towards.*

Subdūcō, ere, dūxī, ductum. *To draw up; to withdraw, lead off.*

Subeō, ire, iī, itum. *To undergo.*

Subiciō,[1] ere, jēcī, jectum. *To throw under, cast under, throw, thrust; to subject.* SUBJECT.

Subitō, *adv.* *Suddenly.*

Sublātus, a, um. See *tollō.*

Sublevō, āre, āvī, ātum. *To assist, support.*

Subministrō, āre, āvī, ātum. *To furnish, supply.*

Submittō, ere, misī, missum. *To send up to, send.* SUBMIT.

Submoveō, ēre, mōvī, mōtum. *To remove, dislodge.*

Subsequor, i, secūtus sum. *To follow close upon, follow.* SUBSEQUENT.

Subsidium, ii, *n.* *Support, reënforcement, aid.* SUBSIDIARY.

Subsistō, ere, stitī. *To make a stand; audācius subsistere, to make a bolder stand.* SUBSIST.

Subveniō, ire, vēnī, ventum. *To come to the help of, succor, aid.*

Succēdō, ere, cessī, cessum. *To go up, come up, approach, succeed.* SUCCEED.

Sudēs, is, *f.* *Stake.*

Suēbī, ōrum, *m. pl.* *The Suebi, Suevi* or *Suabians,* a powerful German tribe.

Suessiōnēs, um, *m. pl.* *The Suessiones,* a tribe of northern Gaul.

Sui. 102, 184. *Of himself, of herself, of itself, of themselves, of him, of her, of it, of them.*

Sulla, ae, *m.* *Sulla,* a celebrated Roman general and statesman.

Sulpicius, ii, *m.* *Sulpicius,* a lieutenant under Caesar.

Sum, esse, fuī. 140, 204. *To be.*

Summa, ae, *f.* *Sum, sum total, total.* SUM.

Summus, a, um, *sup. of* superus. *Highest, greatest; the summit of, top of.*

Sūmō, ere, sūmpsī, sūmptum. *To take.*

Sūmptus, ūs, *m.* *Expense.*

Superbus, a, um. *Proud.* SUPERB.

Superior, us, *comp. of* superus. *Upper, higher; superior; previous.*

---

[1] Pronounced as if spelled *subjicio.*

VOCABULARY.   301

Superō, āre, āvī, ātum. *To surpass; to conquer.*
Supersum, esse, fuī. *To survive.*
Superus, a, um, *comp.* superior, *sup.* suprēmus *and* summus. *Upper.* See *superior* and *summus.*
Supplicătiō, ōnis, *f. Thanksgiving.*
Supplicium, iī, *n. Punishment.*
Suprā, *adv. Above.*
Suscipiō, ere, cēpī, ceptum. *To take up, undertake.*
Suspiciō, ōnis, *f. Suspicion.*
Suspicor, ārī, ātus sum. *To suspect.*
Sustineō, ēre, uī, tentum. *To sustain, resist, withstand.* SUSTAIN.
Suus, a, um. *His, her, hers, its, their.*

T.

Tabula, ae, *f. Table, tablet, record, document.* TABLE.
Taceō, ēre, uī, itum. *To be silent, to keep silent.* TACIT.
Tam, *adv. So, to such an extent.*
Tamen, *adv. Yet, still, nevertheless.*
Tamesis, is, *m. Thames.*
Tametsi, *conj. Although.*
Tantus, a, um. *So great; as great.*
Tardō, āre, āvī, ātum. *To retard, check, hinder, impede.* TARDY.
Tēlum, ī, *n. Dart, weapon.*
Temerārius, a, um. *Rash.*
Temere, *adv. Rashly, unnecessarily.*

Temperantia, ae, *f. Temperance, self-control.* TEMPERANCE.
Tempestās, ātis, *f. Weather; tempest, storm.* TEMPEST.
Templum, ī, *n. Temple.*
Tempus, oris, *n. Time.* [*restrain.*
Teneō, ēre, uī, tentum. *To hold,*
Tentō, āre, āvī, ātum. *To try.*
Tenuis, e. *Thin; feeble.*
Tergum, ī, *n. Back; terga vertere, to turn the back = to retreat, flee.*
Terra, ae, *f. Earth; land.*
Terreō, ēre, uī, itum. *To terrify, frighten.* TERROR.
Terror, ōris, *m. Terror, dread.*
Tertius, a, um. *Third.*
Testāmentum, ī, *n. Will.* TESTAMENT.
Testis, is, *m. and f. Witness.*
Tigurinus, ī, *m. Tigurinus,* one of the four cantons of the Helvetii.
Timeō, ēre, uī. *To fear.* TIMID.
Timor, ōris, *m. Fear.* TIMID.
Titūrius, iī, *m. Titurius,* a lieutenant under Caesar.
Titus, ī, *m. Titus,* a Roman name.
Tollō, ere, sustulī, sublātum. *To lift up; to remove, take away; to exalt, encourage.*
Tolōsa, ae, *f. Tolosa,* a town in southern Gaul.
Tormentum, ī, *n. A military engine for throwing heavy missiles.*
Tōtus, a, um. **45**, 151. *All, the whole of.* TOTAL.
Trādō, ere, dĭdī, dĭtum. *To give up, surrender.* TRADITION.
Trăgula, ae, *f. Javelin, dart.*

Trājectus, ūs, m. *Passage, crossing.*

Trānō, āre, āvi, ātum. *To swim across.*

Trāns, *prep. w. acc. Across, over, beyond.*

Trānslūcō, ere, dūxi, ductum. *To lead across, lead, conduct.*

Trānscō, ire, ii, itum. *To go over, cross.* TRANSIT.

Trānsiciō,[1] ere, jēci, jectum. *To pierce, transfix.*

Trānsportō, āre, āvi, ātum. *To carry over, take over, bring over, transport.* TRANSPORT.

Trēs, tria. 97, 175. *Three.*

Trēveri, ōrum, m. pl. *The Treveri, a tribe of northeastern Gaul.*

Tribūnus, i, m. *Tribune, one of the six principal officers of the legion.*

Triduum, i, n. *Three days, space of three days.*

Trigintā, *indeclinable. Thirty.*

Trini, ae, a. 97, 172, 3. *Three by three, three each, threefold, triple, three.*

Triplex, icis. *Threefold, triple.* TRIPLE.

Tū, tui. 102, 184. *Thou, you.*

Tullia, ae, f. *Tullia, a Roman name.*

Tum, *adv. Then.*

Turma, ae, f. *Troop.*

Turris, is, f. *Tower.*

Tūtō, *adv. Safely.*

Tūtus, a, um. *Safe.*

Tuus, a, um. 102, 185. *Thy, thine, your, yours.*

Tyrannus, i, m. *Tyrant.*

U.

Ubī, *adv. and conj. Where; when.*

Ubii, ōrum, m. pl. *The Ubii, a tribe of western Germany.*

Ulcīscor, i, ultus sum. *To take vengeance on, punish; to avenge.*

Ūllus, a, um. 45, 151. *Any, any one.*

Ūlterior, us, *comp. adj.* 86, 166. *Further;* Gallia Ūlterior, *Farther Gaul, Transalpine Gaul.*

Ūnā, *adv. Together.*

Unde, *adv. Whence, from which place, from which.*

Ūndecimus, a, um. *Eleventh.*

Undique, *adv. On every side, on all sides; from every side, from all sides.*

Ūniversus, a, um. *All, all together.* UNIVERSE.

Unquam, *adv. Ever, at any time.*

Ūnus, a, um. 97, 175. *One, single.* UNIT.

Urbs, urbis, f. *City.* URBANE.

Usipetēs, um. m. pl. *The Usipetes, a tribe of northwestern Germany.*

Usque, *adv. Even.*

Ūsus, ūs, m. *Use, usage, experience; advantage.* USE.

Ut, uti, *conj. That, in order that.*

Ut, *adv. As.*

Uter, tra, trum. 45, 151. *Which (of two).*

Uterque, utraque, utrumque, *inflected like uter. Each; both.*

Ūtilis, e. *Useful.* UTILITY.

---

[1] Pronounced as if spelled *trānsjiciō.*

VOCABULARY. 303

Ūtĭlĭtās, ātis, *f.* *Usefulness; interest, expediency.* UTILITY.
Utĭnam, *interj.* *O that! would that!*
Ūtor, i, ūsus sum. *To use.*
Utrum, *conj.* *Whether;* utrum ... an, *whether* ... *or.*
Uxor, ōris, *f.* *Wife.*

V.

Văcō, āre, āvī, ātum. *To be without, be free from; to be vacant, empty, unoccupied.* VACATE.
Văcuus, a, um. *Vacant, empty, deserted, abandoned.*
Vădum, i, *n.* *Ford; shoal.*
Văleō, ēre, ui, ĭtum. *To avail, prevail, have force or influence.*
Vallum, i, *n.* *Rampart.*
Vastō, āre, āvī, ātum. *To lay waste.*
-Ve, *conj.* *enclitic.*[1] *Or.*
Vectīgal, ălis, *n.* *Tax; revenue.*
Vel, *conj.* *Either; or;* vel ... vel, *either* ... *or.*
Vellem. See *volō.*
Venĕti, ōrum, *m. pl.* *The Veneti, a tribe of western Gaul.*
Venetia, ae, *f.* *Venetia, the country of the Veneti.*
Vĕnĭō, ire, vēni, ventum. *To come, arrive.*
Ventus, i, *m.* *Wind.*
Vēr, vēris, *n.* *Spring.* VERNAL.
Veragri, ōrum, *m. pl.* *The Veragri, a tribe of southeastern Gaul.*
Verbĭgĕnus, i, *m.* *Verbigenus,* one of the four cantons of the Helvetii.
Verbum, i, *n.* *Word.* VERB.
Vercingetorix, igis, *m.* *Vercingetorix, a Gallic chieftain.*
Vergobretus, i, *m.* *Vergobretus, the title of the chief magistrate of the Aedui.*
Vērō, *adv.* *and conj.* *In truth, indeed; but.*
Versor, āri, ātus sum. *To be busied, occupied, engaged.* VERSED.
Vertō, ere, i, sum. *To turn;* terga vertere, *to turn the back* = *to retreat, flee.*
Vērum, i, *n.* *Truth.*
Vērus, a, um. *True.*
Vesontiō, ōnis, *m.* *Vesontio, a town in eastern Gaul, now Besançon.*
Vesper, eri, *m.* *Evening.*
Vester, tra, trum. 102, 185. *Your, yours.*
Vestiō, ire, ivi *or* ii, ītum. *To clothe.*
Veterānus, a, um. *Veteran.*
Vetus, eris. *Old, ancient; former.*
Via, ae, *f.* *Way.*
Viātor, ōris, *m.* *Traveller.*
Vicis, *gen.*, *nom.* *wanting, f.* *Turn;* in vicem, *in turn.*
Victor, ōris, *m.* *Conqueror.*
Victōria, ae, *f.* *Victory.*
Victōria, ae, *f.* *Victoria.*
Vīcus, i, *m.* *Village.*
Vĭdeō, ēre, vidi, visum. *To see.*
Vĭdeor, ēri, visus sum.[2] *To seem.*
Vĭgĭlĭa, ae. *f.* *Watch.*[3] VIGIL.
Vīgintī, *indeclinable.* *Twenty.*

---

[1] See 103, foot-note 2.   [2] See 274.   [3] See 276.

Vincĭo, ire, vinxi, vinctum. *To bind, confine.*

Vinco, ere, vici, victum. *To conquer.*

Vinculum, i, *n. Fetter, bond, chain.*

Vindex, icis, *m. and f. Defender.*

Vir, viri, *m. Man.*

Virgŏ, inis, *f. Maiden.* VIRGIN.

Virtūs, ūtis, *f. Virtue, valor, courage, bravery.* VIRTUE.

Vis, vis, *f. Force, violence;* vim facere, *to use violence;* virĕs, ium, *pl., strength.*

Visus, a, um. See vĭdĕō.

Vita, ae, *f. Life.* VITAL.

Vīto, āre, āvi, ātum. *To avoid, shun.*

Vitrum, i, *n. Woad, a plant used for dyeing blue.*

Vivŏ, ere, vixi, victum. *To live.*

Vocŏ, āre, āvi, ātum. *To call, summon.*

Volŭ, velle, volui. 273, 293. *To wish, to be willing.*

Voluntās, ātis, *f. Wish, good-will, consent.* VOLUNTARY.

Volusēnus, i, *m. Volusenus,* an officer in Caesar's army.

Vŏx, vōcis, *f. Voice, utterance.* VOICE.

Vulgŏ, *adv. Commonly, as a general thing, universally.*

Vulnĕrŏ, āre, āvi, ātum. *To wound.*

Vulnus, eris, *n. Wound.*

Vultis. See volŏ.

Vultus, ûs, *m. Countenance, face;* vultum fingere, *to control the countenance.*

ENGLISH-LATIN VOCABULARY.

A.

A. *See page 18, foot-note 4.*
Able, to be able. *Possum, posse, potuī.* **269**, 290.
About, concerning. *Dē*, prep. w. abl. About, around, *circum*, prep. w. acc.
Above. *Suprā*, adv.
Acceptable. *Grātus, a, um ; acceptus, a, um.*
Accomplish. *Perfĭcĭō, ere, fēcī, fectum ; cōnfĭcĭō, ere, fēcī, fectum.*
Accordance, in accordance with. Often expressed by the Ablative. **158**, 413.
Accuse. *Accūsō, āre, āvī, ātum ; insĭmŭlō, āre, āvī, ātum.* **285**.
Across, over. *In*, w. abl. To lead across, *trānsdūcō, ere, dūxī, ductum.* See **275**, 19.
Adopt. *Capĭō, ere, cēpī, captum ; ĭneō, īre, iī, ĭtum.*
Advance, to advance. *Signa fĕro, ferre, tulī, lātum ; prōgrĕdĭor, ī, prōgressus sum.*
Advise. *Mŏneō, ēre, uī, ĭtum.*
Aedui. *Aeduī, ōrum,* m. pl.
Affair. *Rēs, rĕī,* f. ; military affairs, *rēs mīlĭtāris.*

After. *Post,* adv. ; *posteāquam, postquam,* conj.
Against. *Contrā,* prep. w. acc. ; *in,* prep. w. acc. ; to wage against, *inferō, ferre, intulī, illātum.*
Ahead, to send ahead. *Praemittō, ere, mīsī, missum.*
Aid. *Auxĭlĭum, iī,* n. To aid, *jŭvō, āre, jūvī, jūtum.*
All. *Omnis, e ; tōtus, a, um,* **45**, 151 ; *ūnĭversus, a, um ;* on all sides, *undĭque.*
Alone. *Sōlum,* adv.
Already. *Jam,* adv.
Also. *Etĭam,* adv. and conj. ; *quŏque,* adv.
Although. *Etsī, tametsī,* conj. **254**, 515.
Always. *Semper,* adv.
Ambassador. *Lēgātus, ī,* m.
Among. *Apud,* prep. w. acc. ; *in,* prep. w. acc. and abl.
An. *See page 25, foot-note 1.*
Ancient. *Prīstĭnus, a, um ; antīquus, a, um.*
And. *Et ; que,* **103** ; *atque, āc ;* conj.
Animal. *Anĭmal, ālis,* n.
Announce. *Nūntĭō, āre, āvī, ātum.*

VOCABULARY.

Answer. *Respondeō, ēre, ī, sponsum.*
Any. *Ūllus, a, um,* **45, 131**; anything, n. of *quis* or *aliquis,* **106, 190.**
Appoint. *Indīcō, ere, dīxī, dictum.*
Approach. *Adventus, ūs,* m. To approach, *succēdō, ere, cessi, cessum.*
Approve. *Probō, āre, āvī, ātum.*
Aquitani. *Aquitāni, ōrum,* m. pl.
Arar. *Arar, aris,* m. **128.**
Ariovistus. *Ariovistus, ī, m.*
Arms. *Arma, ōrum,* n. pl.
Army. *Exercitus, ūs,* m.
Arouse. *Excitō, āre, āvī, ātum.*
Arrival. *Adventus, ūs,* m.
Arrogance. *Arrogantia, ae,* f.
Art, work. *Opus, eris,* n.
Artemisia. *Artemisia, ae,* f.
As. *Ut;* as not to, *ut nōn,* **123, 500;** as soon as, *simul, simul atque,* conj.
Ascend. *Ascendō, ere, ī, scensum.*
Ascertain. *Cōgnōscō, ere, nōvī, nītum.*
Ask. *Rogō, āre, āvī, ātum;* to ask for, *rogō.*
Assail. *Aggredior, ī, gressus sum.*
Assault. *Oppūgnō, āre, āvī, ātum.*
Assemble, come together. *Conveniō, īre, vēnī, ventum.*
Assist. *Juvō, āre, jūvī, jūtum.*
Assure. *Cōnfirmō, āre, āvī, ātum.*
At. *Ad,* prep. w. acc.; *in,* prep. w. abl.; often expressed by the Locative or by the Locative Ablative, **185, 425;** at length, *dēmum,* adv.

Attack. *Impetus, ūs,* m. To attack, *oppūgnō, āre, āvī, ātum; aggredior, ī, gressus sum.*
Attempt. *Cōnātus, ūs,* m. To attempt, *cōnor, ārī, ātus sum.*
Audacity. *Audācia, ae,* f.
Authority. *Auctōritās, ātis,* f.
Avail. *Valeō, ēre, uī, itum.*
Avoid. *Vītō, āre, āvī, ātum.*
Avenge. *Persequor, ī, secūtus sum.*
Await. *Exspectō, āre, āvī, ātum.*

B.

Back, to lead back. *Redūcō, ere, dūxī, ductum;* to drive back, *repellō, ere, reppulī, repulsum; repulsō, āre, āvī, ātum.*
Band. *Manus, ūs,* f.
Bank. *Ripa, ae,* f.
Barbarian. *Barbarus, ī,* m.
Barbarous. *Barbarus, a, um.*
Battle. *Proelium, iī,* n.; *pūgna, ae,* f.; line of battle, *aciēs, ēī,* f.; a battle takes place, *pūgnātur.*
Be. *Sum, esse, fuī,* **140, 204;** to be able, *possum, posse, potuī,* **269, 200;** to be eager, *ārdeō, ēre, ārsī, ārsum;* to be free from, *vacō, āre, āvī, ātum;* to be from, to be distant from, *absum, abesse, āfuī;* to be greatly pleased with, *adamō, āre, āvī, ātum;* to be in command of, *praesum, esse, fuī;* to be silent, *taceō, ēre, uī, itum;* to be unwilling, *nōlō, nōlle, nōluī,* **273, 203;** to be well supplied, *abundō, āre, āvī, ātum;* to be willing, *volō, velle, voluī,* **273, 203.**

Bear. *Ferō, ferre, tuli, lātum.*
269, 292.
Beautiful. *Pulcher, chra, chrum.*
Because. *Quod,* conj.
Before. *Ante,* adv., and prep.
w. acc.; *prō,* prep. w. abl.;
antequam, priusquam, conjunction.
Beg. *Ōrō, āre, āvī, ātum; rogō, āre, āvī, ātum.*
Beginning. *Initium, ii,* n.
Behind. *Post,* prep. w. acc.
Belgae, Belgians. *Belgae, ārum,* m. pl.
Believe. *Crēdō, ere, didi, ditum.*
(Followed by the Dative of the person.)
Besiege. *Obsideō, ēre, sēdi, sessum.*
Betake one's self. *Sē mandō, āre, āvī, ātum; sē recipiō, ere, cēpi, ceptum.*
Beyond, across. *Trāns,* prep. w. acc.
Bid. *Liceor, ērī, itus sum.*
Bird. *Avis, is,* f.
Bituriges. *Biturigēs, um,* m. pl.
Blame. *Culpa, ae,* f.
Book. *Liber, brī,* m.
Boundary, natural boundaries. *Nātūra locī.*
Boy. *Puer, erī,* m.
Brave. *Fortis, e.*
Bravely. *Fortiter,* adv.
Bravery. *Virtūs, ūtis,* f.
Bridge. *Pōns, pontis,* m.
Bring. *Portō, āre, āvī, ātum;*
to bring over, *trānsportō, āre, āvī, ātum;* to bring to an end, *cōnficiō, ere, fēci, fectum.*
Britons. *Brĭtannī, ōrum,* m. pl.
Brother. *Frāter, tris,* m.

Build. *Aedificō, āre, āvī, ātum ;*
to make, *faciō, ere, fēci, factum.*
Burn. *Exūrō, ere, ussi, ūstum;*
combūrō, ere, ussi, ūstum; to set on fire, *incendō, ere, i, cēnsum.*
But. *Autem,* conj., see foot-note, p. 316; *sed,* conj.
Buy up. *Redimō, ere, ēmi, emptum.*
By. *Ā, ab,* prep. w. abl.; often expressed by the Ablative alone; 78, 420; by far, *longē, multō,* adv.

C.

Caesar. *Caesar, aris,* m.
Calamity. *Calamitās, ātis,* f.
Call, name. *Appellō, āre, āvī, ātum ; nōminō, āre, āvī, ātum ;* to call together, *convocō, āre, āvī, ātum.*
Camp. *Castra, ōrum,* n. pl.
Can. *Possum, posse, potui.* 269, 290.
Canton. *Pāgus, i,* m.
Captive. *Captīvus, ī,* m.
Carry, take. *Portō, āre, āvī, ātum;*
to bear, *ferō, ferre, tuli, lātum;*
to carry over, *trānsportō, āre, āvī, ātum.*
Carthage. *Karthāgō, inis,* f.
Cassius. *Cassius, iī,* m.
Cause. *Causa, ae,* f.
Celts. *Celtae, ārum,* m. pl.
Censure. *Accūsō, āre, āvī, ātum.*
Centurion. *Centuriō, ōnis,* m.
Check. *Tardō, āre, āvī, ātum.*
Chief. *Prīnceps, ipis ; summus, a, um ;* a chief, chieftain, *prīnceps, ipis,* m.

Cicero. *Cĭcerō, ōnis,* m.
Citizen. *Cīvis, is,* m.
City. *Urbs, urbis,* f.
Civilization. *Hūmānĭtās, ātis,* f.
Civilized. *Hŭmănus, a, um.*
Close. *Claudō, ere, sī, sum.*
Clothe. *Vestĭō, īre, īvī* or *ĭi, ītum.*
Cloud. *Nūbēs, is,* f.
Collect. *Cōgō, ere, coēgi, coāctum.*
Come. *Venĭō, īre, vēni, ventum.*
Command. *Jubeō, ēre, jussi, jussum; imperō, āre, āvī, ātum;* to be in command, *praesum, esse, fui;* to place in command, *praeficiō, ere, fēci, fectum;* under one's command, *dux* in Ablative Absolute.
Commander. *Imperātor, ōris,* m.
Commit. *Admittō, ere, misī, missum.*
Companion. *Comes, ĭtis,* m. and f.
Compel. *Cōgō, ere, coēgi, coāctum.*
Concerning. *Dē,* prep. w. abl.
Conduct. *Dēdūcō, ere, dūxi, ductum.*
Confidence. *Fĭdēs, ĕi,* f.
Congratulate. *Grātulor, ārī, ātus sum.* (Followed by the Dative.)
Conquer. *Superō, āre, āvī, ātum; vincō, ere, vīci, victum.*
Conqueror. *Victor, ōris,* m.
Consider, think. *Putō, āre, āvī, ātum; arbitror, ārī, ātus sum; existimō, āre, āvī, ātum.*
Conspire. *Conjūrō, āre, āvī, ātum.*
Consul. *Cōnsul, ulis,* m.
Consult. *Cōnsŭlō, ere, uī, sultum.*

Contented. *Contentus, a, um.*
Continually. *Continenter,* adv.
Contrary to. *Contrā,* prep. w. acc.
Convention. *Conventus, ūs,* m.
Conversation. *Sermō, ōnis,* m.
Council. *Concilium, ii,* n.; *conventus, ūs,* m.
Counsel. *Cōnsilium, ii,* n.
Country. *Terra, ae,* f.; fields, *agri, ōrum,* m. pl.; one's country, native country, *patria, ae,* f.
Courage. *Virtūs, ūtis,* f.
Crassus. *Crassus, ī,* m.
Crime. *Facĭnus, oris,* n.
Cross. *Trānseō, īre, ĭi, itum.*
Crown. *Corōna, ae,* f.
Custom. *Mōs, mōris,* m.
Cut off. *Interclūdō, ere, si, sum.*

D.

Daily. *Cotīdĭē,* adv.
Danger. *Perīculum, ī,* n.
Dare. *Audeō, ēre, ausus sum.* See 259, *cōnfīdo.*
Dart. *Tēlum, ī,* n.
Daughter. *Fīlia, ae,* f.
Daunt. *Perterreō, ēre, uī, itum.*
Day. *Dĭēs, ēi,* m. and f.
Daybreak. *Prima lūx.*
Daylight. *Lūx, lūcis,* f.
Dear. *Cārus, a, um.*
Death. *Mors, mortis,* f.; to put to death, *interficiō, ere, fēci, fectum.*
Decide. *Cōnstituō, ere, uī, ūtum; statuō, ere, uī, ūtum.*
Defeat. *Superō, āre, āvī, ātum; vincō, ere, vīci, victum.*
Defence, in defence of. *Prō,* prep. w. abl.

Defend. *Dēfendō, ere, ī, fēn-sum.*
Deliberate. *Dēliberō, āre, āvī, ātum.*
Deliberation. Gerund of *dēliberō.*
Delight. *Dēlectō, āre, āvī, ātum.*
Demand. *Postulō, āre, āvī, ātum; flāgitō, āre, āvī, ātum.*
Deserter. *Fugitivus, ī, m.*
Deservedly. *Meritō,* adv.
Desire. *Studium, iī, n.* To desire, *studeō, ēre, uī* (followed by the Dative); *cupiō, ere, īvi or iī, ītum.*
Desirous. *Cupidus, a, um.*
Detain. *Detineō, ēre, uī, tentum.*
Deter. *Dēterreō, ēre, uī, itum.*
Determine. *Cōnstituō, ere, uī, ūtum.*
Detest. *Ōdī, isse.*
Devastate. *Vastō, āre, āvī, ātum.*
Difficulty. *Difficultās, ātis,* f.
Diminish. *Dēminuō, ere, ī, ūtum.*
Direction. *Pars, partis,* f.
Disposition. *Animus, ī, m.*
Distant, to be distant. *Absum, esse, āfuī.*
Distress. *Premō, ere, pressī, pressum.*
Disturb. *Perturbō, āre, āvī, ātum; commoveō, ēre, mōvī, mōtum.*
Divide. *Dīvidō, ere, vīsī, vīsum.*
Divine. *Dīvinus, a, um.*
Division. *Pars, partis,* f.
Divitiacus. *Divitiacus, ī, m.*
Do. *Faciō, ere, fēcī, factum; gerō, ere, gessī, gestum.*
Double. *Duplex, icis.*
Doubt. *Dubitō, āre, āvī, ātum.*
Draw up. *Instruō, ere, strūxī, strūctum.*

Drive back. *Repellō, ere, reppulī, repulsum;* to drive out, *ēiciō, ere, jēcī, jectum.*
Druids. *Druidēs, um,* m. pl.
Dumnorix. *Dumnorix, igis, m.*
During. Usually expressed by the Accusative. 98, 370.
Dwell. *Incolō, ere, uī, cultum; habitō, āre, āvī, ātum.*

E.

Each. *Uterque, traque, trumque,* inflected like *uter*, 45, 151; with each other, *inter sē.*
Eager, to be eager. *Ārdeō, ēre, ārsī, ārsum.*
Easily. *Facile,* adv.
Easy. *Facilis, e;* very easy, *perfacilis, e.*
Eight. *Octo,* indeclinable.
Eighth. *Octāvus, a, um.*
Either. *Aut,* conj.; either . . . or, *aut . . . aut.*
Embassy. *Lēgātiō, ōnis,* f.
Enclose. *Contineō, ēre, uī, tentum.*
End, to bring to an end. *Cōnficiō, ere, fēcī, fectum.*
Endure. *Ferō, ferre, tulī, lātum.* 269, 292.
Enemy. *Hostis, is,* m. and f.; *inimīcus, ī, m.*
Enervate. *Effēminō, āre, āvī, ātum.*
Enlist, enrol. *Cōnscribō, ere, scripsī, scriptum.*
Entangled. *Impedītus, a, um.*
Establish. *Cōnfirmō, āre, āvī, ātum.*
Even. *Etiam,* adv.
Ever, always. *Semper,* adv.

VOCABULARY.

Excellently. *Ēgregiē*, adv.
Except. *Praeterquam*, adv. See 279, sentence 17.
Exchange. *Inter sē dō, dare, dedī, dătum.*
Exile. *Exsul, ŭlis*, m. and f.
Expect. *Exspectō, āre, ātī, ātum.*
Expense. *Sūmptus, ūs*, m.
Experience. *Ūsus, ūs*, m.
Explore. *Explōrō, āre, ātī, ātum.*
Expose. *Nūdō, āre, ātī, ātum.*

F.

Faithful. *Fīdus, a, um ; fĭdēlis, e.*
False. *Falsus, a, um.*
Far. *Longē*, adv.
Father. *Pater, tris*, m.
Father-in-law. *Socer, erī*, m.
Favor. *Grātia, ae*, f. To favor, *faveō, ēre, fāvī, fautum*. (Followed by the Dative.)
Fear. *Timor, ōris*, m. To fear, *timeō, ēre, uī.*
Fertile. *Fertĭlis, e.*
Fertility. *Fertilĭtās, ātis*, f.
Few. *Paucī, ae, a.*
Field. *Ager, grī*, m.
Fierce. *Ferus, a, um.*
Fifth. *Quīntus, a, um.*
Fight. *Pūgnō, āre, ātī, ātum ;* fighting goes on, *pūgnatur;* 281, 301.
Fill. *Compleō, ēre, ēvī, ētum.*
Find. *Reperĭō, īre, repperī, repertum.*
Finish. *Cōnficiō, ere, fēcī, fectum.*
Fire. *Ignis, is*, m; to set on fire, *incendō, ere, ī, cēnsum.*
First. *Prīmus, a, um.*
Five. *Quīnque*, indeclinable.

Flight. *Fuga, ae*, f.
Flow. *Fluō, ere, flūxī, flūxum.*
Foe. *Inimīcus, ī*, m.
Follow. *Sequor, ī, secūtus sum.*
Foot. *Pēs, pedis*, m.
Foot-soldier. *Pedes, itis*, m.
For. *Prō*, prep. w. abl.; *ad*, prep. w. acc.; for, on account of, *ob*, prep. w. acc.; for *is often expressed by the Dative*, 54, 384; for, during. *per*, prep. w. acc.; often expressed by the Accusative alone, 98, 379; to ask for, *rogō, āre, ātī, ātum ;* to wait for, *exspectō, āre, ātī, ātum.*
Force. *Cōgō, ere, coēgī, coāctum.*
Forced marches. *Māgna itinera.*
Forces. *Cōpiae, ārum*, f. pl.
Forest. *Silva, ae*, f.
Form line of battle. *Aciem instruō, ere, strūxī, strūctum.*
Formerly. *Anteā*, adv.
Forth, to go forth. *Exeō, īre, iī, itum ;* to lead forth, *ēdūcō, ere, dūxī, ductum.*
Fortification. *Mūnitiō, ōnis*, f.
Fortify. *Mūniō, īre, ītī or iī, ītum.*
Fortune. *Fortūna, ae*, f.
Forward, to send forward. *Praemittō, ere, mīsī, missum.*
Fourteenth. *Quārtus decimus, quārta decima, quārtum decimum.*
Free. *Līber, era, erum ;* to be free from, *vacō, āre, āvī, ātum.* To free, *līberō, āre, āvī, ātum.*
Freedom. *Libertās, ātis*, f.
Frequent. *Crēber, bra, brum.*
Frequently. *Saepe*, adv.
Friend. *Amīcus, ī*, m.
Friendly. *Amīcus, a, um.*

Friendship. *Amicitia, ae,* f.
From. *A, ab, de,* prep. w. abl.; to be distant from, *absum, esse, afui.*
Front, in front of. *Pro,* prep. w. abl.
Future. *Reliquum tempus;* for the future, in future, *in reliquum tempus.*

G.

Galba. *Galba, ae,* m.
Garrison. *Praesidium, ii,* n.
Gate. *Porta, ae,* f.
Gaul, the country. *Gallia, ae,* f. Gaul, a Gaul, *Gallus, i,* m.
Gem. *Gemma, ae,* f.
General. *Imperator, oris,* m.
Geneva. *Genava, ae,* f.
German. *Germanus, i,* m.
Gift. *Donum, i,* n.
Girl. *Puella, ae,* f.
Give. *Do, dare, dedi, datum;* to give up, *trado, ere, didi, ditum;* reddo, ere, didi, ditum.
Glory. *Gloria, ae,* f.
Go. *Eo, ire, ivi* or *ii, itum,* **277, 295**; to go forth, *exeo, ire, ii, itum;* fighting goes on, *pugnatur,* **281, 301.**
Gold. *Aurum, i,* n.
Golden, gold. *Aureus, a, um.*
Good. *Bonus, a, um,* comp. *melior,* sup. *optimus.*
Grain. *Frumentum, i,* n.
Grandson. *Nepos, otis,* m.
Great. *Magnus, a, um;* so great, *tantus, a, um.*
Greatly, to be greatly pleased with. *Adamo, are, avi, atum.*
Greece. *Graecia, ae,* f.

Greek. *Graecus, a, um;* a Greek, *Graecus, i,* m.
Grief. *Dolor, oris,* m.
Guard. *Custodio, ire, ivi* or *ii, itum.*
Guest. *Hospes, itis,* m. and f.

H.

Hand. *Manus, us,* f.
Happen. *Fio, fieri, factus sum.* **277, 294.**
Happily. *Feliciter,* adv.
Harbor. *Portus, us,* m.
Harm. *Maleficium, ii,* n.
Hasten. *Contendo, ere, i, tum; maturo, are, avi, atum.*
Have. *Habeo, ere, ui, itum;* to have power, *possum, posse, potui,* **269, 290**; to have to, often expressed by the Gerundive, **266, 234.**
He. *Is, ea, id; ille, illa, illud; hic, haec, hoc;* **102, 180**; often only implied in the ending of the verb.
Hear. *Audio, ire, ivi* or *ii, itum.*
Height. *Altitudo, inis,* f.
Help. *Auxilium, ii,* n. To help, *juvo, are, juvi, jutum.*
Helvetii. *Helvetii, orum,* m. pl.
Hesitate. *Dubito, are, avi, atum.*
High. *Altus, a, um.*
Hill. *Collis, is,* m.
Himself. *Sui,* **102, 184**; *ipse, a, um,* **102, 186.**
His. *Suus, a, um;* sometimes expressed by the genitive of *is* or *ille;* sometimes not expressed in Latin.
Hold. *Teneo, ere, ui, tentum;* to regard, *habeo, ere, ui, itum.*

Home. *Domus, ūs,* f.; at home, *domī,* 185, 426; homeward, home, *domum,* 277, 380.
Honor, ornament. *Ornāmentum,* ī, n.
Hope. *Spēs, spĕī,* f.
Horse. *Equus, i,* m.
Horseman. *Eques, itis,* m.
Hostage. *Obses, idis,* m. and f.
Hour. *Hōra, ae,* f.
How. *Quam,* adv.; how large, *quantus, a, um;* how many, *quot,* indeclinable.
Hundred. *Centum,* indeclinable.
Hurl. *Cŏiciō, ere, jēci, jectum.*

I.

I. *Ego, mei.* 102, 134.
If. *Si,* conj. 250, 507.
Implore. *Implōrō, āre, āvī, ātum.*
Import. *Importō, āre, āvī, ātum.*
In. *In,* prep. w. acc. and abl.; in front of, *prō,* prep. w. abl.; in regard to, *dē,* prep. w. abl.; in the vicinity of, *ad, apud, circum,* prep. w. acc.; *to plead in chains, ex vinculis;* in such a way, *ita,* adv.
Incessantly. *Continenter,* adv.
Inflict. *Inferō, ferre, intulī, illātum;* to inflict *punishment, sūmō, ere, sūmpsī, sūmptum,* with *supplicium;* literally, *to take punishment.*
Inform. *Certiōrem faciō, ere, fēci, factum;* to be informed, *certior fierī.*
Inhabit. *Incolō, ere, uī, cultum; habitō, āre, āvī, ātum.*
Inhabitant. *Is qui incolit,* literally, *he who inhabits.*

Inquire. *Quaerō, ere, sīvī* or *sii, sītum.*
Intend. *In animō esse,* w. Dative; I intend, *mihī in animō est;* to intend *is often expressed by the future active participle,* 266, 233.
Intention, it is my intention. *Mihi in animō est.*
Interest, to be for one's interest. *Interest, esse, fuit.* 281, 301.
Interior of. *Interior, us,* in agreement with noun.
Into. *In,* prep. w. acc.
Island. *Insula, ae,* f.
It. *Is, ea, id; ille, a, ud; hic, haec, hŏc;* 102, 186; often only implied in the ending of the verb.
Italy. *Italia, ae,* f.
Its. *Suus, a, um;* sometimes expressed by the genitive of *is* or *ille;* sometimes not expressed in Latin.

J.

Judge. *Jūdex, icis,* m. and f. To judge, *jūdicō, āre, āvī, ātum.*
Justice. *Jūstītia, ae,* f.

K.

Keep. *Teneō, ēre, uī, tentum; contineō, ēre, uī, tentum; retineō, ēre, uī, tentum; habeō, ēre, uī, itum;* to prevent, *prohibeō, ēre, uī, itum.*
Kent. *Cantium, iī,* n.
King. *Rēx, rēgis,* m.
Know. *Sciō, īre, īvī* or *iī, itum; intellegō, ere, lēxī, lēctum.*
Knowledge. *Scientia, ae, f.*

L.

Lake. *Lacus, ūs,* m.
Land. *Terra, ae,* f.; lands, fields, *agri, ōrum,* m. pl.
Large. *Magnus, a, um,* comp. *major,* sup. *maximus;* how large, *quantus, a, um.*
Last, nearest. *Proximus, a, um.*
Latinus. *Latīnus, ī,* m.
Lavinia. *Lāvīnia, ae,* f.
Law. *Lēx, lēgis,* f.
Lay waste. *Vastō, āre, āvī, ātum.*
Lead. *Dūcō, ere, dūxī, ductum;* to lead across, *trānsdūcō, ere, dūxī, ductum;* to lead back, *redūcō, ere, dūxī, ductum;* to lead out, *ēdūcō, ere, dūxī, ductum.*
Leader. *Princeps, ipis,* m. and f.; *dux, ducis,* m. and f.
Learning. *Doctrīna, ae,* f.
Leave. *Relinquō, ere, liquī, lictum.*
Legion. *Legiō, ōnis,* f.
Lemannus. *Lemannus, ī,* m.
Length, at length. *Dēmum,* adv.
Letter of the alphabet. *Littera, ae,* f.; letter, epistle, *epistula, ae,* f.; *litterae, ārum,* f. pl.
Liberty. *Libertās, ātis,* f.
Lieutenant. *Lēgātus, i,* m.
Life. *Vita, ae,* f.
Like very much. *Adamō, āre, āvī, ātum.*
Line. *Aciēs, ēi,* f.; line of battle, *aciēs;* line of march, *āgmen, inis,* n.
Listen to. *Audiō, ire, īvī* or *iī, ītum.*
Live. *Vīvō, ere, vīxī, vīctum.*
Long. *Longē,* adv.; a long time, *diū,* comp. *diūtius,* sup. *diūtissimē,* adv.
Love. *Amor, ōris,* m. To love, *amō, āre, āvī, ātum.*

M.

Magistrate. *Magistrātus, ūs,* m.
Make. *Faciō, ere, fēcī, factum;* to make war, *gerō, ere, gessi, gestum;* *inferō, ferre, intuli, illātum.*
Man. *Homō, inis,* m. and f.; *vir, virī,* m.
Many, much. *Multus, a, um;* how many, *quot,* indeclinable.
March. *Iter, itineris,* n.; forced marches, *magna itinera;* line of march, *āgmen, inis,* n. To march, *iter faciō, facere, fēci, factum.*
Marcus. *Mārcus, ī,* m.
Match, a match for. *Pār, paris.*
May. *Licet, ēre, licuit,* **281, 301.**
Menapii. *Menapii, ōrum,* m. pl.
Merchant. *Mercātor, ōris,* m.
Messenger, *Nūntius, iī,* m.
Midday. *Merīdiēs, ēi,* m.
Mile. *Mille passūs;* **247,** footnote.
Military. *Militāris, e;* military affairs, *res militāris.*
Mind. *Animus, i,* m.; *mens, mentis,* f.
Moat. *Fossa, ae,* f.
Month. *Mēnsis, is,* m.
Mother. *Māter, tris,* f.
Mountain. *Mōns, montis,* m.
Much, to like very much, *adamō, āre, āvī, ātum.*
Must. Often expressed by the Gerundive. **266, 234.**

My. *Meus, a, um.* **102, 185.**
Myself. *Ego, mei,* **102, 184;** *ipse, a, um,* **102, 186.**

N.

Name. *Nōmĭnō, āre, āvī, ātum.*
Nation. *Gēns, gentis,* f.; *nātiō, ōnis,* f.
Natural boundaries. *Nātūra loci.*
Nature. *Nātūra, ae,* f.
Navigate. *Nāvĭgō, āre, āvī, ātum.*
Navigation. Gerund of *nāvigō.*
Near. *Apud, ad,* prep. w. acc.
Nearer. *Propior, us.*
Nearly. *Ferĕ,* adv.; *paene,* adv.
Neighbor. *Fīnitīmus, i,* m.
Neighboring. *Fīnitīmus, a, um; proxĭmus, a, um.*
Nervii. *Nervii, ōrum,* m. pl.
Never. *Nŭnquam,* adv.
New. *Novus, a, um.*
Next. *Proxĭmus, a, um.*
No. *Nūllus, a, um,* **45, 151;** *nihil* w. Partitive Genitive, **28, 397.**
Noble. *Nōbilis, e.*
Not. *Nōn,* adv.; w. imperative or subjunctive of desire, *nē,* adv.; not? *nōnne?* conj., interrogative particle; not yet, *nōndum,* adv.
Number. *Numerus, i,* m.

O.

Obey. *Pāreō, ĕre, uī, ĭtum.* (Followed by the Dative.)
Observe. *Observō, āre, āvī, ātum.*
Obtain possession of. *Potior, īri, ītus sum;* **258, 421;** to obtain one's request, *impetrō, āre, āvī, ātum.*
Occupy. *Occŭpō, āre, āvī, ātum.*
Octodurus. *Octōdūrus, i,* m.
Of. *Dē, ē, ex,* prep. w. abl.; out of, *ē, ex;* in front of, *prō,* prep. w. abl.
Off, to cut off. *Intercludō, ere, si, sum.*
Often. *Saepe,* adv.
On, at. *Ad,* prep. w. acc.; *in.* prep. w. abl.; on the side of, *ā, ab,* prep. w. abl.; on all sides, *undique,* adv.; fighting goes on, *pūgnātur,* **281, 301.**
One. *Ūnus, a, um;* **97, 175;** that one, *is, ea, id; ille, a, ud;* **102, 186.**
Open. *Apertus, a, um.*
Opinion. *Sententia, ae,* f.
Or. *Aut,* conj.; in questions, *an,* conj.
Oration. *Ōrātiō, ōnis,* f.
Orator. *Ōrātor, ōris,* m.
Order. *Imperō, āre, āvī, ātum; jubeō, ēre, jussi, jussum;* in order that, *ut,* conj. **119, 407.**
Other. *Alius, a, ud;* **45, 151;** the remaining, *reliquus, a, um;* with each other, *inter sē.*
Ought. *Dēbeō, ēre, uī, ĭtum;* often expressed by the Gerundive, **266, 234.**
Our. *Noster, tra, trum.*
Out of. *Ex, ē,* prep. w. abl.; to lead out, *ēdūcō, ere, dūxī, ductum;* to set out, *proficiscor, i, profectus sum.*
Over. *Per, trāns,* prep. w. acc.; a bridge over, *in,* prep. w. abl.; to bring over, carry over, *trānsportō, āre, āvī, ātum.*
Owe. *Dēbeō, ēre, uī, ĭtum.*
Own. *Suus, a, um.*

P.

Pain. *Dolor, ōris*, m.
Part. *Pars, partis*, f.
Pass the winter. *Hiemō, āre, āvī, ātum.*
Passionate. *Īrācundus, a, um.*
Patiently. *Patienter*, adv.
Peace. *Pāx, pācis*, f.
Pedius. *Pedius, ii*, m.
Penalty. *Poena, ae*, f.
People. *Populus, ī*, m.
Peril. *Perīculum, ī*, n.
Perilous. *Perīculōsus, a, um.*
Persuade. *Persuādeō, ēre, suāsī, suāsum.* (Followed by the Dative of the *person*.)
Pisistratus. *Pīsistratus, ī*, m.
Place. *Locus, ī*, m., pl. *loca, ōrum*, n.; a battle takes place, *pūgnātur.* To place, *pōnō, ere, posuī, positum; collocō, āre, āvī, ātum; cōnstituō, ere, uī, ūtum;* to place in command, *praeficiō, ere, fēcī, fectum.*
Plan. *Cōnsilium, iī*, n.; *sententia, ae*, f.
Plato. *Plātō, ōnis*, m.
Plead. *Dīcō, ere, dīxī, dictum; agō, ere, ēgī, āctum.*
Pleased, to be greatly pleased with. *Adamō, āre, āvī, ātum.*
Plough. *Arō, āre, āvī, ātum.*
Poet. *Poēta, ae*, m.
Pompey. *Pompēius, iī*, m.
Populace. *Plēbs, plēbis*, f.
Position. *Locus, ī*, m., pl. *loca, ōrum*, n.
Possess. *Habeō, ēre, uī, itum; sum, esse, fuī in* w. abl.; he possesses wisdom, *sapientia in eō est.*

Possession, to obtain possession of. *Potior, īrī, ītus sum,* 258, 421; to take possession of, *occupō, āre, āvī, ātum.*
Power. *Potentia, ae*, f.; regal power, *rēgnum, ī*, n.; to have power, *possum, posse, potuī,* 269, 290.
Praise. *Laudō, āre, āvī, ātum.*
Prefer. *Mālō, mālle, māluī.* 273. 293.
Prepare. *Parō, āre, āvī, ātum; comparō, āre, āvī, ātum.*
Prepared. *Parātus, a, um.*
Present. *Dōnō, āre, āvī, ātum.*
Present, for the present. *In praesentiā.*
Prevail. *Valeō, ēre, uī, itum.*
Prevent. *Prohibeō, ēre, uī, itum.*
Previously. *Anteā*, adv.
Price. *Pretium, iī*, n.
Propose a law. *Ferō, ferre, tulī, lātum,* 269, 292.
Protect, fortify. *Mūniō, īre, īvī* or *iī, ītum.*
Protection. *Praesidium, iī*, n.
Provide. *Prōspiciō, ere, spēxī, spectum; prōvideō, ēre, vīdī, vīsum.* (Followed by the Dative.)
Province. *Prōvincia, ae*, f.
Provisions. *Cibāria, ōrum*, n. pl.
Punishment. *Supplicium, iī*, n.
Pupil. *Discipulus, ī*, m.
Purpose. *Cōnsilium, iī*, n.; *cōnātus, ūs*, m.; for the purpose of, *causā* w. Genitive.
Pursue. *Sequor, ī, secūtus sum; īnsequor, ī, secūtus sum; persequor, ī, secūtus sum.*
Put to death. *Interficiō, ere, fēcī, fectum; occīdō, ere, ī, sum.*

Q.

Quarters, winter quarters. *Hīberna, ōrum,* n. pl.
Queen. *Rēgīna, ae,* f.
Quickly. *Celeriter,* adv.

R.

Rampart. *Vallum, ī,* n.
Rash. *Temerārius, a, um.*
Rather than. *Quam,* conj.
Ravage. *Dēpopulor, ārī, ātus sum.*
Reach, arrive at. *Adeō, īre, iī, itum; venīō, īre, vēnī, ventum; perveniō, īre, vēnī, ventum;* to extend, *pertineō, ēre, uī, tentum.*
Read. *Legō, ere, lēgī, lēctum.*
Readily. *Facile,* adv.
Ready. *Parātus, a, um.*
Rear. *Novissimum āgmen, novissimī āgminis,* n.
Reason. *Causa, ae,* f.; *rēs, reī,* f.
Recollection. *Memoria, ae,* f.
Reference, with reference to. *Dē,* prep. w. abl.
Refinement. *Cultus, ūs,* m.
Regal power. *Rēgnum, ī,* n.
Regard, to regard as. *Habeō, ēre, uī, itum prō* w. abl.; in regard to, *dē,* prep. w. abl.
Region. *Regiō, ōnis,* f.
Reject. *Recūsō, āre, āvī, ātum.*
Rely upon. *Cōnfīdō, ere, fīsus sum.* See 259.
Remain. *Maneō, ēre, mānsī, mānsum; permaneō, ēre, mānsī, mānsum; remaneō, ēre, mānsī, mānsum;* to remain silent, *taceō, ēre, uī, itum.*

Remember. *Reminīscor, ī.* 258, 281.
Reml. *Rēmī, ōrum,* m. pl.
Remove. *Moveō, ēre, mōvī, mōtum; removeō, ēre, mōvī, mōtum.*
Renew. *Renovō, āre, āvī, ātum.*
Renowned. *Clārus, a, um.*
Repent. *Paenitet, ēre, uit;* I repent, *mē paenitet.* 281, 301; 285, 409.
Report. *Rūmor, ōris,* m. To report, *nūntiō, āre, āvī, ātum; ēnūntiō, āre, āvī, ātum.*
Repulse. *Prōpulsō, āre, āvī, ātum; repellō, ere, reppulī, repulsum.*
Reputation. *Auctōritās, ātis,* f.
Request, to obtain one's request. *Impetrō, āre, āvī, ātum.*
Reside. *Habitō, āre, āvī, ātum.*
Rest of. *Reliquus, a, um.*
Restore. *Restituō, ere, uī, ūtum.*
Retain. *Retineō, ēre, uī, tentum.*
Retard. *Tardō, āre, āvī, ātum.*
Return. *Redeō, īre, iī, itum; revertor, ī, reverti, reversum,* deponent in present system.
Revenue. *Vectīgal, ālis,* n.
Revolution. *Rēs novae.*
Rhine. *Rhēnus, ī,* m.
Rhone. *Rhodanus, ī,* m.
Ride toward. *Adequitō, āre, āvī, ātum.*
River. *Flūmen, inis,* n.
Roman. *Rōmānus, a, um;* a Roman, *Rōmānus, ī,* m.
Rome. *Rōma, ae,* f.
Romulus. *Rōmulus, ī,* m.
Route. *Iter, itineris,* n.
Rule. *Regō, ere, rēxī, rēctum.*
Rumor. *Rūmor, ōris,* m.

S.

Safe. *Tūtus, a, um.*
Safeguard. *Praesidium, ii,* n.
Safety. *Salūs, ūtis,* f.
Same. *Idem, eadem, idem.* 102, 186.
Santones. *Santonēs, um,* m. pl.
Say. *Dicō, ere, dīxī, dictum.*
School. *Schola, ae,* f.
Scout. *Explōrātor, ōris,* m.
Sea. *Mare, is,* n.
Second. *Secundus, a, um.*
Secure, win. *Conciliō, āre, āvī, ātum.*
See. *Videō, ēre, vīdī, vīsum.*
Seek. *Petō, ere, ivī or iī, itum;* *quaerō, ere, sivī or siī, situm.*
Seize. *Occupō, āre, āvī, ātum.*
Select. *Dēligō, ere, lēgī, lēctum.*
Senate. *Senātus, ūs,* m.
Send. *Mittō, ere, mīsī, missum;* to send ahead, send forward, *praemittō, ere, mīsī, missum.*
Separate. *Dīvidō, ere, vīsī, vīsum.*
Servitude. *Servitūs, ūtis,* f.
Set fire to. *Incendō, ere, ī, cēnsum.*
Set out. *Proficīscor, ī, profectus sum.*
Setting. *Occāsus, ūs,* m.
Setting out. *Profectiō, ōnis,* f.
Settle. *Cōnsīdō, ere, sēdī, sessum.*
Seventh. *Septimus, a, um.*
Several. *Complūrēs, a* or *ia, ium.*
Severe. *Acer, cris, cre; sevērus, a, um.*
Severely. *Ācriter,* adv.; *graviter,* adv.
Shepherd. *Pāstor, ōris,* m.
Ship. *Nāvis, is,* f.; *nāvigium, iī,* n.; ship of war, *longa nāvis.*

Shut in. *Contineō, ēre, uī, tentum.*
Side, part. *Pars, partis,* f.; on all sides, *undique,* adv.
Sight. *Cōnspectus, ūs,* m.
Signal. *Insignia, e.*
Silent, to be silent, to remain silent. *Taceō, ēre, uī, itum.*
Since. *Cum,* conj.
Singing. *Cantus, ūs,* m.
Single, one. *Ūnus, a, um.* 97, 173.
Six. *Sex,* indeclinable.
Sixth. *Sextus, a, um.*
Skilful. *Peritus, a, um.*
Skin. *Pellis, is,* f.
Slave. *Servus, ī,* m.
Slavery. *Servitūs, ūtis,* f.
Slay. *Occīdō, ere, ī, sum; interficiō, ere, fēcī, fectum.*
Sleep. *Dormiō, īre, ivī* or *iī, itum.*
Small. *Parvus, a, um.* 86, 165.
So, to such an extent. *Tam,* adv.; in such a way, *Ita,* adv.; so great, *tantus, a, um.*
Soldier. *Miles, itis,* m. and f.
Son. *Fīlius, iī,* m. 32, 51, 5.
Son-in-law. *Gener, erī,* m.
Soon, as soon as. *Simul, simul atque,* conj.
Soul. *Animus, ī,* m.
Soundly. *Artē,* adv.
Sovereignty. *Principātus, ūs,* m.
Space. *Spatium, iī,* n.; *locus, ī,* m.
Spare. *Parcō, ere, pepercī, parsum.* (Followed by the Dative.)
Speak. *Dīcō, ere, dīxī, dictum.*
Speedily. *Celeriter,* adv.
Spirit. *Animus, ī,* m.
State. *Cīvitās, ātis,* f. To state, say, *dīcō, ere, dīxī, dictum.*

Station. *Colloco, āre, āvī, ātum; constituō, ere, uī, ūtum.*
Stone. *Lapis, ĭdis,* m.
Storm. *Tempestās, ātis,* f.; to take by storm, *expūgnō, āre, āvī, ātum.*
Story. *Fābula, ae,* f.
Stricken with fear. *Tĭmōre perterrĭtus, a, um.*
Strip. *Nūdō, āre, āvī, ātum.*
Successfully. *Fēlīcĭter,* adv.
Successive. *Continuus, a, um.*
Such, so great. *Tantus, a, um;* in such a way, *ĭta,* adv.
Suebi. *Suēbī, ōrum,* m. pl.
Suffer. *Patior, ī, passus sum.*
Summer. *Aestās, ātis,* f.
Summon. *Vocō, āre, āvī, ātum.*
Sun. *Sōl, sōlis,* m.
Sunset. *Sōlis occāsus, ūs,* m.
Supplied, to be well supplied. *Abundō, āre, āvī, ātum.*
Supply, supplies. *Commeātus, ūs,* m.; supply of grain, supplies, *rēs frūmentāria.*
Support. *Alō, ere, uī, alĭtum* and *altum.*
Surpass. *Praecēdō, ere, cessī, cessum; praestō, āre, stĭtī, stĭtum* and *stătum.*
Surround. *Contineō, ēre, uī, tentum.*
Suspicion. *Suspīciō, ōnis,* f.
Sustain. *Sustineō, ēre, uī, tentum.*

T.

Take. *Capĭō, ere, cēpī, captum; sūmō, ere, sūmpsī, sūmptum;* to carry, *portō, āre, āvī, ātum;* to take by storm, *expūgnō, āre, āvī, ātum;* to take possession of, *occupō, āre, āvī, ātum;* to take from, *efferō, ferre, extulī, ēlātum;* to take vengeance on, *ulcīscor, ī, ultus sum;* a battle takes place, *pūgnātur,* 281, 301.
Teach. *Doceō, ēre, uī, doctum.*
Tell. *Dīcō, ere, dīxī, dictum.*
Temple. *Templum, ī,* n.
Ten. *Decem,* indeclinable.
Tend. *Pertĭneō, ēre, uī, tentum.*
Tenth. *Decimus, a, um.*
Terrify. *Terreō, ēre, uī, ĭtum;* to terrify greatly, *perterreō, ēre, uī, ĭtum.*
Territory. *Fīnēs, ium,* m. pl.
Thames. *Tamesis, is,* m.
Than. *Quam,* conj.
That. *Ille, a, ud; is, ea, id;* 102, 186; that of yours, *iste, a, ud,* 102, 186; that, relative, *quī, quae, quod,* 106, 187; that, repeating a previous noun, is often not to be rendered into Latin; that, in order that, *ut, quō, quōmĭnus,* conj. 119, 497.
The. See page 25, foot-note 1.
Their. *Suus, a, um;* sometimes expressed by the genitive of *is* or *ille,* 102, 186; sometimes not expressed in Latin.
Then. *Tum,* adv.
There. *Ibi,* adv.
Therefore. *Igĭtur,* conj.
Thing. *Rēs, rĕī,* f.
Think. *Putō, āre, āvī, ātum; arbĭtror, ārī, ātus sum; existĭmō, āre, āvī, ātum.*
Third. *Tertius, a, um.*
This. *Hīc, haec, hōc.* 102, 186.
Thou. *Tū, tuī.* 102, 184.
Three. *Trēs, tria.* 97, 175.
Through. *Per,* prep. w. acc.

Throw. *Jaciŏ, ere, jēci, jactum.*
Tidings. *Nūntius, ii, m.*
Time. *Tempus, oris,* n.; *diēs, ēi,* f. (although, when meaning day, usually masculine); for a long time, *diū,* comp. *diūtius,* sup. *diūtissimē,* adv.
To. *Ad,* prep. w. acc.; *often expressed by the Dative,* **54, 384**; with reference to, *dē,* prep. w. abl.; to set fire to, *incendŏ, ere, i, cēnsum.*
Together. *Ūnā,* adv.; to call together, *convocō, āre, āvi, ātum.*
Top of. *Summus, a, um.*
Toward. *Ad,* prep. w. acc.
Tower. *Turris, is,* f.
Town. *Oppidum, ī,* n.
Traitor. *Prōditor, ōris,* m.
Traveller. *Viātor, ōris,* m.
Treason. *Prōditiō, ōnis,* f.
Tribe. *Gēns, gentis,* f.
Tribune. *Tribūnus, ī,* m.
Triple. *Triplex, icis.*
True. *Vērus, a, um.*
Truth. *Vērum, ī,* n.
Try. *Tentō, āre, āvi, ātum.*
Tullia. *Tullia, ae,* f.
Two. *Duo, ae, o,* **97, 175.**
Tyrant. *Tyrannus, ī,* m.

U.

Under. *Sub,* prep. w. acc. and abl.; under the command of, *dux,* in the Ablative Absolute; under the command of Caesar, *Caesare duce.*
Understand. *Intellegō, ere, lēxi, lēctum.*
Undertake. *Suscipiō, ere, cēpi, ceptum.*
Unfortunate. *Infēlix, icis.*
Unite. *Conjungō, ere, jūnxi, jūnctum.*
Unless. *Nisi,* conj. **250, 507.**
Unskilled. *Imperitus, a, um.*
Until. *Dum, quoad,* conj. **337, 519.**
Unwilling, to be unwilling. *Nōlo, nōlle, nōlui.* **273, 203.**
Unworthy. *Indīgnus, a, um.*
Up, to draw up. *Instruō, ere, strūxi, strūctum;* to give up, *trādō, ere, didī, ditum.*
Upbraid. *Accūsō, āre, āvi, ātum.*
Upon. *In,* prep. w. acc. and abl.; against, *in, contrā,* prep. w. acc.
Urge. *Hortor, āri, ātus sum.*
Use. *Ūsus, ūs,* m. To use, *ūtor, i, ūsus sum.*
Useful. *Ūtilis, e.*
Usipetes. *Usipetēs, um,* m. pl.

V.

Valor. *Virtūs, ūtis,* f.
Valuable. *Pretiōsus, a, um.*
Veneti. *Veneti, ōrum,* m. pl.
Vengeance, to take vengeance on. *Ulciscor, i, ultus sum.*
Vergobretus. *Vergobretus, ī,* m.
Very. *Often expressed by the sup.;* very easy, *perfacilis, e;* to like very much, *adamō, āre, āvi, ātum.*
Vessel. *Nāvis, is,* f.
Vicinity, in the vicinity of. *Apud, ad, circum,* prep. w. acc.
Victoria. *Victōria, ae,* f.
Victory. *Victōria, ae,* f.
Village. *Vīcus, ī,* m.
Virtue. *Virtūs, ūtis,* f.
Voice. *Vōx, vōcis,* f.

W.

Wage. *Gerŏ, ere, gessi, gestum;* to wage against, *inferŏ, ferre, intuli, illātum.*
Wait for. *Exspectŏ, āre, āvi, ātum.*
Wall. *Mūrus, i,* m.
Want. *Inopia, ae,* f.
War. *Bellum, i,* n.; ship of war, *nāvis longa.*
Warlike. *Bellicōsus, a, um.*
Warn. *Moneŏ, ēre, ui, itum.*
Waste, to lay waste. *Vastŏ, āre, āvi, ātum.*
Way, in such a way. *Ita,* adv.
Weaken. *Effēminŏ, āre, āvi, ātum.*
Well, to be well supplied. *Abundŏ, āre, āvi, ātum.*
What? *Quis, quae, quid; qui, quae, quod.* 106, 188.
When. *Cum,* conj.
Whether. *Num,* in a single question; *utrum,* in a double question.
Which, who. *Qui, quae, quod,* 106, 187; which? who? *quis, quae, quid; qui, quae, quod;* 106, 188.
Whole. *Omnis, e; tōtus, a, um,* 45, 151; *ūniversus, a, um.*
Why. *Quārē, cūr,* adv.
Width. *Lātitūdŏ, inis,* f.
Willing, to be willing. *Volŏ, velle, volui.* 273, 203.
Winter. *Hiems, emis,* f.; winter quarters, *hiberna, ōrum,* n. pl.
To winter, pass the winter, *hiemŏ, āre, āvi, ātum.*
Wisdom. *Sapientia, ae, f.*
Wise. *Sapiēns, entis.*
Wish. *Cupiŏ, ere, ivi* or *ii, ītum; volŏ, velle, volui.* 273, 203.
With. *Cum,* prep. w. abl.; among, *apud,* prep. w. acc.; with reference to, *dē,* prep. w. abl.; with each other, with one another, *inter sē;* to be greatly pleased with, *adamŏ, āre, āvi, ātum.*
Withdraw. *Subdūcŏ, ere, dūxi, ductum; redūcŏ, ere, dūxi, ductum; dēdūcŏ, ere, dūxi, ductum.*
Without. *Sine,* prep. w. abl.
Withstand. *Sustineŏ, ēre, ui, tentum.*
Witness. *Testis, is,* m. and f.
Word. *Verbum, i,* n.
Would that. *Utinam,* interj. 114, 483, 1.
Wound. *Vulnus, eris,* n. To wound, *vulnerŏ, āre, āvi, ātum.*
Write. *Scribŏ, ere, scripsi, scriptum.*
Wrong. *Injūria, ae,* f.

Y.

Yet, not yet. *Nōndum,* adv.
Yoke. *Jugum, i,* n.
You, thou. *Tū, tui.* 102, 184.
Your. *Vester, tra, trum;* thy, *tuus, a, um.*

APPENDIX.

GENERAL RULES OF SYNTAX

Given here in a body, for convenience of reference, in the order and form in which they occur in the standard edition of Harkness's LATIN GRAMMAR, together with the numbers of sections in which the Rules are given respectively in this Volume, and their grammatical reference numbers.

AGREEMENT OF NOUNS.

RULE I.—Predicate Nouns (59).

362. A noun predicated of another noun denoting the same person or thing agrees with it in CASE:

Brūtus cūstōs lībertātis fuit, *Brutus was the guardian of liberty.*

RULE II.—Appositives (28).

363. An appositive agrees in CASE with the noun or pronoun which it qualifies:

Cluilius rēx moritur, *Cluilius the king dies.*

NOMINATIVE.—VOCATIVE.

RULE III.—Subject Nominative (12).

368. The Subject of a Finite verb is put in the Nominative:

Servius rēgnāvit, *Servius reigned.*

RULE IV.—Case of Address (190).

369. The Name of the person or thing addressed is put in the Vocative:

Perge, Laelī, *proceed, Laelius.*

ACCUSATIVE.

RULE V.—Direct Object (16).

371. The DIRECT OBJECT of an action is put in the Accusative:

Deus mundum aedificāvit. *God made* (built) *the world.*

RULE VI.—Two Accusatives—Same Person (158).

373. Verbs of MAKING, CHOOSING, CALLING, REGARDING, SHOWING, and the like, admit two Accusatives of the same person or thing:

Hamilcarem imperatōrem fēcērunt, *they made Hamilcar commander.*

RULE VII.—Two Accusatives—Person and Thing (273).

374. Some verbs of ASKING, DEMANDING, TEACHING, and CONCEALING admit two Accusatives—one of the *person* and the other of the *thing:*

Mē sententiam rogāvit, *he asked me my opinion.*

RULE VIII.—Accusative of Specification.

378. A verb or an adjective may take an Accusative to define its application:

Capita vēlāmur, *we have our heads veiled.*

RULE IX.—Accusative of Time and Space (98).

379. DURATION OF TIME and EXTENT OF SPACE are expressed by the Accusative:

Septem et trigintā regnāvit annōs, *he reigned thirty-seven years.* Quinque millia passuum ambulāre, *to walk five miles.*

RULE X.—Accusative of Limit (277).

380. The PLACE TO WHICH is designated by the Accusative:

I. Generally with a preposition—ad or in:

Legiōnēs ad urbem addūcit, *he is leading the legions to* or *toward the city.*

II. In names of towns without a preposition:

Nūntius Rōmam redit, *the messenger returns to Rome.*

RULE XI.—Accusative in Exclamations.

381. The Accusative, either with or without an interjection, may be used with Exclamations:

Heu mē miserum, *ah me unhappy!*

DATIVE.

RULE XII.—Dative with Verbs (54).

384. The INDIRECT OBJECT of an action is put in the Dative. It is used—

I. With INTRANSITIVE and PASSIVE verbs:

Tibi servio, *I am devoted to you.*

II. With TRANSITIVE verbs, in connection with the DIRECT OBJECT:

Agros plēbi dedit, *he gave lands to the common people.*

RULE XIII.—Two Datives—To which and For which (281).

390. Two Datives—the OBJECT TO WHICH and the OBJECT OF END FOR WHICH—occur with a few verbs:

I. With INTRANSITIVE and PASSIVE verbs:

Malō est hominibus avāritia, *avarice is an evil to men.*

II. With TRANSITIVE verbs in connection with the ACCUSATIVE:

Quīnque cohortēs castrīs praesidiō rēlīquit, *he left five cohorts for the defence of the camp.*

RULE XIV.—Dative with Adjectives (141).

391. With adjectives, the OBJECT TO WHICH the quality is directed is put in the Dative:

Omnibus cārum est, *it is dear to all.*

RULE XV.—Dative with Nouns and Adverbs.

392. The Dative is used with a few special nouns and adverbs:

I. With a few nouns from verbs which take the Dative:

Jūstitia est obtemperātiō lēgibus, *justice is obedience to laws.*

II. With a few adverbs from adjectives which take the Dative:

Congruenter nātūrae vīvere, *to live in accordance with nature.*

GENITIVE.

RULE XVI.—Genitive with Nouns (28).

395. Any noun, not an Appositive, qualifying the meaning of another noun, is put in the Genitive:

Catōnis ōrātiōnēs, *Cato's orations.*

RULE XVII.—Genitive with Adjectives.

399. Many adjectives take a Genitive to complete their meaning:

Avidus laudis, *desirous of praise.*

RULE XVIII.—Predicate Genitive.

401. A noun predicated of another noun denoting a different person or thing is put in the Genitive:

Omnia hostium erant, *all things belonged to the enemy.*

RULE XIX.—Genitive with Special Verbs.

406. The Genitive is used—

I. With **misereor** and **miserēscō**:

Miserēre labōrum, *pity the labors.*

II. With **recordor, memini, reminiscor,** and **obliviscor**:

Meminit praeteritōrum, *he remembers the past.*

III. With **rēfert** and **interest**:

Interest omnium, *it is the interest of all.*

RULE XX.—Accusative and Genitive (285).

409. The ACCUSATIVE of the PERSON and the GENITIVE of the THING are used with a few transitive verbs:

I. With verbs of *reminding, admonishing:*

Tē amicitiae commonefacit, *he reminds you of friendship.*

II. With verbs of *accusing, convicting, acquitting:*

Viros sceleris arguis, *you accuse men of crime.*

III. With *miseret, paenitet, pudet, taedet,* and *piget:*

Eōrum nōs miseret, *we pity them.*

ABLATIVE PROPER.

RULE XXI.—Place from which (277).

412. The PLACE FROM WHICH is denoted by the Ablative:

I. Generally *with a preposition*—**ā, ab, dē,** or **ex:**

Ab urbe proficiscitur, *he sets out from the city.*

II. In NAMES OF TOWNS *without a preposition:*

Platōnem Athēnīs arcessīvit, *he summoned Plato from Athens.*

RULES OF SYNTAX.

RULE XXII.—Separation, Source, Cause (158).

413. Separation, Source, and Cause are denoted by the Ablative *with* or *without a preposition:*

Caedem á vōbīs dēpellō, *I ward off slaughter from you.* Hōc audīvī dē parente meō, *I heard this from my father.* Ars ūtilitāte laudātur, *an art is praised because of its usefulness.*

RULE XXIII.—Ablative with Comparatives (88).

417. Comparatives without QUAM are followed by the Ablative:

Nihil est amābilius virtūte, *nothing is more lovely than virtue.*

INSTRUMENTAL ABLATIVE.

RULE XXIV.—Ablative of Accompaniment.

419. The Ablative is used—

I. To denote ACCOMPANIMENT. It then takes the preposition cum:
Vīvit cum Balbō, *he lives with Balbus.*

II. To denote CHARACTERISTIC OR QUALITY. It is then modified by an Adjective or by a Genitive:
Summā virtūte adulēscēns, *a youth of the highest virtue.*

III. To denote MANNER. It then takes the preposition cum, or is modified by an Adjective or by a Genitive:
Cum virtūte vīxit, *he lived virtuously.*

RULE XXV.—Ablative of Means (78).

420. INSTRUMENT and MEANS are denoted by the Ablative:

Cornibus taurī sē tūtantur, *bulls defend themselves with their horns.*

RULE XXVI.—Ablative in Special Constructions (258).

421. The Ablative is used—

I. With ūtor, fruor, fungor, potior, vescor, and their compounds:
Plūrimīs rēbus fruimur et ūtimur, *we enjoy and use very many things.*

II. With VERBS and ADJECTIVES OF PLENTY:
Villa abundat lacte, cāseō, melle, *the villa abounds in milk, cheese, and honey.*

III. With dignus, indignus, and contentus:
Dignī sunt amīcitiā, *they are worthy of friendship.*

RULE XXVII.—Ablative of Price.

422. Price is generally denoted by the Ablative:

Vēndidit auro patriam, *he sold his country for gold.*

RULE XXVIII.—Ablative of Difference (236).

423. The Measure of Difference is denoted by the Ablative:

Uno die longiōrem mēnsem, faciunt, *they make the month one day longer.*

RULE XXIX.—Specification (231).

424. A noun, adjective, or verb may take an Ablative to define its application:

Nōmine, nōn potestāte, fuit rēx, *he was king in name, not in power.*

Locative Ablative:

RULE XXX.—Place in which (185).

425. The Place in which is denoted—

I. Generally by the *Locative Ablative with the preposition* in:

Hannibal in Italia fuit, *Hannibal was in Italy.*

II. In Names of Towns by the *Locative*, if such a form exists, otherwise by the *Locative Ablative:*

Rōmae fuit, *he was at Rome.*

RULE XXXI.—Time (93).

429. The Time of an action is denoted by the Ablative:

Octōgēsimō annō est mortuus, *he died in his eightieth year.*

RULE XXXII.—Ablative Absolute (240).

431. A noun and a participle may be put in the Ablative to add to the predicate an attendant circumstance:

Serviō regnante viguērunt, *they flourished in the reign of Servius.*

Cases with Prepositions.

RULE XXXIII.—Cases with Prepositions (64).

432. The Accusative and Ablative may be used with prepositions:

Ad amicum, *to a friend.* In Italia, *in Italy.*

RULES OF SYNTAX.

Agreement of Adjectives, Pronouns, and Verbs.

RULE XXXIV.—Agreement of Adjectives (43).

438. An adjective agrees with its noun in GENDER, NUMBER, and CASE:

Fortūna cæca est, *fortune is blind.*

RULE XXXV.—Agreement of Pronouns (107).

445. A pronoun agrees with its antecedent in GENDER, NUMBER, and PERSON:

Animal, quod sanguinem habet, *an animal which has blood.*

RULE XXXVI.—Agreement of Verb with Subject (12).

460. A finite verb agrees with its subject in NUMBER and PERSON:

Ego rēgēs ējēci, *I have banished kings.*

Use of the Indicative.

RULE XXXVII.—Indicative (112).

474. The indicative is used in treating of facts:

Deus mundum aedificavit, *God made* (built) *the world.*

Moods and Tenses in Principal Clauses.

RULE XXXVIII.—Subjunctive of Desire, Command (114).

483. The Subjunctive is used to represent the action NOT AS REAL, but AS DESIRED:

Valeant cīvēs, *may the citizens be well.*

RULE XXXIX.—Potential Subjunctive.

485. The Subjunctive is used to represent the action NOT AS REAL, but AS POSSIBLE:

Illo quaerat quispiam, *here some one may inquire.*

RULE XL.—Imperative (114).

487. The Imperative is used in COMMANDS, EXHORTATIONS, and ENTREATIES:

Jūstitiam colo, *practice justice.*

APPENDIX.

MOODS AND TENSES IN SUBORDINATE CLAUSES.

RULE XLI.—Sequence of Tenses (119).

491. Principal tenses depend upon principal tenses; historical upon historical:

Enītitur ut vincat, *he strives to conquer.*

RULE XLII.—Purpose (119).

497. The Subjunctive is used to denote PURPOSE—

I. With the relative quī, and with relative adverbs, as ubī, unde, etc.:

Missī sunt quī (= ut iī) cōnsulerent Apollinem, *they were sent to consult Apollo.*

II. With ut, nē, quō, quōminus:

Enītitur ut vincat, *he strives that he may conquer.*

RULE XLIII.—Result (123).

500. The Subjunctive is used to denote RESULT—

I. With the relative quī, and with relative adverbs, as ubī, unde, cūr, etc.:

Nōn is sum quī (= ut ego) hīs ūtar, *I am not such a one as to use these things.*

II. With ut, ut nōn, quīn:

Ita vīxit ut Athēniēnsibus esset cārissimus, *he so lived that he was very dear to the Athenians.*

RULE XLIV.—Conditional Sentences with sī, nisi, nī, sīn (250).

507. Conditional sentences with sī, nisi, nī, sīn, take—

I. The INDICATIVE in both clauses *to assume* the supposed case:

Sī spīritum dūcit, vīvit, *if he breathes, he is alive.*

II. The PRESENT OR PERFECT SUBJUNCTIVE in both clauses to represent the supposed case *as possible:*

Diēs dēficiat, sī velim causam dēfendere, *the day would fail me, if I should wish to defend the cause.*

III. The IMPERFECT or PLUPERFECT SUBJUNCTIVE in both clauses to represent the supposed case as *contrary to fact:*

Plūribus verbīs ad tē scrīberem, sī rēs verba dēsīderāret, *I should write to you more fully* (with more words), *if the case required words.*

RULE XLV.—Conditional Clauses with dum, modo, &c sī, ut sī, etc.

513. Conditional clauses take the Subjunctive—

I. With **dum, modo, dummodo,** 'if only,' 'provided that'; **dum nē, modo nē, dummodo nē,** 'if only not,' 'provided that not':

Manent ingenia, modo permaneat industria, *mental powers remain, if only industry remains.*

II. With **āc sī, ut sī, quam sī, quasi, tanquam, tanquam sī, velut, velut sī,** 'as if,' 'than if,' involving an ellipsis of the real conclusion:

Perinde habēbō, ac si scripsissēs, *I shall regard it just as if* (i. e., as I should if) *you had written.*

RULE XLVI.—Moods in Concessive Clauses (254).

515. Concessive clauses take—

I. Generally the INDICATIVE in the best prose, when introduced by *quamquam:*

Quamquam intellegunt, *though they understand.*

II. The INDICATIVE or SUBJUNCTIVE when introduced by *etsī, etiamsī, tametsī,* or *sī,* like conditional clauses with *sī:*

Etsi nihil sciō quod gaudeam, *though I know no reason why I should rejoice.*

III. The SUBJUNCTIVE when introduced by *licet, quamvīs, ut, nē, cum,* or the relative *quī:*

Licet irrideat, *though he may deride.*

RULE XLVII.—Moods with quod, quia, quoniam, quando.

516. Causal clauses with **quod, quia, quoniam, quandō,** generally take—

I. The INDICATIVE to assign a reason *positively on one's own authority:*

Quoniam supplicātiō decrēta est, *since a thanksgiving has been decreed.*

II. The SUBJUNCTIVE to assign a reason *doubtfully,* or *on another's authority:*

Socrates accūsātus est, quod corrumperet juventūtem, *Socrates was accused, because he corrupted the youth.*

RULE XLVIII.—Causal Clauses with cum and qui.

517. Causal clauses with *cum* and *quī* generally take the Subjunctive in writers of the best period:

Cum vīta metūs plēna sit, *since life is full of fear.*

RULE XLIX.—Temporal Clauses with postquam, etc.

518. In temporal clauses with *postquam, posteaquam, ubi, ut, simul atque*, etc., 'after,' 'when,' 'as soon as,' the Indicative is used:

Postquam vidit, etc., castra posuit, *he pitched his camp, after he saw*, etc.

RULE L.—Temporal Clauses with dum, etc.

519. I. Temporal clauses with *dum, dōnec*, and *quoad*, in the sense of WHILE, AS LONG AS, take the INDICATIVE:

Haec feci, dum licuit, *I did this while it was allowed.*

II. Temporal clauses with *dum, dōnec*, and *quoad*, in the sense of UNTIL, take—

1. The INDICATIVE, when the action is viewed as an ACTUAL FACT:

Delibera hoc, dum ego redeo, *consider this until I return.*

2. The SUBJUNCTIVE, when the action is viewed as something DESIRED, PROPOSED, or CONCEIVED:

Differant, dum deferveścat ira, *let them defer it till their anger cools.*

RULE LI.—Temporal Clauses with antequam and priusquam.

520. In temporal clauses with *antequam* and *priusquam*—

I. Any tense except the Imperfect and Pluperfect is put—

1. In the INDICATIVE, when the action is viewed as an ACTUAL FACT:

Priusquam lucet, adsunt, *they are present before it is light.*

2. In the SUBJUNCTIVE, when the action is viewed as SOMETHING DESIRED, PROPOSED, or CONCEIVED:

Antequam de re publica dicam, *before I* (can) *speak of the republic.*

II. The Imperfect and Pluperfect are put in the SUBJUNCTIVE:

Antequam urbem caperent, *before they took the city.*

RULE LII.—Temporal Clauses with cum.

521. In temporal clauses with *cum*—

I. Any tense except the Imperfect and the Pluperfect is put in the INDICATIVE:

Cum quiescunt, probant, *while they are silent, they approve.*

II. The Imperfect and Pluperfect are put—

1. In the INDICATIVE, when the temporal clause ASSERTS AN HISTORICAL FACT:

Pāruit cum necesse erat, *he obeyed when it was necessary.*

2. In the SUBJUNCTIVE, when the temporal clause simply DEFINES THE TIME of the principal action:

Cum epistulam complicārem, *while I was folding the letter.*

RULE LIII.—Moods in Principal Clauses (262).

523. The principal clauses of the DIRECT DISCOURSE on becoming INDIRECT take the INFINITIVE or SUBJUNCTIVE as follows:

I. When DECLARATIVE, they take the *Infinitive with a Subject Accusative:*

Dīcēbat animōs esse dīvīnōs, *he was wont to say that souls are divine.*

II. When INTERROGATIVE, they take—

1. Generally the *Subjunctive:*

Ad postulāta Caesaris respondit, quid sibī vellet, cūr venīret, *to the demands of Caesar he replied, what did he wish, why did he come?*

2. Sometimes the *Infinitive with a Subject Accusative*, as in rhetorical questions:

Docēbant rem esse testimōniō, etc.; quid esse levius, *they showed that the fact was a proof*, etc.; *what was more inconsiderate?*

III. When IMPERATIVE, they take the *Subjunctive:*

Scrībit Labiēnō cum legiōne veniat, *he writes to Labienus to come* (that he should come) *with a legion.*

RULE LIV.—Moods in Subordinate Clauses (262).

524. The subordinate clauses of the DIRECT DISCOURSE, on becoming INDIRECT, take the *Subjunctive:*

Respondit sē id quod in Nerviīs fēcisset factūrum, *he replied that he would do what he had done in the case of the Nervii.*

RULE LV.—Moods in Indirect Clauses (127).

529. The Subjunctive is used—

I. In indirect questions:

Quaeritur, cūr doctissimī hominēs dissentiant, *it is a question, why the most learned men disagree.*

II. Often in clauses dependent upon an Infinitive or upon another Subjunctive:

APPENDIX.

Nihil indignius est quam eum qui culpâ careat supplicio non carēre, *nothing is more shameful than that he who is free from fault should not be exempt from punishment*.

INFINITIVE.

RULE LVI.—Infinitive (132).

533. Many verbs admit an Infinitive to complete or qualify their meaning:

Haec vitāre cupimus, *we desire to avoid these things*.

RULE LVII.—Accusative and Infinitive (171).

534. Many transitive verbs admit both an Accusative and an Infinitive:

Tē sapere docet, *he teaches you to be wise*.

RULE LVIII.—Subject of Infinitive (171).

536. The Infinitive sometimes takes an Accusative as its subject:

Platōnem Tarentum venīsse reperio, *I find that Plato came to Tarentum*.

SUPINE.

RULE LIX.—Supine in Um (166).

546. The Supine in *um* is used with verbs of motion to express PURPOSE:

Lēgātī vēnērunt rēs repetītum, *deputies came to demand restitution*.

RULE LX.—Supine in û (246).

547. The Supine in *û* is generally used as an Ablative of Specification:

Quid est tam jūcundum audītū, *what is so agreeable to hear* (in hearing)?

ADVERBS.

RULE LXI.—Use of Adverbs (70).

551. Adverbs qualify VERBS, ADJECTIVES, and other ADVERBS:

Sapientēs fēlīciter vīvunt, *the wise live happily*.

TABLE

SHOWING THE ARTICLES IN THIS BOOK CONTAINING ARTICLES FROM THE LATIN GRAMMAR.

Gram.	Lat. Course.	Gram.	Lat. Course.	Gram.	Lat. Course.
1–4	1	211	227	421	258
5–14	2	212	235	422	314
16–18	4	217, 218	246	423	230
22	1	219	250	424	231
30, 31	1	231, 232	258	425, 426	185
33	1	233, 234	260	429	93
38–42	6	289–292	269	431	240
44	6	293	273	432	65
45	8	294, 295	277	438	43
46–48	10	296	281	440, NN. 1 and 2	
51	35	300, 301	281		191, f. n.
55–58	49	346–349	14	445	107
59	53	351–353	106	459, 1	324, 16
60, 61	58	356, 357	14	460	20
62–65	63	302	59	465, N. 2	259, f. n.
66, 4	63	303	31	467, 4	330, 10
69	64	308	20	474	112
105	64	369	100	483	114
111	64	371	25	485	322
116	92	373	153	487	114
120	92	374	273	489	275, 2
146–151	42	376	275, 19	491–493	119
152–154	82	378	200	497, 498	119
155–157	86	379	98	500, 501	123
160–162	86	380	277	503	123
165, 166	86	381	209	506, 507	250
170	86	384	54	513	330
171, 172	97	385, 2	332, f. n. 2	514, 515	254
174–177	97	390	281	516, 517	334
178	247, f. n.	391	141	518, 519	337
179	97	392	303	520, 521	341
182–186	102	395	31	522–524	262
187–190	106	397	31	526	262
192–195	14	399	307	529	127
196	14 and 111	401	307	533	132
197–200	14	406	307	534	171
201–204	140	409	285	536	171
205	152	412	277	541–544	291
206	170	413	158	546	106
207	181	415	158	547	246
208	104	417	88	548–550	291
209	207	419	314	551	70
210	214	420	78		

LATIN TEXT-BOOKS.

BY

ALBERT HARKNESS, Ph. D., LL. D.

A Complete Latin Course for the First Year.

Progressive Exercises in Reading and Writing Latin, with Frequent Practice in Reading at Sight.

An Introductory Latin Book. 12mo.

A Latin Grammar. Edition of 1874. 12mo.

A Latin Grammar. Standard edition of 1881. 12mo.

The Elements of Latin Grammar. 12mo.

A New Latin Reader. 12mo.

A Latin Reader. 12mo.

A Latin Reader. With Exercises in Latin Composition. 12mo.

A Practical Introduction to Latin Composition. 12mo.

Caesar's Commentaries on the Gallic War. 12mo.

Cicero's Select Orations. 12mo.

Cicero's Select Orations. With Explanatory Notes and a Special Dictionary. 12mo.

Sallust's Catiline. With Explanatory Notes and a Special Vocabulary. 12mo.

Preparatory Course of Latin Prose Authors. Large 8vo. Contains Four Books of Caesar's Commentaries, Sallust's Catiline, and Eight of Cicero's Orations.

D. APPLETON & CO., Publishers,

NEW YORK, BOSTON, CHICAGO, SAN FRANCISCO.

STANDARD LATIN SERIES.

Harkness's Standard Latin Grammar.
"The most complete, philosophical, and attractive Grammar ever written." Adapted to all grades. 12mo. Introduction price, $1.12.

Harkness's New Latin Reader.
Especially adapted for use with the "Standard Latin Grammar." 12mo. Introduction price, 87 cents.

Harkness's Complete Course in Latin for the First Year.
Comprising an Outline of Latin Grammar and Progressive Exercises in Reading and Writing Latin, with Frequent Practice in Reading at Sight. Designed to serve as a complete introductory book in Latin—no grammar being required. 12mo. Introduction price, $1.12.

Harkness's Cæsar's Commentaries.
New Pictorial Edition. With full Dictionary, Life of Cæsar, Map of Gaul, Plans of Battles, Outline of the Roman Military System, etc., and Notes to the author's Standard Latin Grammar. Containing numerous colored plates, showing the movements of armies, military uniforms, arms, standards, etc., which, in point of beauty, are superior to any edition of Cæsar yet published. 12mo. Introduction price, $1.20.

Harkness's Cicero's Orations.
With full Notes, Vocabulary, etc. 12mo. Introduction price, $1.22.

Harkness's Course of Latin Prose Authors.
New Pictorial Edition. With full Notes and Dictionary. The work contains four books of "Cæsar's Commentaries," the "Catiline" of Sallust, and eight of Cicero's Orations. 12mo. Introduction price, $1.40.

Frieze's Editions of Vergil.
THE ÆNEID, with Notes only. 12mo. $1.40.
THE ÆNEID, with Notes and Dictionary. 12mo. $1.30.
SIX BOOKS OF THE ÆNEID, GEORGICS, AND BUCOLICS, with Notes and Dictionary. 12mo. $1.30.
VERGIL COMPLETE, with Notes and Dictionary. 12mo. $1.60.

Sallust's Jugurthine War with full Explanatory Notes.
References to Harkness's Standard Latin Grammar, and a copious Latin-English Dictionary. By CHARLES GEORGE HERBERMAN. 12mo. Introduction price, $1.12.

(SEE NEXT PAGE.)

STANDARD LATIN SERIES—*Continued.*

Cornelius Nepos.

Prepared expressly for the Use of Students Learning to Read at Sight. With Notes, Vocabulary, Index of Proper Names, and Exercises for Translation into Latin. Illustrated by numerous Cuts. By THOMAS B. LINDSAY, Ph. D., Professor of Latin in the Boston University. 12mo. Introduction price, $1.22.

THE SAME, for Sight-Reading in Schools and Colleges, with English-Latin Exercises and Index of Proper Names. By THOMAS B. LINDSAY. 12mo. Introduction price, $1.00.

Selections from the Poems of Ovid.

With Notes. By J. L. LINCOLN, LL. D., Professor of Latin in Brown University. The text is very carefully annotated and references made to Harkness's Standard Grammar. 12mo. Introduction price, $1.00.

THE SAME. With Notes and Vocabulary. 12mo. Introduction price, $1.22.

Livy.

Selections from the First Five Books, together with the Twenty first and Twenty-second Books entire; with a Plan of Rome, a Map of the Passage of Hannibal, and English Notes for the Use of Schools. By J. L. LINCOLN, LL. D. 12mo. Introduction price, $1.22.

Horace.

With English Notes, for the Use of Schools and Colleges. By J. L. LINCOLN, LL. D. 12mo. Introduction price, $1.22.

Sallust's Jugurtha and Catiline.

With Notes and a Vocabulary. By NOBLE BUTLER and MINARD STURGUS. 12mo. Introduction price, $1.22.

Germania and Agricola of Tacitus.

With Notes, for Colleges. By W. S. TYLER, Professor of the Greek and Latin Languages in Amherst College. 12mo. Introduction price, 87 cents.

Mailed, post-paid, for examination, at introduction prices. Send for full descriptive circulars.

D. APPLETON & CO., Publishers,

New York, Boston, Chicago, Atlanta, San Francisco.

PROFESSOR LINCOLN'S LATIN TEXT-BOOKS.

Selections from the Poems of Ovid. With Notes. By J. L. Lincoln, LL. D., Professor of Latin in Brown University. 12mo. 238 pages.

This edition of Ovid was prepared at the request of many teachers of Latin who regard the poetry of Ovid more suitable for the use of beginners than that of Vergil, an opinion that governs the course pursued in the European schools generally. The text is very carefully annotated, and references are made to Harkness's Standard Grammar.

Some selections from the "Amores," the "Fasti," and the "Tristia," have been added to those made from the "Metamorphoses," not only on account of the interesting themes of which they treat, but also for the sake of giving the student an opportunity of becoming acquainted with Latin elegiac verse, of which, in Latin poetry, Ovid is the acknowledged master.

With Notes and Vocabulary.

Horace. With English Notes, for the Use of Schools and Colleges. 12mo. 575 pages.

Selections from the First Five Books of Livy, together with the Twenty-first and Twenty-second Books entire; with a Plan of Rome, a Map of the Passage of Hannibal, and English Notes for the Use of Schools. 12mo. 329 pages.

PROFESSOR LINDSAY'S LATIN TEXT-BOOKS.

Cornelius Nepos. Prepared expressly for the Use of Students Learning to Read at Sight. With Notes, Vocabulary, Index of Proper Names, and Exercises for Translation into Latin. Illustrated by numerous Cuts. By THOMAS B. LINDSAY, Ph. D., Assistant Professor of Latin in the Boston University. 12mo. 357 pages.

Among the characteristic features of this new edition of "Cornelius Nepos" are the following: The orthographical accuracy of the text, the results of the investigations of Fleckeisen, Brambach, and others having been kept carefully in view. The notes have been prepared with special reference to the training of the student in *sight-reading*, and to assist him in grasping the main idea of the sentence. The English-Latin exercises make immediate use of the words and idioms of the text, thus fixing them firmly in the mind. The marking of the long vowels and the relation of derivatives to a common root are among the special features of the vocabulary. It is a valuable supplementary reading-book, where the curriculum does not admit of its introduction into the prescribed course.

"Cornelius Nepos" is one of the authors regularly read in the German Gymnasia. The clearness of his style and the interest of the subjects treated by him are especially adapted to engage the attention of the student, and make his study of Latin a pleasure rather than a task.

THE SAME, for Sight-Reading in Schools and Colleges, with English-Latin Exercises and Index of Proper Names. 12mo.

This edition contains the Text, the English-Latin Exercises, and the Historical and Geographical Index, and is designed to meet the wants of students that desire in addition to the regular course to read a Latin author at *sight*.

D. APPLETON & CO., Publishers,
NEW YORK, BOSTON, CHICAGO, SAN FRANCISCO.

RECENT PUBLICATIONS

FOR THE STUDY OF GREEK.

Hadley's Greek Grammar. Revised, and in part rewritten, by FREDERICK DE FOREST ALLEN, Ph. D., Professor of Classical Philology in Harvard University.

This grammar not only presents the latest and best results of Greek studies, but also treats the language in the light received from comparative philology. The work is clear in its language, accurate in its definitions, judicious in its arrangement, and sufficiently comprehensive for all purposes, while it is free from cumbrous details. It is simple enough for the beginner, and comprehensive enough for the most advanced students. 12mo. 405 pages. Introductory price, $1.50.

Greek Lessons. Prepared to accompany the Grammar of Hadley and Allen. By ROBERT P. KEEP, Ph. D., Principal of the Norwich (Connecticut) Free Academy.

An elementary Greek book intended to serve as a companion and guide to the Grammar, and as an introduction to the study of Xenophon. The publishers commend this work to American teachers with great confidence that it will be found to possess important advantages above other books of its class. 12mo. Introductory price, $1.20.

Elementary Lessons in Greek Syntax, designed to accompany the reading of Xenophon's Anabasis. By S. R. WINCHELL, A. M.

A series of lessons on Attic Greek Syntax, designed to follow about one year's study of the etymology of the language. It comprises lessons on the last half of the Grammar, with exercises and vocabularies, all arranged with a view of making the pupil familiar with the fundamental principles of Greek syntax. It is intended as an introduction to a thorough and comprehensive treatise on Greek prose composition. Introductory price, 54 cents.

Harkness's First Greek Book. Comprising an Outline of the Forms and Inflections of the Language, a complete Analytic Syntax, and an Introductory Greek Reader. With Notes and Vocabularies.

Revised and rewritten by the author. Designed especially to accompany Allen-Hadley's Greek Grammar, with references also to Goodwin's and Crosby's Greek Grammars. 12mo. 276 pages. Introductory price, $1.05.

Three Months' Preparation for Reading Xenophon. By JAMES MORRIS WHITON, Ph. D., author of Whiton's "First Lessons in Greek," and MARY BARTLETT WHITON, A. B., Instructor in Greek in Packer Collegiate Institute, Brooklyn.

A concise and practical new introductory Greek book, designed to accompany Allen-Hadley's Greek Grammar. Containing references also to Goodwin's Greek Grammar. 12mo. 94 pages. Introductory price, 48 cents.

Sample copies, for examination, sent to teachers of Greek, post-paid, for examination, on receipt of the introductory price.

D. APPLETON & CO., Publishers,
NEW YORK, BOSTON, CHICAGO, ATLANTA, SAN FRANCISCO.

STANDARD GREEK TEXTS.

Xenophon's Anabasis: with Explanatory Notes for Use of Schools and Colleges in the United States. By JAMES R. BOISE, Ph. D. (Tübingen), LL. D., Professor of Greek in the University of Michigan. 12mo. 393 pages. Introduction price, $1.40.

The First Four Books of Xenophon's Anabasis: with Explanatory Notes with grammatical references to Hadley-Allen's, Goodwin's, and other Greek Grammars; a copious Greek-English Vocabulary; and Kiepert's Map of the Route of the Ten Thousand. By JAMES R. BOISE. 12mo. 451 pages. Introduction price, $1.32.

This work takes the place of the *Three Book* and *Five Book* editions of the Anabasis heretofore published.

THE SAME. Without Vocabulary. 12mo. 324 pages. Introduction price, $1.08.

The First Three Books of Homer's Iliad, according to the Text of Dindorf; with Revised Notes, Critical and Explanatory, and References to Hadley-Allen's, Crosby's, and Goodwin's Greek Grammars. By HENRY CLARK JOHNSON, A. M., LL. B. 12mo. 180 pages. Introduction price, $1.12.

THE SAME. With Vocabulary. 12mo. (*In press.*)

Selections from Herodotus: comprising mainly such Portions as give a Connected History of the East, to the Fall of Babylon and the Death of Cyrus the Great. By HERMAN M. JOHNSON, D. D., Professor of Philosophy and English Literature in Dickinson College. 12mo. 185 pages. Introduction price, $1.05.

The Œdipus Tyrannus of Sophocles; with English Notes. By HOWARD CROSBY, D. D., formerly Professor of Greek Language and Literature in Rutgers College, and Professor in the University of the City of New York. Revised edition, with Notes to Hadley-Allen's and Goodwin's Greek Grammars. 12mo. Introduction price, $1.05.

The Greek Prepositions, Studied from their Original Meanings as Designations of Space. By F. A. ADAMS, Ph. D. A short but comprehensive treatise on the meanings of the verbs as compounded with the prepositions. 12mo. 131 pages. Introduction price, 60 cents.

Specimen copies of the above books, for examination, will be sent, postpaid, to teachers of Greek, on receipt of introduction price.

D. APPLETON & CO., Publishers,
NEW YORK, BOSTON, CHICAGO, ATLANTA, SAN FRANCISCO.

www.ingramcontent.com/pod-product-compliance
Lightning Source LLC
Chambersburg PA
CBHW032352230426
43672CB00007B/679